Boxing in Black and White

Boxing in Black and White

A Statistical Study of Race in the Ring, 1949–1983

ANDREW LINDSAY

McFarland & Company, Inc., Publishers
Jefferson, North Carolina, and London

LIBRARY OF CONGRESS CATALOGUING-IN-PUBLICATION DATA

Lindsay, Andrew, 1965–
    Boxing in black and white : a statistical study of race in the ring, 1949–1983 / Andrew Lindsay.
        p.   cm.
    Includes bibliographical references and index.

    ISBN-13: 978-0-7864-1800-8
    (softcover : 50# alkaline paper) ∞

    1. Boxing — United States — History. 2. Racism in sports — United States — History. I. Title.
GV1125.L56   2004
796.83'0973'0904 — dc22   2004007593

British Library cataloguing data are available

©2004 Andrew Lindsay. All rights reserved

No part of this book may be reproduced or transmitted in any form or by any means, electronic or mechanical, including photocopying or recording, or by any information storage and retrieval system, without permission in writing from the publisher.

On the cover: ©2004 Photodisc

Manufactured in the United States of America

McFarland & Company, Inc., Publishers
  Box 611, Jefferson, North Carolina 28640
    www.mcfarlandpub.com

To Jerry Quarry (1945–1999), a crowd-pleaser, a gutsy competitor, and a world champion where it counted most, in the hearts and minds of his fans.

To the taxpayers of Ohio and Toledo, without whom I never could have pursued and earned a Ph.D.

To Val, who is everything a kind and caring nurse is supposed to be, and a prototype of the warm-hearted and good-natured American.

To my mother, whose generous financial support was essential in the latter stages of this project.

To Donna, who after nineteen years is still the undisputed, undefeated world champion of high school buddies.

And to the 105 men, living and dead, champions and challengers, who make up this study, boxers whose efforts and exploits thrilled so many for so long: Nick, Al, Turkey, Lee, John, Coley, Grant, Billy, Muhammad, Joey, Bob, Tom, Zora, Sonny, Alonzo, Ron, Eddie, Floyd, Bernie, Wayne, Harold, Gus, Charlie, Tony, Roland, Cleveland, Bill, Harry, Ernie, Thad, Dan, Amos, Herbert, Pat, Johnny, Joe, Mike, Jimmy, Leotis, Charlie, Buster, Henry, Bob, Tom, Harold, Rex, Al, Mac, Tom, George, Ron, George, Ken, Earnie, Jerry, Jeff, Larry, Rocky, Billy, Doug, Boone, Jimmy, Larry, Chuck, Johnny, Howard, Duane, Stan, Leon, Willie, Al, Roger, Roy, Elmer, Amos, Randy, Mike, John, Scott, Leroy, Michael, Gerry, Greg, Marty, Tex, James, Renaldo, Pat, Tim, Pinklon, Freddie, S.T., Joe, Pete, Ezzard, Jersey, Joe, Dave, Bob, Clarence, Jimmy, Scott, Terry, Archie, Young Jack, Johnny.

Contents

Acknowledgments   ix
Preface   1

1. American Boxing in Black and White   3
2. Segregation in American Sports Is Dead, but…   23
3. The Great White Hope: Extinct or Dormant?   44
4. Approaching the Summit   76
5. For All the Marbles   127
6. Has the Great White Hope Left the Building?   170

Conclusion: Limitations, Assumptions and Methodological Problems   180

Appendix 1: Records of Opponents   185
Appendix 2: Missing Records   227
Notes   233
References   243
Index   247

Acknowledgments

My opportunity to study at the doctoral level was made possible through the support and encouragement of Dr. Richard Moriarty and Dr. Michael Salter of the University of Windsor. These two scholars recognized my commitment to history and wrote reference letters that helped me win a place in the University of Toledo's Ph.D. history program. They unconditionally supported my doctoral ambitions, ambitions stymied by factors beyond my control. Thank you again, Dr. Moriarty and Dr. Salter, for remembering there are different ways to approach history, that narrative history is not a crime, that independent thinking does not make a graduate student stubborn, and that a master's student does not have to bow to a mentor's views to be a strong doctoral history candidate.

During my studies in Toledo, I was constantly reminded how naturally generous and forthcoming Americans are, in the countless rides my fellow students offered to and from school, in helping me move to a new apartment, and in extending numerous holiday and other social invitations. A hearty thank you to Chris, Andy, Steve, Mark, Tracie, Joe, Colonel Bob, Jamie, Jeff, Mary, Kari and Kathy and, most of all, to Catherine, Beth Ann, and Keith.

A good working relationship between a graduate student and his advisor is an advantage. Dr. Ronald Lora has always been a positive contributor to my academic experience, supporting my historical interests, giving me constructive feedback, allowing me to think independently, taking a genuine interest in boxing history, and treating all his students with civility, courtesy, patience, flexibility and politeness. Having such a historical advisor was a first-time experience for me.

Dr. Charles Glaab, Dr. Timothy Messer-Kruse, Dr. Peter Linebaugh of the University of Toledo History Department, and Dr. Rachel Buff of Bowling Green State University's History Department have all served this study by their willingness to be members of my thesis committee. Each provided a unique perspective on the topic of race, culture and boxing in modern America. Thank you all for your time, input, and support.

My experience in Toledo was made considerably more comfortable by the International Students' Office. From the day I arrived here, this office went the extra mile in welcoming foreign students and helping them acclimate to Toledo and America. A big thank you to the staff at the I.S.O. for helping with my travel documentation and Canadian student loan forms over the past four years.

The Carlson Library staff played an integral role in the successful completion of my coursework and dissertation. My studies would have been more arduous if not for the helpfulness and professionalism of the staff of the circulation desk, reference help desk, and microfilm room.

Gaining an understanding of colonial and antebellum America was the result of extensive readings with Dr. Ruth Herndon and Dr. William Longton, who both served as members of my comprehensive exam committee.

My knowledge of East Asian history has grown light years from a base of zero thanks to my minor field advisor, Dr. William Hoover, whose door was always open and who freely gave advice on the doctoral program and academia in general.

My three graduate assistant assignments with Dr. Marcella Calisto were very positive academic experiences. Thank you, Dr. Calisto, for your friendship and our many conversations.

Dr. Jakobson has been a great academic supporter and friend to all graduate students in the department, always willing to dispense academic direction and career advice to anyone who needed it. On behalf of many graduate students, I thank both Dr. Jakobson and Dr. Herndon for never forgetting their graduate student roots.

Dr. Bruce Way offered me several valuable opportunities to hone my teaching skills and talk about sports in my home country to his Bowling Green classes. He was always willing to discuss the Great White North in person, at least when he was not at Jacobs Field.

I would like to recognize Debbie McDonald, our department secretary, for the many administrative and personal favors she has undertaken for graduate students at Tucker Hall.

I was able to sustain my studies thanks to the Sera-Care Plasma Center of Toledo. Thanks to the staff at Sera-Care for helping me make ends meet.

An equally big thanks to Lisa Yost and Kendra Johnson of the Office of Accessibility and Dr. Sakui Malakpa of the Department of Special Education, for providing valuable and rewarding work opportunities to supplement my income and make a contribution to something other than history.

Thanking those who helped my research into boxing statistics and birth dates could be a chapter in itself. There are dozens of individuals across

North America who gave their time and energy in helping me find what I needed. A few of them really went above and beyond.

A thousand thank yous to Pat Pulcini of UT Computer Services for helping me overcome occasional computer file glitches with this study.

The researchers affiliated with the CyberBoxingZone were unfailingly forthcoming in answering my questions about boxing, or sharing their records with me. Thanks again to Mike Delisa, Dan Cuocuo, Barry Deskins, Luckett Davis, and especially Barry Hugman and Tracey Callis for your insights.

The statistical research of boxers' records for this study was compiled at the Cleveland Public Library and the Joyce Sports Collection of the Hesburgh Library at Notre Dame University. In the latter venue, George Rugg was indispensable in making the complete run of *Ring Record Books* available every time I was in South Bend, or copying and mailing records when I could not get there. Thanks again, George.

A number of boxers, or their surviving relatives, were nice enough to directly share information with me by phone, e-mail, or letter. They included Duane Bobick, Randy Neumann, Johnny Boudreaux, Boone Kirkman, Coley Wallace, Elmer Rush, Linda Benjamin (daughter of Bob Dunlap), and Chuck (brother of Amos) Lincoln.

The following is a list of boxing researchers, graduate students, or amateur historians involved with the USGenWeb site, who helped unravel my topic by researching fights or specific boxers. Some of the following shared hard-to-find boxing records or helped direct me to fighter's birth dates.

Thanks to the Hall Funeral Home in Port Allen, Louisiana, for sharing Henry Clark's birthdate; the International Boxing Hall of Fame, for sharing Chuck Wepner's and Scott LeDoux's birth dates; Jim Beam, of Connecticut, for sharing Bernie Reynolds' birth date; Charlene Todd and Cheryl Viger of Washington State, for helping me find Boone Kirkman; Eileen Holtberg, of Morrison Country, Minnesota, for helping me find Duane Bobick; Jessica Finch, of the California State Athletic Commission, for sharing the birth dates of Marty Monroe, Stan Ward, and Howard Smith; Kim Calame, of the Dishman Community Center in Washington State, who put me in touch with the late Amos Lincoln's brother Chuck; Jeannine Lovgren, formerly of Delta, Ohio, now living in Omaha, Nebraska, who gave me Ron Stander's date of birth. Pat Connolly, Mike Doherty, and Fred Bishop, of Nova Scotia, who went the extra mile in hunting down information about Bert Hardy; Glenn Dowdle, of the Safford City County Library, for uncovering relevant data about Zora Folley's Arizona fights in the 1950s; Martha Bloem, of the Grand Rapids Public Library, for helping my research of Buster Mathis; Art Daly of Spruce Grove, Alberta, for ongoing help with Canadian boxing records; the Amateur Athletic Foundation of Los Angeles, for combing through their microfilm for records of pre-1945 boxers.

Other helpful souls were graduate students who researched newspaper coverage of title fights: Aaron Coleman, University of Louisville; Dan Bubb, University of Nevada, Las Vegas; Dionne Procell, Southern Methodist University; Kenneth Cameron, University of Detroit, Mercy; Paul Raymond Lawrence, University of Toronto; Kim Carey, Cleveland State University; Joyce Chadya, University of Minnesota; Jim Higgins, Lehigh University; Myra Rich, University of Colorado, Denver; Sam Upshaw, Jr., University of Louisville; Paul Lubotina, St. Louis University; John McIntyre, University of Akron; Brandon W. Smith, University of Florida; Peter Pavlovich, Canisius University; Israel Joshua Rubio, Stanford University; Michael Lima, University of Toronto; Elizabeth Moreland, University of Colorado, Denver; Heidi Solber Viar, Western Michigan University; Shelly Martin, Dalhousie University; Cecile Houry, University of Miami; Melissa Gemmler, Tulane University; Todd Cleveland, University of Minnesota; Keith Davey, University of Texas, San Antonio; Koni Benson, University of Minnesota; Tracey Graham, University of Chicago; Jason Bird, University of Windsor.

Preface

The equality or inequality of opportunity along racial lines can be measured in sports just as it can be measured in any other corner of American society. Such measurements are important: Examining how far minority groups have traversed the road to equal opportunity reveals the degree to which white America has become color-blind in at least part of its day-to-day life. Since boxing was once one of the most segregated sports, the ring offers an appropriate forum for a snapshot of what white and black athletes experience pursuing success. *Boxing in Black and White: A Statistical Study of Race in the Ring, 1949–1983* was meant to statistically reveal whether white heavyweight boxers attained success beyond what their talent merited, at a time when sports (it is normally assumed) were a model for fairness and inclusion.

The research strategy of this investigation was to hone in on the most important boxing division in terms of racial symbolism: the heavyweights. No other divisions were considered, because white angst over black athletic dominance focused primarily on the biggest fighters. The study begins with 1949, the year of the retirement of Joe Louis, whose championship reign is seen as a seminal event in the opening of doors to black athletes, and ends in 1983, when the last white heavyweight challenged for the world title. Within this time frame, white and black boxers who reached the pinnacle of this sport were statistically compared as groups to determine how hard they worked to reach the summit. Boxers who did not challenge for the world title or enter the top ten ratings were not considered.

This topic is important to the degree that Americans of all races care about creating a truly color-blind society in terms of achievement through opportunity. Reaching this goal demands particularly close scrutiny of institutions like sports, often expected to be at the forefront of social progress and frequently assumed to be territory already covered in the quest for a fairer society.

Growing up as a sport-obsessed child in the 1970s, I came of age in a time popularly regarded as a golden age of heavyweight boxing. The upper echelon of the sport contained numerous contenders (Lyle, Young, Shavers, Quarry) who probably would have been world champions in other decades, but could not match the standard set by Frazier, Foreman, Ali, and Holmes. The rivalries of these great boxers held my attention at the time. Heavyweight boxing since the 1970s has made that period glow even brighter in the boxing fan's memory. Numerous champions from the 1980s forward would have had difficulty cracking the top ten thirty years ago. Later, when I pursued historical study, I became familiar with the term "Great White Hope," from both the Hollywood portrayal and numerous biographies of former champion Jack Johnson. Coupled with my awareness of the relative rarity of high-profile white heavyweights from the 1970s forward, the question of how far boxing had progressed beyond this phenomenon fascinated me. By the time I first entered university in 1984 (though I could not have known it at the time), the last white boxer's challenge for the undisputed world heavyweight championship had already happened.

The experience of the few white heavyweight contenders in recent decades, their portrayal by the media and the reaction they received from fans (before and after their careers) raised questions. What has been the fate of the Great White Hope fixation in the American sporting psyche? Were the careers of Gerry Cooney, Tommy Morrison, and Lou Savarese propelled upward by a desire for a white champion? And did they disappoint for this reason when they fell short of the title? No attempt had ever been made to statistically measure whether or not white heavyweights have continued to be marketing gold mines for promoters to present to the mainstream boxing audience, subsequently receiving more and easier opportunities to climb their sport's ranks.

1. American Boxing in Black and White

GEORGE KENNEDY: Gosh, Frank! You sure do know your fighters!
LESLIE NIELSEN: All I know is never bet on the white guy.

—The Naked Gun 2½, 1991

A lack of equal opportunity for black citizens has long been as evident in sport as in the rest of American society. In a nation that for nearly two centuries practiced institutionalized discrimination against non-white races in education, business, politics, and housing, it is not surprising that the gridiron, diamond, fairway, and court were also places where white skin meant a quicker, easier road to the top. As many universities were closed to black students until the 1960s, America's National Pastime for over sixty years was as lily white as its foul lines and base paths. Just as thousands of wealthy and middle-class neighborhoods across America were off-limits to darker-skinned citizens looking for a home until three decades ago, so too were most of the nation's university football fields and basketball courts. As the professional golf and tennis tours lacked black faces before the arrival of Sifford, Gibson, Elder, and Ashe, so did most of America's hospitals, law firms, banks, and social clubs. In all the above sports, race was a major factor in widening or narrowing an American athlete's chances at reaching his or her full potential.

In few sports, however, have African Americans faced as uphill a struggle as in professional boxing. Ironically, boxing, a pursuit in which African Americans had more opportunities to participate than in most other nineteenth-century sports, was also one where equal opportunity to excel was not at all forthcoming. In the early years of organized sports, black participation in boxing upset many white Americans to a greater degree than it did in other sports. Interracial competition in the ring frightened them in ways far beyond the unease they felt at whites and blacks sharing other fields of play. This fear made for a sport where black fighters seldom enjoyed equal opportunity to participate, much less excel.

Long before boxing's modern age, the racial dynamic that opened doors to whites closed them in black faces. Most black prizefighters prior to the Civil War were slaves who fought, hopefully, to win enough matches or money for their masters in the hope of winning their freedom. This participation represented opportunity, for obvious reasons, but only an opportunity to pull oneself out of bondage. The nature of such fights did nothing to make the participants forget they were still slaves. They could be ordered to fight to their deaths while wearing dog collars attached to chains that precluded their escape. The opportunity to compete in boxing was only extended to blacks by whites because the dubious stigma afforded sports at the time made black participation seem less threatening to the social order. Since most Americans still saw sports, particularly boxing, as improper, whites could not define it for their kind alone. Whites could not easily decry the morality of boxing, and at the same time cite this sport as a privileged white domain. They could hardly paint boxing as something dubious and illegitimate, while caring enough about it to erect walls around it to keep blacks out and only whites in. Decent nineteenth century society dismissed those Americans who patronized the ring as white riff raff. Such marginalized boxing fans had more immediate things to think about while attending bouts (not the least of which were their bets, their safety, and how to elude the police who could arrive at any moment) than the fact that one of the fighters may have been a black slave.[1]

Accounts of American boxing before the gloved era make reference to Bill Richmond and Tom Molyneaux, who achieved ring prominence in the early 1800s. Richmond and Molyneaux parlayed their fistic skills into freedom, but one finds very few references in African American sports histories of other free blacks making a living from prizefighting. Since the ring lingered in a state of unorganized and erratic competition for so many decades, the market for professional fighters was very small. This could not have made the sport very accessible to aspiring free black pugilists. White Americans did not become obsessed with theories of their own racial supremacy, formally constructing and asserting *scientific* rationales for their superiority, until the 1890s.[2] Prior to that decade, whites typically assumed that blacks were unfit for societal power, without often feeling the need to verbalize such ideas in scholarly journals and in debating halls. Whites in the 1890's, however, felt threatened enough by darker races to prove to all (including themselves) that theirs was the master race. The symbolic significance of interracial competition was not the primary obstacle facing black boxers until that time. Prior to the 1890's, one must conclude that sheer economics had the same effect that segregation later would have on African American boxers or would-be boxers seeking fame and fortune. Few opportunities existed for boxers to make money before the Civil War, and what little there was could only have been monopolized by whites. It was as the century wound down that the story of race and sports in America becomes immediately relevant to the games we watch today.

Boxing first made inroads into respectability in the late 1800s. Black pugilists would remain on the outside looking in. The color line that descended at the close of the nineteenth century separated white from black in sports as it did in all other areas of American life. Jim Crow did not overlook sports more than any other public sphere. Black boxers, particularly, were competing in a sport where their mere involvement scraped white insecurities. Many American whites felt it was scientifically proven that their strain of the Caucasian race was most qualified to lead the world, a belief paralleled by the widespread assumption that non-white races were unfit for full citizenship rights until they caught up with whites mentally, morally, and physically. An entire ideology formed to rationalize why whites and blacks must be kept separate in every avenue of society, including games and recreations.

Organized sports were barely in their infancy when the curtain came down on interracial competition, as white athletes and governing officials squeezed black athletes off the diamond, the horse and pedestrian tracks, and the cycling oval. A handful of elite black athletes shared the playing field with white opponents with considerable success in the 1880's and 1890's, but in each sport, the outcome was the same.[3] The same forces that created black water fountains and railway cars across America also made for Negro sports leagues and separate competitions for black athletes. The descent of Jim Crow policies over sports was often rationalized with the argument that it was clearly pointless to allow athletes of a weaker, slower, less intelligent people to compete against the earth's premier race, since the outcome was preordained. This, in spite of the fact that men like Isaac Murphy, Moses Walker, Frank Hart, and Marshall Taylor had often proven themselves equal or better in competition against white contemporaries.

For white Americans unknowledgeable about boxing, the notion of black inferiority took the shape of outlandish arguments about blacks having weaker stomachs, less endurance, and cowardly temperaments. On the rare occasions when circumstances allowed a fight between men of both races, the key to victory, the thinking went, was for the white man to attack his opponent's midriff and extend a fight into the later rounds when white stamina and perseverance would surely prevail.[4] The ferocity with which respectable whites (outside the boxing audience) opposed interracial sports belied their alleged pointlessness. If white people genuinely felt such contests were a waste of time, one would expect an ambivalence or even bemused tolerance from them towards such scenarios. Another pre-ordained white victory could actually be an effective reinforcement of the racial order, a reminder of where things stood with blacks. But many of those who were the most self-assured about white supremacy were neither indifferent nor smug about such competition. They decried it with almost hysterical overtones. One explanation for this seeming inconsistency was that many whites felt elitist contempt for having anything to do with blacks. To them, mingling with blacks in a sporting event was as beneath their dignity as sitting together in a restaurant or theater. Another contributing factor was a gnawing uncertainty about white supremacy, a fear of the consequences of a wrong outcome.

Many whites secretly feared the image of a black fighter triumphing over a white one, of seeing a black fist drawing blood on a white face, of a black man standing over an unconscious white man. A society that believed in white racial superiority, which sanctioned racial inequality in every corner of America, was horrified at a black merely attacking, let alone proving his physical superiority, over a white. This image could only undercut the white population's monopoly over power, privilege and opportunity. Black Australian Peter Jackson, arguably the best heavyweight contender of the 1890's, waited in vain for a chance to fight for the world championship, while lesser white boxers challenged Jim Corbett. Corbett, who had actually fought Jackson before he won the title, ignored his talented rival and all other black contenders, just as his predecessor John L. Sullivan had done. Jackson had the misfortune of entering his prime as a world-class boxer as a heavy curtain of segregation descended on American society. For years, Jackson patiently and politely appealed to the white American public's sense of sportsmanship and fair play, hoping Corbett would be pressured to do the right thing. He waited in vain. However much criticism rained down on Corbett from anxious and color-blind boxing fans, it was not enough to change what was either his singular determination to respect racial politics, or fear of losing to a dangerous rival.

When his skills finally eroded, Jackson's life went into a tailspin. He failed in acting and in running a boxing school. Turning to the bottle, he returned home heartbroken to Australia, a depressed and bitter man who found an early grave at age forty. Tuberculosis may ultimately have killed him anyway, but his despondency over being denied what his ability so clearly entitled him to, steered him to alcohol, which sapped his strength and motivation to fight the disease. Jackson's life, no matter how long or short, would have been markedly different, in terms of both money and fulfillment, if only he had been allowed to contest the world title.[5]

Jack Johnson was similarly denied a title shot for years because his talent threatened the racial order. Long after this Galveston boxer had established himself as a premier world-class heavyweight, his career had hit a competitive ceiling that appeared permanent. Like many other talented black boxers, Johnson had to cobble together a hard existence, roaming the nation to fight whatever bouts he could arrange. Despite defeating almost every opponent he faced in the first years of the twentieth century, Johnson remained poor. The lucrative, high-profile bouts against top white competition, the type that led to the world championship, were for a long time beyond his reach. He had to build his record with multiple bouts against a handful of fellow African American fighters, only occasionally landing fights with unmarketable or over-the-hill white boxers who would cross the color line.[6] The world champion at this time, Jim Jeffries, remained just as committed to keeping his title in white hands as did Sullivan, Corbett, and Fitzimmons before him. Jeffries retired undefeated in 1904, claiming he had no worthy challengers left to fight when he merely had no worthy white rivals. The outgoing champion actually staged his own succession by refereeing an elimination bout between two lackluster white contenders named Marvin Hart and Jack Root, neither of whom could hold a candle to Johnson's talent. Year after year, Johnson stewed at racist indignities of his childhood and the injustice of a society and sport that allowed him to aspire no higher than winning the Negro heavyweight championship, a title which had no prestige with the white media outside California.[7]

Only through a combination of circumstances was the color line lifted for Johnson. In 1906, the title fell into the hands of a Canadian, Tommy Burns, who was not handcuffed by American racial convention. After Jeffries's retirement, boxing's popularity and economic viability declined significantly, steering more white sentiment in favor of lowering the color bar for a fight that could catch the public's imagination. This was possible because there had also long been aspects of boxing which, at times, opened more opportunity to black Americans than other sports did, factors which could push a boxer at least within striking distance of the championship. Perhaps because boxing had traditionally been at the margins of respectable American society, it was the only professional sport where black Americans could excel prior to World War II. To understand this seeming anomaly, one must consider the responses of different Americans to this sport.

Boxing's traditional enemies were found in the morally upright and righteous old middle class, which fueled reform movements in the nineteenth and twentieth centuries, and had provided the most stubborn opposition to the growth of sports in general since the days of the Puritans.[8] That social class had long seen sports as a waste of time, if not immoral. They particularly loathed blood sports like boxing for its association with gambling and the character of its participants.[9] High-minded Americans would feel the need for a bath if forced to sit ringside for a typical fight in the late 1800's, with the boxers inside the ropes sometimes the safest individuals present. It was not unheard of for local police chiefs to deal with crime waves by taking a contingent of constables to a prizefight where they could more easily round up their quarry. To critics, the mere act of wagering on a sporting outcome and the unruliness of the crowds were reasons enough to ban boxing. The dishonesty and fraud seemingly entrenched in the sport also offended many sensibilities. Well after Sullivan and Corbett had begun changing minds about the value of the sport, contempt persisted in some circles due to boxing's lack of any organizational structure, a void of control often resulting in fixed matches that defrauded the public. The lack of gambling activity for the 1900 title bout between Corbett and Jeffries has been cited as just one example where the mere perception of impropriety clung to the sport like paint.[10] Few spectators would wager on fights like this one when rumors circulated that the outcome was set before the fighters ever set foot in the ring.

The list of objections to boxing did not end there. Even if no money had ever been wagered for a fight on American soil, the ring would still have had ample warts to disqualify it from acceptance. Protestant sensitivities could not abide a sport whose specific purpose was to injure another human being, a defilement of God's image: Darwinists saw in the sport a societal move backward, away from civilization. Law and order advocates condemned an activity whose participants and spectators flaunted the law.[11]

For all these objections, however, many boxing fans were from the restless urban male working class. Boxers themselves, of course, were drawn almost exclusively from those trying to escape the clutches of nineteenth-century poverty, typically immigrants, with Irish Americans leading the way into the nation's rings. It was much the same story for the sport's audience. Savoring distraction from their brutal existences, underpaid laborers in America's burgeoning cities took to a variety of commercial spectator sports in the Gilded Age, when they could afford a ticket. In New York, where organized sports first took root on a large scale, the typical boxer was an urban street tough working as political muscle for Tammany Hall or other urban political factions. The political machines benefited from having such men work as "shoulder hitters" on election day, while the boxers were given jobs working as bartenders or bouncers in gang-allied taverns to sustain themselves during their long intervals between fights. Such men clearly were not among the class that could afford to turn its nose up at boxing. The sport was a pathway to escape the slums.[12]

Better compensated workers, including the nation's new and rapidly growing industrial middle class, had more disposable income and free time than previous generations. They also had to cope with an increasingly structured workplace that allowed them less power, input, and opportunity for advancement. This white-collar crowd found in boxing and other sporting events the fulfillment lacking in their repetitive desk jobs.[13] Few jobs in the emerging Industrial America offered the thrill of witnessing another victory by the great John L. Sullivan or other eminent ring heroes. The Boston Strong Boy's ability to emphatically settle matters (often with a single punch) must have seemed intoxicating to paper-pushing office types who could not leave work a minute early or express an opinion to their supervisors.

At the other end of the economic spectrum, America's wealthy elite had long found entertainment in sporting spectacles hated by reformers, and its patronage in the 1890's had elevated prizefighting's reputation (though less its reality) into the more regulated and upright sport of modern boxing. Amidst the boisterous throng that made up most early boxing audiences, there was consistently a representation of the gentlemanly sporting crowd. Wealthier fans could more easily salve their consciences after attending a boxing contest because the rough-hewn backgrounds of the fighters emphasized the moral distance between athlete and spectator. Blueblood sport enthusiasts were less bothered by moral reservations in sports where they did not have to otherwise interact with the participants. They were likely to apply more rigorous moral standards if the athletes in front of them were their social peers. Boxers were clearly far below such fans in everyday life, thus the opportunity to enjoy without feeling morally compromised.[14] The view from above was apparently a less self-conscious one.

In all economic classes, there were fans who liked the sport for its creation of heroes. Americans enjoyed less and less individualism in an age when work increasingly meant standing next to a machine alongside hundreds of co-workers. The ring reasserted this yearning of Americans to define themselves as unique, as having their own identity at a time when the workplace offered them less opportunity to feel this way. Seeing a fighter's gloved hand raised in victory was inspiring to Gilded Age urbanites whose name was still unknown by his long-time boss at work, a promise (no matter how realistic) that one could still rise to the top through dedication and hard work. In boxing, there was no need to get into the right school (or even finish high school), have the right social connections, or know how to operate a machine. No other sport better personified the dominant ethos of the late 1800's, the belief in survival of the fittest, of the inherent rightness of rigorous competition to root out the weak and push the strong to greater heights. Like no other contests, boxing defined genuine winners and losers.[15]

Regionally, one could also find more favorable terrain for boxing by moving westward where frontier Americans had less use for moral crusades. Jeffrey Sammons emphasizes that during boxing's most vulnerable period at the turn of the century, when the sport suffered heavy legal and political blows from outraged critics in the East, it found a haven in places like Nevada, Texas, Wyoming, and California.[16] Progressive calls for a morally pure society through more government control and intervention did not ring as loudly in chaotic mining towns and railway camps. The rugged social climate of the West attracted a breed of American who was obviously less cowed by the social norms of the urban East. As with the teeming blue-collar masses who toiled in America's older urban centers, farming, ranching, and mining were hard enough existences for many Westerners without deferring to big-city prigs when the workday was over.

This diverse boxing constituency enjoyed the sheer entertainment value of the ring, the sport's drama and excitement. Such boxing fans were certainly a minority of white America, but they were plentiful and enthusiastic enough to keep the sport alive even during its darkest days.[17] Specific to this discussion, those who were more open-minded (or immoral) in regard to the existence of boxing were naturally less hidebound about other objections to it. Many whites who loved the thrill of human combat could forget the color line when a marketable black-white bout was in the works. By simply patronizing boxing matches, they were already challenging social convention. For many fans of the sport, buying a ticket to see an interracial bout was merely one step further in the direction of recreating on the wild side. At the same time, such aficionados admitted qualities in boxers to which the rest of upright America was slowly coming to appreciate. With the White House occupied by a former police chief and range cowboy, a man whose pores virtually breathed rugged individualism, the traits of courage, sacrifice and persistence would soon be celebrated in America by more than the small boxing gentry. There was a growing sense that America's future goals, the greatness it aspired to, could not be realized without rigorous sporting pursuits to instil the qualities more and more workplaces did not provide.

Within the sport's hard core audience, rumblings in favor of a black versus white heavyweight title were growing especially loud by 1908. Boxing writers were wistful about the sport's golden days, when icons like Jeffries and Sullivan ruled the roost and generated great crowds, profits, and press coverage. Sufficiently bored with second-rate champion Tommy Burns's defenses against mediocre competition, boxing writers and white fans were ready to accept interracial fights. The prospect of a marketable fight between the Canadian champion and Johnson became more attractive. Sammons points out that American support, or at least tolerance, for a Burns-Johnson match, was also a calculated ploy to reassert white racial supremacy. Such white boxing interests genuinely believed that Burns's expected victory would stem directly from his race. Even if he lost, they reasoned, a native son would quickly set things straight, for there was no white like an American white.[18] This inevitable victory would once again clarify which race was superior. A short-term sullying of the world heavyweight title would hopefully pay off large dividends in dissuading American blacks from becoming too proud. With some white Americans fully expecting such a fight to be a textbook lesson in the natural order of things (by Burns if possible, by an American later on if necessary), the boxing audience and powers in the United States raised its color line and did not object too strenuously when Tommy Burns finally signed to fight Johnson in Sydney.[19] Ultimately, no American in or out of the boxing world had the power to stop a Canadian world champion from defending his title against a black American in Australia if the money was right. America's media, however, was more receptive to such a championship bout than ever before. Johnson was that good, Burns was that mediocre, and boxing was in bad enough financial straits to make the fight worth the temporary risk to race relations. Desperate times (for boxing) called for desperate measures.

Johnson made the most of this opportunity by destroying Burns to win the title. Whites who were unhappy at the fight even happening became angry when Johnson let spew the rage he had felt toward white racial discrimination since his childhood. Both in the ring against Burns, and in public when he arrived home, he gave Americans a taste of what his reign would be like. Continuing a habit already obvious before he fought Burns, Johnson arrogantly taunted the Canadian throughout a fourteen-round slaughter. Humiliating his white opponent with a steady stream of dismissive comments, the black challenger had toyed with his smaller foe as a man would with a child. Verbally, the Texan did more than pull Burns's psychological chain during the beating. He infuriated the white audience by mugging and bantering with ringside observers. With scores of punches to the champion's face, the Galveston challenger exacted revenge on a white establishment that would not allow his mother to ride streetcars with white tramps, that pushed him into gutters as an adult, that made him wait outside posh doors for hours and be spat upon by boy servants while his manager negotiated fights inside.

Any chance of Johnson distinguishing between his white opponent and the white society that had dehumanized him for three decades was lost in the weeks leading up to the fight. Overconfident and contemptuous toward his black challenger, Burns had taunted him with common racial epithets of that time, calling him "coon" and "nigger" publicly.[20] Johnson's response was to cut Burns to ribbons before the police stopped the fight. If the new champion was not the only black American in 1908 who could assault and verbally emasculate a white man for over forty minutes with impunity, he was part of a very exclusive club.

Knowing exactly what his prescribed place was as a black man living among whites, "Little Arthur," the champion, set out to live his life exactly as any wealthy white man could. Even before beating Burns, Johnson had been increasingly bold in crossing over the color line. Asserting himself verbally and sometimes physically around white men, failing to pay debts to white creditors, and flaunting his wealth (when he had some) in white faces, Johnson was not only unconcerned about raking white sensitivies, he at times intentionally stuck a knife in racist convention. Sizing up the fame and fortune the world title offered, the first black heavyweight champion feasted on his celebrity. Like a thirsty barfly *accidentally* locked in a bar overnight, Johnson enjoyed the privilege of world recognition as much as any white champion ever had. In America, being a famous sporting hero had become a key to the good life, and Johnson would enjoy his stature while wiping his feet on white assumptions and norms. Randy Roberts has compared this fighter to a sadistic dentist searching for the most delicate nerves to drill in white America's teeth, in cold repayment for the brutality and indignities he had suffered as a black man. Another biographer described Johnson as behaving like the honored guest at a never-ending party.[21]

The heavyweight title lessened what few social inhibitions he had when he sailed to Australia. Smiling at and belittling his opponents, deliberately carrying them long after he could have knocked them out, and repeatedly baiting white hecklers at ringside, continued to be his trademarks in the ring. These acts alone would have made him unpopular with white fans, but like other champion boxers, Johnson would fight rarely. Millions of whites who only saw or heard about his ring behavior one or twice a year would have to endure far more common offensive images in his public life.

Johnson wore the finest clothes, and in the tradition of a dandy, changed outfits multiple times every day, employing a maid solely to take care of his suits. He frequented hotels and restaurants that few whites could ever afford, in a time when few whites could abide the idea of blacks even being equal. He routinely carried silver canes, wore diamond stickpins while out on the town, and had a gold straw made to sip his favorite drink in bars and restaurants. If there were any white racists not sufficiently offended by seeing gold fillings in Johnson's mouth, he had a diamond mounted on top of one such tooth. For many infuriated whites, Johnson was already a "bad nigger" for his fearless disdain for white convention. Such displays of wealth on a black man's person now spelled out "uppity nigger." This was a black man who was not at all dependent on white favor to live his life. Photographs of Johnson's public life show a man who looked dressed for a day at an exclusive golf or riding club. He owned six luxury automobiles and drove them as recklessly as he spurned white convention, with no regard for safety or traffic tickets. He said exactly what was on his mind, with no deference to white sensitivities about race issues. Long before Johnson's championship years, and decades after, millions of blacks learned it was safer to shuffle and lower their heads in the presence of whites, to doff their hat no matter how un-

1. American Boxing in Black and White 13

comfortable the sun. A black man who walked with his head high, looked straight into white men's eyes as an equal, and did not smile ingratiatingly, was treading on dangerous ground. The slightest hint of anger or resentment in black eyes could result in a white lynch mob reasserting the racial order. White supremacists did not merely want a society where blacks were treated as inferiors, they wanted blacks to smilingly acknowledge their inferiority, thus soothing white fears about a bloody race war. The burden of keeping the racial peace lay entirely on black people knowing what was what, and behaving accordingly. The new heavyweight champion, however, had shuffled little in his first thirty years of life. After he became the heavyweight king, he never did so again.[22]

All of the above, however, paled next to his ultimate faux pas in white eyes. He openly courted and romanced white women. Johnson was routinely seen in public with a white prostitute on his arm, often showing them off as trophies that seemed to compliment his mastery over white boxers. He appeared, probably intentionally, as the white man's superior in the ring and between the sheets. If this did not make him enough of a rebel, he went one step further, marrying three white women, two of them while champion. Interracial marriage was outlawed in many states, as this was a time when southern black men could be murdered for merely being accused of staring suggestively at a white woman.[23] There was more than sexual insecurity and pride involved. Many vocal politicians, clergy, and editors of this era warned that miscegenation threatened to contaminate the white race, creating a mongrel human breed. For those confident of white America's destiny as the world's leading nation, black men could not be kept far enough away from white women.

Johnson's celebrity status meant that whites offended by interracial sex could do little but seethe. Public criticism did nothing to make him alter his taste in women anymore than the other outlandish aspects of his lifestyle. White patrons of Johnson's Chicago nightclub could not help but be aware of his choice in romantic companions. They were greeted inside the door by a huge wall photograph of the fighter embracing his first white wife. Perhaps the most blatant, if crude, example of Johnson flaying white insecurities occurred when he was training. While changing into his boxing garb, he would wrap his penis to look larger under his tight shorts when he ventured into the ring. This behavior ripped open another scab in white men's minds, the fear that their wives fantasized about black men. All of the above behaviors had to be swallowed by white America on top of the dangerous symbolism of seeing Johnson dominate white men in the ring, an image not lost on millions of black men. He held the heavyweight title during what has been called the nadir of black history in America. In the four decades spanning the turn of the century, black men had more reason than ever before to watch their step and mind their tongues around whites. Determined to maintain a racial caste system, whites were nervous at even the hint of a challenge to the social order. During the six full years of Johnson's reign, 359 black Americans were lynched, an average of five every month, while this black champion rubbed his physical superiority, sexual conquests, and wealth in white faces.[24] The vast majority of these mob murders were for crimes either petty or imaginary, many carried out under the pretext that a white woman's virtue or safety had been violated. These lynchings spelled out to the black population where it stood, and must remain. If not for his celebrity, Johnson could have been killed many times over for a litany of social transgressions in early twentieth century America. His belt and crown were all that kept him from becoming the "strange fruit" that Billie Holiday would later sing of hanging from so many American trees prior to World War II.

Johnson's public behavior could have been a brief aberration if a white champion had quickly been found to win back the world title and racial pride for the supposed master race. This did not happen, in spite of feverish searches for such a hero. One opponent after another climbed into the ring and lost to this grinning thorn in white America's side. White desperation shone through in the man who would become the nation's greatest white hope. Former champion Jim Jeffries, age thirty-five, six years retired, and grotesquely out of shape at 300 pounds, was pressured by appeals to race loyalty and huge financial offers to train for a return to the ring against Johnson in Reno, on Independence Day, 1910. For months, the attention of virtually the entire nation, black and white, focused on this looming conflict and its presumed meaning for race relations. No matter how fashionable moral opposition was to boxing at this time, no newspaper could afford to ignore the fight, given how fixated Americans were on the outcome of this racial holy war. The white public trumpeted the unbeaten and supposedly unbeatable Jeffries like none of Johnson's previous half dozen white championship opponents, certain he was the best white specimen for the job, the hero who would set things straight. Under a scalding Nevada sun, Jeffries's fans watched in horror as Johnson easily outclassed his ring-rusty opponent, knocking him down three times before the fight was stopped.

With Johnson having emphatically proven his superiority over white America's best hope, the passions that had been building nationwide for so long spilled over for days afterward. In almost every region of the country, the jubilation and defiance of celebrating blacks collided with white bitterness, frustration, and fear, with predictable results in a country that had placed so much symbolic importance in a boxing match. Nineteen people were killed and over 200 injured in confrontations stemming from black euphoria and white resentment over the outcome. White America would have to tolerate a black world champion for a long time yet, and was none too happy about it. There were no more white hopes on the immediate horizon, at least none that could seriously challenge Johnson. Even a relative progressive, Teddy Roosevelt, spoke for many worried whites when he called for boxing to be abolished in the aftermath of Reno. This from a man who himself boxed in the White House and spent eight years as president selling Americans on the value of rugged, manly sports, the first U.S. president to encourage citizens to become strong through exercise and games.[25]

White newspapers had confidently publicized the fight beforehand as a true indication of racial superiority. With Jeffries's destruction, they now twisted themselves into pretzels trying to deflate the symbolism of the fight. Johnson's supremacy had no significance beyond the ring, they now explained to their worried white readers and emboldened black ones. Some editorials even warned blacks not to read anything into the result, white insecurity and rage screaming off the page at the same time.

> Do not point your nose too high. Do not swell your chest too much. Do not boast too loudly. Do not be puffed up. Let not your ambition be inordinate or take a wrong direction.... Remember, you have done nothing at all. You are just the same member of society today you were last week.... You are on no higher lane, deserve no new consideration, and will get none.... No man will think a bit higher of you because your complexion is the same as that of the victor at Reno.[26]

Ultimately, the white establishment did to Johnson in the courts what it could not do in the ring. The champion's recklessness inevitably gave the authorities a means to punish him for his misdeeds. The federal government successfully prosecuted him on a dubious infraction of the federal Mann Act, a statute banning the interstate transportation of prostitutes. This law had to be stretched to the breaking point of credibility in Johnson's case. Johnson had routinely traveled the country with white girlfriends who also happened to be prostitutes, but there was no evidence he had ever personally profited as a pimp from them, which was clearly the original intent of the law. His conviction was blatantly about his being a black man who did not know his place in relation to white women.[27] Sentenced to one year in jail in 1913, the world heavyweight champion fled the country. Two years later, his finances low from living in Europe, the thirty-seven year-old champion agreed to fight another white challenger, Jess Willard, in Havana, Cuba. Whites who detested Johnson finally got what they had wanted for seven years, a fighter who could reassert the supremacy of the master race. The larger and much younger Willard knocked out Johnson in the twenty-sixth round.

Johnson's image would limit the prospects of black heavyweights for more than two decades. Once the crown was safely on Willard's head, many Caucasians did not want to revisit the uneasy feelings they had when Johnson toyed with white fighters or courted white women. How many more Jack Johnsons were waiting in the wings to make a mockery of white values and assumptions, and encourage blacks to question and challenge the color line? Still decades away from supporting equal civil rights for minorities, whites concluded that for the sake of American (white) society, no more blacks should be allowed to fight for the heavyweight crown. Few promoters, politicians, and legal authorities wanted to again deal with the violence that unfolded on Independence Day, 1910, or with the insufferable sight of Johnson smiling while flaunting his wealth and taste in women.

Talented black heavyweights between 1915 and 1937 are largely unknown to the popular boxing memory because no matter how skilled, they labored under Johnson's shadow, a shadow that stranded them far from the world title. Their quest for the heavyweight crown was futile. The color line was written in harder stone than it had ever been before 1908. White America was more committed to keeping the world champion white than it was to the vitality of heavyweight boxing. The accolades for Johnson's successor, Willard, died out quickly as he proved both unable and unwilling to capture the public's imagination as a champion. Willard defended his title once in four years, much to the derision of the boxing public. Still, a lazy and inactive white champion was infinitely preferable to any black one. Superb contenders like Sam Langford, Joe Jeannette, Sam McVey, and Bill Tate remained anonymous outside of boxing solely because of their skin color.[28] Willard never considered making the same mistake as Tommy Burns had a decade earlier, and its doubtful the white public would have allowed him to waive the color line even if he had been tempted.

When Willard lost his championship, his successor, Jack Dempsey, ruled the heavyweight roost for seven years without ever fighting a black opponent. Another black contender, the aging but still dangerous Harry Wills, spent years lobbying for a fight with Dempsey to no avail. By 1923, Dempsey had almost run out of qualified opponents. Wills was conspicuously the leading contender throughout Dempsey's championship reign, but this did not stop the Manassa Mauler, like his predecessor, from taking an extended vacation from fighting, leaving his belt in moth balls from 1923 to 1926. Jess Willard's reputation as a heavyweight champion never recovered from defending his title just once in four years (for a draw, even!) before being deposed. Even media and political pressure from whites who recognized Wills's rightful claim to a championship bout was not enough to overcome the legacy of Jack Johnson. In 1924, a bout between the two seemed finalized, but Dempsey's handlers paid Wills off with $50,000 rather than go through with a contest. Whether the decision emanated from the world champion, his manager Tex Rickard, New York state boxing officials, legislators, or some combination therein, the fear that Dempsey might lose to a black challenger and the racial turmoil of fourteen years earlier hung over this dilemma like a dark cloud. Wills was passed over and forgotten.[29] Dempsey's aura has never dimmed in spite of a thirty-six month vacation in which he spurned one of the best rivals of his time.

In the 1930's, a combination of slowly changing attitudes and the negative financial impact on boxing caused by both the Depression and a decline in the quality of heavyweight champions, finally broke down the world title's color line. In the seven years after Gene Tunney's retirement, the world title may have been safely on white heads, but in the eyes of the ticket-buying public, they were anemic white heads. Five champions in seven years wore the mantle of world heavyweight champion, and none of them would capture the imagination of boxing fans, whose yearning for excitement and greatness in the ring eroded many lingering white reservations about racial symbolism in the ring. German fighter Max Schmeling came from a nation that America had been at war with twelve years earlier, making him an unlikely candidate to win over the boxing fancy on this side of the Atlantic. Jack Sharkey may have done patriotism a good deed by toppling Schmeling's crown, but he had eight losses on his spotty record, and lost the title in his first defense. Italian Primo Carnera was a more tolerable foreigner, hailing from an allied nation in World War I, but he was viewed more as a muscular carnival freak than a skilled boxer, and it was an open secret that his rise to the top of the division was the result of mafia-fixed fights. Carnera's conqueror, Max Baer, was colorful and popular with both media and fans, but his playboy lifestyle even after winning the title was compelling proof of his lack of intensity and commitment to his sport. Having upset Baer, Jim Braddock was a heartwarming rags-to-riches Depression story, but he had twenty-one losses on his record when he became champion, and froze his title through two years of inactivity. These five champions stand historically as boxers who kept the heavyweight crown lukewarm between the Dempsey-Tunney era, and another great champion waiting in the wings.

The desire for a boxing legend erased the division's color line, and this played to the advantage of a highly touted black fighter from Detroit. His undeniable talent, and the willingness of cash-starved promoters to allow him to fight white opponents would shake America far beyond the confines of sports. Joe Louis seized this opportunity and made the most of it by beating one white opponent after another until he knocked out Jim Braddock in 1937 to become world champion. Holding the crown for twelve years, Louis's thrashing of white boxers did not result in race riots like those of 1910. His possession of the heavyweight title came to be widely accepted, and cherished by the racial majority. Louis, a black man, would become one of America's most cherished sports icons. In barely more than a decade, his greatness in the ring, and his deportment out of it, would make whites question their ideas about their society, about their black brethren, and about fairness and justice.[30]

Louis would stand as one of the most seminal figures in the softening of American racist attitudes before, during, and after World War II. The seismic shift in American race relations from the time Louis first burst onto the national sports pages in 1935 to his hanging up of his gloves in 1951 is difficult to overestimate. As millions of white sports fans got to know Joe Louis, their support for the drawing of the color line weakened, first in boxing, then in other sports, and ultimately in society in general. The more America witnessed Joe Louis's grace, dignity, and class as a sports hero, the harder it was to rationalize countless forms of discrimination against blacks.

Louis biographer Chris Mead illustrates just how far attitudes changed toward integration in sports when Joe Louis was champion. When he first entered the nation's consciousness, the description of Louis in the white press alternated between patronizing and fearful, similar to the way that white America saw blacks generally. They either painted him in animal metaphors, as an expressionless and remorseless killing machine one step removed from the jungle, or as a stereotypical lazy and dumb southern darkie, quoting him in Uncle Remus dialect. That the media blithely, shamelessly used such demeaning caricatures in their coverage of a fighter who many genuinely liked, compellingly shows how narrow white thinking was at this time. On the rare occasion when the white press publicized a black figure, they were made to fit cookie-cutter stereotypes conveying childlike ignorance. Media behavior that would seem ghastly to all but the most bigoted Americans today was a periodic trial of Louis's patience. One photographer attempted to force a watermelon on Louis so as to have his picture snapped in an image apparently comfortable to a white audience.[31] This proclivity toward condescension was made worse by Louis's shy personality, as well as his demeanor during filmed interviews. He was strictly coached by his handlers to be unfailingly polite and formal around whites. Forever conscious of his facial expressions, it is doubtful Louis could have projected himself in a way that would undermine assumptions about blacks. If he had demonstrated a robust, exuberant, or humorous personality, it would have been easy for writers to paint him in Amos and Andy terms. As it was, his passive, reserved, and methodical demeanor made it easy for reporters to depict him as a sleepy-eyed, indolent, and limited black man beyond the ring. Carrying an armload of preconceived racial assumptions, many white reporters saw what they expected to see in Louis for years

At first, promoters and boxing fans in the 1930's were similarly unable or unwilling to accept Louis on the same terms as white athletes. Promoters were reluctant to stage bouts with black fighters out of fear that white fans would not pay to see them compete. Even one black boxer in the ring was seen as a risky marketing venture. White spectators consistently rooted for Louis's overmatched white opponents before and after he won the title. On the night Louis lost his first match to Max Schmeling, after many months of seeming acceptance and praise by the media and public, America's response was to hail a white foreigner's triumph over a black American. Schmeling's treatment as a conquering white hero early on laid bare the tenuous nature of Louis's claim on the affections of white America.[32]

By the latter stages of Louis's career, America's racial dynamic had taken several large steps forward. Through the initiative of eminent African Americans like the Brown Bomber and many others, combined with the greater receptivity of whites to social justice, neither integrated boxing matches or a black world champion seemed as frightening or radical as they had a decade before. No one thought it newsworthy when Louis chose two black men, Ezzard Charles and Joe Walcott, to contest his vacated belt in 1949. Fans actually cheered louder for Louis in his last fight two years later when he stepped into the ring to fight a white fighter, Rocky Marciano. The empathy felt by many whites at the sight of Louis being conquered by Marciano was in sharp contrast to the giddy celebration that greeted Jack Johnson's demise in Cuba thirty-six years earlier. Even Marciano cried in the celebratory aftermath of his victory over the faded legend.[33] Five decades later, sports fans still allude to Louis's bittersweet loss to Marciano and father time, to the undignified image of boxing's greatest champion stretched unconsious over the ropes in the eighth round, when they wax nostalgic about athletes who hang on too long. The media had come to express almost universal admiration for Louis, placing him on a pedestal of respect given to few white athletes. Louis's decency, graciousness, military service, patriotic persona, and reverence for his society had reassured countless whites that their worst fears about integrated sports were unfounded. To many whites who doubted it, the Brown Bomber demonstrated that blacks could handle success responsibly, could be public figures who lived up to middle-class America's cherished ideals, and could seize opportunity without bitterness or revenge on their minds. He succeeded in reassuring America that black athletes could compete at the highest levels without stirring up racial tensions. Journalists had become reverential toward him after the war. Racial stereotypes had virtually disappeared from newspaper accounts of him, as white sports columnists depicted him with sentimental, almost saintly overtones as someone worthy of the highest admiration.

Clearly, Americans had evolved considerably in their views toward who should be allowed on the field of play during Joe Louis's boxing career. But for all that Joe Louis accomplished to open doors for other black athletes, there were very real limitations to what his career meant for white acceptance of black participation in sports and other institutions. The willingness of whites to offer equal opportunity to black athletes received a tremendous boost from his achievements, but opportunity still lagged considerably behind their embrace of Louis himself. For the Brown Bomber to be accepted as a black celebrity in a white society required painstaking public relations efforts by his handlers to make him presentable to middle-class America, to make him non-threatening to core white values and beliefs. Louis was never free to be himself publicly as champion, never had the latitude to live on his own terms, the latitude most white athletes possessed simply by being white. To break down longstanding racial barriers, he had to be very different from Jack Johnson, the complete opposite of prevailing racist stereotypes about blacks. Early on, his handlers actually spelled out what acceptable public behavior would be in the public eye. He was never to have his picture taken with a white woman, go into a nightclub alone, or gloat over a fallen opponent. He was always to keep a deadpan expression in front of cameras. Such advice was meant to put whites at ease so as to maximize Louis's career prospects. The success of Louis and his handlers in doing this benefited not only Louis, but opened doors to countless other blacks in sports and other endeavors. This public persona was successfully sold to America for years, permitting Louis (and Black America with him) the opportunity to change many white attitudes about integration.

The image was not all contrived. In many ways, Louis was what the white media presented him as being. He was decent, modest, disciplined, polite, uncontroversial, generous, a true sportsman, a patriot to the core, and did not cuss or smoke. Journalists had to downplay other aspects of his personality, however, to project the right image for his career to be successful. Obscured was the fact that Louis was a womanizer between and during multiple marriages, hopelessly inept in saving his riches, and (when not in training) an active participant in the urban nightlife.[34] In short, Louis's image had to be managed carefully for white America to feel comfortable with giving him a title fight, and he had to maintain this public posture for white approval for twelve years as the world's most celebrated athlete. Falling short of this finely tuned image would have provided ammunition for opponents of racial integration, who would argue *this is what happens when equality is given those who are not ready for it.*

Louis's career was a huge breakthrough in American race relations, and a major step in the fight for integration that would peak in the 1960's. He is credited as having opened sports to blacks and with putting athletics at the forefront of the civil rights movement.[35] Enough whites liked and respected what they saw in Louis to become more accommodating toward black boxers and other athletes. The underlying rationales for segregation would never again be as secure after he became a fixture in American lives. Even before he retired, the three major team sports had all accepted their first black athletes. When Louis hung up his gloves, he left behind an America where blacks were far more inspired and emboldened to assert their rights, and whites were far more willing to listen, agree with and sometimes support such efforts. White America was more aware of racial injustice in their midst, of the harm done by racial stereotypes. This greater awareness gained while Louis was champion made this nation ripe for significant social change. In short, Louis's uncanny ability to dominate a sport and represent his race without confirming racist fears stood as an early and major crack in the walls of American segregation.[36]

But Louis's acceptance did not testify to his receiving equal opportunity for fame and fortune in his profession, if equal opportunity means being free to express oneself openly and live one's own life on one's own terms. In the 1930's, the racial status quo of America made that impossible. That Louis was one of America's favorite sports figures hardly proved the nation was completely comfortable with integrated sports, with seeing black athletes on the same teams as whites, with black domination in the ring or any other field of play, or with discarding any need for symbolic white victories in sports. The door opened for this fighter because he was so talented in a time when his sport was in dire economic straits. His value as a box office attraction outweighed the memory of his black predecessor. But Louis remained a black boxer who succeeded on white America's terms, on white America's schedule, and as far as white America cared to permit. If Louis, in 1936, had publicly cavorted with white prostitutes, grinned and boasted while pummeling inferior white boxers, or criticized America for its treatment of blacks, his name would be unknown to most Americans today. His career would have met an invisible wall long before he came near a title shot.

To whatever degree Louis was accepted by America, most black heavyweights in the 1930's and 1940's did not walk through the same narrow doorway and share the same opportunity he did, any more than every qualified black baseball player reached the major leagues upon Jackie Robinson's breaking of the color barrier in 1947. Josh Gibson was one of many deserving black diamond greats tragically stranded in Major League Baseball's lobby early in 1947 when Walter O'Malley first imagined Jackie Robinson in Dodger Blue. Robinson was chosen as much for his suitability (age, personality) for a brutal racial experiment as for his skills. The 35-year-old Gibson seems to have never been even considered to integrate baseball, even though he had been comparable to Babe Ruth in his batting prowess. Gibson's premature death at 35, before Robinson ever suited up, in no way changes the fact that white attitudes would change too slowly for all but a select few black players to join the big leagues prior to the 1960's. In the same vein, the hole Louis punched in boxing segregation's wall was not big enough to carry many other black heavyweights with him to color blind opportunity. He did not defend his crown against a true black heavyweight until his two bouts with Jersey Joe Walcott in the final two years (1947–48) of his reign. That twenty-two of Louis' twenty-five defenses were against white challengers was no accident. There were credible black heavyweight challengers at the time, but however much Louis won over white hearts, the white audience still wanted a white champion if possible, something that obviously could not happen if Louis fought other African Americans.[37]

Countless black athletes who entered professional sports after Louis benefited immensely from his impact and example. The walls of segregation in sports were ultimately shattered by the Brown Bomber and other men named Cooper, Lloyd, Washington, Strode, Robinson, and Doby. These developments tempt one to believe that whites no longer have any problem with unfettered black participation and opportunity for success in the games they watch. How could race still be a problem in sports when so many black athletes make up the rosters of professional teams, have garnered so many laurels for their play, and become many of white America's most famous and cherished heroes? Were there not tens of millions of white fans who idolized the outfield artistry of Willie Mays and power of Hank Aaron? How many white football followers were not thrilled by the toughness of Jim Brown and the speed of Jerry Rice? Did the creativity of Magic Johnson and intensity of Michael Jordan not reach far beyond the black community? How many white sports fans would have wanted to miss the exploits of these giants of sports, instead seeing lesser talented white athletes in their place? The throngs of whites who cheered for these athletes and asked for their autographs certainly make it appear they became as ready to accept black sports heroes as white ones. The story of American sports in recent decades, however, indicates white acceptance and enthusiasm for racially equal sports opportunity is complex and qualified.

2. SEGREGATION IN AMERICAN SPORTS IS DEAD, BUT...

> QUESTION: Do you know any good white basketball players?
> RESPONSE: There are no good white basketball players.
>
> —*Top Secret*, 1984

The on-the-field success enjoyed by countless great black athletes over the past fifty years, the fame and financial rewards they have received, and their huge over-representation in some sports, tempt us to think that skin color stopped being an important factor in sports a long time ago. But the white adulation of men like Joe Louis and Jackie Robinson that gave rise to these developments was still just a stepping stone toward a more racially just society. For all the rewards blacks have reaped from sports, they still today do not enjoy the same range of opportunities and rewards when they try to make a living in this field. Opening the door of sports was one thing; allowing black athletes to freely join the party has been another story for five decades. Segregation itself was broken down slowly, especially in America's showcase sport of baseball. White baseball fans congratulated themselves for their open-mindedness about Jackie Robinson, but there was no rush by most teams to overturn seventy years of racial tradition.

The initial wave of black players signed to major league rosters was very thin, as if owners knew there was no going back to segregation, but waited and wondered who would field a black athlete next. By the end of the 1950s, a full decade after the Dodgers broke the Jim Crow mold and well after Robinson's 1956 retirement, the game's white establishment approached integration with little more enthusiasm than one heading to a dentist for root canal surgery. Six years after Robinson's first at bat, ten of sixteen major league teams still did not have a black on their roster. It was not until four more years had passed that the final holdout, the Boston Red Sox, fielded a non-white player. Although Major League Baseball's showcase franchise, the dynastic Yankees, had earlier signed Elston Howard, the New York Club dug its heels in for years against criticism of its milk-white roster. All the while, their front office insisted it was looking for appropriate talent, with little tangible evidence to show for it. At the league level, the Junior Circuit was particularly reticent about integrating; by 1959, the American League employed only half as many African Americans as the National League. This determination not to tap into a gold mine of black talent was apparently more powerful than the embarrassment of three decades worth of All-Star Game domination by a more quickly integrating Senior Circuit. All told, Major League Baseball had found room for exactly eighteen black players a full decade after Robinson faced his first racist epithet at Ebbets Field, an average of less than two players per year.[1]

If the spirit of integration was tarnished by baseball's best team, it was dragged through the mud by the football franchise in the nation's capital. Long after every other NFL team had integrated rosters, the Washington Redskins, sharing a city with the most powerful democratic government in the world, had no black players. George Preston Marshall gave in to the winds of change only when his need for a federally funded new stadium forced him to sign Bobby Mitchell in 1962. This was sixteen years (!) after Kenny Washington and Woody Strode had first worn Los Angeles Ram horns, and Bill Willis and Marion Motley had donned the orange of the Cleveland Browns in the All-American Football Conference. In the intervening period, Marshall was willing to endure eleven losing seasons, only two winning ones, no playoff appearances, and a pair of one-win seasons immediately before he finally capitulated. For this owner, losing with white players was clearly preferable to winning with black ones.

The media gave up old habits slowly. Joe Louis's growth into an American icon eventually shielded him from the demeaning "darkie" portrayals directed at him by so many newspapers before World War II. This advance in white journalists' racial sensitivity did not extend far beyond the Brown Bomber himself. Baseball players who integrated the game in the early 1950s experienced the same demeaning depictions fifteen years after Louis fought his way to the title. Even the very best black players did not escape the shadow of *Amos and Andy* in mainstream editorial cartoons, depicted as speaking in buffoonish, uneducated dialect. Author Jules Tygiel cites a cartoon in which Willie Mays proudly says, "Ah aims to go up in the world."

Those black athletes who rode Robinson's coattails into the major leagues had numerous stories of how the degrading shadow of Jim Crow hung over their daily lives. Segregation reared its head for many years in baseball, as white-owned establishments that benefited directly from the major leagues' business continued to tiptoe around the racist sensitivities of white customers. In some Florida spring training towns, black ballplayers had little opportunity to enjoy themselves after hours. They could seldom walk far from their training complexes without colliding with still very entrenched racial codes that restricted them from patronizing white beaches, theaters, and restaurants. Long after teams broke camp to head north for the regular season, the stadium remained the only place where black ballplayers could expect nominally equitable treatment. Some suffered the indignity of being boarded by black families while their white teammates stayed at top-flight hotels. When this practice faded, and integrated teams were typically accepted by most hotels, the dining room, lobby or pool might be off limits to black members, and some noticed the keys they were assigned were routinely for the worst rooms on the premises. At the ballpark, segregated seating died a slow death, with African American fans still crudely roped off in their own sections into the early 1950s. Because it took this long for the most egregious symptoms of racism to be ironed out of major league baseball, it is even less surprising that other, more subtle forms of racial inequality still persist in American sports.[2]

Blacks who have ever been National Football League head coaches or Major League Baseball managers are few indeed. In baseball, there is an ongoing "old-boys network" in which a familiar cast of experienced white baseball managers are often at the front of the line for open jobs. Recently, black managers have made a breakthrough of sorts, with men like Cito Gaston, Dusty Baker, Don Baylor, and Hal McRae managing major league teams, but they represent a fraction of available and qualified African American candidates to run a baseball team. Along with Frank Robinson, Maury Wills, and Larry Doby, these men were all former star, or near-star players. Few black men have ever managed a baseball team without first having an on-field career. Legendary white skippers Sparky Anderson, Walter Alston, Earl Weaver, and Tommy Lasorda all reached the Hall of Fame as managers despite little, if any, experience as major league players.[3] Without an in-uniform reputation of greatness on their resumes, such managers clearly moved strictly through baseball acumen, leadership and organizational skills. As of yet, only white managers have had the opportunity to learn the game solely from the bench and prove their credentials over time. Black candidates have needed to bring on-field greatness and fame with them into the interview room to have a chance. For four decades, it was not even a good chance. The experience of Jackie Robinson, himself, was an omen for countless subsequent black superstars of the diamond. Any thought Robinson had of staying in baseball after his retirement as a player was wasted energy; the interest of the major league community in his talents amounted to a deafening silence. Robinson became a highly successful businessmen in the restaurant field. Olsen recounts the frustrations of men like Bill White and Larry Doby, former players who would have jumped at an opportunity to remain connected to the game with managing or front office type positions, but noticed the door to the stadium slamming loudly behind them upon their retirement. It was years after their playing careers were over before either had an offer from a major league team. Four decades' worth of retired black major leaguers produced who knows how many qualified coaching candidates who never became coaches, because most baseball owners were happy that integration stayed on the field. Should it surprise anyone that the love affair between black Americans and baseball has cooled in recent decades? While Latin American players were becoming more common on the field, the percentage of black players on major league rosters dropped by a third between the late 1960s and late 1980s, and black fans were avoiding ballparks in droves.[4] Clearly, black America's enthusiastic response to the pioneering efforts of Branch Rickey are an old memory.

Football lags even further behind in integrating head coaching positions, with Art Shell taking over the Raiders fourteen years (1989) after Frank Robinson first led the Indians. Dennis Green, Ray Rhodes, Sherman Lewis, Herman Edwards, and Tony Dungy have followed in Shell's footsteps, but for each individual who has broken through the barrier, there are outstanding black football minds languishing in assistant coaching jobs. A vivid illustration of how the head coach line forms behind many whites was the hiring of Dick Vermeil four years ago. It has been compellingly argued that Vermeil, who had been out of coaching for fifteen years, had no business being a front-running candidate when there were black assistant coaches like Sherman Lewis and Emmit Thomas who had long been cooling their heels waiting for a job interview. In 2009, Art Shell will be fifteen years removed from being fired as head coach of the Oakland Raiders, winners of three Super Bowls with Shell as a player, including a rout of Vermeil's own Eagles. One anxiously awaits this year to see which NFL teams will actively court Shell with the same fervor the Rams pursued Vermeil in 1997. (Vermeil, who retired from the Rams after winning the Super Bowl after the 1999 season, came out of hiatus again to coach Kansas City in 2001.) In 1998, when NBA, NFL and MLB players were 80 percent, 65 percent, and 25 percent black, respectively, the three leagues' coaches were 14 percent, 7 percent, and 2 percent African American. Equal racial opportunity is well off in the future in this area.[5]

Aspiring black head coaches in college sports have similarly struggled to find employment. With many hundreds of prestigious coaching jobs having been available in NCAA football and basketball for decades, black candidates have faced long odds in getting hired, even with many black players on the floor. Black head coaches are now a more common sight on the sidelines of televised college basketball games, including some at the nation's strongest basketball schools. As of 1995, however, there were still only thirty-nine black coaches at 296 (13 percent) Division I men's basketball programs, a percentage that agrees with the African American presence in the United States' population, but is far lower than their presence in basketball. The picture in college football was far worse. Only six (of 108) Division I head coaches were filled by African Americans in 1995.[6] This, in spite of the fact that, in recent years, blacks make up 67 percent and 44 percent of the athletes in the above two sports. The personal and professional networks that steer favored candidates toward open jobs are clearly white ones. Black activist groups were particularly incensed in 1994 when the University of Colorado replaced its long-time coach Bill McCartney with an outside candidate, passing over a long-serving black assistant coach who was respected by his players.[7] While the Buffaloes' head coaching choice ultimately proved a good one, African American observers perceived an all-too-familiar (to them) trend in which a black who had paid his dues seemed barely an afterthought in the hiring process. In 2002, the University of Notre Dame hired its first black football coach after 109 seasons of play, and this only after its initial hire had been exposed for falsifying his résumé and embarrassing a university long heralded for its integrity.

These well-publicized examples merely illustrate that many blacks are still stranded at the level of assistant coach long after their credentials and experience merit a head coach position. Whether this is caused by alumni pressures, fan expectations, the fear of either or both by athletic directors, or outright old boys networking, white coaches still call most of the plays for many games in which the players are mostly black.

The ability of the black athlete to fully benefit educationally and professionally from playing college sports offers more disturbing findings. To the extent that athletic scholarships are supposed to be paths to better economic opportunity for those with few other options, the scholarly and journalistic attention devoted to the NCAA over the past two decades has revealed shocking evidence of low graduation rates for those involved in the major revenue sports of football and basketball. Thousands of athletes, black and white, are poorly served every year by coaches and athletic departments that blatantly force them to focus heavily on their sport to the detriment of their studies, many of them discarded without a degree once their eligibility (and usefulness) is used up. This tragedy is particularly the fate of black athletes, who were graduating at barely half the rate of their white cohorts in 1990 and 1991. Steered by their coaches into taking easy courses, nursed by inflated grades and low expectations, their daily routines consumed by practice, training, and travel, the fate of many black high school football and basketball stars has been to help generate huge revenues for a college only to drift into anonymity and a bleak future when their playing days are done.

The popular metaphor of "plantation sports" being played on college campuses is hard to discount. It was twenty years after Jackie Robinson became a Dodger that college sport officials even acknowledged institutionalized racist practices in their programs. A wave of male black athletes in the late 1960s protested at having their on-campus social lives closely monitored and restricted by their coaches so as not to violate local racial customs. They protested at alternately being told not to leave campus, while being racially excluded from activities on campus. Sports sociologist Harry Edwards described such athletes being discriminated against from the first moment they stepped on campus as invited recruits, of their being handed money to amuse themselves on their own while the white recruits were feted with the entire campus experience they would have access to if they signed a letter of intent. After committing to such schools, many such athletes experienced borderline apartheid conditions in their university experience. Many complained of blatant discrimination in both the under-the-table perks of high-profile sports and in the basic treatment they received as athletes and students. Those interviewed by Jack Olsen in 1968 bitterly indicted their schools' alumni for making summer jobs and cash payments available to white athletes alone, school authorities for providing substandard housing for black recruits, local communities for denying them decent off-campus quarters near the university, and lily-white fraternities and other student organizations for excluding them from participation. None of these realities, of course, were made known to the black athletic recruit when they were being courted and feted by their white coach.

Perhaps no racial barrier was harder to swallow than the subtle but powerful pressure placed on them to obey local custom and not date white women visibly, if at all. This made for a bigger problem than an infringement on their freedom to date women of their choice. Many major athletic power colleges recruiting black athletes in earnest for the first time had general student populations almost completely white. Since there were often virtually no black female students on campus, white women stood as the only social choice for black men stranded at a college for four years of their lives. Yet the response to seeing them even talking or walking with white co-eds, both on campus and in the community, was often enough to elicit frozen stares, angry phone calls, threats from faculty, and warnings from coaches. In addition, then, to not being welcome in various student activities and hangouts at their school, black football, basketball and track team members at many whitebread colleges were stranded socially, with few romantic outlets. Harry Edwards's account of his college days speaks of the loneliness and boredom of a black athlete seemingly invisible on campus, welcome almost nowhere outside his own dorm, of being implored to think of the team on Saturday afternoon by white teammates who had ignored and slammed doors in his face all week long![8]

Even their time spent at practice and games was not always a refuge from the prevailing racial order for African American athletes. No less than their professional counterparts, black college athletes were segregated in their hotel room assignments by their coaches. Having college teammates sleeping in side by side hotel beds was apparently less comfortable for athletic departments than having them line up next to each other in the trenches of the line of scrimmage. Age-old stereotypes of blacks being lazy shirkers manifested on courts and gridirons as many African American athletes complained of having their injuries doubted by skeptical trainers and coaches. White athletes, they claimed, were generally taken at their word when they claimed to be hurt, while blacks were expected to be impervious to pain, always ready to perform. When the whistle blew and the games began, African American team members were convinced they had to be near perfect to stay on the field, that they were benched after making a fraction of the mistakes their white teammates made. Finally, verbal and physical abuse seemed to many a black athlete to be directed their way far more often and intensely than at their white counterparts.[9]

Such shabby treatment and transparent exploitation by white coaches, athletic officials, and administrators appears to have been par for the course on many American campuses right through the 1960s. Such treatment was so widespread in 1968 that black athletes launched organized protests at more than three dozen American universities, often threatening boycotts of their games if their grievances were not heard or addressed.[10] Clearly, these developments were a disturbing pattern for those convinced that Jackie Robinson's first at bat forever ushered in fairness in sports. The only place where many black college athletes came close to equality (not quite, even there) was on the playing field. Elsewhere in the college experience, they often routinely collided with the same ugly racial caste system, the same second-class citizenship status that had long confronted millions of African Americans not playing organized sports. Being allowed on the same field ended formal segregation, but it did not stop inequality in sports. If such angry resentment was so common barely three decades ago, can anyone doubt that more subtle racist attitudes (if not practices) endured long after?

The experience of Connie Hawkins as a scholarship athlete in the early 1960s illustrated both the loneliness and exploitation of naïve black college recruits brought onto campus solely to win games for the glory and profit of white colleges. A New York City basketball court legend as a teenager, the naïve Hawkins may as well have been an alien from another planet when he was recruited to play for the University of Iowa. Essentially a hoops mercenary hired to entertain whites and raise his college's profile, with virtually no one demanding he measure up academically, Hawkins was little more than a glorified serf, hurtling along toward the "faceless, hopeless, ignominious existence" Edwards described as the destination of so many used-up non-student black athletes. Ultimately expelled from Iowa for accepting a loan from alumni sources closely associated with his school, and under investigation for a point-shaving scandal, a crime he was too naïve to even understand, Hawkins was barred from the NBA for almost a decade, his potential superstar career cut tragically short. His biggest crime was going along with an entrenched system of financial favors for star athletes, and being too green to recognize gamblers. His ultimate fate as the sacrificial lamb of an NCAA investigation stands as a metaphor for the limitations of integration in college athletics, for the unwillingness of white fans, coaches, students, and alumni to accept black athletes as total persons, rather than numbers in running shoes or pads.[11]

The dumb jock stereotype has allowed many white college athletes to drift academically as long as they produce on Saturday, but their black counterparts suffer from an additional label, the dumb black stereotype. This double caricature results in even worse non-education and mis-education for African American athletes while they fill stadiums and win multi-million dollar trips for their schools to play in the Rose Bowl or Final Four.[12] In short, the white belief that blacks are less intelligent and less likely to want or benefit from rigorous education makes the involvement of many in college sports exploitative. One can almost visualize the freshman scholarship black athlete arriving on an American campus in the 1960s, being introduced to every corner of an athletic facility, while being handed a map to the rest of campus as an afterthought.

If examples from the 1960s seem safely removed from the present-day status quo of college sports, there are ample illustrations of more recent exploitation of black talent by white coaches and athletic departments. In 1985, Memphis State's trip to the Final Four was an inspiring story for those who could overlook that a black athlete had not graduated while playing for coach Dana Kirk in twelve years! Bob Huggins's Cincinnati program has a black athlete graduation rate of less than 10 percent, something that has not stopped his Bearcats from the publicity and NCAA tournament appearances normally given Top Twenty-Five teams.[13]

Professional sport front offices reveal nowhere near as much diversity as on the field, with the vast bulk of owners, executives, and high-ranking administrative staff almost as white as they were before Jackie Robinson. The decision-making authority for the three major team sports with hundreds of black entertainers still rests almost exclusively with whites. A persistent white belief that blacks are not cut out for leadership and management responsibilities still bars many of them from coaching and front office roles. This assumption was going strong in the 1980s, never more controversially articulated than in 1987. Los Angeles Dodgers executive Al Campanis stunned Ted

Koppel and a live national audience when he defended the dearth of blacks in baseball front offices on the grounds that they lacked the necessities for such jobs.[14] Black Americans associated with baseball, having claimed for decades that this attitude was prevalent in organized sports, could feel some rueful satisfaction at hearing the soon-to-be fired Campanis's immolation in front of millions for blithely stating what major league executives had denied so fervently.

It was not until 1975, a quarter century after white fans began accepting blacks in their end zones and on their base paths, that a black golfer, Lee Elder, was allowed to participate at the Masters Championship in Augusta, Georgia. Charlie Sifford spent an entire career being denied entry into major or southern tournaments for which he was qualified but was the wrong color to set foot on the course. The first two PGA-sponsored tournaments Sifford won, in 1957 and 1960, conveniently became *unofficial* for record-keeping purposes. Professional golf's "powers that be" at that time made baseball owners look like the NAACP. At the 1962 Canadian Open in Montreal, Sifford was leading after the first two rounds, a tournament that would have automatically qualified him for the Masters championship. A quick phone call from PGA authorities changed the rules arbitrarily on that very Saturday and announced that tournament was no longer a qualifier. With a crass transparency that would have been comical if not so offensive, Masters tournament officials altered their own eligibility rules on several occasions to leave Sifford on the outside. Being amongst the top money-winners, capturing a PGA-sponsored event, finishing in the top sixteen of the U.S. Open, were the criteria for being good enough to play amongst the Georgia pines under normal circumstances. A black man reaching these goals, however, was not what the Masters wanted to think of as normal.

Sifford's pioneering 1961 entry as the first black man to play a PGA event in the South turned into a nightmare. On the tournament's second day, he was followed, harassed with racial insults and threatened by a dozen white men who were strangely not kicked off the course by PGA officials until the fourteenth hole. Sifford, in front after the opening day, lost and never regained the lead.

The 1990 PGA Championship was scheduled at an exclusive Birmingham, Alabama, golf club whose whites-only membership policy was an open secret. The same was true for seventeen of the tour's thirty-nine events in 1990. It was only after embarrassing stories like these cost the tour $2 million in advertisement revenue that golf's ruling authority laid down rules demanding that golf courses lobbying for PGA events must have minority club members. This barely qualified as a moral victory for minority advancement. The Birmingham course that spawned the controversy kept the PGA Championship by promising to admit one black member. Aside from Tiger Woods, the complete list of black golfers known by most American sports fans might include Sifford, Lee Elder, Calvin Peete, Jim Thorpe, and very few, if any others.[15]

In team sports, it has long been observed that black players are over-represented in positions demanding pure physical attributes like agility, speed, and reflexes, while under-represented in those demanding more poise, leadership and intelligence. Team roles that are closest to the action and central to the strategy of the game are occupied by black athletes to a much lower degree than their representation in such sports would predict. Pitchers, catchers, and infielders, positions most involved in the strategic control of a baseball game, have long been filled disproportionately by whites, while the outfield positions, which require less thinking and more explosive reactions, are still most commonly played by blacks.

Racial stacking is also evident in football, where positions like center, middle linebacker, and punter, where athletes must show poise, leadership, and intelligence are filled by white athletes far more often than their presence in the NFL would predict by talent alone. Meanwhile, defensive backs, running backs and receivers, those positions calling for pure speed and instinctive reactions, are almost totally monopolized by black athletes. No position, however, has seen more stacking than the football quarterback. One of American culture's most heroic and admired leadership roles, the quarterback epitomizes many of the traits Americans most want to see in themselves, qualities like coolness under pressure, cunning, resourcefulness, and persistence. Americans have seen two black starting quarterbacks in thirty-eight Super Bowls: Doug Williams and Steve McNair. An entire Hall of Fame could exist for talented black college quarterbacks from the 1950s onward who entered a supposedly integrated NFL and were steered into playing defensive back, receiver, or running back because they were deemed somehow lacking in the qualities needed to lead the team's offense. What blocked so many would-be quarterbacks were assumptions that blacks were not smart enough to run a professional offense. Other coaches felt black athletes were too lacking in intelligence to win the respect and trust of white teammates. Men like Marlin Briscoe, Joe Gilliam, James Harris, and Warren Moon felt the sting of this label, none of them receiving the full opportunity to be quarterback they deserved. (Moon did have a long career as an NFL starter, but he first had to prove himself by playing six dominant seasons in Canada.) Well into the past decade, black college quarterbacks entered the professional ranks with their abilities somehow (though more subtly) doubted, their credentials held up to more critical scrutiny than their highly touted white cohorts. In the early 1990s, a series of outstanding black college quarterbacks were drafted lower into the professional ranks than white counterparts who finished beneath them in the Heisman Trophy balloting. Unpolished white college quarterbacks can be drafted as "project" players given time to learn and grow into the job. Few black NFL quarterback "projects" come to mind. Their lot has typically been to produce or go home.[16]

In addition to racial assumptions about their abilities, black quarterbacks are felt to suffer from owner's fears that the racial symbolism of a black athlete leading white teammates would discourage white fans from buying tickets. There is too much evidence to doubt that a lot of white football fans, coaches, and owners still seem uncomfortable with the image of a black athlete shaping the fate of a team full of whites. In 1990, the NFL was 60 percent black, but 93 percent of its quarterbacks were white, despite the availability of scores of black college quarterbacks. That cannot be interpreted as anything but racial bias.[17]

Barely a quarter century ago, Hank Aaron received thousands of hate letters and death threats as he closed in on Babe Ruth's all-time home run record, many of the letters openly racist. Twenty years after America had first started accepting the sight of Aaron in a baseball uniform, there was still a white element that could not abide the symbolism of a cherished white icon's record being toppled by a black player.[18] Having more home runs, runs batted in, and All-Star Game appearances than any other player in history did not make Aaron's skin color any more acceptable to a disturbingly large portion of baseball's audience when he threatened a symbol of white racial pride. Apparently, the willingness to allow opportunity to blacks in baseball still had strings attached in 1974. Even though he was well aware that most of white America was behind him, Aaron was traumatized for years by this exposure to the ugly underbelly of American racism.

As black athletes have filled professional basketball rosters, allegations of racial preference have emerged. In an 80 percent black NBA, some black players believe the owners are determined to hold at least one, preferably two spots on their rosters for white players to soothe their mostly white fans. This fear is not merely a product of the last two decades when blacks became the majority of players. As early as the 1960s, when whites still made up a sizable portion of the league, concerns were being expressed that white fans might soon reject a growing black presence on the floor. The commissioner himself, Maurice Podoloff, worried at a league owner's meeting about the box office impact of a sport dominated by blacks. It required many years for professional team owners and college administrations to be comfortable with having more blacks than whites on the field of play. The machinations that went on to keep a white majority in the game could be in spite of the team's best chances for victory. Well into the 1960s, talented black athletes still faced an invisible, but very real wall, in that a black majority of players in action was beyond the threshold of white sensitivities.[19] A popular adage (of unknown origins) was that the wise 1960s college basketball coach played one black player at home, three on the road, and five when they were losing.

While few worry anymore about white and black majorities on the field, racial selectivity is felt to have persisted in different forms. An entirely black 1979–80 New York Knicks team improved their record by eight wins, but their attendance dropped lower than it had in many years. The following season the Boston Celtics (with several key white players) and Philadelphia 76ers were equally dominant over the rest of the league on the court, but the former left the latter far behind in ticket sales. Winning clearly was not enough for the mostly black Knicks and 76ers to fill their stands in two of the largest, and historically fertile basketball cities in America. Given this context, it is small wonder the Knickerbockers were called the "Niggerbockers" by some white fans and the Dallas Mavericks (of the rival American Basketball Association) actually cut four of their ten black players to win back disinterested white spectators. In 1991, Charles Barkley verbalized this suspicion of white fan preferences when he commented to the media that the 76ers lone white player in training camp was the surest bet to make the team. Barkley was implying that talent was not the sole factor determining which players landed jobs in the NBA, that white fans were still not completely comfortable with equal opportunity based solely on merit.

Long after black superstars became a regular presence on NBA floors, it was a given that the last three player spots on a twelve-man roster would be filled by white players. Who can guess how many good but not great black players in the 1960s and 1970s never set foot in an NBA arena, remaining anonymous simply because they were a notch or two below Russell, Chamberlain, Baylor and Wilkens in skill? When Barkley made the above statement in the 1990s, three positions on NBA rosters were no longer automatically reserved for whites. Black players, however, still believed the league's white owners were jealously hanging on to a small core of white athletes to soothe the insecurities or appeal to the tastes of white fans. Few NBA teams even today have attempted to field an all-black roster, understandable given one study's findings that replacing a black with an equally talented white raises NBA team's home attendance by 8,000 to 13,000 fans per year. This form of white customer discrimination, the author's claim, motivates owners to offer salary premiums to white players, premiums that account for at least part of a demonstrable gap between white and black salaries. A white basketball player is thought to be a more marketable commodity with a racially selective white audience, and gets paid accordingly. If these scholars are correct, one can expect that the NBA has reached a ceiling in how many black and how few white players it keeps under contract.[20]

Black athletes are squeezed for jobs throughout their careers by the expectation they must out-produce whites and perform closer to superstar status to take the field. They sense they must be among the best, and contributing regularly, to have job security. The evidence exists to indicate that black professional athletes are the absolute elite from the ranks of black candidates in their sports, those whom whites cannot afford to leave out of their games. Throughout the age of integrated sports, black athletes have taken it as given they must excel to find a job in sports. They have long suspected that situations in which black and white athletes of equal ability are fighting over a roster spot will normally go to the latter. In all three major team sports, and in the awarding of college scholarships, it has been proven that even into the 1970s and 1980s, marginal talent was a luxury granted far more often to whites.[21]

Average ability was something few black athletes could afford. Lapchick found this phenomenon to be going strong in the 1990s. He demonstrated that active black athletes are more likely to be found in the statistical leaders of various sports while whites are more commonly found in the ranks of those role-playing athletes whose contributions are more modest. In both baseball and basketball, one sees a huge discrepancy in the overrepresentation of blacks in the performance leaders, and an equally conspicuous discrepancy in more whites than blacks hanging onto jobs in spite of marginal contributions. Whether one looks at rookie athletes freshly drafted out of college, veteran players at the peak of their game, or over-the-hill players trying desperately to squeeze a few more paychecks from their sport, blacks have to do more to remain in the professional ranks.

Promotional opportunities for athletes have long been cited as much more lucrative for white players than black ones. The classic example of this trend was seen when Baltimore's Frank Robinson and Boston's Carl Yastrzemski won the rare Triple Crown title in consecutive years in the 1960s. A stellar accomplishment that has not been won since, the Triple Crown signifies a superbly balanced batter who can hit for both average and power. Along with the trophy, Robinson, whose team also won the World Series, reaped barely $1,000 in commercial endorsements for his achievement, probably not much more than many star players routinely earned for advertising work at that time. Frank Robinson's 1966 Triple Crown was apparently special everywhere except Madison Avenue. One year later, Yaz duplicated the feat. Over the next three years, Yastrzemski would reap about $200,000 worth of advertising income from his fame as the Triple Crown winner. Does it need to be emphasized which player was white and which was black?[22]

One of the only rivals to Michael Jordan's reputation as the greatest basketball player ever is Oscar Robertson. The consummate ball-handling guard, the superbly talented Robertson is still the only NBA player ever to have a triple-double for an entire season, meaning he averaged at least ten points, rebounds, and assists for an entire year. It is a feat that not even Jordan attained. Yet through the prime of his career, Robertson's phone was silent as far as advertising offers went. Being one of the most superbly skilled, all-around players the league had ever seen was not enough to make him a spokesman for American business. There was, furthermore, never the slightest question about this Cincinnati Royal's upstanding character as a pitchman.[23]

Five decades after the integration of the three major team sports, when blacks comprised a far greater proportion of player rosters than their 12 percent representation in the general population, eight of the ten athletes deemed most popular with America's fans were black. Yet only one, Michael Jordan, stood in the top ten for money earned through commercial endorsements. Clearly there is athletic popularity, and advertising popularity, the latter helping pull white athletes up the money-making ladder, leapfrogging over higher profile black ones.

Even in the recent past, the amount of adulation black athletes receive for their exploits between the lines has clearly not been proportional to how often their images have been used in magazine and television advertisements. Black quarterback Doug Williams reaped $175,000 in the year following his winning of the Super Bowl Most Valuable Player Award in 1988, a pittance compared to the $1,000,000 and $750,000 that came the way of his two white predecessors, Jim McMahon and Phil Simms. Neither McMahon nor Simms threw five touchdown passes in a quarter, as Williams did, yet the latter's unparalleled accomplishment earned him relative pocket change compared to his white counterparts. In the advertisements that black athletes do appear in, they have often been portrayed as successful because of physical ability, while whites are much more likely depicted as achieving greatness due to character or intellectual traits.[24] Can anyone remember a television commercial that emphasized God-given physical skills as the primary factor behind the success of Cal Ripken, Larry Bird, or Joe Montana? How many advertisements have hawked a product by emphasizing the grit, dedication or character of Shaquille O'Neal, Randall Cunningham, or Ken Griffey?

Other perks come with the territory of playing professional sports, and such privileges in the local community also indicate that reverence of white fans for black athletes often does not extend beyond the stadium. Black NBA superstar Bill Russell recounted that early in his career, a Boston social club offered him one-third the speaking fee that was first tendered to his white (but unavailable) teammate Bob Cousy. Lest anyone think this story from forty years ago is buried in a different time, a Florida establishment in the 1980s left free entrance coupons in the lockers of every white member of the Boston Red Sox during exhibition training camp, and only ended this practice in the face of a public outcry by black Red Sox coach Tommy Harper. When he was ultimately let go by the Red Sox, Harper felt his assertive stand was the cause.[25]

Long after white fans were cheering loudly for black athletes on the field, the latter were expected to respect segregated white neighborhood boundaries. Even seemingly beloved superstars like Wilt Chamberlain and Willie Mays were barred from living in posh neighborhoods of their choosing in San Francisco, supposedly one of America's most liberal cities. Cowboys running back Don Perkins endured substandard housing for years, and lived a lonely life separated from his family, simply because his team's stadium was surrounded by exclusive white communities, even though he made more than enough money to live where he pleased.[26] Perkins, a key element of the Cowboys' growth into a championship caliber team and one of the NFL's best runners in the late 1960s, lived in an apartment with cockroaches.

Those who make a career reporting on, or announcing sports, also continue to be disproportionately white compared to the racial makeup of the players in the game. The lens through which sport is interpreted and understood by the mainstream public is still the perception of white Americans. Ron Thomas informs that in both the print and broadcast media, aspiring black journalists find it close to impossible to break into entry jobs, making up a tiny percentage of the regular beat reporters, editors, and on-air personalities who cover professional teams and events. Of the nation's 1,600 daily newspapers, there were seven full-time black sports columnists in the mid-1990s. Unless one assumes that understanding and knowledge of sport evaporates the moment a black American steps off the playing field, these numbers are a stunning indictment of sports media hiring practices, even after taking into account that one in eight Americans are black. If talented young African Americans are not applying for sports writing jobs, can one reasonably argue this is solely a lack of interest?

With so few black journalists around even today, what whites feel and think about the games they watch is greatly vulnerable to unconscious racial stereotypes and assumptions. One study found thirty newspaper stories nationally between 1988 and 1990 in which athletes were accused of sexually assaulting women. Seventy percent (twenty-one) of the accused athletes were white, but *Sports Illustrated* addressed the issue with a cover story that focused exclusively on black athlete suspects at two universities.[27] Such developments do little to make black athletes think they get a fair representation from the media.

The image of the hyper-sexed, out-of-control black lives on in sports reporting. In citing the O.J. Simpson murder trial, one scholar argues that the American media still pigeonholes black athletes (and all other black male celebrities) into the same derogatory stereotypes prescribed for them on the antebellum plantation. From studying *Time* and *Newsweek* covers, he concluded the print media used many photographs of black men which served the same agenda of slave owners terrified by the prospect of a rebellion. They legitimize discrimination and the perception that blacks need more direction, supervision, and control than whites. With sports specifically, such portrayals hold black men guilty until proven innocent if they are suspected of anti-social behavior. Simpson's mug shot cover photo was cited as an example of how a white media still perpetuates the primitive *black brute* image that defines African American men unfit for societal opportunities and roles reserved for whites.[28] Athletic greatness is argued to be no more a shield against this uncivilized portrayal for black athletes today than it was for Jim Brown or Jack Johnson.

Finally, there is an ongoing controversy as to whether blacks are physically superior to whites, giving them a genetic (and ostensibly unfair) advantage on the field of play. In both the popular and scholarly literature, there have been ongoing attempts to explain black success in terms of natural attributes. For decades, black competitors have been poked, prodded and analyzed in an elusive and vain quest by white America to scientifically account for their sporting dominance. The ground zero literature of this volatile debate was a lengthy series of articles written by Martin Kane in *Sports Illustrated*. Kane speculated in detail about the physiological advantages enjoyed by African Americans on the field of play, asserting that blacks had superior relaxation powers and looser joints owing to their musculature.[29] Black athletes and spokespersons were outraged by Kane's sketchy scientific research and what they believed to be racist motivations for his study. Whatever Kane's attitudes and leanings, the conclusions he reached appeal to a considerable American audience even today, and within that audience are those with cynical motivations for believing that blacks must be more naturally endowed for sports. Kane's questions and answers were not the first, nor the last of their kind. Whites have theorized about virtually every corner of the black body as being a source of athletic advantage: hands, tendons, muscles, joints, blood, thighs ... even eye color. "But," the narrow thinking goes, "not their minds." Seldom suggested as critical factors are qualities like dedication, drive, character, motivation, persistence, mental toughness, and intelligence. Whether or not blacks enjoy an advantage over whites in physical competition, the ease with which so many white Americans unconsciously accept the notion indicates an unwillingness to take black athletic success at face value.

African American scholars, activists, politicians and professionals, not surprisingly are angered that black athletic success is rarely explained by qualities that would justify opening doors of opportunity elsewhere in American society. The acknowledged ability to dunk a basketball or catch a football does not persuade whites to open up graduate study, law schools, medical programs, or boardrooms any more than is already the case. This obsessive quest to find a physical explanation for athletic accomplishments has never been evident for white ethnic groups which previously dominated American sports. Irish Americans dominated nineteenth-century boxing, Jews succeeded like no other group in early twentieth-century basketball, and Slavs were over-represented on the offensive and defensive line positions in football in the 1930s, but none of these white groups' successes prompted a fraction as many scientific inquiries into how their bodies must be different.[30] Their successes were either unquestioned or assumed to be the result of admirable character traits.

This tendency to reduce black athletic achievement to mere genetic endowment has been evident in how white sportscasters describe the abilities and actions of black and white athletes in the same game. On major televised sporting events, there has been a clear tendency for commentators to use adjectives of raw physical ability, at times even animal metaphors, more often when they are describing black athletes, while painting white players as disciplined, smart and hardworking.[31] Some observers have suggested that one could close their eyes while watching the NCAA Final Four and know the color of the players being referred to, so entrenched is the pattern of thinking underlying such descriptions by white announcers. In his 1996 autobiography, Negro League legend Buck O'Neil reflected that the "natural black athlete" syndrome he was familiar with from his playing days was still evident decades later. He commented on the media describing black major leaguers as underachievers, while white players with the same statistics were tagged as overachievers.[32]

Such discrepancies can only feed a pervasive mindset that black athletes are explosive and agile beings not far removed from the jungle, players who merely react and conquer, while their white teammates provide the needed control, guile, patience, and gritty courage to win games.

Whatever its merit, the belief that blacks are born athletes has a convenient appeal to those whites seeking to minimize their accomplishments on the field, so as to deny the former equal opportunity in other areas. Less than fifteen years ago, African American made up roughly 7 percent of the first-year enrollments of law and medical schools nationally, ratios barely half that of the black portion of America's population.[33] These figures are more likely to continue to grow if black success in sports and entertainment are credited to drive and work ethic, rather than genetic gifts of birth. The notion that blacks succeed naturally in sport makes it very easy to believe (for those already predisposed) that blacks are lazy and ignorant. By grudgingly conceding the domain of sport as a place where blacks are predestined to succeed, whites who doubt black mental ability can salve their feelings and still rationalize the racial status quo most everywhere else. The natural black athlete is a more subtle line of segregation drawn in the sand which costs intolerant whites nothing in their narrow outlook. The negative impact is borne entirely by black athletes who unendingly hear their achievements portrayed as if they required no effort. Intolerant whites have come full circle from the days when they barred black athletes from tracks, rings, and diamonds because blacks were genetically doomed to laziness, cowardice, and stupidity. For more than half a century now, they have cherry-picked from pseudo-science enough quackery to conclude that blacks are born athletes, a theory they hope will confine black advances to sports alone.[34]

The examples cited above indicate that total acceptance of black athletes by white fans has been elusive, at least if acceptance is measured by the experience of blacks and whites involved in sports. Such discrepancies raise doubts about the degree of freedom black athletes have, relative to whites, to participate in sports on the same terms as whites.

In short, how equal *is* opportunity for blacks? Although sports provide far greater opportunity for blacks to find fame and fortune than most other pursuits, and more equitable opportunity relative to whites, black athletes are still not experiencing the same rewards as white athletes. The push toward equal opportunity in sports that began in earnest with Joe Louis' career was strong, and countless black athletes have since enjoyed opportunity by following his path. Over the past five decades, thousands of black athletes have participated in professional football, basketball, baseball, boxing, and elite track and field. Most earned a better standard of living, at least during their athletic careers, than would have been otherwise possible. Scores earned multiple millions of dollars and became revered household names in the consciousness of whites. Many have parlayed their success and income on the field into opportunity when their playing days were over. Over the past five decades, black athletes have made these tremendous strides toward equal opportunity in sport through their own determination, and because tens of millions of white Americans accepted interracial sports competition. Stepping on a football field or baseball diamond alongside whites without having to face hostility is a freedom black athletes have asserted by passing through the door that Joe Louis opened in 1937.

But American sport still has the shadow of race hanging over it. White America has long been so accepting of integrated sports competition, it is almost inconceivable we will ever see a black athlete meet the same legal fate as Jack Johnson. Yet long after white racial supremacy has been laid to rest in the minds of all but the most bigoted, some Caucasians still care, consciously or unconsciously, about the skin color of those they see on the field. If whites did not have a racial preference in who they want to see triumph between the lines, blacks would constitute more than roughly 12–13 percent of NFL quarterbacks. Blacks would be as well represented on the sidelines and in team administrative positions as they are on the field. Black athletes would have their success attributed to God-given ability no more than white athletes, would be as well represented as pitchers and catchers as they are in major league outfields, and their voices and faces would be as much a part of the sport media as their numbers in American society would warrant. Blacks would reap the same endorsement rewards and salaries as whites. This is not the reality of American sport. Like many other social victories won by African Americans over the past sixty years, Louis and Robinson did not (clearly could not) succeed as much in overcoming the entrenched white racial attitudes, attitudes which manifested in the kinds of inequality cited here, which continued long after segregation ended.

Tolerating interracial competition is hardly the same thing as liking it. Accepting blacks on the same fields, courts and diamonds as whites was only one contested terrain in American racial history. Less visible, but more persistent, racial barriers have survived in sport. The examples cited earlier clearly prove that white acceptance of black participation in sports is still not absolute, and this partial tolerance translates into something less than equal opportunity for black athletes. Skin color still matters in sport. But to what extent? White fans being intolerant of black excellence in sports may seem an absurd notion for one who has turned on television to see an Olympic Games in which every single American short distance runner is black, a closed circuit boxing presentation in which almost every fighter is African American, or an NBA All-Star Game in which only a handful of the league's twenty-four best stars are white. These scenarios have become commonplace and few whites seem to notice, much less make them an issue. Such realities from other sports make it appear the thought of a Great White Hope has become a dead letter in the minds of white America.

It is tenuous to assume, however, that white sports fans do not want a Great White Hope when there are no such boxers around to test that belief. White America has long outgrown any anger or fear about interracial fights, as well an any hostility to black champions. This does not prove the absence of white sentiment for a white champion. It could merely depict their acquiescence to a mostly black sport, in which the world championship appears to be pre-ordained to rest on African American heads.

However loud some white fans scream at the victories of Evander Holyfield or George Foreman, many could still prefer a white champion. White fans not complaining about a dearth of white faces in boxing, or sports in general, is not by itself an indication they would not be happier at seeing more whites in the game, and more importantly, in the winner's circle. White cheering for superstar black athletes could just as easily be resigned acceptance as genuine tolerance; the desire for white supremacy expressed through sport may have never left the minds of the gallery.

How much has integration in sports and white support of black heroes reflected a change in white feelings toward sharing success on the playing field? Is it really a voluntary sharing of success when whites have less to share in sports like boxing and basketball? Is it a case of whites welcoming blacks onto a previously taboo terrain or rather politely resigning themselves to a fait accompli, a new reality that was not their preferred choice? In specific regard to boxing, did white adulation of the Brown Bomber signify the beginning of the end for interest in white hopes? Was tacit acceptance of forty-five years of black heavyweight supremacy matched by a deeper change in racial attitudes, whereby white fans became immune to racial symbolism in the ring? Did white fans become just as willing to cheer for a black contender as a white one in the decades after Louis handed over his crown? If so, over-hyped white contenders would have climbed the heavyweight ranks no more quickly than their talents merited, while deserving black fighters would have broken into the Top Ten when they paid their competitive dues, or soon after. The loss of interest by white fans in Great White Hopes should have been paralleled by a competitive setting in which black fighters have attained equal opportunity to reach the world championship. The disappearance of the former should have enabled the latter.

In front of the Philadelphia Spectrum, a statue of a famous boxer from the City of Brotherly Love stands proudly, arms raised in triumph. The boxer has come to symbolize hard work, dedication, grit, as well as the historic reputation of Philadelphia as a vibrant boxing center. The statue is instantly recognizable to tens of millions of Americans over the age of thirty, and many others younger than that. The figure is not of the flesh and blood black Philadelphian Joe Frazier, one of the greatest world champions ever. Frazier, who still resides in this city as a boxing trainer, and was the epitome of the rugged, courageous, Philadelphia fighter Frazier, apparently was never even considered. Instead, the boxing statue that has become a tourist landmark is a likeness of one Rocky Balboa, a white heavyweight who has existed solely on the celluloid screen since 1976. The white citizenry of Philadelphia is more comfortable heralding an imaginary white ring hero than a black champion who brought acclaim to the city for a decade.

The original *Rocky* movie screenplay was written by an unknown actor, Sylvester Stallone, who had formed the idea sitting at ringside when white heavyweight Chuck Wepner challenged Muhammad Ali for the world championship. The parallels between the real life white-black ring confrontation and that of the film are too obvious to deny, and were framed squarely within popular cultural notions about race and boxing. The perceived differences in the fighting styles and abilities of whites (Wepner) and blacks (Ali) were perfectly recreated in the movie's title fight between Rocky Balboa (Stallone) and the dominant black champion Apollo Creed (Carl Weathers). Like Wepner, Rocky is strong but slow, courageous but limited, plodding and durable in taking punishment, a marginal neighborhood club fighter (Wepner actually had some national name recognition) seeking unlikely glory. Like Ali, Creed is lightning fast, slick, boastful, overconfident, a seemingly natural talent with far more skill than his doomed challenger. In both fights, the overmatched but gritty white challenger scores a moral victory, Wepner by pushing an undertrained Ali into the fifteenth round before being knocked out, Rocky by being the first challenger ever to push Creed the full distance before losing the decision. Stallone's film resonated strongly with its American audience. One likely reason is that by 1976, the image of a game, white heavyweight triumphing simply by lasting fifteen competitive rounds with a superior black (a redundancy to many?) champion had considerable appeal to a growing, young, white American sporting audience that had never seen a white champion. The movie's debut was twenty years after Marciano had retired.

Where exactly is white America at in the process of letting go of white hopes on the field? How far have whites traveled toward acceptance of black achievement in sports, especially boxing?

3. THE GREAT WHITE HOPE: EXTINCT OR DORMANT?

> Everybody in boxing says white guys can't fight. White guys can fight. White American guys can't fight. White Russian guys can fight.
>
> —*Bob Arum*[1]

How might one measure how much white Americans still care about race in their fan loyalties and preferences while watching sports? This question calls for a comparison of the opportunity enjoyed by white and black athletes in recent times. The examples discussed earlier offer glimpses of how opportunity for success and rewards continue to be somewhat less than equal for black athletes. Lesser endorsement opportunities, stereotypes about black genetic advantages, fewer coaching opportunities, unequal media coverage, stacking, lower salaries, and lesser job security are all disturbing reflections of inequality in sport. They reveal nothing directly, however, about how far white America has evolved in relation to what was once its greatest fear about black participation in sports: whites losing to blacks. Because this scenario has unfolded countless times in the five plus decades since the three major team sports were integrated (and six decades since Joe Louis won the title), the temptation is to conclude that black athletic supremacy is not, could not, be an issue anymore in the minds of whites — even though some whites may still want to rationalize it. Theories about black genetic superiority aside, one wants to assume that, at the very least, the outcome on the field has long been a forum for equal opportunity, that American sport's white audience has surmounted any bias in favor of seeing white faces in the winner's circle over black ones. But is this the case? With the freedom to root for whichever athlete or team they want, can it be said that white fans no longer have any racial motivation to want to see whites beat blacks? If they do, can it be assumed this desire is not enough to actually influence competitive opportunity in sports? How far have white Americans come in the decades since so many of them prayed for Jim Jeffries to set things straight in the scorching heat of Reno, Nevada?

Today, however much the racial dynamic of American sports has changed, boxing could still be considered as the litmus test of how whites welcome black athletic success, especially in interracial competition. If a white sports fan is tolerant of a black boxer beating a white opponent into unconsciousness, they are almost certainly even more accepting toward seeing black victory in less aggressive interracial sports confrontations. Someone whose racial world view was not the least bit bothered by seeing Muhammad Ali defeat Chuck Wepner in 1975 was unlikely to be upset at Arthur Ashe beating Jimmy Connors in the Wimbledon final of that year. A white fan who yawned when Mike Tyson destroyed Lou Savarese in thirty-nine seconds of the first round can hardly have felt any disturbing racial significance at Tiger Woods dominating white golfers on the PGA Tour. Losing at tennis or golf to a member of another race is hardly as symbolically powerful as taking multiple punches in the face from them. No lynching on record has ever originated from an eighteenth hole or center court.

Just as in 1910, one must look to boxing for a valid indication of where America is in terms of race relations and equal opportunity. Since it was black success at white expense that terrified so many in 1910, boxing is a valuable measure of how comfortable white America has become with watching blacks beat whites, with seeing championship laurels resting on black heads. Since boxing was a sport where African American dominance was the most threatening to whites, where the color line was drawn so ruthlessly, the ring can reveal how much white tolerance has enabled black competitive opportunity. Only in boxing has there ever been a national campaign by white Americans to find an athlete specifically to depose a black one. To topple Jack Johnson, organized efforts on American soil and far beyond were launched to establish the most talented fighter to restore white pride and confidence. Such white desperation then was revealed in the ragtag assortment of would-be prospects who were welcomed to audition for the title of white champion. Football players, construction workers, truck drivers, factory workers, circus strong men, farmhands, saloon bouncers, and just plain street brawlers were induced to try their hands at prizefighting.[2]

Only in boxing has there ever been a Great White Hope. No black athletes in any other sport were the targets or organized searches for a white-skinned hero of the magnitude of the campaign launched at Jack Johnson. It was in boxing that Caucasian America once felt a hysterical desperation to have one of their own be the best, boxing where they felt the most insecurity about their race's security and strength. For white peace of mind, Jack Johnson needed to be put in his place to a far greater degree than Paul Robeson, Isaac Murphy, or Fleetwood Walker. Boxing was the sport where interracial contests were the most risky, the most frightening to whites. Jack Johnson's dominance in the ring and behavior out of it was far more uncomfortable for millions of whites than the careers of the above athletes. No other black athlete's victories resulted in the assault on hundreds of black citizens. No other black athlete had films of their victories over white opponents banned from showing. No other black athlete was legally hounded from American soil.

Boxing is also a valid measure of white fans' racial tolerance because, unlike team sports, boxers share neither the blame for failure nor the credit for success. The outcome is placed squarely on their shoulders; there can be no finger-pointing at teammates. All eyes are on the boxer, and whatever acceptance a white fan might feel toward black success is more evident than in team sports where an intolerant fan might root for a team, in spite of numerous blacks being on the roster. With boxing, racial intolerance has fewer places to hide in the hearts and minds of the spectator. White fans willing to cheer for a black boxer are unlikely to feel any racial discomfort at seeing black athletes score touchdowns or hit home runs, since these team sports inherently demand the sharing of adulation with others, including many whites. The glory of the ring leads straight to a single person, the fighter himself. A white racist who does not like the idea of blacks "taking over" can insist the San Francisco 49ers won the Super Bowl through Joe Montana's passes, not Jerry Rice's catches. They can argue that Larry Bird's work ethic won the Boston Celtics a world championship, not the poise of a Robert Parish, or that the Yankees won the World Series on the arm of Roger Clemens, not the bat of Series MVP Derek Jeter. One cannot rationalize away the superiority of a black boxer as one can the greatness of black athletes in team sports.

Even compared to other individual sports, boxing is a more compelling indicator of white willingness to open doors and allow full opportunity to blacks. The inherent aggression and domination of boxing is what made interracial contests in the ring so unnerving to whites in Johnson's time. Black golfers, tennis players, and jockeys do not walk off the field of play and leave behind battered and bloodied humiliated whites. A century ago, millions of whites were unnerved at sitting on a racial caste system that had become a powder keg of injustice and black resentment. In 1908, how many blacks fantasized about picking up a tennis racket and acing a white opponent, or challenging the racial majority to eighteen holes of golf? Undoubtedly, millions of blacks thought of defending their dignity with the same physical force that had trampled them for centuries, of venting the rage inside them and settling matters with their fists. The desire of so many frustrated blacks to lash out at the injustices they encountered daily could not have been lost on many whites. Their fear of the racial order being overturned made them far more disturbed at seeing a grinning Jack Johnson toy with white opponents than anything that could happen on a tennis court, race track, or fairway. The race war they feared would have involved physical assault, not backhands and chip shots.

Professional boxing, then, is where one can find a vivid illustration of how far whites have progressed in accepting the possibility of black dominance in sports, this degree of acceptance in turn shaping how easy or hard it is for blacks to pursue sporting excellence. One must focus on the heavyweight division, since it has usually garnered the most boxing publicity. The heavyweight champion has generally received the greatest accolades for being the toughest, most courageous, and able physical specimen on earth. In the early 1900s, whites kept the heavyweight crown among their own race for these reasons. Interracial combat at lower weights could offend them, and did so when black pugilists thrashed white adversaries, but the jewel in the crown of the white supremacy theory was the heavyweight title. Black champions at the lightweight and middleweight level could be rationalized away, but the biggest champion had to be white to prevent millions of disenfranchised blacks from challenging the racial order. For racial pride, the heavyweight championship was what mattered.[3] As long as this crown sat on a white head, the racial caste system was legitimized. Jack Johnson was denied the chance to fight for this title for years after he was clearly the world's top contender. Allowing him to climb into a ring with the heavyweight title at stake was to threaten one of the basic social foundations of American society. One lucky punch could turn the notion of white superiority on its head.

Heavyweight boxing and boxers have typically received more media attention because most boxing fans have preferred the excitement of punching power and dramatic knockouts they entail relative to smaller weight divisions. With more interest in the heavyweights, one would expect to find the strongest indication of whether America has largely maintained or mostly left behind its need to assert white control on the playing field.

As with football, basketball, baseball, and track, one can easily assume that the number of black boxers in American rings since Joe Louis, as well as the scores of black fighters who reached the pinnacle, proves that white America could not possibly have any racial biases working in favor of their own at the expense of black boxers. How could whites care about a heavyweight Great White Hope when there have been so few white boxers of world title caliber since the 1950s? So many hundreds of black boxers have appeared on our television screens, the boxing audience could not possible notice enough to care anymore? Or could it?

It is easy for a white bigot to be outwardly tolerant of black boxing heroes when there have been so few quality white boxers to root for in recent decades. This kind of *acceptance* is more about lack of choice than genuine open-mindedness. The acid test of racial tolerance in boxing is revealed when there has been legitimate white contender on which white ring followers could pin whatever racial insecurities they might have. It is when a white audience has the opportunity to celebrate a seemingly genuine white prospect that our question can be answered. It is entirely possible that the Great White Hope has still not disappeared from the consciousness of whites and that it simply went into hibernation, lying dormant as white heavyweight faces became a rarer sight in the ring. If this affection for a white champion has survived underneath a façade of acceptance, it would have reemerged every time a white heavyweight has been sold to the public as a credible championship contender. This enthusiasm would have opened some competitive doors closed to black heavyweights, smoothing the white heavyweight's road to the top. And this support from the boxing industry and public would have only faded away when such a fighter was exposed as less than advertised. It is when a white audience has the opportunity to celebrate a white prospect that reveals just how much race means to them as they watch a fight.

In 1982, undefeated white heavyweight Gerry Cooney challenged black world champion Larry Holmes in Las Vegas. The first serious white contender for the world crown in many years, Cooney received a conspicuously large amount of publicity in the months leading up to this fight, certainly far more than any of Holmes's previous black challengers. *Time* ran on its cover the white face of Cooney, the challenger, not the champion Holmes, who had already successfully defended his title eleven times over four years. The immediate pre-fight publicity was more of the same in raking the black champion's sensitivities and sense of fairness. Holmes noticed a recurring pattern that hints at a white America gearing up for a coronation of a new white icon and sporting role model. In Las Vegas, where the fighters trained, a steady stream of celebrities were photographed with Cooney. The challenger was consistently portrayed by the media in the most friendly, smiling, baby-kissing manner; newspaper pictures of Holmes were invariably of a scowling visage. High-profile boxing analysts picked Cooney to win to a degree that seemed more about wanting than predicting.[4]

On the night Cooney was knocked out in the thirteenth round, it was rumored that the Reagan White House had arranged for a direct telephone line into the Long Island challenger's dressing room to offer congratulations if he won. No conversation took place between the president and Larry Holmes after the latter's victory because no such phone connection had been made to his dressing room.[5] One can visualize thousands of Wheaties box covers displaying Gerry Cooney's face lying forgotten in a basement twenty years later.

What other likely conclusion is there but that Cooney's camera-friendly white face had become a welcome novelty in a black sport, so that the media, even the president, was caught up in the symbolism? Cooney had received the same purse for the fight as Holmes, almost unheard of in a sport where the champion controls the crown and can choose his opponents. Yet Cooney's marketing appeal gave his handlers the bargaining power to push for such equity. One wonders how much of Holmes's intensity for this fight was spawned by the indignity of this fifty-fifty financial split. Sixteen years later, Holmes was still rankled enough about this to mention it in his autobiography.[6] This leads to a hypothetical, but tantalizing question: Can one visualize the opposite scenario, a white champion settling for financial parity when defending against a black challenger?

Perhaps the most compelling racial dynamic to the Holmes-Cooney fight was that two of the three white judges had the fight scored even into the thirteenth round of Cooney's demise. Although certainly a tough fight, the challenger had clearly taken greater punishment, the cumulative effect of Holmes's punches had Cooney close to defeat. Yet two of the scoring officials had Holmes ahead by only two points on their ring cards, a margin that disappears when one remembers the referee had penalized Cooney one point for each of two low blow infractions earlier.[7] That two professional ring judges imagined they were watching an even fight going into the last three rounds harkens back to Muhammad Ali's decision *victories* over Joe Frazier (1974), Jimmy Young (1976), Ken Norton (1976), and Earnie Shavers (1977).[8] However high the integrity of these judges, they were seeing what they wanted to see, or perhaps they were caught up in the passion of what the mostly white audience wanted to see. Larry Holmes was clearly ahead of Gerry Cooney when the fight was stopped, yet the contest somehow transformed into a neck-and-neck race in the minds of two of the judges. Such scoring makes one wonder what the black champion's chances would have been of winning by decision if Cooney had survived the last three rounds.

There were big plans in the works to capitalize on this Irish-American's magnetic appeal if he could beat the champion.

> Gerry has the potential to make $50 million from endorsements and advertising once he's got the title. He's got everything going for him. He'll not only be champion of the world, but also the champion of Wall Street.
>
> — Mike Jones (Cooney's manager)[9]

Inflated predictions are a staple offering from boxer's managers. Yet this type of hyperbole was missing from the early promotional machines of great black heavyweights like Frazier, Foreman, Patterson, and Ali, all fighters who had won Olympic gold medals, something not part of Cooney's resume. In the early years of these four African American heavyweight's careers, there were no predictions of earning $50 million, or the time-adjusted equivalent. If America had been as interested or receptive in facilitating the careers of these truly great black fighters, Joe Frazier's family would not have been living on the edge of desperation for almost a year after he returned home an Olympic champion from Tokyo, his career delayed by a broken thumb. Similarly, Floyd Patterson would have had more to show for his efforts than a gold medal as he and his family lived in modest circumstances while he clawed his way through the professional ranks in the early 1950s.[10] Winning a gold medal in 1952, only one Olympics ahead of the privileged Peter Rademacher, couldn't keep Patterson from experiencing genuine need in the early days of his ring career.

Mike Jones's grandiose managerial praise was either wishful thinking, indicating his perception that Cooney would be box office gold, or an accurate read of public receptiveness, even more powerful evidence of such a public desire. Either way, white America was conspicuously more interested in Holmes's defense against Cooney than any of his previous or subsequent challengers, including the other white ones. His one previous, and two subsequent white challengers did not generate anywhere near as much attention from mainstream America. No matter how white LeDoux, Cobb, and Frank were, they were not as marketable to the white boxing public as Cooney. Their records were either quantitatively inferior (LeDoux had eight losses and four draws), or even less qualitatively impressive. Frank had not a single notable victim on his record, while Cobb had lost to the same Ken Norton who could not last a minute with Cooney. Perhaps white America had a yardstick with which to measure white challengers, a threshold of perceived quality that needed to be reached before they would allow themselves to get their hopes up again.

Whatever the explanation, America embraced Gerry Cooney like they had never fawned over Wepner, Stander, Daniels, or Zyglewicz as those fighters set out to win the title. The adulation was excessive alongside an objective analysis of his credentials. However good his unblemished twenty-five wins looked on paper, Cooney's major victories consisted of destroying a thirty-one-year-old Jimmy Young who had lost four of his previous six fights, caving in the ribs of a *thirty-nine-year-old* Ron Lyle, who had served seven years for murder and started his career at thirty, and a fifty-four second devastation of a faded, thirty-five-year-old Ken Norton. Those three name opponents were all that was needed to propel him into the public consciousness and sign to fight for the world title. One of his other victories came at the expense of Joe Maye, who had lost seventeen fights in a row when he tested Cooney. Another was over Bill Jackson, who Holmes later claimed had lost eighteen straight bouts.[11] The hard-scrabble Holmes had already defeated Norton in his prime, Earnie Shavers (twice), former champion Leon Spinks, one-time European champions Alfredo Evangelista and Lorenzo Zanon, undefeated Ossie Ocasio, a young and dangerous Top Ten contender in Renaldo Snipes, and future title claimants Trevor Berbick and Mike Weaver.

The point here is not to assume that Cooney was unqualified for the title challenge against Holmes. He may well have been the best possible opponent for the Easton Assassin at the time, and no one can blame Cooney for accepting the opportunity to fight for the crown when it was offered. Who could reasonably expect Cooney to place higher demands on himself than the sport around him? If he landed a title shot without having high enough credentials, the fault lies elsewhere, in the boxing establishment itself, and the public watching it. To his credit, Cooney did nothing to encourage his persona as a Great White Hope. That he did not have to establish a better record before his big break against Holmes can most plausibly be explained by the receptiveness for a potential white champion. The only other possible explanation that would not support a white public desire for a white champ is that the quality of the heavyweight division had declined so much by the early 1980s, that all challengers (black and white) were similarly *qualified* title contestants.

How would one establish whether black heavyweights have had equal opportunity to succeed as their white cohorts since Louis's reign? Since the world title is boxing's ultimate accomplishment, one must compare the paths heavyweight boxers have taken toward the championship. If talented black boxers have continued to be hindered (relative to white pugilists) from achieving the success their talents merit, having had to work harder to reach the summit, one would conclude that white America still has a strong preference for their own kind ruling the ring. If blacks have enjoyed the same chance at upward mobility as whites, their skill dictating their success, white fans clearly have become more color blind when watching fights, supporting boxing heroes for reasons other than race.

How would one compare the relative experiences of black and white boxers chasing success in the heavyweight division, to prove or disprove racial preference in the sport's white audience? What criteria would demonstrate whether or not white fighters have an easier ride to the top, whether or not white fans have left a candle burning in the window for a white champion?

Quantitative Credentials

A boxer's career performances offer a variety of measures for numerical comparison. The complete results of virtually all fighter's efforts in the ring are a matter of record. One can consult where and when they fought, against which opponent, and the outcome of each bout. Thus, there are ready means of determining how equal or unequal opportunity along racial lines has been for heavyweight boxers of recent vintage. By creating two data bases of white and black heavyweights who reached common standards of achievement, one can find whether the latter's path to success has been steeper. If this is the case, the numbers showing a smoother white ascension to boxing's penthouse suggest the forces shaping boxing in a mostly white America have continued to favor white hopes.

A boxing periodical first published in 1922 will provide both a means of creating our data bases, and quantitative criteria that will place the career experience of black and white heavyweights alongside each other for comparison. Aside from the narrow criteria of separating world champion boxers from those who are not, the most objective standards of elite boxing quality are Top Ten rankings. Contenders rated in the Top Ten receive most opportunities to fight for the championship belt. A Top Ten rating is ostensibly given only to those fighters who have accumulated an impressive record against quality competition, fighters who objectively figure to present a challenge to the reigning world champion. One expects a fighter to enter the Top Ten by having few, if any, defeats on his record, and many victories, including a few wins against stiff competition. Typically, a young boxer breaks into the ratings by defeating a former champion or Top Ten contender on the downside of his career. On a rising star's record, such over the hill opponents are called "names" in boxing parlance, bolstering a fighter's credentials the same way relevant job experience or education strengthens a job résumé. When such a boxer has victories under his belt against names recognizable to the broad boxing audience, he is making the transition from being a merely regional fighter to a nationally recognized challenger with a name recognized by fans reading the morning sports pages across the country. When this happens, his competitive and financial horizons widen. Having paid his dues, and having run out of worthy competition fighting in small- and medium-size venues in their hometown, this boxer will often become the number ten (or sometimes even higher) contender. But more importantly than a reward for prior success, such a status allows the pugilist access to more important and lucrative bouts against other Top Ten fighters, a stepping stone (if he continues to win) before challenging the reigning champion. No professional boxer is ever satisfied with merely being a contender. The driving motivation behind every elite boxer is to make that final step toward the world title. After coming this far, at so much expense and sacrifice, a fighter would be foolish not to strive to reach his highest potential. The Top Ten contenders typically offer the stable of potential opponents for the king of the division.

World champions are expected to defend their titles against challengers among the ten boxers just below them. Their reputations as worthy champions depend on it, for defending against weak challengers invites public ridicule. Furthermore, the income potential is greater for a defense against a serious rival. Few fans will pay to see a championship mismatch whose outcome seems preordained. For this reason, once a boxer becomes one of the select ten contenders within a stone's throw of the champion, his career has taken a huge step. Many boxers are unknown to the general public until they are ranked, and they fight for miniscule purses compared to what they earn once they are rated. Ken Norton was mostly unknown outside his home state of California, fighting for purses of a few hundred dollars until his shocking upset of Muhammad Ali in 1973. Overnight, he became a household name, and a rich boxer. Even fighters who never win the title can reap considerable financial reward from being a known contender. Because a world ranking is an achievement enjoyed by a select few boxers, this accomplishment offers a criteria for limiting the number of boxers under investigation.

Only ranked heavyweights will be considered in this study. How such elite boxers gained this ranking, in terms of how much time and effort they had to put forward to get there, will provide benchmarks for comparing how hard it has been for black and white heavyweights to succeed in their profession. Since ranking the ability of many boxers who have never competed against each other is largely subjective, one must hope for the most objective ratings available. For most of the past eighty years, the monthly periodical *The Ring* has provided the most credible assessments of the world's best fighters.[12] Each month, the magazine has published ratings of the best ten contenders in each division, with constant juggling of fighters based on their recent performances, talent, and age. This study will identify Top Ten contenders and arrange them in black and white groupings. The complete ring record for such boxers will be evaluated quantitatively and qualitatively to establish their level of accomplishment when they cracked the Top Ten barrier.

Many questions will be considered. What did the average black and white boxer have to do to reach this level, relative to each other? How long did they have to compete before breaking into the rankings, how old were they, how many fights did they have under their belt, and how often did they compete per year? How many wins, how few losses, what winning percentage, how many knockouts, and what knockout percentage was on their resume that first month they were acclaimed as a rated contender? How many notches on their belts did they have in the form of victories over already ranked Top Ten opponents, what was the average record of the opponents in their wake? What quality of opponent did they beat in their fights immediately leading up to the time when *The Ring* took notice of them, the fights that turned the heads of this magazine's writers and editors?

Further inspection of these boxers' careers after they became ranked by *The Ring* will provide more insight as to how color blind opportunity has been in the heavyweight division. How long did such boxers remain in the ratings, and what did they have to do to maintain their status? How often did they have to fight and keep winning to move up through the ten spots, or even just to hang on to their rating? When age began to take a toll on their stock as a ranked contender, how many losses did it take for them to slip from this exalted status? How many white and black contenders ever entered the ratings a second time after being dropped? A third time? A fourth? What did such boxers have to do to win back this distinction in *The Ring*'s eyes?

Another means of comparing opportunity for heavyweights racially is the rarer achievement of fighting for the championship. The ranks of boxers who fight for a world title are even smaller than those who dent the Top Ten ratings. The same statistical measures used for rated contenders will be used for these heavyweights. It might be found there is little or no difference in achievement when black and white fighters became world ranked contenders or fight for the world championship. If this is the case, whatever yearnings whites may have for a Great White Hope (if any at all), have not been strong enough to significantly restrict blacks from success relative to their white fighters. If the average black heavyweight has had to fight longer, more often, and have a closer to perfect record to enter the elite ratings or challenge for the championship, it is likely that a sizable part of boxing's white audience still wants a white champion, and that this desire has skewed competitive opportunity in favor of white prospects. These queries offer potential insight as to whether race has continued to have a say in which heavyweights climb to the top or close to it.

Time Frame

When should such an investigation begin? What is being asked is how much race matters to white fans cheering for and supporting the fighters they watch. The period from 1949 to 1983 offers a workable period of analysis to identify whether black boxers have continued to climb a steeper hill to the summit. It is taken as given that prior to Joe Louis, it was the norm for blacks to have nowhere near the opportunity whites had to pursue heavyweight success. Before Louis, only Jack Johnson ever had the chance to contest the world championship. The color line that kept the title belt around white flesh could only have restricted the earning potential of countless black contenders, for elite white heavyweights had both competitive reasons and social pressures steering them away from fighting credible African American opponents. The pathway to the heavyweight crown was a lot clearer without blacks in the way, and a white fighter's reputation (and future purses) could easily be damaged by treading on the sensitivities of white fans not ready to deal with a black champion. Joe Louis's twelve-year reign as world champion was a transition period in which Americans made huge steps in at least superficially accepting integration in sports. When Louis was introduced to the crowd the night he fought for Jim Braddock's title in 1937, the ring announcer felt compelled to plead with the crowd to ignore the former's race. In the first years after Louis won this fight, the sporting media were almost obsessed with the issue of this new champion's skin color, using an endless stream of color-laden monikers to describe him that never allowed readers to forget he was not white.

By 1949, such attitudes already seemed quaint, if not embarrassing, to a broad swath of white sports fans. When Louis handed over his belt in that year, his contribution to opening doors to black athletes was mostly in the history books. Further advances in knocking down racial barriers would be made by other black athletes, but the Brown Bomber's accomplishments and grace inside the ring and out set sports squarely on the path toward integration. Never again would it be as easy for white racists to justify denying black athletes the opportunity to compete with whites. Millions of whites who had previously thought little about or opposed the idea of integration, saw in Louis a truth whose logic would carry well beyond the ring, and then further beyond the domain of sports. One is tempted to think that when he retired from boxing, Louis left behind an America where the Great White Hope was destined to disappear from the minds of boxing fans. A myriad of evidence today, however, indicates that white acceptance of black dominance on the playing field is not absolute. Since Louis's career struck such a huge blow against the attitudes that justified the color line in boxing, and what is in doubt is how much his impact on interracial competition was matched by genuine acceptance of black participation in sports, it is appropriate to hone in on the period beginning with his pioneering contribution in the books. His leaving the stage offers a symbolic benchmark from which one can establish how far the racial majority had moved, and would continue to move toward true integration in sport. This study, then, will begin in 1949.

The year 1983 will serve as the end point of this investigation. In this year, the last challenge for the undisputed heavyweight crown by a white fighter took place, with Scott Frank vying for Larry Holmes's title. Since this was the last time one of their own was within one punch of being a world champion, 1983 is an appropriate end bracket for finding how America's racial majority feels, if anything at all, about the skin color of the most famous athlete on the planet. If they still wanted a white champion, such feelings would be more prevalent in a time when there was a chance for this to happen. Since 1983, no white American fighter has challenged for the world crown when it was unified, or for one of the two or three most respected splinter belts (WBC, WBA, IBF) when it was not. Tommy Morrison won a title belt from the dubious WBO in 1994, a claim to heavyweight supremacy that no knowledgeable boxing fan would take seriously.

To identify progress in racial attitudes and competitive opportunity for heavyweights (if any) over this study's span of almost thirty-five years, the interval period will be divided into three, roughly equal sub-periods. The comparisons will be made between black and white heavyweights across the periods of 1949–59, 1960–69, and 1970–83. These three and a half decades could be analyzed in their entirety, but heavyweight boxing, like all sports in America, did not sit still during this span. It evolved from a sport populated by hundreds of whites to one in which they became the subject of tongue-in-cheek jokes and assumed to be inferior. The racial evolution of the ring did not happen overnight, and any inequalities in competitive opportunities are not likely to have done so either; thus these three sub-periods offer a looking glass to spot changes along racial lines over time.

Foreign-born heavyweights could add considerable validity to the findings if there were a comparable sample of foreign-born black heavyweight contenders and challengers to balance off the several dozen white ones who challenged for the title or became ranked during the period of focus. Between 1949 and 1983, only Jamaican-born Trevor Berbick (of Canada) and Bunny Johnson (of England) challenged for the world heavyweight title or broke into the Top Ten rankings. Without a large counterbalancing sample of black foreign heavyweights for direct statistical comparison to the white foreigners, one is left with several dozen European, South African, Canadian, and Latin American fighters who could still be statistically compared to the African American sample. Such boxers cannot be neatly included in a study of America's racial perceptions of sports. Many whites with racial biases have undoubtedly held more favorable attitudes toward white foreigners than their black brethren but, as discussed earlier, the theory of white racial supremacy on this soil always had a nationalistic tone. White skin was always deemed on a higher plane, but within this category, there were assumptions that Yankee muscle and fortitude could set straight what other Anglos might struggle with. America's mainstream audience was nowhere near as angry when Tommy Burns lost to Jack Johnson as when one of their own was beaten two years later. A white Canadian being thrashed by a grinning Black American could somehow be rationalized as simply distasteful, rather than a genuine threat staring in the face of white supremacy. Americans who believed in racial supremacy assumed they were the flagbearer for all the white races of the world. Foreign white boxers winning did not give white Americans as much satisfaction, nor did their losing to black opponents feel as painful, as when one of their own was involved. When John Sullivan lost his crown to Jim Corbett, his assessment of his downfall was as jingoistic as it was gracious. "Gentlemen, all I've got to say is I stayed once too long. I'm glad the championship remains in America, with one of our own people." Curiously enough, this chauvinistic desire to see the heavyweight title as an inherent birthright of Americans has extended across racial lines. In 1959, black heavyweight Floyd Patterson rang the same nationalist bell in his feelings about losing his title to a Swede, Ingemar Johansson. "Losing a championship was bad enough, but losing it to a foreigner was even worse."[13] One can recall that American sport fans for years felt it was their nation's birthright to count the world's fastest human (100 meter sprint) among their ranks. When the Russian Valery Borzov took the 1972 Munich gold in this event, the glaring sports page headline in the otherwise liberal *New York Times* lamented the apocalypse that the world's fastest man was a Commie. It required some swallowing for the U.S. track establishment to accept that the laurel previously monopolized by their own speed demons was now on the mantle of a Soviet runner.

Overlying the racial dynamic of boxing's history in America has been a strong nationalist sentiment, in which American citizenship has influenced the public's feelings about fighters in general, and champions specifically. In this study, white foreign challengers like George Chuvalo (Canada); Henry Cooper, Don Cockell, and Brian London (England); Karl Mildenberger (Germany), Alfredo Evangelista and Lorenzo Zanon (Spain); Jean Pierre Coopman (Belgium); Gerry Coetzee (South Africa); and numerous other Anglo or European challengers will not be included for analysis. They represent a confounding variable which cannot be easily analyzed for the statistical comparisons of this study. None of these men could be groomed into a Great White Hope because they were not American. After Jeffries's defeat in 1910, the obsessive search by the white American boxing establishment, media and fans for a Great White Hope was directed primarily across America. The names of such hyped prospects were overwhelmingly American, indicating that white America needed, wanted, and expected the Jack Johnson problem to be solved by one of their own, as Jeffries had been. While any non-black champion would undoubtedly have been preferable to the self-assured, gloating Johnson from Galveston, both in 1910 and long after, Caucasian boxing fans in the United States derived far more satisfaction from American world titleists than from any other white champions. European heavyweight kings like Primo Carnera of Italy, Max Schmeling of Germany (even before the rise of Hitler), and Ingemar Johannson of Sweden, elicited little more warmth from mainstream America than socialism, soccer, the metric system, and public transportation.

Inclusion of foreign heavyweights is even more problematic given the complexity of integrating Latin American boxers into the comparisons. Hispanics have always been visible minorities in America. Their history in this country provides ample evidence of mistreatment and inequality, as well as examples of cultural and racial disdain stretching back to the age of Jack Johnson and earlier. Those of Latin descent did not escape the ugly mindset of white supremacy in the time when the color line was the norm in American sports. No better example of this can be found than in the frustration President Teddy Roosevelt expressed when the Colombian government refused to sell Panamian land for the building of a canal at the price offered by Washington. Roosevelt referred to Bogota's regime, and by implication its entire nation, as "dagoes" and "contemptible little creatures."[14] Clearly, for many Gilded Age whites, the racial pinnacle of mankind lay north of the Mexican-U.S. border.

Still, the racial disdain felt by whites in high places toward Latin Americans does not conveniently place such boxers in an assessment of the Great White Hope appeal, both in 1910 and the 1949–83 period. A century ago, when the theory of white racial supremacy was burning at a fever pitch in the psyches of some Caucasian Americans, the mindset was vocalized and aimed at African Americans. By far the nation's largest, most visible racial minority, blacks were as well the group victimized by the most violent abuse and virulent hatred in day-to-day American life. It was a black insurrection, a bloody race war with blacks, that was first and foremost in the minds of those whites worried about the purity and surivival of their race. Thus, black heavyweights like Jack Johnson were shunned as a threat to the racial order for what they might do in the ring. There were nowhere near as many Americans of Mexican, Cuban, Puerto Rican, or Central or South American descent proportionally, so white supremacy could not have been as threatened by them as they were by blacks.[15] As well, there were virtually no elite Latin American heavyweight boxers fighting on American soil in the late nineteenth and early twentieth century. If there had been, they would have been part of boxing's historical record, since the brutal color line in boxing did not stop frustrated black heavyweights like Joe Jeanette, Sam McVey, Harry Wills, and Sam Langford from entering the consciousness of the boxing media and press through their superb skills.[16] If there were topnotch Hispanic heavyweights plying their trade on American soil, there is no reason why they would not have at least been heard of, even if they were barred from the world title by the color line.

With Latin Americans making up a much smaller part of America's population, and with there being no such boxers threatening to upset white America's racial apple cart, both the theory of white racial supremacy and the Great White Hope campaign were much less identified with the dynamic of white and Hispanic relations than the relationship between white and black Americans. A major premise of this study is to examine how far white America has come in tolerating equal sporting opportunity along racial lines, using the Great White Hope era as a frame of reference, as the starting point in a century-long process of accomodation versus resistance. Since the Great White Hope was born primarily from the perceived threat black American advancement and assertiveness posed to the status quo, it is problematic to include Latin American fighters in this study on the same methodological terms. Put simply, it was not an Argentinian heavyweight who made white fans squirm in their seats by thrashing the best white heavyweights in the world, not a Mexican heavyweight who was dating Caucasian women while white passers-by seethed, nor a Puerto Rican who openly flaunted his wealth and opinions in white faces, between 1908 and 1915. It was a black man. There is no way of knowing how white supremacy advocates would have reacted to such scenarios. Would they have been half as horrified? Two-thirds as outraged? Would there have been three-quarters as many race murders, arrests, and injuries if the aftermath of Jim Jeffries losing to a Venezuelan champion? A Cuban titleholder? Or would it have even been deemed necessary to lure the faded Jeffries out of retirement to put a Peruvian or Chilean heavyweight king in his proper place? Would white Americans have even needed a Great White Hope to defeat such a symbol, so as to sleep better at night? Less than a decade after Johnson's downfall, Jack Dempsey defended his title against Argentinian Luis Firpo. There is no record of any public opposition to Dempsey risking his title against a Latin American, no concern that white racial strength and security were at stake in this fight. The white boxing public lapped up this promotion with nary a peep of discomfort. Latin American heavyweights, as few as there were, did not seem to bother white racial sensitivities, suggesting Caucasian Americans perceived them as close enough to being white to be non-threatening on the playing field. This makes it questionable to include the careers of 1949–83 Latin fighters for comparison to the opportunity received by white heavyweights, since there is little evidence that white America had much problem with such a boxer winning the title at the time when the Great White Hope phenomenon was born.

It is anyone's guess whether a white American desire for a Great White Hope would work in favor, or to the disadvantage of Latin heavyweights in recent times. Such a yearning (if it existed) might solely benefit white American, Anglo, or European boxers, stranding Hispanic boxers on the margins of opportunity where black heavyweights resided in the early 1900s, and presumably still do. In this case, Manuel Ramos (Mexico), Oscar Bonavena, Abel Cestac, Domingo D'Elia, Eduardo Corletti, Gregorio Peralta, Cesar Brion, and Alejandro Lavorante (Argentina), Jose Luis Garcia (Venezuela), and Bernardo Mercado (Colombia), would have to be compared statistically against white American heavyweights, to assess whether their race worked against their careers. If white American boxing fans who needed a Great White Hope saw Latin Americans as more alike than different, the above fighters would have to be included in the white grouping, as the prospect of such a champion would be assumed to be soothing or reassuring to a white public anxious for something other than a black titleholder.

In short, it is clear that white supremacists who recoiled at the Johnson-Jeffries fight, would have reacted with somewhat less hostility to a foreign Hispanic champion. White American attitudes toward lighter-skinned minority peoples like Latinos have never been exactly the same as those they have held toward African Americans. With the exception of the World War II internment of over 100,000 Japanese Americans, it has generally been true that the lighter one's skin, the less overt hostility and victimization minorities have received in American history. There is less of a history of racial symbolism hinging on Latin participation in American boxing; not as much evidence exists of tension surrounding the outcomes of bouts between whites and Hispanics. The very history of New World colonization and intermarriage south of the American-Mexican border by itself would call for nothing less than a dissertation in any discussion of racial identity. In Central and South America, and the Caribbean, attitudes range from those who proudly celebrate their mixed ancestry to those who angrily deny any identity with "blackness." Such a reality represents a statistical wild card for any study arbitrarily dividing boxers into black and white categories through the cultural and historical lenses of the United States.

Sitting somewhere between white and black racial identities in any measurement of white American boxing fans' loyalties, Latin American boxers cannot be pigeonholed into an *us versus them* black-white dichotomy of advantage versus disadvantage. It is possible that if white fans between 1949 and 1983 were dismayed at their race being shut out of the heavyweight title for decades, this could have made foreign Hispanic boxers more attractive than they once were. The assumption here is that any boxer who is close to being white (whatever that means in a given white fan's mind) could offer partial satisfaction to those Causcasian boxing followers whose security is somehow connected to the racial identity of the world champion. It is also possible that the only prescription for white American insecurity about black dominance in boxing could be a Waspy, whitebread champion, with no pscyhological relief to be gained from a Mexican or South American titleholder.

Because one of this study's major pillars is the development of white-black American relations as a result of the Great White Hope phenomenon, the most valid approach is to limit the comparisons of boxer credentials to black and white American fighters. Assessing whether nationalism trumps race or vica versa in the hearts of American sports fans is a study in itself. The relative importance of the two factors is murky enough to justify an exclusive focus on American-born fighters.

Of major relevance is that the past five decades have seen the world heavyweight championship monopolized by an almost unbroken string of

3. The Great White Hope: Extinct or Dormant? 61

African American fighters, no white American heavyweight has been an undisputed champion since Rocky Marciano retired in 1956. Nearly a half century of domination by black boxers has hardly gone unnoticed by the racial majority. The stranglehold over the crown by the black fighters and the apparent disappearance of elite white heavyweights has been even more stark than the racial shift in the NBA, where four-fifths of the players are black. Since credible white heavyweights have become the dodo birds of American sports, the opportunity enjoyed by those that have been around could easily have been affected. If there are still Americans who need a white champion, such a desire has long been an unfulfilled wish, a yearning frustrated since before many white sports fans were born. This blocked desire could make for racial inequality in the sport's competitive workings. That is, although the disappearance of white contenders from the ring has obviously aided black opportunity in that a sport that may be 90 percent black, unequal opportunity could be even more evident. If an average of only five of the best 100 American heavyweights are white over a long period, and two or three of the Top Ten contenders are consistently white, one might suspect a racial dynamic is at work, that white pugilists are enjoying competitive and financial advantages in moving up the ladder simply because they are white. The novelty of world-class white boxers may have made white boxing fans think more about race than would have been the case if there had been several white champions over the past few decades. The absence of credible white heavyweights could have made the white fan's heart grow fonder.

If white boxers still have an easier ride to the top, it would be an expression of white racial preferences working through those factors that shape success in the ring. In other words, what influences how high any boxer climbs the competitive ranks would also be the means through which whites would express their desire for a Great White Hope. Media publicity, fan support, financial backing, promotion, and favorable ratings are a web of inter-related factors that open or close opportunity to boxers pursuing the world title, often in ways having nothing to do with fairness. Acting together, these five factors are mechanisms that could work to the advantage of white boxers and the detriment of black ones. A white media could demonstrate a preference toward white boxers by trumpeting the skills of a less talented white fighter over better black pugilists, creating the perception in the public's mind that he *must* be great because he is receiving all this media attention. Such fans would be more likely to buy tickets to see this boxer compete, thus helping his career financially and competitively. Concurrently, the white boxing public could be predisposed to rave about any credible white fighter placed in front of them, and this greater interest could steer the media into singing the praises of a mediocre white heavyweight to give their paying readers what they want. Both media and fans could honestly argue they are not biased in favor of white hopes, but both contribute to a cyclical process that manufactures such boxers instead of proven entities in the ring. The media could defend its glowing coverage of a white heavyweight by claiming the public wants to read about him, while boxing fans insist the only reason they cheer for him is because he has been written about so much.

Financial backing, promotional efforts, and the ratings of governing bodies are similar competitive levers within the boxing world that could (if fans still wanted a white hope) operate to boost a white heavyweight's fortunes faster and further than their black rivals. Promotional magnates like Don King and Bob Arum have ample power to push white contenders on the market if they feel the boxing public is receptive, without having to justify why more talented black ones are not included as often on their fight cards. A yearning for a white hope spells dollar signs in any boxing promoter's eyes, and who are they to deny the fans what they want?

Young boxers are as much at the mercy of their bank accounts as their opponents in the ring. Being discovered and supported well by a patron or financial group often makes a huge difference in a fighter's ability to even continue his career, let alone move up through the division. Such economic backing does not have to have any connection to genuine talent potential, opening a wide door for race to have its say in which fighters can and cannot continue their careers. Like promoters, the management teams that sustain young boxers' quest for success could easily be inclined to fund a white hope of lesser ability if they suspect the public would rave about him long enough to make a tidy profit.

Finally, the world rankings of some boxing governing bodies, to a far greater degree than *The Ring*, have long been characterized by seedy motives in the fighters they rate, for reasons other than performance. It is an open secret that some bodies have operated as virtual hand puppets to powerful boxing promoters. At times, they have moved dubious boxers into the Top Ten ratings solely to legitimize potentially lucrative world title fights, as their bylaws decree that all world title defenses must be against ranking contenders. Such boxing officials have been no more immune to the sight of green paper than promoters. Since their willingness to illegitimately fast-track boxers into their rankings has been purely about money, inflated white hopes with massaged reputations and starry-eyed fans can benefit as much as any other bogus fighter.

For many individuals associated with professional boxing, the questions asked by this study will seem like asking if the sky is blue. It is taken as a given by many boxers, boxing writers, and promoters that white boxers benefit competitively and financially from their skin color. The inside word in boxing is that white skin is money in the bank from a marketing standpoint. A 1991 source of boxing quotations reveals some powerful gems from the sport's power brokers, the following names all being men who became eminent, quotable boxing figures in the 1980s.

> Any white fighter, if he becomes a good fighter, has big money box office potential. There's no question about that. You must be able to deal with the fact that you have racism out there. A white fighter is platinum gold if he can fight.
>
> — Don King, promoter

> Let's be honest. In the sport of boxing, black-white fights happen to be more attractive to the public. A Cooney-Spinks match, on the safe side, is worth five to ten million dollars. Holmes-Spinks is worth three to four million.
>
> — Butch Lewis, promoter

> As boxing has become more and more controlled by black fighters, white fighters are a must from a marketing standpoint. This is the way it is in every major city across the nation. Even if a white fighter is not that good, he will draw well, if he is a winner, and is entertaining.
>
> — Ernie Terrell, promoter[17]

All three of the above quotes lend credence to the belief that America still yearns for white boxing heroes, a desire that manifests itself in big profits for Caucasian fighters and those who promote them. It is worth noting that all three of the above promoters are black men who are convinced that white fans still want to buy tickets to see white hopes. Since all three make a living from marketing boxing cards (particularly lucrative livings for Lewis and King), their unanimity is compelling.

This notion is not limited to black Americans involved with the ring, nor does it have to involve the embracing of white American boxers. One of the sport's most eminent white promoters, Bob Arum, described the initial promotional allure of 1984 Canadian Olympic boxing hero Shawn O'Sullivan as being almost entirely about skin color. Arum stated that if O'Sullivan had not been white, nobody would have given him a second thought.[18] In O'Sullivan's first stiff test against a Black American, Simon Brown, he was soundly thrashed in three rounds. His career never went any higher.

Some observers go even further, not merely suggesting that white Americans would feel good seeing a white heavyweight do well, but directly linking white infatuation with Great White Hopes to a desire for a white world champion.

> If one fighter is black and the other is white, pride is almost automatically at stake. It is a race war every time it happens. These days, it is what the public — especially white people, hoping for a white champion after so many years — will always pay to see.
>
> — Larry Holmes, as told to Phil Berger[19]

The perception (if not reality) that America's racial majority still wants or needs a white champion obviously could be financially exploited as easily by black promoters as white ones. The irony, if this belief is factual, is that almost a century after Jack Johnson spilled into the laps of an unhappy white America, the color line in boxing may have transformed into a lucrative money cow to be milked by America's racial minority. A white preference for white boxing heroes, like any other consumer market, could be a gravy train with room for black boxers and promoters as well. Why fight it when one can profit from it? Who could fairly blame black promoters for working this status quo to their own advantage? Who could judge elite African American heavyweights for seeking out fair-to-middling white opponents who represent more green in the wallet than better-talented black rivals? If that seems to be what the white public wants, why not give it to them, and laugh all the way to the bank with a larger bag of money than would otherwise be the case? If this attitude has been the norm among black champions, it would not have been a particularly noble or idealistic mindset, given that one would hope that such fighters would care about helping their fellow brethren gain the same opportunity they had. But idealism and nobility have seldom found fertile ground in boxing.

One writer alludes as to why white boxers see bluer competitive and economic skies than black fighters.

> Boxing is the last overtly racist professional sport, especially in the United States where battles between black men and white men are still a draw for all the wrong reasons. Reaching the affluent portion of the white public who are only casual boxing fans is easiest with an attractive white fighter. Blessed with one, any promoter can seem a genius.
>
> — Stephen Brunt[20]

If whites still favor a white heavyweight champion, however quietly, one inevitable question must be asked: do they feel this way? Both the question and the answer are relevant far beyond the realm of sports and it brings up more questions. Why is it that more than nine decades since July 4, 1910, that whites should feel better if the world heavyweight champion shares the same skin color? What kind of satisfaction or security would this afford them in a society that has made huge, though long overdue leaps toward racially equal opportunity? In what way would millions of white Americans sleep better at night simply because the world champ was Caucasian kin?

Some would insist that it is perfectly natural for anyone to identify with someone of their own race in any endeavor, to feel more empathy for one of their own. It may well be true that no matter how tolerant and equal in providing opportunity America may become, it will always be that plenty of whites will feel a deeper satisfaction at seeing fellow whites succeed in sports or any other pursuit. Perhaps racial identification is such a strong element in shaping attitudes, it is naïve to expect that White American sport fans, or those of any other race, could ever be totally color blind in choosing what sporting heroes to support. If there is a core yearning in white minds to see one of their own excel over athletes of other races, a yearning that has nothing to do with animosity toward other races, whites would hardly be the only race to feel this way. Does anyone seriously think that no African, Asian, or Native Americans cheer for members of their race in interracial competition, solely because of their race? Is it racism against whites when a black barfly screams in celebration at Tiger Woods winning a golf tournament over a field of white opponents? Is it called racism when Hispanic Americans cheer lustily for boxer Oscar De La Hoya? If minorities have the thumbs up to root for their own without being criticized or called racists for it, then surely whites deserve no less. Americans of Irish, Italian, Polish, German, and Anglo descent are no less entitled to feel proud of their heritage, or celebrate it through athletic success, than the above. While this study may conclude that many whites still lean toward cheering for white boxers, that will only indicate the possibility of racism, not its existence. This study can only assess whether black fighters still have to climb a steeper hill to reach the top than do white ones, and whether professional boxing is shaped toward this outcome by the conscious or unconscious preferences of whites boxing fans for a Great White Hope. Liking the idea of a white champion can not be perfectly reduced to disliking or marginalizing black athletes.

The presence of a strong white bias in favor of Great White Hopes will not by itself demonstrate white racism, or hostility toward black success. Similarly, if it is discovered that opportunity in heavyweight boxing has become equal, that no distinguishable bias toward Great White Hopes can be attributed to the white audience, this will obviously imply a racial acceptance or color blindness in boxing, and to a lesser degree, sports. This would represent a significant step toward racial tolerance, to be sure, but extrapolating this change in attitude beyond the world of sports would be tenuous. More or less equal competitive opportunity represents a significant racial hurdle cleared in sports, but it could be another form of intolerance or racial preference. Whites could simply have abandoned interest in boxing and turned their attention to sports where white athletes put up a better show. This potential outcome could be defined as whites, realizing they cannot have the heroes they want, simply taking their boxing gloves and going home.

The practical purpose of this study is twofold. At least two injustices would be prevalent in boxing if a persistent white audience's yearning for a Great White Hope has continued to slant opportunity unequally.

First, talented black heavyweights would have had to work harder for lesser rewards in their chosen profession, making less money than their skills and commitment to their trade merited. In an America that still subtly pines for a Great White Hope, how many hundreds of black fighters have only risen part of the way that their potential predicted, only earned half or three quarters of what they would have reaped if they had been white with the same talent? How much more financial sponsorship would they have received that would have allowed them to focus on their craft instead of having to hold down another job while competing? How many more competitive and profitable fights would have come their way if they had been allowed to climb to their true potential? Since the vast majority of boxers struggle to even make a living, the lack of unequal opportunity looms as large in its unfairness here as it does in many other sectors of the economy. What is being discussed is not the unionized football, basketball, or baseball player of today who makes a minimum salary of several hundred thousand dollars, but boxers who toil for years for perhaps one chance to make big money. In the former sports, salaries have occasionally been proven to be slightly unequal along racial lines, but the difference between white players averaging $240,000 and black ones earning $220,000 would seem trivial to boxers striving to climb their sport's rankings. An average player on the worst team in the NFL makes enough money, if wisely invested, to last a lifetime. Few professional boxers can realistically dream of this windfall.

The other injustice, if Great White Hopes are still being manufactured and fast-tracked through the division, is that legitimate white contenders of the past will not have received the full credit their accomplishments called for, while present and future ones can expect more of the same. Even the perception that white boxers leapfrog over black ones who have paid greater dues can elicit sneers of disdain, reflexive assumptions that a given fighter advanced as much for his skin as his performance. One can only empathize with a boxer who is dismissed as another Great White Hope simply because he did not win the title. One can be an outstanding boxer, and have a very proud and rewarding career, without being a world champion. The respect that should be part of this accomplishment is less likely for a white heavyweight when it is assumed that the rare market appeal of his skin has accounted for much of his success. Jerry Quarry won over fifty fights in his career, with notable victories over a series of elite heavyweights.[21] Yet for many years, the defining image of his career seemed to be his four losses to Muhammad Ali and Joe Frazier. Never counted out on the canvas, five of his eight losses came as a result of facial cuts. The rivulets of blood pouring down Quarry's face against Frazier, Ali, and Ken Norton still linger in American boxing fans' collective memory, an image that captures the perceived futility of white heavyweights matching their skills against black champions. On his biggest nights, when greatness hung in the balance, Quarry always seemed to be fighting desperate, uphill battles against his own skin as well as his African American opponents.

Did the respect and recognition Quarry was due as a Top-Ten contender for a decade get lost in the disappointment of another white fighter falling short of the championship? When Quarry was pounded into a swollen mess by Frazier, or cut open by Ali, were white fans disillusioned or cynical enough to take their frustrations out on Quarry's reputation? Did whites express their disappointment by discarding Quarry as someone who let them down? If the boxing audience has continued to visualize a white champion, it might explain why a fighter like Quarry seems to have gotten the short shrift in boxing literature. This attitude, if it was an accurate reflection of white boxing fans' thinking, could be expressed as, "You raised our hopes and failed to deliver, AGAIN!" Even today, when Quarry is referred to in popular sports literature, the allusion is often as a "bridesmaid" from the past, trotted out to be equated to a contemporary boxer (often white) who has fallen short of the title and fans' expectations. Such is the reputation of Jerry Quarry. Four of his eight losses were to two of the greatest heavyweight champions of all time, Frazier and Ali. Two more defeats came at the hands of superb title claimants Ken Norton (who beat Ali) and Jimmy Ellis, who beat Quarry in a close fifteen-round decision even though he was fighting with a broken back. One loss was to a man popularly respected as the toughest and most durable heavyweight ever, the almost indestructible Canadian, George Chuvalo. Another was to Eddie Machen, a wily and seasoned Top Ten contender for a decade; Chuvalo was in his prime, twenty-one years old, when he fought Quarry. Which of these losses are unforgivable in the eyes of those who denigrate Quarry? Does anyone ridicule Jimmy Young, Ken Norton, or Earnie Shavers, black fighters with comparable defeats who never won the title in the ring? Was the inability to win the world championship by African Americans Ernie Terrell, Eddie Machen, or Zora Folley to win the world championship, ever a similar source of contempt?

How many black heavyweights with forty-eight wins, only four losses, and forty-two knockouts elicit smirks and eye rolls at the mere mention of their name, which has been the fate of Duane Bobick, a white contender of the mid-1970s? This fighter's name has often been regarded as a synonym for inflated white boxing prospects. More than twenty years after his retirement, his career is summoned up by boxing aficionados and analysts denigrating the latest white heavyweight making waves in the division. Did Bobick really disappoint, or were the expectations too high from the beginning? From the moment he was upset in the 1972 Munich Olympics by Cuban legend Teofilo Stevenson, Bobick seemed to labor under a shadow of suspicion by white fans, who were reluctant to invest their hearts and cheers in a fighter who might be another "Great White Hoax," "Great White Hype," or "Great White Hopeless." Thirty-eight consecutive victories were erased in the public's mind when he was knocked out at fifty-eight seconds of the first round by Ken Norton in 1977, making him the butt of comedians' jokes, including America's favorite late-night humorist.

> "Hey, did you hear about the Duane Bobick doll? Wind it up and it falls down?"
>
> "Hey, did you hear about the one-minute commercial Duane Bobick did? It lasts 58 seconds!"
>
> — Johnny Carson[22]

But how many fighters, even Top Ten contenders, would be thrilled to retire with Bobick's record? That Bobick's popular legacy is of a white disappointment, rather than a very good heavyweight who won most of his fights, reveals more about white America's unfulfilled hopes than any major failing on Bobick's part. Was Bobick's record any more stuffed with creampuff opponents than the typical contender (black or white) of the 1970s? At the very least, Bobick had worked his way through thirty-eight opponents before his ill-fated bout with Norton, representing more work than many boxers were (and still are) willing to invest in their careers.

Gerry Cooney's reputation took a similar beating after his loss to Larry Holmes. It was one thing to approach Cooney's pre-1982 record with caution. But against Holmes, Cooney put up a better effort than most of the champion's opponents, black or white. Losing to a champion of this caliber was nothing to be ashamed of for great black fighters. Few have ridiculed Ken Norton, Leon Spinks, or Earnie Shavers for being conquered by the Easton Assassin, yet Cooney's loss seems to have defined his entire career. The social and cultural stakes appear to have been much higher when Quarry, Bobick, and Cooney, climbed into the ring to contest the world title, and with it the derision that followed their losses. On the biggest nights of their careers, being white novelties in a black sport might well have amounted to an albatross around their necks, a five hundred-pound white gorilla placed on their backs by an anxious public.

Could such merciless scrutiny have reduced the number of young white boxers in recent years, discouraging would-be Caucasian fighters with potential from setting their sights high? Having heard so much denigration directed at Quarry, Bobick, and Cooney, white amateur pugilists since the 1970s might have needed as much self-confidence as Caucasian youths who set out to be competitive sprinters or win basketball scholarships. One can imagine the bemused stares and dismissive snorts that could face such aspiring white fighters by skeptics who *needed* Quarry to beat Ali, had their hearts set on Bobick trouncing Norton, or invested themselves emotionally in Cooney defeating Holmes, and were bitterly disappointed when none of the above happened. Such injustices to both white and black boxers, if they exist, call out for remedy as do all areas of society in which race skews the opportunity people have to pursue their goals, and the meaning attributed to their achievements.

The possibility that, from 1949 to 1983, white America continued to need a Great White Hope to the degree that more deserving black fighters were hindered in the heavyweight title chase in favor of more pedestrian white challengers, is strongly alluded to in the newspaper coverage of interracial championship fights during that span. In 1950, the *New York Times* almost damned a white challenger to death with faint praise. On the day of Ezzard Charles's second defense of his title against Fred Beshore in Buffalo, the paper reassured (?) its readers that the white challenger, although an underdog, was "not exactly despised."[23] Perhaps this compliment was meant to sway attention from the fact that Beshore was not even a Top Ten contender when the fight transpired, and had not been on *The Ring*'s pages for seventeen months! Not unless one one believes it was a coincidence that the magazine airlifted Beshore into its ninth spot effective August 15, the day of the fight. The reporting of this fight's outcome almost makes the reader forget who was the champion and who was the challenger, whether the winner or the loser was the real story. The headlines read "Loser Exhibits Courage," that Beshore "Moves Forward Despite Severe Beating." The narrative's depiction of Charles's fourteenth-round knockout was cold, clinical, and almost completely submerged in the paper's syrupy adulation of the white challenger's doomed heroism. One can almost visualize John Wayne heroically staring down America's enemies.

> He (Beshore) had gone about as far as he could against ring experience, boxing skill and sharp solid punching which proved an insurmountable barrier for Beshore from the fifth round.
>
> To his everlasting credit, however, be it said that Beshore fought to the limit of his ordinary best in as game an exhibition as any heavyweight has provided in ring combat through recent years. That he went as far as he did under the battering to which he was subjected, and what is more, without once taking a backward step, spoke volumes for the courage, strength and resistance to punishment of that sturdy ex-gob, who crashed down to defeat, suffering his third knockout in a battle in which he gambled his all on a bid for victory that was pitifully weak.
>
> That Beshore didn't crumple reflected the lack of finishing power in Charles' blows, as it testified to the amazing resistance to punishment which carried Beshore almost to the limit of this one-sided struggle.
>
> ...Onlookers were wondering how any human could withstand such a pounding. He was hardly able to lift his hands, but still Beshore kept moving forward, instinctively, doggedly, in the face of a versatile punching gale.[24]

The reporting of Nick Barone's unsuccessful quest for Charles's title four months later in Cincinnati was similarly focussed on white bravery, rather than the black champion's superior skill in the eleventh-round stoppage.

> Battered from pillar to post through nine of the ten rounds which preceded the finish, Barone nevertheless kept tearing at Charles as 10,085 who paid receipts of $53,334 watched, unbelievingly, and wondering how any human could withstand the battering to which the Syracuse ex-Marine was subjected. What Barone did was a testimony to his courage and his amazing resistance to punishment.
>
> But he never had a chance tonight. However, he fought bravely, fearlessly, recklessly, and with an astounding determination from the time the first bell sent them on their journey until finally he crumpled under the punches of a champion Barone said is underrated.[25]

It took the bloodied Barone to say what was so conspicuously missing from the *Times* correspondent James P. Dawson's account of the fight, that Charles was a talented champion worthy of respect. Both Beshore and Barone's resoluteness and nobility in defeat were a preoccupation of the *Times* boxing writer. The black heavyweight king's clear supremacy was something of an afterthought.

Eight years later, the same newspaper could not clench its teeth hard enough to sell Roy Harris as a credible opponent to challenge for Floyd Patterson's title in Los Angeles, sharing that "...whether he could make even a decent showing ... was entirely uncertain."[26]

By fast-forwarding through the *Times* three more annums, one reads the following assessment of Tom McNeely's chances against Patterson in a 1961 Toronto tilt. "He has a chance all right. So has Outer Mongolia of becoming the first nation to send a man to the moon." Subsequent descriptions of the Massachussetts challenger's prospects included the observation, "The only two persons in this sparkling Canadian metropolis who think that the challenger has even the remotest chance of winning the crown are McNeely and Fuller (McNeely's manager)." Although Outer Mongolia would show more grit and fire more satellites at Patterson than skeptics predicted, the fight would be a slow motion rout. Having little chance against the world champion, McNeely's showing would have done any Irish Boston tavern brawler proud. He pulled himself off the floor eight times in less than four rounds of mayhem, the last time not beating the count. Of course, courageously getting off the canvas eight times only happens when one is knocked *down* eight times. One does not prove oneself a worthy challenger to the world title by proving how much abuse one can take. If this were the case, the world heavyweight crown would have rested on Tex Cobb's head, and might still be there today.

What is compellingly alike about the coverage of the Harris and McNeely challenges, and with the Barone and Beshore fights a decade earlier, is the dominant meaning stamped on the bouts by the *Times* reporters. Like Charles's defenses, Patterson's lop-sided victories were reported by the same reporter, and there is a glaring uniformed to the way Arthur Daley's defined these bouts in his introduction.

3. The Great White Hope: Extinct or Dormant?   71

> The flaming courage of Roy Harris, the educated backwoodsman from Cut 'n' Shoot, deep in the heart of Texas, carried him through twelve rounds with Floyd Patterson tonight. But blazing spirit wasn't enough.[27]

Three years later, Daley was no less determined to place the white challenger at enter stage of the event, to make the white fighter the story, without even changing his opening.

> The flaming courage of Tom McNeely made an exciting drama of his fight with Floyd Patterson at Maple Leaf Gardens tonight. But the champion chopped him down with the methodical precision of a butcher going to work on an obstreporous steer. Eight times Patterson felled him. The eighth was for keeps.
> But even then the bould brother of a boy from The Boston suburb of Arlington made one last valiant gesture. At the count of 7, he struggled to get up...[28]

That Beshore, Barone, Harris and McNeely all went above and beyond in trying to win against unbeatable odds is obvious, and it is hardly suspicious that the reporting made note of their fortitude in the face of brutal beatings. They deserved to be praised for their efforts. That such white challenger's noble heroism virtually pushed the black champions' victory into the background, though, makes it seem as if there was a yearning (to the extent that popular *New York Times* sportswriters were representative of broad white sentiment) for a white miracle victory. In 1955, the African American light-heavyweight champion, Archie Moore, challenged the white heavyweight king, Rocky Marciano. Before being knocked out in the ninth round, Moore fought as heroically in defeat as the others mentioned, getting off the floor four times (the same as Harris, more than Beshore and Barone) before losing. Yet the opening sentence to the *Times* report of the fight referred to Rocky Marciano.[29] In all fairness to the *Times*, its coverage included ample praise of Moore's gutsy effort. Yet the subtle difference in first introducing the story as Marciano's victory, in contrast to Charles's victories where the courage of the white challenger was front and center, raises the question whether it was instinctively easier for sportswriters to celebrate white defeat in the absence of a white champion.

Three years after America beat Outer Mongolia to the moon, New Yorkers read that Joe Frazier, training for a New Orleans title defense against Terry Daniels, had been dislodged from his hotel to another to make room for one of the football teams playing in a Super Bowl game also held in the Big Easy that same weekend. A *Times* sportswriter glibly explained that, in having Frazier politely evicted, a hotel reservation clerk had done what no boxer had yet accomplished; he had handled the undefeated champion. He then joked that "Quite possibly, the reservation clerk could handle Terry Daniels,"[30] speaking volumes about the media perception of Daniels's prospects. Years later, Frazier openly admitted in his autobiography that Daniels was chosen as contender specifically because he represented little threat, an easy payday after the champion's grueling victory over Muhammad Ali the previous year. During training, when Frazier was asked by the media if his Texan opponent was better than his own sparring partners, the champ admitted, "A little."[31] Daniels, a student at Southern Methodist University, gave it the old college try, rising four times after being decked by Frazier. The referee finally ended the massacre in the fourth round.

> ...Frazier defended his title in a bout whose result was not in doubt for an instant. It was a routine slaughter that left the beaten challenger in tears.
> [Daniels observed,] "It was just about the most one-sided fight in the history of boxing."[32]

Four months after Daniels was served as a courageous delicacy to Smokin' Joe, the Philadelphia champion defended against Ron Stander of Omaha. Stander, a popular local brawler, no more figured to lift Frazier's belt than Daniels. His ruggedness and durability as a fighter promised the fans nothing less than an exciting confrontation. His chances of winning were an open secret in the sports pages. The *Times* correspondent quipped that "most observers doubt that he'll last fifteen minutes." While training, Stander appeared "easy to hit," and "his skin looked as if it might crack like plaster." The *Times* also wrote that the Iowan[33] "seldon threw a clever combination." One gymside media observer watching Stander work on the speed bag reportedly said, "Going into this round, I've got the bag leading." The following day, readers learned there was no serious wagering on the fight, that Stander was ranked thirty-first in *Boxing Illustrated Magazine*, that his opponents had been inconsequential, that his local popularity was his dominant attribute for the bout, and that Stander was likely to emerge from the fight as red, white, and blue as the gloves Frazier planned to wear.[34] Even the challenger's wife was not completely on her husband's promotional bandwagon as he got ready for his big night. Darlene Stander shared that she thought her spouse should have lost one of his showcase fights, a draw with Mexican contender Manuel Ramos, that he was never in shape for his fights, and he was already suffering the effects of too many punches![35] The Bluffs Butcher fought as bravely as any title challenger ever has, and his face at the end of the contest testified to his fortitude like no sportswriter's words ever could. After five rounds of walking into the maelstrom of Frazier's superior artillery, the fight was mercifully halted with Stander staggering around the ring blindly, his face having been bloodied ghoulishly for several rounds.

In 1975, the gamblers took another holiday from a title fight, as Muhammad Ali put his championship on the line against Chuck Wepner of Cleveland. For the third time in three years, the prospect of a white challenger actually winning the title was placed roughly alongside that of nailing jelly to a wall. Wepner was seemingly chosen from the same marginal hinterland of boxing as Daniels and Stander.

Dave Anderson of the *New York Times* said the same thing about the three boxers:

> If he [Daniels] were to win, it would be the biggest upset in boxing history.[36] (January 1972).
>
> If he [Stander] were to win, it would be boxing's biggest upset.[37] (May 1972).
>
> Ali is such an obvious favorite that no betting has been established by the oddsmakers except for the round in which Ali will win.... If Wepner were to win, it would rank as the most astonishing upset in boxing history.... Ali's lack of conditioning represents, as the fight posters proclaim, the "Chance of a Lifetime for Chuck Wepner."[38] (March 1975).

That the promoters of this title fight were pushing the champion's flabbiness as the challenger's best chance does not inspire the belief that America had outgrown its interest in a Great White Hope. Wepner defied the odds, and pushed an undertrained Ali into the fifteenth round before the champ's superior boxing skills wore him down to the point of exhaustion. If Wepner could come this close to going the distance against the champ, it becomes easier to understand Ali's steadfast refusal to give an immediate rematch to the black former champion George Foreman, from whom the Louisville Lip had lifted the belt the previous October.

The above examples of media coverage all shed light on the seeming long odds facing the white men privileged to fight for the title. Further newspaper accounts testify not only to the perception of white heavyweights being plucked from national obscurity into the glare of a championship bout, but also of ongoing flare-ups of Great White Hope discourse. In preparation for his challenge of Larry Holmes's title, readers of the *Times* learned that Scott LeDoux had "attempted to 'hype' the fight by playing up the race angle. He is white, Holmes is black and the champion believes LeDoux 'is trying to turn white folk against me.'" Irritated at LeDoux's press conference accusations that he was avoiding white challengers, Holmes advised his challenger, "Sit down, white boy." The outburst (Holmes believed) precipitated an influx of racist hate mail. Holmes was talked into fighting LeDoux by his handlers at the expense of a black opponent thought by Holmes himself (Leon Spinks) to be more qualified.[39] Like others before him, LeDoux's best accomplishment of the night was showing how much punishment he could withstand without complaint. Holmes finished LeDoux off in the seventh round, the challenger complaining of being thumbed in the eye.

> Larry Holmes scored his seventh straight knockout in defense of his world heavyweight boxing title tonight when the referee stopped a one-

sided bout with Scott LeDoux, a 236-pound heavy bag with courage and determination, in the seventh round.... LeDoux, who had landed only one solid blow...Holmes, who said later he was thinking of Earnie Shavers, who needed an operation to reattach a retina after last year's title fight, stopped fighting several times in the seventh and beckoned to (referee) Pearl to halt the bout.[40]

Perhaps it was a sign of progress that the black champion's name came first in the article's opening sentence. LeDoux insisted afterward that the fight was going exactly the way he had planned, his strategy being to let Holmes exhaust himself from punching. All that can be said for certain is that the champion obliged, dishing out enough punishment that the referee stopped the proceedings long before LeDoux's fight plan bore fruit.

Three years afterward, New Jerseyite Scott Frank finagled his way into a bout with the Easton Assassin. Specifically, Frank revealed the cojones of a door-to-door salesman, calling on Holmes directly by phone and asking for a title fight. Frank's chutzpah paid off; Holmes's handlers talked him into defending against this nationally obscure interloper. Unlike the Cooney or LeDoux bouts, there was little racial symbolism to this fight's coverage, but not necessarily because racial sentiment did not exist. Peter Alfano of the *New York Times* wrote:

> As was the case with Gerry Cooney and Randall (Tex) Cobb, among others, Frank has heard others call him "a white hope." The "white hope" angle has been played down in this fight because Frank is not perceived as having a chance to beat Holmes."[41]

The steep odds facing Frank were confirmed three days later, when the same newspaper reported, "There are not many boxing people who give Frank a chance against Holmes."[42] The Oakland, New Jersey fighter, battling Holmes 150 miles up the road in Atlantic City, landed few punches against the legendary champion and was ultimately stopped in round five, also claiming he had been thumbed in the eye by Holmes.

> From the very beginning, it was apparent that the warnings that this fight would be a mismatch were correct. Larry Holmes, the World Boxing Council heavyweight Champion, bloodied and bruised an outclassed Scott Frank repeatedly tonight until Referee Tony Perez stopped the bout at 1:28 of the fifth round with Frank bleeding from cuts over the eye and from the nose.... He looked amateurish against Holmes as he fruitlessly tried to walk past the champion's stinging left jab, which reddened his face in the opening minute of the fight.... All of Frank's punches looked as if they were being thrown in desperation.[43]

Having enjoyed the financial payoff of a championship title bout, Frank retired after the Holmes's bout, though he returned for one-fight comebacks in 1987 and 1997.

Such media coverage at least hints at a perception that a Great White

3. The Great White Hope: Extinct or Dormant?   75

Hope is needed, through lesser-talented white challengers reaching boxing's penthouse while more deserving black ones have a slower ride in the sport's freight elevator. Discourse about Great White Hopes obviously persisted into the early 1980s, when LeDoux, Frank and Cooney stepped into the limelight with the world title dangling tantalizingly in front of their noses. The 1996 comedy, *The Great White Hype*, pulled no punches in its hilarious spin on race and professional boxing in the 1990s. In this film, a powerful black boxing promoter (Don King in everything but name), and his gullible minion, a dominant black world heavyweight champion (an equally transparent representation of Mike Tyson), are at their wits' end trying to financially revitalize the sport for lack of worthy opposition. The promoter openly admits "I need a white heavyweight contender worse than white America needs one.... If there ain't a white guy out there for you, I'm going to create you one." The promoter subsequently digs up an objectively ridiculous white opponent, and successfully sells him as a credible challenger to a fatuous white American audience. The challenger is even given the moniker "Irish" in front of his name, with bagpipes blazing at press conferences and a huge publicity machine depicting him as the hero of wheelchair-bound children, fawning female groupies, and senior citizens across the land. The white challenger is subsequently knocked out in the first round, but not before making the cash registers ring and Las Vegas betting boards teem with action.

That both this story and the film's title had enough cultural resonance to even be made, much less be a popular comedy, indicates that even by the mid-1990s, the notion of an American need for a Great White Hope was part of the nation's consciousness. Satirical movie spoofs can only be made if enough of the audience is familiar with the real story, the straight truth from which the jokes are being derived. If such a movie could be made in 1996, it is small wonder that so many boxing insiders claim with such conviction that a Great White Hope is a diamond in boxing's rough.

To what degree, if any, then, has there been unequal opportunity between white and black heavyweight boxers since Joe Louis punched a hole in the walls of sports segregation? Do white Americans still need a white heavyweight champion, a desire that pushes white fighters up the sport's ladder more quickly and easily than black pugilists? Can this be statistically proven? Can it be quantified that white heavyweights were still being helped along by a white audience in America's recent past?

4. Approaching the Summit

> LES NESSMAN: We have a good chance of winning this softball game. I happen to know that Venus here is an outstanding athlete.
> VENUS FLYTRAP: Well, thanks, Les. What makes you say that?
> LES: Simple. You're black.
>
> —*1970s TV comedy,* WKRP in Cincinnati

Between Joe Louis's retirement in 1949 and Scott Frank's challenge of Larry Holmes's title in 1983, ninety-two heavyweights entered *The Ring*'s Top Ten monthly ratings for the first time. This study makes no pretense of having a completely valid biological dichotomy of race. The heavyweights were slotted into black and white categories based on how they were perceived by the mainstream American public, or by the author's subjective impressions of the skin color and facial features of more obscure boxer's black and white photographs. The story of race and racism in America has been shaped by an all or nothing assumption that a very small amount of black heritage makes a person other than (and less than) white. For those predisposed to believe in white superiority, the view was that one drop stains the entire rug, so to speak. Very few of the black boxers included here have skin color as light as or lighter than Muhammad Ali, someone who is associated with black America as closely as any celebrity has ever been, even though his bronze skin is obviously the result of interbreeding. Every *black* boxer is assumed to have had dark enough skin to be categorized as black in the eyes of whites, or perhaps dark enough to have been a potential target of discrimination.

In addition to the ninety-two ranked contenders, thirteen more fighters were included. This latter group consisted of seven unusually lucky boxers who fought for the heavyweight title without even being ranked in the Top Ten, and six who had already entered the Top Ten before 1949, and fought for the title after Louis's first retirement. Of these, seventy-three (70 percent) were black while thirty-two (30 percent) were white, figures that make sense of the subjective impression most Americans today have that boxing has long been a black sport. Statistical comparisons of the credentials needed by black and white heavyweights to become ranked are made below, with the numbers of those who fought for the title in the next chapter.

Number of Fights

There is no evidence that skin color did anything to limit the access of black heavyweights to the Top Ten rankings in any of the three periods. In fact, in two of the three time spans, the white fighters had significantly more bouts under their belts before denting the Top Ten. As late as three decades ago, the average white boxer who actually reached the hallowed land of being rated, laced up his gloves considerably more often to get there than his black counterpart. Every single white heavyweight contender in the 1970s entered the rankings with at least twenty fights, whereas eight of the nineteen black pugilists had fewer than that. Stan Ward and Leon Spinks had fifteen fights between them at their points of entry into the ratings. Such numbers testify to a racially blind or apathetic white boxing audience, at least so far as *The Ring* might have been pandering to white biases in opening its door to the elite level of the sport.

Average Number of Fights at Entry Into *The Ring*'s Top Ten

White Contenders (1949–59)		*Black Contenders (1949–59)*	
Bernie Reynolds	46	Al Hoosman	23
Gus Lesnevich	76	Turkey Thompson	57
Grant Butcher	13	John Holman	15
Roland LaStarza	37	Bob Baker	14
Rocky Marciano	26	Clarence Henry	18
Harry Mathews	87	Coley Wallace	15
Dan Bucceroni	42	Bob Dunlap	30
Roy Harris	21	Tommy Harrison	27
Pat McMurtry	26	Bob Satterfield	47
Mike DeJohn	38	Jimmy Slade	33
Charlie Norkus	38	Archie Moore	172
Rex Layne	26	Tommy Jackson	16
Willie Pastrano	43	John Summerlin	34
		Young Jack Johnson	16
		Harold Carter	20
		Eddie Machen	13
		Floyd Patterson	30
		Zora Folley	30
		Wayne Bethea	21
		Harold Johnson	61
		Sonny Liston	21
		Charlie Powell	25
		Tony Anthony	49

		Alonzo Johnson	17
		Billy Hunter	22
		Bill Gilliam	46
Average >	39.9	Average >	33.5

| *White Contenders* | | *Black Contenders* | |
(1960–69)		*(1960–69)*	
Tom McNeely	22	Cleveland Williams	54
George Logan	29	Cassius Clay	10
Jerry Quarry	28	Billy Daniels	18
Boone Kirkman	18	Doug Jones	25
		Ernie Terrell	35
		Thad Spencer	27
		Amos Johnson	19
		Hubert Hilton	15
		Elmer Rush	15
		Amos Lincoln	40
		Johnny Persol	21
		Joe Frazier	13
		Jimmy Ellis	29
		Leotis Martin	25
		Buster Mathis	23
		Henry Clark	20
		Al Lewis	20
		Mac Foster	18
		Al Jones	31
		Roger Rischer	36
Average >	24.3	Average >	24.7

| *White Contenders* | | *Black Contenders* | |
(1970–83)		*(1970–83)*	
Chuck Wepner	37	George Foreman	20
Duane Bobick	33	Ron Lyle	16
Randy Neumann	37	Ken Norton	28
Scott LeDoux	36	Earnie Shavers	47
Gerry Cooney	21	Jeff Merritt	21
Tex Cobb	20	Larry Middleton	19
		Jimmy Young	20
		Larry Holmes	20
		Johnny Boudreaux	20
		Howard Smith	17
		Stan Ward	8
		Leon Spinks	7
		Mike Weaver	26
		John Tate	18
		Leroy Jones	25
		Michael Dokes	16
		Greg Page	11
		Marty Monroe	24
		James Tillis	20
		Renaldo Snipes	22
		Tim Witherspoon	14
		Pinklon Thomas	20
		S.T. Gordon	29
Average >	30.7	Average >	20.3

Black heavyweights between 1949 and 1983 were at no disadvantage in attaining the competitive and financial benefits of world class recognition, in terms of simple contest experience. In two of the three sub-periods, they had considerably fewer fights behind them before they found their way onto *The Ring*'s pages. From 1950–59, whites had almost six more fights on average (39.9–34) and more than ten more contests (30.7–20.3) in the 1970–83 time frame. Only in the 1960s did we see essential parity between the two groups, both having about twenty-four fights before being rated.

Average Record

To become a ranked contender in the years 1949–83, the average black heavyweight also did not have to scale a significantly higher wall in terms of wins and losses than white ones. Once again, as with the number of fights, the data reveals that in at least one of the three periods, the former broke into *The Ring*'s heralded pages with inferior win-loss-draw records. In the first ten years, thirteen white boxers became world ranked with an average record of 35–4–1. The twenty-six black heavyweights were first anointed as one of the world's ten best with an inferior average record of only 27–5–1. The 1960s saw almost perfect equality, with the four whites entering at 21–2–1, while the twenty blacks reached this level at 22–2–1. The 1970s, however, saw the tables turn, as twenty-three black fighters averaged a 19–1 record upon their initial ranking, while the six white boxers were a clearly inferior 26–4–1.

With one period indicating that black boxers had an easier time becoming ranked, one era of equal credentials, and one suggesting that whites reached this benchmark with lesser records, this criteria does not indicate a white audience preference working to the advantage of white heavyweights. That the last period saw the first evidence of whites becoming rated with considerably more losses is potentially meaningful, given that by the 1970s, it had been two full decades since the last white champion. Once can intuitively accept that a marked discrepancy in white and black credentials is less surprising the longer a white drought goes on in the heavyweight class, if the white audience was motivated to care about this. If year after year, the crown remained on black heads, it is not completely surprising that white challengers for the title would be dug up (no pun intended) to carry the white race's banner between the ropes. The difference between having one and four setbacks on one's record is hard to dismiss, but it is hardly sufficient evidence by itself to conclude that the inner workings of boxing were slanting the sport's riches toward white heroes.

Average Win-Loss-Draw Record of Contenders Entering *The Ring's* Top Ten

White Contenders (1949–59)	Wins-Losses-Draws	Black Contenders (1949–59)	Wins-Losses-Draws
Bernie Reynolds	42–4	Al Hoosman	19–4
Gus Lesnevich	58–13–5	Turkey Thompson	46–9–2
Grant Butcher	10–1–2	John Holman	13–2
Roland LaStarza	37–0	Bob Baker	14–0
Rocky Marciano	26–0	Clarence Henry	16–1–1
Harry Mathews	78–3–6	Coley Wallace	14–1
Dan Bucceroni	39–3	Bob Dunlap	23–6–1
Roy Harris	21–0	Tom Harrison	19–7–1
Pat McMurtry	24–1–1	Bob Satterfield	31–14–2
Mike DeJohn	34–3–1	Jim Slade	20–9–4
Charlie Norkus	26–12	Archie Moore	147–19–6
Rex Layne	25–1	Tom Jackson	14–1–1
Willie Pastrano	35–5–3	John Summerlin	28–4–2
		Young Jack Johnson	12–5–1
		Harold Carter	17–1–2
		Eddie Machen	13–0
		Floyd Patterson	29–1
		Zora Folley	27–2–1
		Wayne Bethea	13–6–2
		Harold Johnson	53–8
		Sonny Liston	19–1
		Charlie Powell	20–3–2
		Tony Anthony	41–7–1
		Alonzo Johnson	16–1
		Billy Hunter	14–6–2
		Bill Gilliam	27–17–2
Average >	35–4–1	Average >	27–5–1

White Contenders (1960–69)	Wins-Losses-Draws	Black Contenders (1960–69)	Wins-Losses-Draws
Tom McNeely	22–0	Cleveland Williams	50–4
George Logan	22–6–1	Cassius Clay	10–0
Jerry Quarry	23–1–4	Billy Daniels	17–1
Boone Kirkman	17–1	Doug Jones	21–3–1
		Ernie Terrell	31–4
		Thad Spencer	24–3
		Amos Johnson	16–2–1
		Hubert Hilton	12–2–2
		Elmer Rush	13–1–1
		Amos Lincoln	33–4–3
		Johnny Persol	17–3–1
		Joe Frazier	13–0
		Jimmy Ellis	24–5
		Leotis Martin	24–1
		Buster Mathis	23–0
		Henry Clark	15–3–2
		Al Lewis	19–1
		Mac Foster	18–0

4. Approaching the Summit

		Al Jones	29–1–1
		Roger Rischer	26–8–2
Average >	21–2–1	Average >	22–2–1

White Contenders (1970–83)	Wins-Losses -Draws	Black Contenders (1970–83)	Wins-Losses -Draws
Chuck Wepner	26–9–2	George Foreman	20–0
Duane Bobick	33–0	Ron Lyle	16–0
Randy Neumann	31–6	Ken Norton	27–1
Scott LeDoux	25–7–4	Earnie Shavers	45–2
Gerry Cooney	21–0	Jeff Merritt	20–1
Randy Cobb	18–2	Larry Middleton	17–1–1
		Jimmy Young	14–4–2
		Larry Holmes	20–0
		Johnny Boudreaux	19–0–1
		Howard Smith	16–1
		Stan Ward	6–0–2
		Leon Spinks	6–0–1
		Mike Weaver	18–8
		John Tate	18–0
		Leroy Jones	24–0–1
		Michael Dokes	16–0
		Greg Page	11–0
		Marty Monroe	22–1–1
		James Tillis	20–0
		Renaldo Snipes	22–0
		Tim Witherspoon	14–0
		Pinklon Thomas	20–0
		S.T.Gordon	24–5
Average >	26–4–1	Average >	19–1

For the white and black contenders and challengers between 1949 and 1983, four of the six statistical measures relating to wins, losses, and draws, indicated black fighters having a harder time getting opportunity. Yet one of these four differences was minuscule. All in all, there has not been a consistent bias in favor of white hopes across the entire study. From 1949 to 1969, blacks did not have to use a different (or harder to open) door than whites to break into the elite ranks or vie for the championship. It is equally true that in both 1970–83 measures, the numbers testify to whites earning their stripes with inferior resumes, the challengers having five fewer wins, the contenders being rated by *The Ring* with three more losses.

Average Winning Percentage Per Fighter

Averaging the records of the fighters for comparison has its limitations in terms of making valid conclusions about the quality of the boxers as grouped by era. Since the number of fights varies widely from one boxer to the next, some have a greater impact on the totals. One can control for this by analyzing the winning percentage of each fighter the month they were heralded by *The Ring* or climbed the steps to look across at the world champion, thus giving them equal weighting.

The average winning percentage of contenders revealed an interesting trend. In the 1950s, there was no evident discrimination, conscious or otherwise, working in favor of white heavyweights. Not only did they not have an easier time showing up on *The Ring*'s exalted list, the average rated white boxer actually had a clearly better winning percentage (88 percent to 82 percent) than their black cohorts. In the 1960s, the numbers pulled even to a virtual dead heat, with blacks becoming ranked with marginally better averages (89 percent to 88 percent) than whites. Then, in the 1970s and early 1980s, the average black contender attained this plateau with a much higher success rate, ninety-three to eighty-six percent.

Average Winning Percentage of Contenders Entering The Ring's Top Ten

White Contenders (1949–59)	Percent	Black Contenders (1949–59)	Percent
Bernie Reynolds	91.3	Al Hoosman	82.6
Gus Lesnevich	76.3	Turkey Thompson	80.7
Grant Butcher	76.9	John Holman	86.7
Roland LaStarza	100	Bob Baker	100
Rocky Marciano	100	Clarence Henry	88.9
Harry Mathews	89.7	Coley Wallace	93.3
Dan Bucceroni	92.9	Bob Dunlap	76.7
Roy Harris	100	Tommy Harrison	70.4
Pat McMurtry	92.3	Bob Satterfield	66
Mike DeJohn	89.5	Jim Slade	60.6
Charlie Norkus	68.4	Archie Moore	85.5
Rex Layne	96.2	Tom Jackson	87.5
Willie Pastrano	81.4	John Summerlin	82.4
		Young Jack Johnson	66.7
		Harold Carter	85
		Eddie Machen	100
		Floyd Patterson	96.7
		Zora Folley	90
		Wayne Bethea	61.9
		Harold Johnson	86.9
		Sonny Liston	95.2
		Charlie Powell	80
		Tony Anthony	83.7
		Alonzo Johnson	94.1
		Billy Hunter	63.6
		Bill Gilliam	58.7
Average >	88.8 %	Average >	81.7 %

4. Approaching the Summit

White Contenders (1960–69)	Percent	Black Contenders (1960–69)	Percent
Tom McNeely	100	Cleveland Williams	92.6
George Logan	75.9	Cassius Clay	100
Jerry Quarry	82.1	Billy Daniels	94.4
Boone Kirkman	94.4	Doug Jones	84
		Ernie Terrell	88.6
		Thad Spencer	88.9
		Amos Johnson	84.2
		Hubert Hilton	80
		Elmer Rush	86.7
		Amos Lincoln	82.5
		Johnny Persol	81
		Joe Frazier	100
		Jimmy Ellis	82.8
		Leotis Martin	96
		Buster Mathis	100
		Henry Clark	75
		Al Lewis	95
		Mac Foster	100
		Al Jones	93.6
		Roger Rischer	72.2
Average >	88.1 %	Average >	88.9 %

White Contenders (1970–83)	Percent	Black Contenders (1970–83)	Percent
Chuck Wepner	70.3	George Foreman	100
Duane Bobick	100	Ron Lyle	100
Randy Neumann	83.8	Ken Norton	96.4
Scott LeDoux	69.4	Earnie Shavers	95.7
Gerry Cooney	100	Jeff Merritt	95.2
Tex Cobb	90	Larry Middleton	89.5
		Jimmy Young	70
		Larry Holmes	100
		Johnny Boudreaux	95
		Howard Smith	94.1
		Stan Ward	75
		Leon Spinks	87.5
		Mike Weaver	69.2
		John Tate	100
		Leroy Jones	96
		Michael Dokes	100
		Greg Page	100
		Marty Monroe	91.7
		James Tillis	100
		Renaldo Snipes	100
		Tim Witherspoon	100
		Pinklon Thomas	100
		S.T. Gordon	82.8
Average >	85.6 %	Average >	93 %

Knockouts

The goal in boxing is to defeat one's opponent as quickly as possible. Most fighters would happily choose to knock their opponent out for a count of ten rather than endure ten to twelve rounds of pain and then have to trust the subjective decision of three judges for a decision victory. Since one's opponent is always a threat to inflict defeat with one punch (possibly a fluke blow), and since the amount of physical punishment one can endure through a career is finite, scoring a knockout is far more appealing to a boxer. It is also the preferred outcome to the vast majority of ring fans. It is almost universally acknowledged that the larger casual audience of the sport (and many hardcore buffs as well) enjoy seeing the drama, the emotional release, the raw thrill of a knockout, as opposed to a fight that goes the distance. The knockout is boxing's answer to the most exciting plays in other sports.

So-called baseball purists who appreciate the strategy of a tense, 2–1 pitching duel, are far outnumbered by the multitudes who enjoy a 10–8 slugfest with seven home runs. Rightly or wrongly, contact hitters like Tony Gwynn and Rod Carew do not capture the imagination of the public like deep swinging home run hitters like Mark McGuire and Sammy Sosa. It is doubtful that one could find more than a handful of American football fans who would want to return to the game that was played in the 1920s, when *three yards and a cloud of dust* was the only strategy by which the rules allowed the ball to be moved downfield. The electrifying seventy-yard touchdown runs of Red Grange captured the imaginations of fans in a way the slogging mass formation game never could. Few NBA fans today would prefer to see an easy lay-up basket over a violent, backboard shaking slam dunk. The dunk is perceived by both player and fan alike as an assertion of in-your-face machismo, an act of intimidation that serves psychologically as a legal substitute for attacking an opponent. The home run, the long touchdown play, and the dunk symbolize the expression of power over methodical plodding.

So too have boxing fans long cheered the loudest for hard-hitting fighters who can end a fight at any time. Jack Dempsey forever remained far more popular than his conqueror Gene Tunney. The former carried a knockout in either hand, and wanted to win fights as unequivocally as possible. The latter was a meticulous strategist who safely piled up points while taking no unnecessary chances in the ring, no matter what the crowd wanted. Joe Louis's successor as heavyweight champion, Ezzard Charles, was a superbly skilled ring technician who dominated his rivals with speed, skill, and defense. But Charles was never embraced by boxing public in spite of eight successful title defenses in two years. Part of the reason was the inevitable coldness shown by the public toward those who replace their loved icons. Charles handily defeated Louis when the ring-rusty Brown Bomber came out of retirement, a sobering reality lesson that many Louis fans never forgave. But conquering Louis did not ultimately stop Rocky Marciano from being a fan favorite. At least part of the difference had to be power. Marciano, like Louis, bludgeoned most of his opponents into dreamland long before the final bell could ring. Charles did not knock out anywhere near as many opponents as Louis or Marciano, knocking out less than half of his adversaries (58 of 122). Boxing fans responded accordingly. More recently, Mike Tyson's meteoric rise to the world title was clearly the result of dominant ability, but his attainment of multi-million dollar contracts was as much about the shrewd marketing of his knack for first-round destruction. His handlers even compiled a promotional video (*Mike Tyson's Greatest Hits*) to illustrate their fighter's brutal "don't blink or you'll miss it" conquests. This video contributed greatly to Tyson's lucrative persona as an angry destroyer in the ring, and pushed his earning potential into a stratosphere that no stylist like Charles or Tunney will likely ever reach. Mike Tyson's persona as a brutal knockout machine persisted long after his skills had eroded, thus persuading millions of boxing fans that he had a chance of victory against Lennox Lewis. If Tyson had built his record and reputation from 1985 to 1990 by winning fights stylishly on points decisions, few followers of the ring would have been fatuous enough to bet on him twelve years after he lost his title. (It should be noted that technical boxers depend on reflexes that erode before hitting power does.) It is almost certain that the Tyson-Lewis fight would never have been promoted as lavishly, nor would $54 have been charged pay-per-view fans if Tyson had the reputation of being a boxer rather than a slugger.

Boxers have long been motivated to go for knockouts because an abundance of KO's indicates domination far more than winning by decision. Unless they are fighting conspicuously weak opposition, a fighter who only has to put in nine or twelve minutes work to conquer an opponent looks more impressive than one who must toil through twelve three-minute rounds. Boxers who win 80–90 percent of their fights by KO have the term *great* applied to their name much more readily than wily strategists who patiently wait all night for an opening than might never come.

One can then analyze these two racial samples of heavyweights by comparing how often they ended their adversaries' nights early.

Knockouts Scored by Contenders Ranked in *The Ring*'s Top Ten

White Contenders (1949–59)	KO's	Black Contenders (1949–59)	KO's
Bernie Reynolds	29	Al Hoosman	12
Gus Lesnevich	21	Turkey Thompson	33
Grant Butcher	4	John Holman	8

Roland LaStarza	17	Bob Baker	11
Rocky Marciano	23	Clarence Henry	110
Harry Mathews	57	Coley Wallace	12
Dan Bucceroni	27	Bob Dunlap	17
Roy Harris	9	Tom Harrison	5
Pat McMurtry	20	Bob Satterfield	24
Mike DeJohn	25	Jim Slade	5
Charlie Norkus	16	Archie Moore	108
Rex Layne	18	Tom Jackson	5
Willie Pastrano	8	John Summerlin	19
		Young Jack Johnson	8
		Harold Carter	9
		Eddie Machen	10
		Floyd Patterson	22
		Zora Folley	18
		Wayne Bethea	6
		Harold Johnson	23
		Sonny Liston	12
		Charlie Powell	15
		Tony Anthony	30
		Alonzo Johnson	5
		Billy Hunter	8
		Bill Gilliam	7
Average >	274/ 13 = 21	Average >	443/ 26 = 17

White Contenders (1960–69)	*KO's*	*Black Contenders (1960–69)*	*KO's*
Tom McNeely	17	Cleveland Williams	41
George Logan	13	Cassius Clay	7
Jerry Quarry	13	Billy Daniels	8
Boone Kirkman	14	Doug Jones	13
		Ernie Terrell	16
		Thad Spencer	12
		Amos Johnson	9
		Hubert Hilton	5
		Elmer Rush	14
		Amos Lincoln	21
		Johnny Persol	4
		Joe Frazier	12
		Jimmy Ellis	11
		Leotis Martin	14
		Buster Mathis	17
		Henry Clark	2
		Al Lewis	11
		Mac Foster	18
		Al Jones	17
		Roger Rischer	13
Average >	57/ 4 = 14	Average >	265/ 20 = 13

White Contenders (1970–83)	*KO's*	*Black Contenders (1970–83)*	*KO's*
Chuck Wepner	9	George Foreman	17
Duane Bobick	30	Ron Lyle	14
Randy Neumann	11	Ken Norton	22

Scott LeDoux	17	Earnie Shavers	44
Gerry Cooney	17	Jeff Merritt	14
Tex Cobb	17	Larry Middleton	10
		Jimmy Young	3
		Larry Holmes	15
		Johnny Boudreaux	7
		Howard Smith	10
		Stan Ward	4
		Leon Spinks	5
		Mike Weaver	12
		John Tate	14
		Leroy Jones	12
		Michael Dokes	8
		Greg Page	10
		Marty Monroe	14
		James Tillis	16
		Renaldo Snipes	11
		Tim Witherspoon	11
		Pinklon Thomas	17
		S.T. Gordon	21
Average >	101/ 6 = 17	Average >	311/ 23 = 14

Becoming a contender was actually more difficult for the average white heavyweight throughout the entire study, in terms of scoring knockouts. In all three sub-periods, black contenders became rated with fewer KO's, seventeen to twenty-one in the 1950s, thirteen to fourteen in the 1960s, and fourteen to seventeen in the final period. To whatever degree KO's influenced *The Ring*'s editors when picking the world's ten best heavyweights, a knockout was a knockout was a knockout for *The Ring*'s editors, regardless of skin color.

Individual Knockout Rate

As with the record comparisons above, simply analyzing the number of knockouts scored by the white and black heavyweights can be skewed by the wide differences in the number of bouts, meaning fighters like Archie Moore and Harry Mathews can have a misleading influence on the group total. This possibility can again be eliminated by counting equally the knockout percentage rates of every boxer.

The contender groupings, consistent with several of the above measures, do not reveal anything as simplistic as a uniform slant of opportunity in favor of whites over blacks. One actually sees the Caucasian fighters becoming rated with superior KO percentages than black ones in both the 1950s (53.9 percent to 49.9 percent) and the 1960s (61.6 percent to 54.5 percent). The white members of the Top Ten had no advantage here. They reached this milestone having stopped their opponents at a higher rate for twenty years after Joe Louis handed over his belt. In the final time frame, the situation did reverse, and black contenders were reaching the elite level with notably higher knockout ratios.

Knockout Percentage of Contenders Rated in *The Ring*'s Top Ten

White Contenders (1949–59)	KO Percentage	Black Contenders (1949–59)	KO Percentage
Bernie Reynolds	29/ 46 = 63	Al Hoosman	12/ 23 = 52.2
Gus Lesnevich	21/ 76 = 27.6	Turkey Thompson	33/ 57 = 57.9
Grant Butcher	4/ 13 = 30.8	John Holman	8/ 15 = 53.3
Roland LaStarza	17/ 37 = 45.9	Bob Baker	11/ 14 = 78.6
Rocky Marciano	23/ 26 = 88.5	Clarence Henry	11/ 18 = 61.1
Harry Mathews	57/ 87 = 65.5	Coley Wallace	12/ 15 = 80
Dan Bucceroni	27/ 42 = 64.3	Bob Dunlap	17/ 30 = 56.7
Roy Harris	9/ 21 = 42.9	Tom Harrison	5/ 27 = 18.5
Pat McMurtry	20/ 26 = 76.9	Bob Satterfield	24/ 47 = 51.1
Mike DeJohn	25/ 38 = 65.8	Jimmy Slade	5/ 33 = 15.2
Charlie Norkus	16/ 38 = 42.1	Archie Moore	108/ 172 = 62.8
Rex Layne	18/ 26 = 69.2	Tom Jackson	5/ 16 = 31.3
Willie Pastrano	8/ 43 = 18.6	John Summerlin	19/ 34 = 55.9
		Young Jack Johnson	8/ 18 = 44.4
		Harold Carter	9/ 20 = 45
		Eddie Machen	10/ 13 = 76.9
		Floyd Patterson	22/ 31 = 71
		Zora Folley	18/ 30 = 60
		Wayne Bethea	6/ 21 = 28.6
		Harold Johnson	23/ 61 = 37.7
		Sonny Liston	12/ 21 = 57.1
		Charlie Powell	15/ 25 = 60
		Tony Anthony	30/ 49 = 61.2
		Alonzo Johnson	5/ 17 = 29.4
		Billy Hunter	8/ 22 = 36.4
		Bill Gilliam	7/ 46 = 15.2
Average >	53.9 %	Average >	49.9%

White Contenders (1960–69)	KO Percentage	Black Contenders (1960–69)	KO Percentage
Tom McNeely	17/ 22 = 77.3	Cleveland Williams	41/ 54 = 75.9
George Logan	13/ 29 = 44.8	Cassius Clay	7/ 10 = 70
Jerry Quarry	13/ 28 = 46.4	Billy Daniels	8/ 18 = 44.4
Boone Kirkman	14/ 18 = 77.8	Doug Jones	13/ 24 = 54.2
		Ernie Terrell	16/ 35 = 45.7
		Thad Spencer	12/ 27 = 44.4
		Amos Johnson	9/ 19 = 47.4
		Hubert Hilton	5/ 15 =33
		Elmer Rush	14/ 16 = 87.5
		Amos Lincoln	21/ 40 = 52.5
		Johnny Persol	4/ 21 = 19.1
		Joe Frazier	12/ 13 = 92.3
		Jimmy Ellis	11/ 29 = 37.9
		Leotis Martin	14/ 25 = 56
		Buster Mathis	17/ 23 = 73.9
		Henry Clark	2/ 20 = 10
		Al Lewis	11/ 20 = 55
		Mac Foster	18/ 18 = 100
		Al Jones	17/ 31 = 54.8
		Roger Rischer	13/ 36 = 36.1
Average >	61.6%	Average >	54.5%

White Contenders (1970–83)	KO Percentage	Black Contenders (1970–83)	KO Percentage
Chuck Wepner	9/ 37 = 24.3	George Foreman	17/ 20 = 85
Duane Bobick	30/ 33 = 90.9	Ron Lyle	14/ 16 = 87.5
Randy Neumann	11/ 37 = 29.7	Ken Norton	22/ 28 = 78.6
Scott LeDoux	17/ 36 = 47.2	Earnie Shavers	44/ 47 = 93.6
Gerry Cooney	17/ 21 = 81	Jeff Merritt	14/ 19 = 73.7
Tex Cobb	17/ 20 = 85	Larry Middleton	10/ 19 = 52.6
		Jimmy Young	3/ 20 = 15
		Larry Holmes	15/ 20 = 75
		Johnny Boudreaux	7/ 20 = 35
		Howard Smith	10/ 17 = 58.8
		Stan Ward	4/ 8 = 50
		Leon Spinks	5/ 7 = 71.4
		Mike Weaver	12/ 26 = 46.2
		John Tate	14/ 18 = 77.8
		Leroy Jones	12/ 25 = 48
		Michael Dokes	8/ 16 = 50
		Greg Page	10/ 11 = 90.9
		Marty Monroe	14/ 24 = 58.3
		James Tillis	16/ 20 = 80
		Renaldo Snipes	11/ 22 = 50
		Tim Witherspoon	11/ 14 = 78.6
		Pinklon Thomas	17/ 20 = 85
		S.T. Gordon	21/ 29 = 72.4
Average >	59.7%	Average >	65.8%

Age

The window of opportunity for many professional athletes to earn acclaim and maximize their profits is small relative to other high profile careers. The typical professional team sport athlete is lucky to compete a handful of years before injury or skill erosion sends him to the sidelines. Past age thirty, when the careers of doctors, lawyers, and academics are taking off in terms of finances and status, many athletes are already looking backward at their greatest accomplishments and largest paychecks. As much as any athlete, and more than most, age is an ever present shadow hanging over the professional boxer. There are scores of golfers on the PGA Tour over 30, many of them late bloomers who have yet to peak. Billy Jean King, Rod Laver, Chris Evert, and Jimmy Connors were winning lucrative tennis paychecks well into their thirties. The lavish contracts enjoyed in the three major American team sports offer such athletes lifetime financial security after only a few seasons. Average boxers have never enjoyed this kind of prosperity. Their sport, for a long time, has been a much steeper hierarchy in terms of prosperity. Only with the impact of Muhammad Ali on the sport, and the advent of casino boxing cards and pay-per-view fights, did fight purses explode upward. But even this growth in profits did not bring the typical American boxer anywhere near parity with his counterparts in other sports.

Whereas a marginal NFL player can ride the bench and still earn the league minimum of several hundred thousand dollars per year, run-of-the-mill boxers seldom come within shouting distance of this money in their entire careers.

Only the very best boxers emerge from anonymity into the national audience's consciousness, the promised land where marketability translates into riches. For every fighter who appears on an HBO or Showtime boxing card, there are many more who never break into the sport's lucrative limelight. This is why the biological clock ticks so loudly for a boxer, and why a comparison between black and white boxers is in order to throw another light on the equality or inequality of opportunity in the sport. The beatings that boxers take in every fight exact a toll on their bodies, a toll that often comes due long before their thirtieth birthday. Many boxers progress from being at their physical peak to being an empty shell, a spent force between the ropes from one fight to the next. Thus, every day that a boxer waits to become ranked, every day that passes without a title opportunity for a rated fighter, looms large against their ambitions. It's impossible to estimate how many worthy boxers have simply aged out of title contention. That one big chance never came their way because of corruption or politics within the sport, or simply because they spent the prime of their career in a line-up of equally worthy rivals, with only a few lucking into a championship bid.

Once a boxer hits his peak, his chances of beating the reigning champion go downward the longer he spends cooling his heels waiting for a match with the latter. It is readily obvious why champions are attracted to defending their beloved belts against older fighters. Over-the-hill challengers are less of a threat, a safer defense of the title so long in achieving. It is a rare exception when a forty-five-year-old George Foreman regains his crown after twenty years, capturing lightning in a bottle and separating a Michael Moorer from his senses, or when an ancient Jersey Joe Walcott defies the calendar and finally beats Ezzard Charles on the third try for the crown. Much more typical are scenarios when the king of a division judiciously selects long-in-the tooth opponents, who can be promoted as better challengers (for ticket sales) than they really are. Muhammad Ali's 1960s defenses of his title against Cleveland Williams and Zora Folley are perfect examples of this cherry picking trend. These two fights are ironically celebrated by Ali fans as being great victories for the Louisville Lip. In reality, although Ali fought superbly, both Folley and Williams were years past their primes when they were served up as sacrificial lambs to the champion. In all fairness to Ali, overmatched ring veterans like Folley and Williams are usually all too happy to take on fights like this in which they have no chance of winning, for the one-time windfall of a title bout can mean financial security that previously eluded them through years of fighting. Williams and Folley might have been troublesome adversaries for Ali in their prime.

4. Approaching the Summit

How old, then, has the typical white and black heavyweight been upon first being rated or fighting for the world crown? Is there any evidence that that black heavyweights have been relative graybeards when they have entered the spotlight compared to white ones, thus reducing their competitive chances to become the champion?

Average Age of Contenders Entering *The Ring*'s Top Ten
Age is given in years/months

White Contenders (1949–59)	Born	Entered Top Ten	Age
Bernie Reynolds	9/3/24	1/15/49	21/7
Gus Lesnevich	2/22/15	6/16/49	34/4
Grant Butcher	7/21/28	9/15/49	21/2
Roland LaStarza	5/12/27	1/16/50	22/8
Rocky Marciano	9/1/23	4/15/50	26/7
Harry Mathews	12/9/22	6/18/52	31/6
Dan Bucceroni	12/3/27	2/18/53	25/2
Roy Harris	6/29/33	5/23/57	23/11
Pat McMurtry	1/5/32	6/20/57	25/5
Mike DeJohn	12/29/31	10/25/57	25/10
Charlie Norkus	7/15/28	12/16/54	26/5
Rex Layne	7/7/28	8/15/50	22/1
Willie Pastrano	11/27/35	1/17/56	21/2

Average > 25 years, 3 months

Black Contenders (1949–59)	Born	Entered Top Ten	Age
Al Hoosman	10/4/20	8/15/49	28/10
Turkey Thompson	12/25/19	8/15/49	29/7
John Holman	8/3/27	2/15/50	22/6
Bob Baker	10/26/26	4/15/50	23/6
Clarence Henry	3/27/26	6/15/50	24/3
Coley Wallace	5/19/27	2/18/52	24/9
Bob Dunlap	3/3/25	3/18/52	27/0
Tom Harrison	11/8/29	4/18/53	23/4
Bob Satterfield	11/9/23	7/18/53	29/8
Jim Slade	8/14/26	5/20/54	27/9
Archie Moore	12/13/13	5/21/55	41/5
Tom Jackson	8/9/31	3/18/54	22/7
John Summerlin	1/23/32	11/17/55	23/10
Young Jack Johnson	10/26/28	1/17/56	27/3
Harold Carter	5/23/34	11/17/55	21/6
Eddie Machen	7/15/32	4/19/56	23/9
Floyd Patterson	1/4/35	5/21/56	21/5
Zora Folley	5/27/32	12/22/56	24/7
Wayne Bethea	3/27/32	1/22/57	24/10
Harold Johnson	8/29/28	3/19/57	28/7
Sonny Liston	5/8/32	8/22/58	26/8
Charlie Powell	10/10/32	3/19/59	26/5
Tony Anthony	2/6/35	9/23/59	24/8
Alonzo Johnson	11/6/34	6/26/59	24/7
Billy Hunter	7/16/34	11/19/59	25/4
Bill Gilliam	5/?/24[1]	3/18/54	29/10

Average > 26 years, 1 month

White Contenders (1960–69)

	Born	Entered Top Ten	Age
Tom McNeely	2/27/37	1/19/61	23/11
George Logan	8/19/36	1/23/62	25/5
Jerry Quarry	5/15/45	7/18/67	22/2
Boone Kirkman	2/6/45	5/20/68	23/3

Average > 23 years, 8 months

Black Contenders (1960–69)

	Born	Entered Top Ten	Age
Cleveland Williams	6/30/33	5/22/61	27/11
Cassius Clay	1/17/42	1/23/62	20
Billy Daniels	1/28/37	11/21/62	25/10
Doug Jones	2/27/37	12/20/62	25/10
Ernie Terrell	4/4/39	4/24/63	24/1
Thad Spencer	3/28/43	4/15/65	22/1
Amos Johnson	1/4/39	4/15/65	26/3
Hubert Hilton	8/18/39	6/20/65	25/10
Elmer Rush	1/23/37	9/20/65	28/8
Amos Lincoln	8/12/36	12/20/65	29/4
Johnny Persol	6/12/40	11/20/66	26/5
Joe Frazier	1/12/44	12/20/66	22/11
Jimmy Ellis	2/24/40	4/20/67	27/2
Leotis Martin	3/10/39	7/18/67	28/4
Buster Mathis	6/5/44	1/20/68	23/7
Henry Clark	3/5/45	5/20/68	23/2
Al Lewis	12/11/42	8/19/68	25/8
Mac Foster	6/27/42	6/20/69	27
Al Jones	12/28/43	8/20/69	25/8
Roger Rischer	3/20/34	12/19/64	30/9

Average > 25 years, 10 months

White Contenders (1970–83)

	Born	Entered Top Ten	Age
Chuck Wepner	2/26/39	7/15/73	34/5
Duane Bobick	8/24/50	12/15/75	25/4
Randy Neumann	7/21/48	1/15/76	27/6
Scott LeDoux	1/7/49	9/8/79	30/8
Gerry Cooney	7/24/56	11/9/79	23/4
Tex Cobb	12/10/54	10/29/81	26/11

Average > 28 years

Black Contenders (1970–83)

	Born	Entered Top Ten	Age
George Foreman	1/22/48	5/20/70	22/4
Ron Lyle	2/11/42	8/15/72	30/6
Ken Norton	8/9/45	9/15/72	27/1
Earnie Shavers	7/31/45	7/15/73	27/11
Jeff Merritt	1/1/462	2/15/74	28/1
Larry Middleton	1/24/42	1/15/72	30
Jimmy Young	11/14/48	3/15/75	26/4
Larry Holmes	11/3/49	12/31/75	26/2
Johnny Boudreaux	7/17/52	3/15/76	23/8
Howard Smith	1/12/47	7/18/76	29/6
Stan Ward	5/9/49	9/15/76	27/4
Leon Spinks	7/11/53	11/15/77	24/4

Mike Weaver	6/14/52	1/28/79	26/7
John Tate	1/29/55	2/25/79	24/1
Leroy Jones	2/10/50	7/25/79	29/5
Michael Dokes	7/10/58	2/9/80	21/7
Greg Page	10/28/58	7/10/80	21/8
Marty Monroe	10/26/53	10/4/80	26/11
James Tillis	7/5/57	3/19/81	23/8
Renaldo Snipes	7/15/56	9/22/81	25/2
Tim Witherspoon	12/27/57	5/1/82	24/4
Pinklon Thomas	2/10/58	8/20/82	24/6
S.T. Gordon	4/18/59	6/25/83	24/2

Average > 25 years, 11 months

To become rated, black heavyweights were at a disadvantage for the first two periods, not being rated until they were older than their white colleagues. From 1950 to 1959, black heavyweights were ten months older (26 years, one month to 25 years, three months) than the latter when first ranked. In the 1960s, the average black age for entry into the Top Ten was almost two years older (25 years, ten months to 23 years, eight months) than whites. Then, from 1970–83, the numbers reversed, when whites entered *The Ring*'s pages at an average age twenty-five months older (28 years to 25 years, eleven months) than the age at which blacks appeared.

Career Length

The older a boxer is at reaching plateaus of success, the longer the odds against him reaching his fullest potential, or garnering the full rewards his talents merited. How long a fighter has been competing professionally before they move upward is another measure that speaks to the equality or inequality of boxing opportunity along racial lines. In a racially just society, one expects that, given roughly equal qualifications and work ethics, white and minority employees should toil for the same periods of time before they are promoted to better positions, and the rewards that come with them. What does the evidence say about the length of heavyweights' careers before their big chances?

Career Length of Contenders Entering *The Ring*'s Top Ten

Intervals are given in years/months

White Contenders (1949–59)	*Pro Debut*	*Top Ten Entry*	*Interval*
Bernie Reynolds	4/23/46	3/15/49	2 y/11m
Gus Lesnevich	5/5/34	6/16/49	15/1
Grant Butcher	10/4/48	9/15/49	0/11
Roland LaStarza	7/7/47	1/16/50	2/6
Rocky Marciano	3/17/47	4/15/50	3/1
Harry Mathews*	6/1/37	6/18/52	15/1

Dan Bucceroni	11/6/47	2/18/53	5/3
Roy Harris	4/26/55	5/23/57	2/1
Pat McMurtry	2/4/54	6/20/57	3/5
Mike DeJohn	4/12/51	10/25/57	6/6
Charlie Norkus	11/30/48	12/16/54	6/1
Rex Layne	5/23/49	8/15/50	1/3
Willie Pastrano	9/10/51	1/17/56	4/4

Average > 5 years, 3 months

*After sixty-five years, the first year of Harry Mathews's professional career is still a mystery. There is no reliable record of the dates of his first bouts in Ontario, Oregon, save that they happened in 1937. For the purpose of this measure, the impact on the total average for the white 1950s contender's sample was one month fewer with a January 1937 former estimate (5 years, 6 months), or no change at all with a December 1937 estimate. It was estimated for statistical purposes that he began fighting on June 1, 1937.

Black Contenders (1949–59)	Pro Debut	Top Ten Entry	Interval
Al Hoosman	6/18/43	8/15/49	6/2
Turkey Thompson	5/9/39	8/15/49	10/3
John Holman	9/22/47	2/15/50	2/5
Bob Baker	4/21/49	4/15/50	1/0
Clarence Henry	7/7/48	6/15/50	1/11
Coley Wallace	3/15/50	2/18/52	1/11
Bob Dunlap	1/7/48	3/18/52	4/2
Tom Harrison	1/12/51	4/18/53	2/3
Bob Satterfield	3/19/45	7/18/53	8/4
Jim Slade	7/25/49	5/20/54	4/10
Archie Moore	7/14/36	5/21/55	18/10
Tom Jackson	7/14/52	3/18/54	1/8
John Summerlin	8/2/50	11/17/55	5/3
Young Jack Johnson	3/28/53	1/17/56	2/10
Harold Carter	5/30/53	11/17/55	2/6
Eddie Machen	3/22/55	4/19/56	1/1
Floyd Patterson	9/12/52	5/21/56	3/8
Zora Folley	9/22/53	12/22/56	3/3
Wayne Bethea	8/12/54	1/22/57	2/5
Harold Johnson*	5/1/46	3/19/57	10/7
Sonny Liston	9/2/53	8/22/58	5/0
Charlie Powell	3/7/53	3/19/59	6/0
Tony Anthony	11/5/52	9/23/59	6/11
Alonzo Johnson	1/19/57	6/26/59	2/5
Billy Hunter	4/19/54	11/19/59	5/7
Bill Gilliam	6/1/43	3/18/54	10/10

Average > 5 years, 1 month

*As with Harry Mathews, the date of Harold Johnson's first fight in 1946, in Wilmington, Delaware, is seemingly lost to the historical record. His first confirmed fight date was in October of that year, meaning his debut was somewhere between January and September. It was discovered that regardless of when in this nine month span he began fighting, the impact on the overall average for the 1950s black contenders was nil either way. It was estimated he began fighting on May 1, 1946, roughly half way across the mystery span.

White Contenders (1960–69)	Pro Debut	Top Ten Entry	Interval
Tom McNeely	7/17/58	1/19/61	2/6
George Logan	9/18/57	1/23/62	4/4

	Pro Debut	Top Ten Entry	Interval
Jerry Quarry	5/7/65	7/18/67	2/2
Boone Kirkman	4/1/66	5/20/68	2/2
Average > 2 years, 10 months			

Black Contenders (1960–69)	Pro Debut	Top Ten Entry	Interval
Cleveland Williams	12/11/51	5/22/61	9/5
Cassius Clay	10/29/60	1/23/62	1/3
Billy Daniels	5/20/60	11/21/62	2/6
Doug Jones	7/22/58	12/20/62	4/5
Ernie Terrell	5/15/57	4/24/63	5/11
Roger Rischer	10/5/53	12/19/64	11/2
Thad Spencer	5/3/60	4/15/65	4/11
Amos Johnson	3/11/60	4/15/65	5/1
Hubert Hilton	6/4/63	6/20/65	2/1
Elmer Rush	6/25/62	9/20/65	3/3
Amos Lincoln	10/5/54	12/20/65	9/1
Johnny Persol	1/5/63	11/20/66	3/10
Joe Frazier	7/16/65	12/20/66	1/5
Jimmy Ellis	4/19/61	4/20/67	6/0
Leotis Martin	1/26/62	7/18/67	5/6
Buster Mathis	6/28/65	1/20/68	2/7
Henry Clark	5/28/64	5/20/68	4/0
Al Lewis	6/21/66	8/19/68	2/2
Mac Foster	11/28/66	6/20/69	2/7
Al Jones	6/11/64	8/20/69	5/2
Average > 4 years, 7 months			

White Contenders (1970–83)	Pro Debut	Top Ten Entry	Interval
Chuck Wepner	7/5/64	7/15/73	9/0
Duane Bobick	4/10/73	12/15/75	2/8
Randy Neumann	7/18/69	1/15/76	6/7
Scott LeDoux	2/4/74	9/8/79	5/5
Gerry Cooney	2/15/77	11/9/79	2/9
Tex Cobb	1/21/77	10/29/81	4/9
Average > 5 years, 2 months			

Black Contenders (1970–83)	Pro Debut	Top Ten Entry	Interval
George Foreman	6/23/69	5/20/70	0/11
Ron Lyle	4/23/71	8/15/72	1/4
Ken Norton	11/14/67	9/15/72	4/10
Earnie Shavers	11/6/69	7/15/73	3/8
Jeff Merritt	2/23/68	2/15/74	6/0
Larry Middleton	9/23/65	1/15/72	6/4
Jimmy Young	6/22/69	3/15/75	5/9
Larry Holmes	3/21/73	12/31/75	2/9
Johnny Boudreaux	2/12/73	3/15/76	3/1
Howard Smith	5/8/71	7/18/76	5/2
Stan Ward	6/25/74	9/15/76	2/3
Leon Spinks	1/15/77	11/15/77	/10
Mike Weaver	9/14/72	1/28/79	6/4
John Tate	5/7/77	2/25/79	1/10
Leroy Jones	7/30/73	7/25/79	6/0
Michael Dokes	10/15/76	2/9/80	3/4

Greg Page	2/16/79	7/10/80	1/5
Marty Monroe	5/2/74	10/4/80	6/6
James Tillis	11/18/78	3/19/81	2/4
Renaldo Snipes	11/18/78	9/22/81	2/10
Tim Witherspoon	10/30/79	5/1/82	2/6
Pinklon Thomas	8/29/78	8/20/82	4/0
S.T. Gordon	2/23/77	6/25/83	6/4

Average > 3 years, 9 months

The evidence indicates white contenders fought longer before being ranked in two of the three time spans. The 1950s saw white contenders achieve this career step needing two more months of than their black counterparts. In the 1960s, it took white boxers nineteen fewer months to be ranked following their debuts. In the final era, however, the situation reversed with the black contenders hitting the Top Ten seventeen months earlier. There is no pattern of white heavyweights consistently breaking into boxing's elite class with shorter careers than black heavyweights between 1949 and 1983.

Rate of Fighting Activity

Having already compared the racial samples for the number of fights and length of career as measured by months, there is an even more cogent variable that assesses to what degree these boxers paid their dues on the way to the peak. The career length of a fighter can be misleading if he had long periods of inactivity, as can the number of fights if he fought many times in a short period, than seldom leading up to his ascension into the elite level. Their fighting frequency over the totality of their career reduces these distortions. Boxers who have fought at a steady rate seem more credible and deserving of opportunity than those who disappear from the rings for long stretches of time because of laziness or poor motivation. Did the white and black pugilists in this sample enter the ring to test their skills with the same regularity?

Rate of Fighting by Contenders Ranked in *The Ring*'s Top Ten

White Contenders (1949–59)	Career Length (Months)		Fights		Months Between Fights
Bernie Reynolds	35	/	46	=	.8
Gus Lesnevich	181	/	76	=	2.4
Grant Butcher	11	/	13	=	.8
Roland LaStarza	30	/	37	=	.8
Rocky Marciano	37	/	26	=	1.4
Harry Mathews	180	/	87	=	2.1
Dan Bucceroni	63	/	42	=	1.5

4. Approaching the Summit 97

Roy Harris	25	/	21	=	1.2
Pat McMurtry	41	/	26	=	1.6
Mike DeJohn	78	/	38	=	2.1
Charlie Norkus	73	/	38	=	1.9
Rex Layne	15	/	26	=	.6
Willie Pastrano	52	/	43	=	1.2

Average > 1 fight per 1.4 months

Black Contenders (1950–59)	Career Length (Months)		Fights		Months Between Fights
Al Hoosman	73	/	23	=	3.2
Turkey Thompson	122	/	57	=	2.1
John Holman	29	/	15	=	1.9
Bob Baker	12	/	14	=	.9
Clarence Henry	23	/	18	=	1.3
Coley Wallace	23	/	15	=	1.5
Bob Dunlap	50	/	30	=	1.7
Tommy Harrison	27	/	27	=	1
Bob Satterfield	100	/	47	=	2.1
Jimmy Slade	58	/	33	=	1.8
Archie Moore	226	/	172	=	1.3
Tommy Jackson	20	/	16	=	1.3
John Summerlin	63	/	34	=	1.9
Young Jack Johnson	34	/	18	=	1.9
Harold Carter	30	/	20	=	1.5
Eddie Machen	13	/	13	=	1
Floyd Patterson	44	/	30	=	1.5
Zora Folley	39	/	30	=	1.3
Wayne Bethea	29	/	21	=	1.4
Harold Johnson	131	/	61	=	2.1
Sonny Liston	60	/	21	=	2.9
Charlie Powell	72	/	25	=	2.9
Tony Anthony	83	/	49	=	1.7
Alonzo Johnson	29	/	17	=	1.7
Billy Hunter	67	/	22	=	3.0
Bill Gilliam	130	/	46	=	2.8

Average > 1 fight per 1.8 months

White Contenders (1960–69)	Career Length (Months)		Fights		Months Between Fights
Tom McNeely	30	/	22	=	1.4
George Logan	52	/	29	=	1.8
Jerry Quarry	26	/	28	=	.9
Boone Kirkman	26	/	18	=	1.4

Average > 1 fight per 1.4 months

Black Contenders (1960–69)	Career Length (Months)		Fights		Months Between Fights
Cleveland Williams	114	/	54	=	2.1

	Career Length (Months)		Fights		Months Between Fights
Cassius Clay	15	/	10	=	1.5
Billy Daniels	30	/	18	=	1.7
Doug Jones	53	/	25	=	2.1
Ernie Terrell	71	/	35	=	2.0
Thad Spencer	59	/	27	=	2.2
Amos Johnson	61	/	19	=	3.2
Hubert Hilton	25	/	15	=	1.7
Elmer Rush	39	/	15	=	2.6
Amos Lincoln	134	/	40	=	3.4
Johnny Persol	46	/	21	=	2.2
Joe Frazier	17	/	13	=	1.3
Jimmy Ellis	72	/	29	=	2.5
Leotis Martin	66	/	25	=	2.6
Buster Mathis	31	/	23	=	1.3
Henry Clark	48	/	20	=	2.4
Al Lewis	26	/	20	=	1.3
Mac Foster	31	/	18	=	1.7
Al Jones	62	/	31	=	2
Roger Rischer	134	/	36	=	3.7

Average > 1 fight per 2.2 months

White Contenders (1970–83)	Career Length (Months)		Fights		Months Between Fights
Chuck Wepner	108	/	37	=	2.9
Duane Bobick	32	/	33	=	1.0
Randy Neumann	79	/	37	=	2.1
Scott LeDoux	65	/	36	=	1.8
Gerry Cooney	33	/	21	=	1.6
Tex Cobb	57	/	20	=	2.9

Average > 1 fight per 2.1 months

Black Contenders (1970–83)	Career Length (Months)		Fights		Months Between Fights
George Foreman	11	/	20	=	.6
Ron Lyle	16	/	16	=	1
Ken Norton	58	/	28	=	2.1
Earnie Shavers	44	/	47	=	.9
Jeff Merritt	72	/	21	=	3.4
Larry Middleton	76	/	19	=	4
Jimmy Young	69	/	20	=	3.5
Larry Holmes	33	/	20	=	1.7
Johnny Boudreaux	37	/	20	=	1.9
Howard Smith	72	/	17	=	4.2
Stan Ward	26	/	8	=	3.3
Leon Spinks	10	/	7	=	1.4
Mike Weaver	76	/	26	=	2.9
John Tate	22	/	18	=	1.2
Leroy Jones	72	/	25	=	2.9
Michael Dokes	40	/	16	=	2.5
Greg Page	17	/	11	=	1.5
Marty Monroe	78	/	24	=	3.3
James Tillis	28	/	20	=	1.4

Renaldo Snipes	34	/	22	=	1.5
Tim Witherspoon	30	/	14	=	2.1
Pinklon Thomas	48	/	20	=	2.4
S.T. Gordon	76	/	29	=	2.6

Average > 1 fight per 2.3 months

Throughout the study, white heavyweights were more consistent in chasing their dreams. Whatever the truth was about white and black credentials, one cannot conclude that less-motivated white fighters butted in line in front of more active black ones. In all three time spans, the white contenders had shorter gaps (1.4 months, 1.4, 2.1) between fights than did the black boxers (1.8 months, 2.2, 2.3) on their way to being rated, although the gap had shrunk to its smallest by the last phase. Caucasian contenders had earned their stripes by at least competing at a better rate than their black contemporaries. A caveat is that this measure assumes both white and black young fighters had equal opportunity to fight on professional cards from the beginning of their careers. This assumption is impossible to prove or disprove, since there is no way of measuring the motivation and work ethic of a fighter at present, much less ones who fought twenty, thirty, even fifty years ago. Boxers are responsible for their own careers, which is why this measure has to assume that the average boxer who fights one bout per month is more deserving of ranked status than one who laces up the gloves once every three months. Moving on up in boxing demands fighting, not excuses. Yet the entire premise of this study is that forces might be working against the opportunity of black boxers at the elite level, factors beyond the control of the pugilists themselves. It is not a great leap to consider that such a possible racial discrepancy could also be in play in the rest of the sport. It is no secret that professional boxers in America had often languished in activity because of inability to get fights, which always require a promoter's blessing. Fighters cannot demand a bout, so ones lacking effective management or promotional pull can develop ring rust for lack of opportunity. It has always been true that truly elite boxers have increasing difficulty finding opponents willing to enter the same ring. As he ascended the heavyweight division in the late 1950s, Sonny Liston had such an intimidating reputation that he could only get fights by offering terrified would-be opponents larger shares of the proceeds than he himself received for thrashing them in a few rounds.

If simple talent could hinder a boxer from having regular work, racial sentiments among promoters could only have prevented some black contenders from fighting as often as they wanted. Such attitudes could also have reduced the size of their purses in the fights they did land. This could have forced them to work second jobs outside boxing, leaving less time for training that would have drawn out their true potential. It is possible that longtime ring veterans like Walcott, Charles, and Moore, whose careers began in the Depression faced greater barriers to competing or being compensated for their work, than white heavyweights. Many of the other 1950s and 1960s black contenders were fighting in a time when institutionalized segregation was the norm in much of the United States, and de facto segregation existed in many other American locales. It is extremely likely some African American heavyweights were fighting as often as white promoters allowed, not as often as they wanted. This measure, then, shows no quantifiable evidence of white fighters receiving equal opportunity while competing at a more leisurely pace due to the color of their skin. One must stop short of concluding they were more ambitious and dedicated simply because of such numbers.

Entering and Leaving the Top Ten Ratings

The Top Ten list of contenders is not merely the last springboard to the championship. Each spot in the list can be thought of as a step in itself toward the crown. There have historically been few mechanisms at the disposal of governing bodies to force the heavyweight champion to fight the top ranked challenger, but there has generally been pressure to fight someone closer to the number one spot, where ostensibly the second best boxer in the world resides. As mentioned earlier, there have been myriad examples of champions bypassing true threats to their perch in favor of nonentity opponents there has also been the counterbalancing pressure of media and public favor, as well as the financial incentive to steer the king of a boxing division toward stiffer contests. Assuming the rankings to be a valid measure of ring skill, the better-ranked contenders promise a bigger payday for the champ, owing to greater public interest. The reputation of a champion who fights several consecutive opponents more *rank* than ranked, begins to take on a bad smell of his own. Any chance of being recognized in retirement as one of the great champs of all time is destroyed if most of a titleholder's defenses were against lower or unranked opponents. No credible boxing authority could cite Floyd Patterson as a great champion, given the reluctance of his over-protective manager, Cus D'Amato, to risk his pupil against tough opposition. This sheltering of Patterson, and the rationalizations used by D'Amato to justify his avoidance of elite challengers, became an open joke in the boxing world. It was almost universally accepted that Patterson was the heavyweight champion only on paper from 1958 or 1959 onward. At this time, Sonny Liston was decimating the heavyweight division, but had to wait for years before pride forced Patterson to overrule his timid (or shrewd) manager and fight the ex-convict. Eddie Machen and Zora Folley were both superb candidates for a title bout, but they were too good for D'Amato to allow into the ring with Patterson.[3] Both fighters had to wait for title fights against less timid champions: Machen lost to Ernie Terrell in 1965, Folley was defeated by Ali in 1967.

A champion's quest for greatness and fame depends, then, on risking their title against higher ranked contenders, so these spots are a much better place to be for aspiring boxers. Since each Top Ten spot roughly represents progression toward the pinnacle and an increased chance at a title shot, there is another statistical comparison one can make to determine how quickly elite black and white fighters have climbed the ranks of the sweet science. Finding out what numerical ranking has been awarded to white and black contenders when they first entered the ratings, will reveal whether or not any glaring favors have been done for the careers of the former. Unless an unranked fighter scores a huge upset over a high-ranking contender, it normally happens that they are first included in *The Ring*'s ratings at the tenth or ninth position. Initial rankings at each subsequent upward position are increasingly rare, for being introduced to the Top Ten at number six or five means this magazine's boxing experts have decided that such a fighter has leapfrogged over four or five established contenders in the space of only month. Such a step forward would depend on a very impressive victory, indeed.

What if one were to find the average white contender landing in the ratings in front of several standing rivals, while the black contenders typically gained a tentative foothold on the ninth or tenth rung of the ladder? This, if true, would strongly suggest a desire to fast-track white heavyweights toward a title showdown, while black ones were forced to struggle more to move upward, scraping and clawing for every rank.

First Monthly Ranking of Top Ten Contenders Rated by *The Ring*

White Contenders (1949–59)	Entry Rank(s)	Black Contenders (1949–59)	Entry Rank(s)
Bernie Reynolds	9	Al Hoosman	8
Gus Lesnevich	7	Turkey Thompson	10
Grant Butcher	10	John Holman	6, 6, 10
Roland LaStarza	10, 10	Bob Baker	8, 8
Rocky Marciano	9, 9	Clarence Henry	10, 7
Harry Mathews	6, 9, 9, 9	Coley Wallace	10, 7, 9
Dan Bucceroni	10	Bob Dunlap	8
Roy Harris	9, 6	Tom Harrison	6
Pat McMurtry	10, 10	Bob Satterfield	6, 7, 4, 8
Mike DeJohn	8, 7, 10, 9	Tommy Jackson	8
Charlie Norkus	10	Jim Slade	4, 5
Rex Layne	7, 7, 9, 9	Archie Moore	1, 5, 4,
Willie Pastrano	5	John Summerlin	5, 7
		Young Jack Johnson	9
		Harold Carter	9, 8, 9
		Eddie Machen	9

		Floyd Patterson	4
		Zora Folley	10
		Wayne Bethea	10, 9
		Harold Johnson	6
		Sonny Liston	9
		Charlie Powell	9
		Tony Anthony	10
		Alonzo Johnson	9
		Billy Hunter	8
		Bill Gilliam	10
Average > 223/ 26 = 8.6		Average > 315/ 42 = 7.5	

White Contenders (1960–69)	Entry Rank(s)	Black Contenders (1960–69)	Entry Rank(s)
Tom McNeely	10	Cleveland Williams	8, 10
George Logan	10	Cassius Clay	9
Jerry Quarry	8	Billy Daniels	10, 8, 10
Boone Kirkman	9, 10, 9	Doug Jones	4, 9, 6
Willie Pastrano	10	Ernie Terrell	10
Mike DeJohn	10	Thad Spencer	9
		Amos Johnson	10, 10
		Hubert Hilton	10
		Elmer Rush	10
		Amos Lincoln	6, 7
		Johnny Persol	10, 10
		Joe Frazier	6
		Jimmy Ellis	10, 7
		Leotis Martin	10, 6
		Buster Mathis	10, 6
		Henry Clark	10, 10
		Al Lewis	8
		Mac Foster	10
		Al Jones	10
		Roger Rischer	8
		Billy Hunter	10
		Sonny Liston	7
		Eddie Machen	8
		Floyd Patterson	8
		Archie Moore	6
Average > 76/ 8 = 9.5		Average > 316/ 37 = 8.5	

White Contenders (1970–83)	Entry Rank(s)	Black Contenders (1970–83)	Entry Rank(s)
Chuck Wepner	10	George Foreman	10
Duane Bobick	9	Ron Lyle	9
Randy Neumann	10	Ken Norton	10, 10
Scott LeDoux	10, 9	Earnie Shavers	5, 10, 10, 4
Gerry Cooney	10, 10	Jeff Merritt	10
Tex Cobb	9	Larry Middleton	10, 10
Jerry Quarry	3	Jimmy Young	7, 10
		Larry Holmes	10
		Johnny Boudreaux	10
		Howard Smith	7
		Stan Ward	10

4. Approaching the Summit 103

Leon Spinks	9, 10, 10
Mike Weaver	10
John Tate	10, 9
Leroy Jones	8, 10
Michael Dokes	8
Greg Page	10
Marty Monroe	6
James Tillis	10, 8
Renaldo Snipes	10
Tim Witherspoon	9
Pinklon Thomas	7
S.T. Gordon	8
Ernie Terrell	7
Jimmy Ellis	7, 8

Average > 80/ 9 = 8.9   Average > 326/ 37 = 8.8

For this, and the exit rank averages compilation below, the entry ranking tabulations were grouped by period, rather than anchored within the first period in which the boxer entered the rankings. Numerous fighters in the study joined the Top Ten in one period, then exited (and sometimes re-entered) in the following period. With other measures in this study, it was decided to attribute the statistics of each boxer to the 1950s, 1960s and 1970–83 groupings, the logic being that such measures were cumulative, spanning the division years of 1960 and 1970. The number of wins, knockouts, length of career, and age, are obviously variables that cannot be isolated within these artificial decade designations. With this statistic, one can focus in on the time period, since boxers enter and exit the rankings at a specific point in time. The numerical ranking that Floyd Patterson was dropped from in July 1966, and re-entered the same year, can hardly be attributed to the 1950s black cohort group in any reliable or valid way, since *The Ring*'s rationale for these decisions had to be based on his performance at that time.

There is no evidence that *The Ring* was anything but color-blind in where it first slotted new arrivals into its ratings. In all three periods, black contenders first showed up in this magazine's rankings at higher spots than the white heavyweights. In the 1950s, the average black newcomer to the ratings was ranked more than a full position ahead (7.5 to 8.6) of the average white one. In the 1960s, this margin barely closed, blacks averaging a ranking a shade above whites (8.5 to 9.5) upon their respective arrivals. In the final period, the two races joined the list at almost the same average black ranking, but with black heavyweights first rated slightly better (8.8 to 8.9) than the white pugilists. Nothing in these numbers suggests any favors were done for white heavyweights by *The Ring*.

One can gain further insight by considering how quickly white and black heavyweights have dropped from the ranks after their careers have ostensibly peaked. How fast *The Ring* has discarded the two groups of boxers from its list could also support or refute the conclusion of unequal opportunity in boxing. In the latter stages of their career, elite fighters seek to hold onto their Top Ten ranking as long as possible, hanging on by their fingernails in the hope of one more shot at the title, one more big payday. If white heavyweights tended to hold their place closer to the bottom of the Top Ten than their black counterparts, one would think that the system was geared toward giving whites every last opportunity to win the title. If over-the-hill white heavies sat for months in the nine or ten spots while blacks plummeted off the page from the sixth or seventh rank, one would conclude there were levers of boxing influence which, consciously or unconsciously, were maximizing the public relations value of having a white fighter in the Top Ten. Such forces would be acting on behalf of white fan interest, or the perception of it, holding white heavies up longer, pulling the rug out from under black ones more quickly. Has the average white contender conspicuously held onto lower rungs on the Top Ten list than their black contemporaries?

Final Monthly Ranking of Top Ten Contenders Rated by *The Ring*

White Contenders (1949–59)	Exit Rank	Black Contenders (1949–59)	Exit Rank
Bernie Reynolds	10	Al Hoosman	8
Gus Lesnevich	7	Turkey Thompson	3
Grant Butcher	10	John Holman	10, 8, 9
Roland LaStarza	8, 8	Bob Baker	9, 8
Rocky Marciano	7	Clarence Henry	10, 6
Harry Mathews	6, 10, 9, 9	Coley Wallace	5, 10, 10
Dan Bucceroni	10	Bob Dunlap	4
Roy Harris	7, 10	Tom Harrison	10
Pat McMurtry	10, 9	Bob Satterfield	6, 9, 7, 8
Mike DeJohn	8, 7, 10	Jim Slade	10, 9
Charlie Norkus	10	Archie Moore	3, 5, 6,
Rex Layne	10, 8	Tom Jackson	9
Willie Pastrano	8	John Summerlin	7, 10
		Young Jack Johnson	9
		Harold Carter	9, 3, 10
		Wayne Bethea	10, 10
		Harold Johnson	4
		Charlie Powell	9
		Tony Anthony	9
		Alonzo Johnson	10
		Bill Gilliam	10
Average >191/ 22 = 8.7		Average > 292/ 37 = 7.9	

White Contenders (1960–69)	Exit Rank	Black Contenders (1960–69)	Exit Rank
Tom McNeely	9	Cleveland Williams	8, 3
George Logan	10	Billy Daniels	10, 9, 10
Boone Kirkman	10, 10, 10	Doug Jones	10, 7, 6
Willie Pastrano	10	Ernie Terrell	10

4. Approaching the Summit

Mike DeJohn	9, 10	Thad Spencer	8
		Amos Johnson	10, 10
		Hubert Hilton	10
		Elmer Rush	10
		Amos Lincoln	7, 7
		Johnny Persol	9, 10
		Jimmy Ellis	10
		Leotis Martin	10
		Buster Mathis	10, 9
		Henry Clark	10, 10
		Al Lewis	9
		Mac Foster	10
		Al Jones	9
		Roger Rischer	9
		Billy Hunter	9, 10
		Sonny Liston	5
		Zora Folley	8
		Eddie Machen	1, 10
		Floyd Patterson	9, 8
		Archie Moore	9
Average > 78/ 8 = 9.8		Average > 319/ 37 = 8.6	

White Contenders (1970–83)	Exit Rank	Black Challengers (1970–83)	Exit Rank
Chuck Wepner	9	Ron Lyle	8
Duane Bobick	9	Ken Norton	8, 9
Scott LeDoux	10, 10	Earnie Shavers	8, 9, 9, 5
Gerry Cooney	10, 10	Jeff Merritt	10
Tex Cobb	10	Larry Middleton	9, 10
Jerry Quarry	5	Jimmy Young	7, 10
		Johnny Boudreaux	10
		Howard Smith	7
		Stan Ward	10
		Leon Spinks	9, 10, 9
		Mike Weaver	10
		John Tate	9, 9
		Leroy Jones	9, 10
		Michael Dokes	10
		Greg Page	5
		Marty Monroe	9
		James Tillis	7, 8
		Renaldo Snipes	7
		Tim Witherspoon	5
		Pinklon Thomas	10
		S.T. Gordon	8
		Ernie Terrell	8
		Jimmy Ellis	10, 10, 9
Average > 73/ 8 = 9.1		Average > 310/ 36 = 8.6	

With this measure, one can identify a discrepancy working in favor of white heavyweights. In two of the three eras, black contenders were dropped from the Top Ten from lower numerical (or higher quality) places in the ratings. From 1949 to 1959, they dropped from an average rating almost one spot higher (7.9 to 8.7) than the white contenders. The 1960s saw this gap grow, as the average black fighter disappeared from an average ranking more than one place better in the Top Ten (8.6 to 9.8) than their white rivals. In the study's final thirteen years, the margin had shrunk to an almost incidental difference (9.1 for whites, 8.6 for blacks) yet it was still black contenders who were sliding a greater distance out of contention when they finally lost their grip on their ratings. Consistent with many of the above 1970–83 measures, white contenders seemed to cling to a lower rung of the Top Ten until it was absolutely certain they were not championship material, and they had to be discarded until they proved themselves worthy of re-enter. The black contenders did not get shown the door quickly or easily, but they did slip farther when they were sent packing from the pages of *The Ring*.

Re-Entering the Ratings

Many of the contenders in this study did not merely enter the ratings when they were young and improving, then leave for good when they passed their prime. It has often happened that elite boxers have career hills and valleys, whereby they drop from the elite when their fortunes take a downturn, then re-enter the Top Ten when they regain their former level of excellence. Injuries, fluctuating confidence and motivation, financial and managerial troubles, personal problems, all can make a boxer's career resemble a roller-coaster. Successful pugilists seem prone to retiring in front of lavish press conferences, only to be lured back into the gym the moment they feel bored with their post-boxing lives (or in need of more cash). Sugar Ray Leonard, Roberto Duran, and Larry Holmes are only three of many famous boxers whose retirements required two hands for counting. With so many fighters experiencing variable career fortunes, there are many in this sample who left *The Ring*'s ratings and then climbed their way back into recognition. Some of them even left and returned to the elite several times. Were white and black contenders equally likely to get a second chance? Was there equality in the likelihood of both groups earning this valuable status on multiple occasions? If a much greater ratio of whites were dusted off by *The Ring* for second or third inclusion in the rankings, one would suspect a concerted attempt to keep serving the public with a Great White Hope to support. Has the door slammed more quickly behind black contenders than white contenders leaving the ratings?

Ratio of Contenders Re-Entering *The Ring*'s Top Ten

White Contenders (1949–59)	Number of Entries
Bernie Reynolds	Entered once
Gus Lesnevich	Entered once

4. Approaching the Summit

Grant Butcher	Entered once
Roland LaStarza	Re-entered Top Ten on February 15, 1951
Rocky Marciano	Re-entered Top Ten on October 15, 1950
Harry Mathews	Re-entered Top Ten on July 18, 1953, February 18, 1954, and June 21, 1954
Dan Bucceroni	Entered once
Roy Harris	Re-entered Top Ten on June 26, 1959
Pat McMurtry	Re-entered Top Ten on October 22, 1958
Mike DeJohn	Re-entered on January 23, 1958, January 21, 1959, November 19, 1959, and August 20, 1962
Willie Pastrano	Re-entered on June 20, 1962
Charlie Norkus	Entered once
Rex Layne	Re-entered Top Ten on December 15, 1950, July 18, 1952, and December 16, 1954

Entered Once > 5/ 13 = 38.5%
Entered Twice > 5/ 13 = 38.5%%
Entered Three Times > 0/ 13 = 0%
Entered Four Times > 2/ 13 = 15.4%
Entered Five Times > 1/ 13 = 7.7%
Total > 13 fighters entered 28 times = 2.2/contender

Black Contenders (1949–59)

Al Hoosman	Entered once
Turkey Thompson	Entered once
John Holman	Re-entered Top Ten on May 21, 1955 and October 20, 1955
Bob Baker	Re-entered Top Ten on January 18, 1953
Clarence Henry	Re-entered Top Ten on November 15, 1950
Coley Wallace	Re-entered Top Ten on December 18, 1952
Bob Dunlap	Entered once
Tom Harrison	Entered once
Bob Satterfield	Re-entered Top Ten on December 18, 1953, December 17, 1955, and December 20, 1957
Jim Slade	Re-entered Top Ten on November 17, 1955
Archie Moore	Re-entered Top Ten on December 20, 1957, March 26, 1958, and April 20, 1962
Tom Jackson	Entered once
John Summerlin	Re-entered Top Ten on January 17, 1956
Young Jack Johnson	Entered once
Harold Carter	Re-entered Top Ten on March 19, 1956
Eddie Machen	Re-entered Top Ten on September 17, 1963
Floyd Patterson	Re-entered Top Ten on October 20, 1966
Zora Folley	Entered once
Wayne Bethea	Re-entered Top Ten on October 25, 1957
Harold Johnson	Entered once
Sonny Liston	Re-entered Top Ten on August 19, 1968
Charlie Powell	Entered once
Tony Anthony	Entered once
Alonzo Johnson	Entered once
Billy Hunter	Re-entered Top Ten on November 23, 1960
Bill Gilliam	Entered Once

Entered Once > 12/ 26 = 46.2%
Entered Twice > 11/ 26 = 42.3%
Entered Three Times > 1/ 26 = 3.8 %
Entered Four Times > 2/ 26 = 7.7%
Totals > 26 fighters entered Top Ten 45 times = 1.7/ contender

White Contenders
(1960–69)

Tom McNeely	Entered once
George Logan	Entered once
Jerry Quarry	Re-entered Top Ten on March 15, 1973
Boone Kirkman	Re-entered Top Ten on June 16, 1970

Entered Once > 2/ 4 = 50%
Entered Twice > 2/ 4 = 50%
Totals: 4 fighters entered Top Ten 6 times = 1.5/ contender

Black Contenders
(1960–69)

Cleveland Williams	Re-entered Top Ten on May 20, 1966
Cassius Clay	Re-entered Top Ten on July 10, 1980
Billy Daniels	Re-entered Top Ten on January 20, 1963 and September 11, 1964
Doug Jones	Re-entered Top Ten on October 20, 1965 and January 20, 1967
Ernie Terrell	Re-entered Top Ten on November 15, 1972
Thad Spencer	Entered once
Amos Johnson	Re-entered Top Ten on February 20, 1966
Hubert Hilton	Entered once
Elmer Rush	Entered once
Amos Lincoln	Re-entered Top Ten on January 20, 1967
Johnny Persol	Re-entered Top Ten on February 20, 1967
Joe Frazier	Entered once
Jimmy Ellis	Re-entered Top Ten on August 15, 1967
Leotis Martin	Re-entered Top Ten on June 20, 1968
Buster Mathis	Re-entered Top Ten on February 20, 1969
Henry Clark	Re-entered Top Ten on August 15, 1972
Al Lewis	Entered once
Mac Foster	Entered once
Al Jones	Entered once
Roger Rischer	Entered once

Entered Once > 8/ 20 = 40%
Entered Twice > 10/ 20 = 50%
Entered Three Times > 2/ 20 = 10%
Total > 20 fighters entered Top Ten 34 times = 1.7/ contender

White Contenders
(1970–83)

Chuck Wepner	Entered once
Duane Bobick	Entered once
Randy Neumann	Entered once
Scott LeDoux	Re-entered Top Ten on April 1, 1980
Gerry Cooney	Re-entered Top Ten on December 1, 1984
Tex Cobb	Entered once

Entered Once > 4/ 6 = 67%
Entered Twice > 2/ 6 = 50%
Total > 6 fighters entered Top Ten 8 times = 1.3/ fighter

Black Contenders
(1970–83)

George Foreman*	Re-entered Top Ten on December 20, 1990 and March, 1995

4. Approaching the Summit

Ron Lyle	Entered once
Ken Norton	Re-entered Top Ten on December 10, 1980
Earnie Shavers	Re-entered Top Ten on April 15, 1975, March 15, 1977, and March 25, 1979
Jeff Merritt	Entered once
Larry Middleton	Re-entered Top Ten on April 15, 1974
Jimmy Young	Re-entered Top Ten on March 1, 1980
Larry Holmes*	Re-entered Top Ten on February 19, 1992, April, 1994, and February, 1995
Johnny Boudreaux	Entered once
Howard Smith	Entered once
Stan Ward	Entered once
Leon Spinks	Re-entered Top Ten on October 6, 1979 and January 10, 1980
Mike Weaver	Re-entered Top Ten on December 3, 1987
John Tate	Re-entered Top Ten on July 25, 1983
Leroy Jones	Re-entered Top Ten on November 4, 1980
Michael Dokes	Re-entered Top Ten on July 6, 1988
Greg Page	Entered once
Marty Monroe	Entered once
James Tillis	Re-entered Top Ten on July 25, 1983
Renaldo Snipes	Re-entered Top Ten on April 19, 1990
Tim Witherspoon*	Re-entered Top Ten on July, 1995, December 1996, February 1997 and January 1998
Pinklon Thomas	Entered once
S.T. Gordon	Entered once

*Although this study has 1983 as its chronological end date, this particular measure, how many times boxers entered the Top Ten, needs to include data from beyond that year for two reasons. First, restricting this measure's data to 1970–83 would present a distorted picture of this factor. All of the boxers in this time frame began establishing their credentials fighting before 1983. What is being measured is *The Ring*'s color-blindness in rating heavyweights. It would be inaccurate and unfair to this magazine if the younger boxers within this cohort, those who began fighting in the late 1970s and early 1980s, did not have post-1983 entries acknowledged, since some may have reached their primes after the arbitrary cut-off point represented by that year. This would reflect less on any potential bias of *The Ring* than on the simple fact the younger boxers had not matured enough as fighters to merit Top Ten status. Secondly, considering entries into the rankings after 1983 is consistent with the data-gathering pattern for contenders and challengers in the 1949–59 and 1960–69 eras. Some of the fighters from those decades climbed back into the ratings in the following arbitrarily defined period. Since *The Ring*'s decision-making processes for ratings inclusion cannot help but take into account boxers' past performances and reputations, any re-admittance of 1970–83 fighter's after 1983 is at least partially an expression of their careers spanning that year.

Entered Once > 9/ 23 = 39.1%
Entered Twice > 9/ 23 = 39.1%
Entered Three Times > 2/ 23 = 8.7%
Entered Four Times > 2/ 23 = 8.6%
Entered Five Times >1/ 23 = 4.3%
Total: 23 fighters entered 46 times = 2/ contender

This measure, as much as any, indicates that at the level of ranked contender, the sport reveals no significant racial bias in favor of white opportunity. Examining how many, and what ratio of heavyweights in both groups have fought their way back into contention, reveals that for much of the thirty-five-year study, black boxers have had either an equal or better chance of re-entering *The Ring*'s ratings relative to the white heavyweights.

The 1950s was the only era when white contenders made multiple entries into the *Top Ten* at a higher rate than their black rivals. Then, the ratings door was opened to thirteen white heavyweights on twenty-eight occasions, an average of more than two stints per fighter. The twenty-six black boxers rated in this decade entered *The Ring*'s monthly list, an average of less than two per contender. Where two black heavyweights out of twenty-six were accepted into the ratings four times, two of *thirteen* white contenders enjoyed the same reward. One must not exaggerate this margin. The discrepancy (2.1 to 1.7) was hardly large enough to signify a major trend easing the path of whites toward the title at the expense of blacks. There were many black boxers in this set (fourteen of twenty-five) who made at least two trips into the ratings. It is compelling, however, that the only heavyweight who dropped out of the rankings four times and made it back in for a fifth visit (before the 1990s when the quality of the sport had undeniably declined) was white. The enormous Mike DeJohn seemed irresistible to *The Ring*'s editors in the late 1950s and early 1960s. Every opportunity, and then some, was taken to introduce this heavyweight as elite caliber to boxing fans and promoters.

From the 1960s forward, *The Ring* was slightly more likely to rank black heavyweights on multiple occasions. From 1960–69, twenty blacks broke into the Top Ten thirty-four times, an average (1.7) marginally higher than that (1.5) of the four white contenders who entered six times. The gap grew slightly larger after 1970 (2.0 to 1.3) with six whites climbing into the ratings eight times while twenty-three blacks were rated on forty-five occasions. Five of the twenty-three African American heavyweights were ranked on at least three occasions, a recognition that none of the white boxers attained.

The Ring had no affinity for Great White Hopes in giving second and third chances to heavyweights. Black heavyweights could, and did, regenerate their title prospects by clawing their way back onto this magazine's pages, with twenty-six of forty-three African Americans (60 percent) from 1960 forward having been rated on at least two occasions. This compared to only four of the ten white prospects (40 percent) being similarly rewarded.

Performance to Remain in and Re-Enter the Top Ten

A spot in the Top Ten is a prized accomplishment that greatly facilitates a boxer's career prospects, so both getting there and staying there is something that is supposed to be earned. Contenders' records the first time they broke into the ratings have already been compared, as well as the number of times such heavyweights were able to re-enter the rankings. What they did to hold onto that privilege for as long as they could, or regain it if they lost it, can also be quantified. A contender who sits in the rankings for months on end without fighting is not supposed to stick around in this rarified atmosphere for very long. One who fights and loses to an unranked opponent, or several fights in a row, is hard to recognize as one of the best ten fighters in the world. Fairness and objectivity dictate that performance must remain at a high level for a boxer to stay rated. There are scores of hungry motivated boxers howling on the front porch of the Top Ten, anxiously waiting for their big break. Have the two races averaged similar records during their stint in the rankings? Has there been a tendency for one group to have to fight and win more to remain there, or get back in after being dropped?

Average Records to Remain in and Re-enter *The Ring*'s Top Ten

White Contenders (1949–59)	In Top Ten	Out	In
Bernie Reynolds	4–1		
Gus Lesnevich	0–1		
Grant Butcher	0–1		
Roland LaStarza	2–1	4–0	10–5
Rocky Marciano	2–0	1–0	13–0
Harry Mathews	0–1	3–0–1	0–1
Dan Bucceroni	6–2		
Roy Harris	2–1		
Pat McMurtry	2–1		
Mike DeJohn	0–0	0–0	0–0
Charlie Norkus	0–1		
Rex Layne	1–0–2	1–0	8–2
Willie Pastrano	13–4–1	7–2–2	0–0
Average > 32–14–3	16–2–3	31–8	
	= 65.3%	= 76.2%	= 79.5%

Only the records for the contenders' first three entries into the Top Ten were included as the data base for subsequent stays in the rankings was miniscule, unlikely to yield valid or reliable numbers.

Black Contenders (1949–59)	In Top Ten	Out	In
Al Hoosman	1–1		
Turkey Thompson	3–1		
John Holman	0–2	1–0	0–1
Bob Baker	12–1–1	3–1	2–1
Clarence Henry	2–1	2–0	10–0
Coley Wallace	2–1	1–0	0–0
Bob Dunlap	4–2		
Tom Harrison	8–2		
Bob Satterfield	0–0	1–0	0–1
Jim Slade	1–3	3–2	0–1
Archie Moore	14–2	4–0	1–0
Tom Jackson	15–6		

John Summerlin	0–0	0–0	3–2	
Young Jack Johnson	0–1			
Harold Carter	0–0	0–0–1	5–1	
Eddie Machen	29–4–2	0–0	5–2–1	
Floyd Patterson*	14–4	1–0	2–0–1	
Zora Folley	47–6–3			
Wayne Bethea	0–0	3–1	1–1	
Harold Johnson	1–0			
Sonny Liston*	16–2	7–0	8–1	Died in Top Ten
Charlie Powell	0–1			
Tony Anthony	0–1			
Alonzo Johnson	1–2			
Billy Hunter	1–1	1–0	0–1	
Bill Gilliam	0–0			
Average > 171–44–6	27–4–1 = 77.4%	37–12–2 = 84.4%	= 72.5%	

Patterson and other champions below (Ali, Frazier, Ellis, Foreman, Spinks, Holmes, Tate, Weaver, Dokes) are considered to have been in the Top Ten during the time they were heavyweight champions. Since wearing the crown is a cut above being a rated contender, one can hardly depict a boxer as having dropped out of the Top Ten by performance when they are actually more accomplished and talented than the ten rated contenders.

White Contenders (1960–69)	*In Top Ten*	*Out*	*In*	
Tom McNeely	1–1			
George Logan	0–1			
Jerry Quarry	20–5	2–0	5–2	Retired in Top Ten
Boone Kirkman	0–0	4–0	1–1	
Average	21–7 = 75%	6–0 = 100%	7–3 = 70%	

Black Contenders (1960–69)	*In Top Ten*	*Out*	*In*	
Cleveland Williams	12–1–1	3–0	1–1	
Muhammad Ali*	46–4	0–0	0–1	
Billy Daniels	0–0	1–0	0–4	
Doug Jones	3–3	2–0	3–2	
Ernie Terrell	8–3	6–0	1–2	
Thad Spencer	8–4			
Amos Johnson	0–0	3–0	0–0	
Hubert Hilton	1–2			
Elmer Rush	1–0			
Amos Lincoln	3–1–1	1–0	0–0	
Johnny Persol	0–0	0–0	0–1	
Joe Frazier	13–4*			
Jimmy Ellis	0–0	1–0	3–1*	
Leotis Martin	0–1	2–2		Retired from Top Ten (Eye Injury)
Buster Mathis	1–1	5–0	0–1	
Henry Clark	1–1	8–3–1	0–0	

Al Lewis	1–1		
Mac Foster	10–2		
Al Jones	1–0–1		
Roger Rischer	0–2		
Average >	109–30–3	32–5–1	8–13
	= 76.8%	= 84.2%	= 38.1%

Like the above measure in which post-1983 entries into the Top Ten were included, the records of such boxers between and during such stints will be considered for the same reasons. Clay/Ali won the heavyweight title in 1964, and held it until he was stripped of the championship and his license to fight in 1967 for refusal to serve in the military. *The Ring* continued to recognize Ali as the world champion under the assumption that it was unfair to strip him of his title when he had not lost it inside the ring. In 1970, when it appeared after three years of inactivity that Ali might never fight again, the magazine finally gave in to practicality and recognized the Frazier-Ellis elimination winner as the new champ. Ironically, shortly thereafter the ex-champ won his legal battle to fight again, and was immediately recognized as *The Ring*'s number one contender with his first victory over Jerry Quarry. Since this measure is focused on contenders' records after they have earned their way into the Top Ten, and similarly fallen out by performance, Ali's career from his first entry into the ratings in 1962, all the way to his first retirement in late 1978, is considered one continuous stretch as a rated fighter.

White Contenders (1970–83)	*In Top Ten*	*Out*	*In*
Chuck Wepner	7–2		
Duane Bobick	7–2		
Randy Neumann	0–0	Retired from Top Ten	
Scott LeDoux	1–1	1–0	0–1
Gerry Cooney	4–1	1–0	0–1
Tex Cobb	3–1		
Average >	22–7	2–0	0–2
	= 75.9%	= 100%	= 0%

Black Contenders (1970–83)	*In Top Ten*	*Out*	*In*
George Foreman*	25–2	24–0	2–0
Ron Lyle	20–5–1		
Ken Norton	14–5–1	1–0	0–1
Earnie Shavers	0–1	3–1–1	3–1
Jeff Merritt	0–1		
Larry Middleton	3–1	1–2–1	0–1
Jimmy Young	8–4	2–1	1–0
Larry Holmes*	29–2	6–1	0–1
Johnny Boudreaux	3–2		
Howard Smith	1–1		
Stan Ward	2–1		

Leon Spinks*	1–2	0–0	0–0
Mike Weaver*	10–5–1		
John Tate*	5–2	6–0	1–0
Leroy Jones	0–1		
Michael Dokes*	14–1–2		
Greg Page	13–5		
Marty Monroe	0–1		
James Tillis	2–2	4–1	0–1
Renaldo Snipes	1–4–1		
Tim Witherspoon	23–4	4–0	4–0
Pinklon Thomas	9–3–1		
S.T. Gordon	0–1		
Average >	183–56–7 = 74.4%	51–6–2 = 86.4%	11–5 = 68.8%

This measure indicates an initial advantage for white contenders in the 1950s, which disappeared from the 1960s forward. In their first stint on *The Ring*'s pages, African American heavyweights held onto their perch by winning 77 percent of their bouts, while their white counterparts held the keys to that kingdom by winning only 67 percent of theirs. After being dropped for the first time, the black contenders needed a rate of victory of 7 percentage points higher than the white pugilists to be invited back into the party.

The above trend indicates white boxers having an easier time clinging to their precious ratings and getting through the door again with less effort in the 1950s. This pattern was turned on its head in subsequent periods. In the 1960s, the measures revealed the elite black fighters as having held and re-acquired their place in the Top Ten with similar or lower winning percentages. For instance, their initial place in the ratings was maintained by winning 77 percent of their fights, while 1960s white contenders remained there by defeating 75 percent of their opponents. Clawing their way back into the elite ranks required whites to win 100 percent of their contests, while blacks broke through for the second time having won 84 percent of theirs. African American fighters were not dropped by *The Ring* without a considerably worse winning percentages (70–38 percent) than their counterparts.

The 1970s saw the continuance of this black advantage as whites both held their rated status, and regained it with better records than blacks. Holding their initial ranking and working to regain it a second time was accomplished with better win ratios (76–74 percent, 100–86 percent) than the latter. Taken in their entirety, the numbers reveal *The Ring* showed no evidence from the 1960s forward of pampering white heavyweights while in the rankings, or yanking them in through the door more quickly when they stepped outside. Five of the nine measures indicated black advantage, while four hinted of whites having an easier time.

Opponents' Records

The most comprehensive indicator of a boxer's credentials, although a crude one, is to look at the win-loss record of every single opponent he has fought. One cannot ask a more direct question about the worthiness of a fighter than to analyze the success of the men they beat. Did the white and black heavyweight contingents build their pre-ranking or pre-title fight reputations on the same oppositional foundation? Did they compile their records against opponents with comparable numbers of wins and losses on their own resumes?

Average Records for Opponents of Contenders Upon the Latter's Entry Into *The Ring*'s Top Ten

White Contenders (1949–59)	Opponents' Average Record	Black Contenders (1949–59)	Opponents' Average Record
Bernie Reynolds	13–7–1	Al Hoosman	34–13–2
Gus Lesnevich	39–8–4	Turkey Thompson	28–10–2
Grant Butcher	17–4–2	John Holman	20–6–1
Roland LaStarza	11–7–1	Bob Baker	12–8–1
Rocky Marciano	16–8–1	Clarence Henry	21–7–2
Harry Mathews	24–10–3	Coley Wallace	15–7–1
Dan Bucceroni	14–7–1	Bob Dunlap	14–6–3
Roy Harris	18–7–1	Tommy Harrison	21–6
Pat McMurtry	16–7–1	Bob Satterfield	29–8–2
Mike DeJohn	9–5–1	Jimmy Slade	27–8–2
Charlie Norkus	16–5–1	Archie Moore	37–10–3
Rex Layne	12–6–2	Tommy Jackson	17–4–1
Willie Pastrano	26–8–2	John Summerlin	9–4–1
		Young Jack Johnson	24–12–2
		Harold Carter	13–5–2
		Eddie Machen	12–6–1
		Floyd Patterson	27–11–3
		Zora Folley	13–8–2
		Wayne Bethea	19–5–1
		Harold Johnson	33–11–2
		Sonny Liston	13–6–1
		Charlie Powell	11–9–2
		Tony Anthony	21–8–2
		Alonzo Johnson	12–6–1
		Billy Hunter	12–4–1
		Bill Gilliam	19–6–1
Average > 18–7–2		Average > 20–7–2	
White Contenders (1960–69)		**Black Contenders (1960–69)**	
Tom McNeely	9–6–1	Cleveland Williams	13–8–1
George Logan	19–8–1	Cassius Clay	20–8–1
Jerry Quarry	13–5–1	Billy Daniels	15–5–1

116   Boxing in Black and White

Boone Kirkman	19–10–1	Doug Jones	20–4–1
		Ernie Terrell	14–7–1
		Thad Spencer	13–8–1
		Amos Johnson	11–5–1
		Hubert Hilton	10–4–1
		Elmer Rush	15–6–1
		Amos Lincoln	12–6–1
		Johnny Persol	27–7–1
		Joe Frazier	13–6–1
		Jimmy Ellis	26–10–2
		Leotis Martin	12–9–2
		Buster Mathis	6–5–1
		Henry Clark	18–5–1
		Al Lewis	10–5–1
		Mac Foster	10–8–1
		Al Jones	15–7–1
		Roger Rischer	22–7–2
Average > 15–7–1		Average > 15–7–1	

White Contenders (1970–83)	Opponents' Average Record	Black Contenders (1970–83)	Opponents' Average Record
Chuck Wepner	12–5–1	George Foreman	13–7–1
Duane Bobick	12–9–1	Ron Lyle	15–13–2
Randy Neumann	10–4–1	Ken Norton	11–8–1
Scott LeDoux	17–6–1	Earnie Shavers	10–9–1
Gerry Cooney	9–7–1	Jeff Merritt	8–7–1
Tex Cobb	14–6–1	Larry Middleton	9–6–1
		Jimmy Young	15–5–1
		Larry Holmes	9–6–1
		Johnny Boudreaux	10–10–1
		Howard Smith	12–5–1
		Stan Ward	18–4–1
		Leon Spinks	15–9
		Mike Weaver	12–3
		John Tate	13–9–1
		Leroy Jones	11–6
		Michael Dokes	8–5
		Greg Page	9–3
		Marty Monroe	7–3–1
		James Tillis	11–8–1
		Renaldo Snipes	9–5–1
		Tim Witherspoon	8–3
		Pinklon Thomas	5–5–1
		S.T. Gordon	16–5–1
Average > 12–6–1		Average > 11–6–1	

The record averages above, presented in the appendix at the end of this study, were taken primarily from what was long considered the most reliable source available for boxer's records, *The Ring Record Book and Boxing Encyclopedia* series published annually by *The Ring* from 1942 to 1986. Each year, the magazine's editors would compile up-to-date records for several thousand active boxers around the world. While inaccuracies can occasionally be found in this publication, its records are as accurate as a researcher is ever going to find while studying wins and losses of professional boxers.

The one gap in this data base is that the vast majority of boxers who retired without winning the world championship would disappear from the following year's compendium, without any record of their last fights. Obscure boxers who fought irregularly, or who made brief comebacks from retirement(s), would also have gaps in their careers missing from this source, because only fighters who were officially still active at the end of the previous year (when the record book went to press) were included. The 105 heavyweights who made up this study counted roughly 3,500 fights prior to their inclusion into the ratings or their challenges for the world title.

For approximately 90 percent of the opponents involved in these fights, confirmed, up-to-date records were found for the time when the opponent in question fought against the fighter relevant to this study. For the remaining 10 percent of incomplete or completely missing records, the careers of the boxers in question were consulted through several other sources, including the CyberBoxingZone (*www.cyberboxingzone.com*), BoxRec (*www.boxrec.com*), numerous American newspapers whose sports coverage sometimes included the records of boxers involved in upcoming local fight cards, and many private boxing researchers who generously shared their record collections for the benefit of this study.

Boxing records have always called for cautious interpretation given the inherent temptation for boxers and their handlers to enhance the former's marketability by inflating their wins and *forgetting* losses. Even relying heavily on *The Ring Record Book*, there could be as many as several hundred inaccuracies in this data bank, one too many losses here, one too many draws there. It is believed, however, that the size of the sample is large enough to reduce the distortive effect that such inaccuracies would have on the interpretation of the numbers. After a year of hunting down this data, the researcher senses the records are 90–95 percent accurate. There are roughly 500 fighters below designated as having incomplete or missing records. If the boxers themselves, their surviving relatives, or boxing researchers with corrections, read this, they are encouraged (begged, actually) to send complete and accurate records along to the author in care of the publisher.

The Ring welcomed white and black heavyweights into its ratings with equal credentials by this measure. The average records of both groups' opponents were remarkably similar, indicating no bias whereby white fighters earned rankings by beating inferior opponents as defined by simple wins and losses. The 1950s saw the average white contender join the Top Ten having fought against adversaries with an average record of 18–7–2, while the black contender's past opponents averaged a record of 20–7–2. From 1960 to 1969, the average opponent record for both groups was exactly the same: 15–7–1. The last period saw a white average of 12–6–1, a black one of 11–6–1. Using the crude measure of wins and losses by opponents, there was virtual equality over the entire 1949–83 span for the black and white samples. White heavyweights were no more likely to be invited into the ratings having thrashed a greater ratio of opponents with records like 3–19 or 1–12.

Top Ten Victims

A fighter's record only testifies to his ability against the range of opponents he has faced. Since their sport's lack of any organizational structure forces boxers to find their own opponents, wins and losses can have limited value in objectively measuring skill. The two contestants in virtually any fight share no more than a handful of common opponents. But not only do won-loss records need to be taken with a grain of salt, they can sometimes be misleading. One may have a gaudy record of twenty wins and no losses, and actually be inferior to the seventeen-win and six-loss boxer in the opposite corner, if the latter has been facing stiffer competition. A longstanding boxing practice has been for a young prospect with elite potential to be safely groomed toward the big-time with a steady diet of cannon fodder opponents; these sacrificial lambs are no threat to upset the prospect's promotional apple cart. This is virtually the expected norm today for highly-touted young pugilists, especially for Olympic gold medallists.

The credentials of the boxers in this study must be analyzed qualitatively as well as quantitatively. Their fighting resumes are as much defined by *who* as by *how many*. One or several victories over reputable opponents carries as much weight in knowledgeable fight circles, perhaps even more, than a dozen wins over fighters known in boxing parlance as tomato cans, stiffs, and bums. For example, Joe Frazier began his career with eleven straight victories against opponents whose names would be lost on all but the most obsessive boxing aficionados. Frazier could have spent eternity fighting opponents like Woody Goss and Abe Davis and never come within earshot of the bigtime. Even better wins over past one-time contenders like Doug Jones and Billy Daniels would not have been sufficient to propel Frazier into championship opportunity, since Jones and Daniels were both well past their prime. What rocketed Smokin' Joe into the championship limelight, what separated him from the pack and legitimized his quality, were victories over Oscar Bonavena, Eddie Machen, and George Chuvalo. These fights destroyed any remaining doubts about Frazier's talent in a way that the earlier wins could not. Bonavena was already the heavyweight champion for all of South America, while Chuvalo had challenged Muhammad Ali for the heavyweight title and pushed him the full fifteen rounds. The Machen fight, particularly, symbolized Frazier's transition into the elite ranks. Although Chuvalo and Bonavena were big powerful sluggers, Machen had once been the number one ranked contender in the world, had held his Top Ten ranking for almost a decade (1956–65), and, in spite of being past his prime, still had the boxing savvy and wiliness of a ring technician. At thirty-five, Machen had forgotten more about boxing skill and strategy than most fighters ever know, the kind of know-how that often presents problems for younger boxers moving up the ranks. He had already out-boxed one rising young heavyweight, taking a ten-round decision over Jerry Quarry. When Frazier's management signed to fight Machen, so-called boxing experts had enough reverence for Machen to doubt Frazier's chances.[4] Yet the Philadelphia slugger methodically dissected his more experienced foe. Such a victory proved Frazier to be the *real deal* in the heavyweight division. To use an academic hiring metaphor, beating Machen and the others got Frazier past the phone interview and put him on the shortlist for a tenured teaching position. Such is the case with most elite boxers, their arrival in the spotlight is usually defined by beating a handful of impressive opponents rather than a boatload of unknown ones.

For this reason, any study comparing boxer's qualifications must include a measure of opposition quality. If one can visualize a heavyweight fighter as a hunter, his skill is defined by the big game heads on his study wall, not the deer that is no threat to the hunter. Have elite white and black boxers from 1949 to 1983 had the same number of lions and tigers on their walls when they were presented to the public as elite caliber?

Victories Over Top Ten Opponents By Contenders Ranked by The Ring

White Contenders (1949–59)	Top Ten Victims	Black Contenders (1949–59)	Top Ten Victims
Bernie Reynolds	None	Al Hoosman	None
Gus Lesnevich	Mauriello (2)	Turkey Thompson	Daniels, Rivera
Grant Butcher	Kahut	John Holman	Ray, Thompson
Roland LaStarza	None	Bob Baker	None
Rocky Marciano	LaStarza	Clarence Henry	Holman
Harry Mathews	None	Coley Wallace	None
Dan Bucceroni	LaStarza (2)	Bob Dunlap	Beshore, Brion

Roy Harris	None	Tom Harrison	Bivins (2)
Pat McMurtry	None	Bob Satterfield	Oma, Baker
Mike DeJohn	Miteff	Jim Slade	Henry, Jackson
Charlie Norkus	LaStarza	Archie Moore	Riley, Dunlap
Rex Layne	None		Valdes, Bivins (3)
Willie Pastrano	None		
		Tom Jackson	Henry
		John Summerlin	None
		Young Jack Johnson	Charles
		Harold Carter	None
		Eddie Machen	Valdes
		Floyd Patterson	Slade (2)
		Zora Folley	None
		Wayne Bethea	None
		Harold Johnson	Bivins, Henry
			Charles
			Satterfield
		Sonny Liston	None
		Charlie Powell	Valdes
		Tony Anthony	Alonzo Johnson
		Alonzo Johnson	Valdes
		Billy Hunter	Miteff, Anthony
		Bill Gilliam	None

Average > 8/ 13 = .6   Average > 33/ 26 = 1.3

White Contenders (1960–69)	*Top Ten Victims*	*Black Contenders (1960–69)*	*Top Ten Victims*
Tom McNeely	None	Cleveland Williams	None
George Logan	Lavorante	Cassius Clay	None
Jerry Quarry	None	Billy Daniels	DeJohn
Boone Kirkman	None	Doug Jones	Folley
		Ernie Terrell	Williams
		Thad Spencer	None
		Amos Johnson	None
		Hubert Hilton	None
		Elmer Rush	Machen
		Amos Lincoln	Spencer
		Johnny Persol	Lincoln
		Joe Frazier	Bonavena
		Jimmy Ellis	Persol
		Leotis Martin	None
		Buster Mathis	None
		Henry Clark	None
		Al Lewis	Corletti
		Mac Foster	None
		Al Jones	None
		Roger Rischer	None

Average > 1/ 4 = .3   Average > 9/ 20 = .5

White Contenders (1970–83)	*Top Ten Victims*	*Black Contenders (1970–83)*	*Top Ten Victims*
Chuck Wepner	Terrell	George Foreman	None
Duane Bobick	None	Ron Lyle	None
Randy Neumann	None	Ken Norton	None

Scott LeDoux	None	Earnie Shavers	Ellis
Gerry Cooney	None	Jeff Merritt	Terrell
Tex Cobb	None	Larry Middleton	Bugner
		Jimmy Young	Lyle
		Larry Holmes	None
		Johnny Boudreaux	None
		Howard Smith	Boudreaux
		Stan Ward	None
		Leon Spinks	Righetti
		Mike Weaver	None
		John Tate	None
		Leroy Jones	None
		Michael Dokes	None
		Greg Page	None
		Marty Monroe	None
		James Tillis	None
		Renaldo Snipes	Coetzee
		Tim Witherspoon	None
		Pinklon Thomas	Tillis
		S.T. Gordon	Berbick

Average > 1/ 6 = .2   Average > 9/ 23 = .4

To make it into *The Ring*'s Top Ten, black boxers repeatedly needed more quality victories over men already in the ratings. The significance is that both a career, and the championship hopes that go with it, can be derailed with a single loss. These losses are far more likely to occur when one bites the bullet and signs to fight a ranked contender. An off night, a lucky punch, biased judges who favor an established or hometown contender, even an accidental head butt, can all result in a devastating loss that undercuts a rising contender's marketability, sending him back down the mountain of his profession, where he has to start climbing again. Madison Square Garden's promoters were grooming Johnny Persol toward a title opportunity in 1967, when his career was permanently sidetracked by a shocking one-round knockout at the hands of Kentuckian Jimmy Ellis.[5] In 1951, Harry Mathews was introduced to New York boxing circles as a sensational title prospect who had piled up dozens of victories in the West. Mathews's promotional machine came crashing down when he was knocked out by Rocky Marciano in the second round. Mathews was exposed as a world class light heavyweight, not a championship caliber heavyweight. Having scored knockouts in all of his first twenty-four fights, Mac Foster was being touted as a possible title challenger, but his first real test resulted in a devastating knockout by Jerry Quarry, a loss from which his career never recovered. Thus, the true potential of a would-be prospect is never established until he faces quality opposition, and contenders who have faced more such rivals have traversed a wider mine field, commanding more respect and legitimizing their credentials.

In all three periods, the black men who appeared in the rankings for the first time had risked their careers more often. Completely independent of the racial dynamic shaping this study, the numbers reveal a stark decline in the quality of elite boxers from the middle twentieth century. Becoming ranked has become considerably easier for aspiring boxers than it was five decades ago. Elite heavyweights once had to have far more impressive wins on their calling cards before they were rated by *The Ring*. But even within this general trend of decay in performance, white fighters made it through the door with less rather than more. The thirteen white contenders of the 1950s averaged less than one victory over a Top Ten opponent, while the twenty-five rated black boxers averaged more than double that tally. In the 1960s, the margin almost disappeared as rated blacks had averaged one half of a victory over elite contemporaries, bare percentage points above their white brethren. In the final era, the qualifications of African Americans continued to drop (to .4 such wins), but not as fast as those of whites. Of the seven Caucasian heavyweights ranked from 1970 to 1983, *only one had a single victory over a ranked opponent.* Chuck Wepner entered the rankings with a controversial decision victory over a thirty-four year old Ernie Terrell. The other five white boxers had not climbed a single Top Ten mountain, so to speak, before being included among the world's ten best heavyweights. In the final two sub-periods, both black and white contenders had very few signature triumphs on their records, making this measure less compelling than numerous others. Still, this is yet another statistical variable where blacks had to accomplish more to earn the same opportunity.

Ranking of Previous Opponent

If one can illuminate boxers' credentials by unveiling how many top-notch rivals are on their trophy cases, one can further unveil their credentials by focusing on the most conspicuous fight of all, the last bout before they reached the dual plateaus of Top Ten standing, and a championship challenge. Not having many Top Ten victims would not be as dubious an indictment of a contender's ability, if at the very least, they won impressively over top-notch competition right before they entered the spotlight.

Both *The Ring* magazine and boxing's promotional establishment have a vested interest in presenting contenders and title challengers as valid and worthy. When a name first appears in the rankings, it is *The Ring*'s reputation and readership numbers on the line. When a contender sits before a packed press conference to sign for a title match, the financial backers stand to make more money if the challenger appears more credible. While the above boxers' records will usually be scrutinized in their entirety before the media decide whether to support or denigrate such a bout, their most recent fight will loom larger than any other. To reach rated status or a championship bout, a pugilist is supposed to have progressed, to have improved drastically over their career. This creates the expectation they have been fighting generally tougher opposition along the way, and the reasonable assumption that their most recent bout, if not the hardest, would have at least been a stiff test. This last bout before hitting the big time is what makes up the minds of *The Ring*'s editors (for inclusion in the rankings) and the sport's governing bodies (to sanction their challenge for the title) that such fighters have arrived, have proved themselves worthy of the next career step upward.

Every boxer in this sample fought an ostensibly "worthy" opponent in order to be ranked or awarded a title shot. What does this array of penultimate opponents reveal about the quality of the subject fighters? How many of the former were rated pugilists themselves, and how many were unknown quantities, who simply represented another line on the latter's record? In short, before they became rated or secured the ultimate boxing opportunity, how many of the elite boxer's final opponents were ranked in the Top Ten themselves? What was the average ranking of the opponents who were rated? With these measures, one again expects comparable numbers for white and black pugilists.

Ranking of Last Opponent Fought by Contenders Before Being Ranked by *The Ring*

White Contenders (1949–59)	Previous Oppt and Ranking	Black Contenders (1949–59)	Previous Oppt and Ranking
Bernie Reynolds	Hafer (UNR)	Al Hoosman	Spaulding (UNR)
Gus Lesnevich	Maxim (5)	Turkey Thompson	Spaulding (UNR)
Grant Butcher	Whitlock (UNR)	John Holman	Thompson (3)
Roland LaStarza	Brion (UNR)	Bob Baker	Payne (UNR)
Rocky Marciano	LaStarza (10)	Clarence Henry	Holman (10)
Harry Mathews	Layne (UNR)	Coley Wallace	Wilson (UNR)
Dan Bucceroni	Jones (UNR)	Bob Dunlap	Brion (6)
Roy Harris	Baker (4)	Tom Harrison	Bivins (9)
Pat McMurtry	Romero (UNR)	Bob Satterfield	Baker (4)
Mike DeJohn	Miteff (8)	Jim Slade	Jackson (3)
Charlie Norkus	LaStarza (8)	Archie Moore	Valdes (1)
Rex Layne	Thompson (UNR)	Tommy Jackson	Henry (8)
Willie Pastrano	Layne (UNR)	John Summerlin	Cab (UNR)
		Young Jack Johnson	Charles (UNR)
		Harold Carter	Satterfield (8)
		Eddie Machen	Valdes (6)
		Floyd Patterson	Williams (UNR)
		Zora Folley	Bethea (UNR)
		Wayne Bethea	Folley (10)
		Harold Johnson	Satterfield (6)
		Sonny Liston	Daniels (UNR)

		Charlie Powell	Valdes (2)
		Tony Anthony	Johnson (10)
		Alonzo Johnson	Valdes (6)
		Billy Hunter	Anthony (9)
		Bill Gilliam	Morrow (UNR)

Average > 35/ 5 = 7
Unranked Opponents > 8/ 13

Average > 101/ 16 = 6.3
Unranked Opponents > 10/ 26

White Contenders (1960–69)	*Previous Oppt and Ranking*	*Black Contenders (1960–69)*	*Previous Oppt and Ranking*
Tom McNeely	Logan (UNR)	Cleveland Williams	Miteff (7)
George Logan	Lavorante (4)	Cassius Clay	Besmanoff (UNR)
Jerry Quarry	Patterson (3)	Billy Daniels	DeJohn (10)
Boone Kirkman	Copeland (UNR)	Doug Jones	Folley (3)
		Ernie Terrell	Williams (4)
		Thad Spencer	Daniels (UNR)
		Amos Johnson	Gorman (UNR)
		Hubert Hilton	Bodell (UNR)
		Elmer Rush	Herring (UNR)
		Amos Lincoln	Spencer (4)
		Johnny Persol	Lincoln (3)
		Joe Frazier	Machen (UNR)
		Jimmy Ellis	Persol (10)
		Leotis Martin	Daniels (UNR)
		Buster Mathis	DeBruyn (UNR)
		Henry Clark	Martin (UNR)
		Al Lewis	Corletti (9)
		Mac Foster	Spencer (UNR)
		Al Jones	O'Halloran (UNR)
		Roger Rischer	Cooper (UNR)

Average > 7/2 = 3.5
Unranked Opponents > 2/ 4

Average > 50/ 8 = 6.3
Unranked Opponents > 12/ 20

White Contenders (1970–83)	*Previous Oppt and Ranking*	*Black Contenders (1970–83)*	*Previous Oppt and Ranking*
Chuck Wepner	Terrell (7)	George Foreman	Johnson (UNR)
Duane Bobick	Neumann (UNR)	Ron Lyle	Rondon (UNR)
Randy Neumann	Bobick (UNR)	Ken Norton	Woody (UNR)
Scott LeDoux	Norton (6)	Earnie Shavers	Ellis (5)
Gerry Cooney	Dennis (UNR)	Jeff Merritt	Stander (UNR)
Tex Cobb	Terrell (UNR)	Larry Middleton	Bugner (10)
		Jimmy Young	Lyle (3)
		Larry Holmes	Gholston (UNR)
		Johnny Boudreaux	Atlas (UNR)
		Howard Smith	Boudreaux (6)
		Stan Ward	Merritt (UNR)
		Leon Spinks	Righetti (7)
		Mike Weaver	Ward (UNR)
		John Tate	Bobick (UNR)
		Leroy Jones	Beattie (UNR)
		Michael Dokes	Tripp (UNR)
		Greg Page	Alexander (UNR)

	Marty Monroe	Lopez (UNR)
	James Tillis	Fischer (UNR)
	Renaldo Snipes	Coetzee (6)
	Tim Witherspoon	Acosta (UNR)
	Pinklon Thomas	Tillis (7)
	S.T. Gordon	Berbick (3)
Average > 13/ 2 = 6.5	Average > 47/ 8 = 5.9	
Unranked Opponents > 4/ 6	Unranked Opponents > 15/ 23	

In regard to the quality of their last opponent before the big time, the white contenders became ranked after winning their previous contests against better quality rivals in two of the three eras, but the difference seems slight in both. In the 1950s, the average penultimate victim of a newly-minted white contender was ranked at the seventh spot, marginally more impressive than the boxers most recently dispatched by black boxers (6.3) rated by *The Ring*. In the years 1970 to 1983, the gap (6.5 to 5.9) again testified to a small advantage in white opportunity. The conclusive value of these findings must be weighed against the results from the 1960s, in which black contenders on average received their first ranking after beating opponents sitting above six in the Top Ten, while the two white fighters broke in after conquering adversaries rated almost three spots (3.5) better. Any infatuation with a Great White Hope is not strongly supported by the caliber of the most recent victim on white and black fighting résumés.

There was no clear pattern, as well, with the number of unranked victims in the most recent bout of white and black contenders. In the 1950s, white heavies were far more likely to show up on *The Ring*'s pages having just beaten an unranked rival, eight of thirteen having done so compared to only ten of twenty-five African American fighters. This scenario was reversed in the 1960s when two of the four white contenders found recognition with a somewhat dubious conquest in their immediate past, while more than half (12 of 20) of the black contenders did the same. The two group's performance were almost identical from 1970 forward, as four of six white contenders received their coronation after beating an unranked rival, while fifteen of twenty-three black fighters did the same.

The investigation of the above variables revealed an unexpectedly compelling statistic. The abnormally lucky heavyweight who gained entry into the rankings in spite of not winning his most recent bout was far more likely to be white. Such recognition would logically demand a very impressive effort, perhaps a decision loss to or draw with an already rated opponent. Very few boxers in this study have enjoyed this scenario, but since 1960, all three who did have been white. There was virtual equality from 1950 to 1959 as one of thirteen (7 percent) white fighters (Lesnevich, who lost to Maxim) and two of twenty-five (8 percent) black heavyweights (Carter, who drew with Satterfield, and Bethea who lost to Folley) became ranked without winning their previous fight. From 1960 to 1969, one of the four white contenders, Jerry Quarry, became rated after drawing with former heavyweight king Floyd Patterson. All of the twenty black contenders in this decade had victories before they became Top Ten pugilists. Two of the six white fighters entering the ratings from 1970 onward impressed the judges enough without winning to become rated, Randy Neumann in spite of being knocked out by Duane Bobick, Scott LeDoux by scoring a draw with an aging Ken Norton. Not one of the twenty-three black boxers cleared such a hurdle, all of them won to unlock the last door into the elite grouping. Three of the last ten white contenders did not need a win to become rated in this study, while none of the forty-three rated African Americans since 1960 had the same privilege!

5. For All the Marbles

EDDIE GRIFFIN: Behind every strong black man, there's what?
NEIL PATRICK HARRIS: A lot of slow white athletes?

— *Undercover Brother*, 2002

White and black heavyweights pursuing rated, contender status in *The Ring* took similar paths between 1949 and 1983. The measures presented in the previous chapter showed as many statistical comparisons where blacks had lesser credentials as ones showing white advantage. At that level of success, boxing was color blind in meting out opportunity. An entirely different story emerges from analyzing the numbers of those even more select boxers who fought for the world heavyweight championship over these thirty-five years. Breaking into the Top Ten rankings is signified by a boxer walking the last few steps to the pot of gold at the end of the rainbow. Actually opening the last door to the treasure is the opportunity to challenge the world titleholder. Here, although it would be an exaggeration to use the historic metaphor of a white door and a black door, African American heavyweights had to work through a larger ring of keys before entering the Broadway stage of professional boxing: a world title fight opportunity.

Number of Fights

That blacks were becoming ranked with an equal or sometimes smaller number of fights than whites was undoubtedly a positive sign of progress in that skin color was not preventing them from reaching this plateau. But long after Joe Louis was on the golf links, black heavyweights needed a bigger final push to boxing fame and wealth, in the form of having more fights on their resumes. From 1949 to 1959, white challengers for the crown averaged a healthy fifty-three contests before they landed a title bout. The black heavyweights averaged a staggering eighty-four matches to reach a fight for the belt.

A difference of thirty-one fights separating the white and black challengers is glaring when one considers the sacrifice and preparation that goes into a single boxing match, as well as the punishment fighters take in the ring. In the 1950s, thirty-one fights represented a sizable chunk of most boxers' careers. Many pugilists today do not even fight this many times in their entire career. The pain, sweat, and concentration expended on a single match, multiplied thirty-one times, indicates a huge discrepancy in white versus black opportunity. The forces shaping opportunity for heavyweight boxers in America were clearly holding the bar higher for blacks than whites. The former had to punch and be punched many more times for a chance at the crown.

This discrepancy did not disappear after 1959. In the 1960s, there was still a significant chasm separating how much work black and white fighters had to log in the ring before their big title chance. The only four white challengers in this decade — Tom McNeely, Dave Zyglewicz, and Jerry Quarry (twice) — were deemed title-worthy after an average of thirty bouts. Their sixteen black counterparts needed forty-two fights to enjoy the same privilege. A fighter's marketability can decline with one fluke loss; one lucky punch by an opponent can forever derail title dreams. Career-ending injuries can be inflicted by the most overmatched opponent. Even twelve extra fights, then, represent a huge minefield that can eliminate a boxer from title contention. As in the previous decade, who can say how many deserving black boxers were sifted from the title chase within this twelve-fight discrepancy? Breaking into the Top Ten with ten or thirteen fewer bouts is an advantage, but the number of fighters historically stranded at this level, never to fight for the championship, make the former statistic seem dwarfed by the significance of the latter discrepancy. By the 1970–83 era, a more equitable scenario had developed. Twenty-seven African Americans challenged for the championship with an average of thirty-three contests behind them. Seven white fighters vied for the crown with twenty-nine fights' experience. Much of the discrepancy had evaporated, but it still worked in favor of white heavyweights.

Average Number of Fights for World Title Challengers

White Challengers (1949–59)		Black Challengers (1949–59)	
Gus Lesnevich	76	Ezzard Charles	69
Pat Valentino	56	Joe Walcott	60
Freddie Beshore	37	Joe Louis	61
Nick Barone	52	Joe Walcott	67
Lee Oma	92	Joe Walcott	68
Joey Maxim	95	Ezzard Charles	82
Rocky Marciano	42	Joe Walcott	71

5. For All the Marbles

Roland LaStarza	56		Ezzard Charles	97
Pete Rademacher	0		Ezzard Charles	98
Roy Harris	23		Archie Moore	173
			Floyd Patterson	31
			Archie Moore	185
			Tommy Jackson	35
Average >	53		Average >	84

White Challengers (1960–69)

Black Challengers (1960–69)

Tom McNeely	23		Sonny Liston	34
Jerry Quarry	31		Floyd Patterson	37
Dave Zyglewicz	29		Cassius Clay	19
Jerry Quarry	37		Sonny Liston	37
			Floyd Patterson	41
			Ernie Terrell	40
			Eddie Machen	52
			Doug Jones	36
			Floyd Patterson	53
			Cleveland Williams	71
			Ernie Terrell	43
			Zora Folley	85
			Jimmy Ellis	30
			Joe Frazier	19
			Buster Mathis	23
			Floyd Patterson	47
Average	30		Average	42

White Challengers (1970–83)

Black Challengers (1970–83)

Terry Daniels	33		Joe Frazier	24
Ron Stander	25		Jimmy Ellis	30
Chuck Wepner	41		Bob Foster	45
Scott LeDoux	38		Muhammad Ali	31
Gerry Cooney	25		George Foreman	37
Randy Cobb	23		Ken Norton	32
Scott Frank	21		Muhammad Ali	46
			Ron Lyle	34
			Joe Frazier	34
			Jimmy Young	23
			Ken Norton	40
			Earnie Shavers	58
			Leon Spinks	7
			Muhammad Ali	58
			Larry Holmes	27
			Mike Weaver	27
			Earnie Shavers	65
			Leroy Jones	25
			Muhammad Ali	59
			Leon Spinks	14
			Renaldo Snipes	22
			Tim Witherspoon	15
			John Tate	19
			Mike Weaver	30

		James Tillis	20
		Michael Dokes	26
		Mike Weaver	34
Average	29	Average	33

Average Record

Not only did they need more contests to reach a title fight, black heavyweights carried better win-loss records into the championship spotlight. In all three periods, one finds black fighters bringing better records to a title fight than white ones. From 1949 to 1959, black title challengers were introduced to fans with an average record of 70–11–2, while the average for white ones was 43–8–2. In terms of winning percentage, needing twenty-seven more wins to enjoy the same career privilege is glaring. In the years 1960 to 1969, the advantage was still in favor of white heavyweights, but the margin had become infinitesimal. Both groups met for the world championship having won about 90 percent of their bouts. In the next thirteen years, the pendulum swung back in favor of white pugilists again. Black challengers between 1970 and 1983 averaged a record of 30–3, while the white title opponents had logged a tally of 25–3–1 on the night of their big chance. Five extra wins could loom very large in assessing the credentials of the two groups, depending on the quality of competition.

In two of the three periods, the total cumulative winning percentages of the black title contestants were noticeably higher, the numbers being a virtual dead heat in the third.

Average Win-Loss-Draw Record of Title Challengers

White Challengers (1949–59)	Wins-Losses -Draws	Black Challengers (1949–59)	Wins-Losses -Draws
Gus Lesnevich	58–13–5	Ezzard Charles	63–5–1
Pat Valentino	42–10–4	Joe Walcott	46–13–1
Freddie Beshore	29–6–2	Joe Louis	60–1
Nick Barone	43–8–1	Joe Walcott	51–15–1
Lee Oma	63–26–3	Joe Walcott	51–16–1
Joey Maxim	75–16–4	Ezzard Charles	75–6–1
Rocky Marciano	42–0	Joe Walcott	53–17–1
Roland LaStarza	53–3	Ezzard Charles	86–10–1
Pete Rademacher	0–0	Archie Moore	144–20–8
Roy Harris	23–0	Floyd Patterson	30–1
		Archie Moore	156–21–8
		Tommy Jackson	27–4–1
Average	43–8–2 (81%)	Average	70–11–2 (85%)

White Challengers (1960–69)	Wins-Losses -Draws	Black Challengers (1960–69)	Wins-Losses -Draws
Tom McNeely	23–0	Floyd Patterson	35–2
Jerry Quarry	26–1–4	Sonny Liston	33–1

5. For All the Marbles

Dave Zyglewicz	28–1	Floyd Patterson	38–3
Jerry Quarry	31–2–4	Cassius Clay	19–0
		Sonny Liston	35–2
		Ernie Terrell	36–4
		Eddie Machen	46–4–2
		Floyd Patterson	43–4
		Doug Jones	29–6–1
		Cleveland Williams	65–5–1
		Ernie Terrell	39–4
		Zora Folley	74–7–4
		Jimmy Ellis	25–5
		Joe Frazier	19–0
		Buster Mathis	23–0
		Floyd Patterson	46–6–1
Average	27–1–2 (90%)	Average	38–3–1 (91%)

White Challengers (1970–83)	Wins-Losses -Draws	Black Challengers (1970–83)	Wins-Losses -Draws
Terry Daniels	28–4–1	Joe Frazier	24–0
Ron Stander	23–3–1	Jimmy Ellis	27–5
Chuck Wepner	30–9–2	Bob Foster	41–4
Scott Ledoux	26–8–4	Muhammad Ali	31–0
Gerry Cooney	25–0	George Foreman	37–0
Randy Cobb	21–2	Ken Norton	30–2
Scott Frank	20–0–1	Muhammad Ali	44–2
		Ron Lyle	31–2–1
		Joe Frazier	32–2
		Jimmy Young	17–4–2
		Ken Norton	37–3
		Earnie Shavers	52–5–1
		Leon Spinks	6–0–1
		Muhammad Ali	55–3
		Larry Holmes	27–0
		Mike Weaver	19–8
		Earnie Shavers	57–7–1
		Leroy Jones	24–0–1
		Muhammad Ali	56–3
		Leon Spinks	10–2–2
		Renaldo Snipes	22–0
		Tim Witherspoon	15–0
		John Tate	19–0
		Mike Weaver	21–9
		James Tillis	20–0
		Michael Dokes	25–0–1
		Mike Weaver	24–10
Average >	25–3–1 (86%)	Average >	30— 3 (91%)

Average Winning Percentage Per Fighter

The wide variation in the number of fights for each boxer again raised the possibility of statistical distortion, and calls for closer analysis in which all fighters are weighed equally, by averaging their individual winning percentages. But even placing equal value on each individual fighter's record, one still finds black heavyweights having won a greater percentage of their contests in all three time frames.

Average Winning Percentage of Title Challengers

White Challengers (1949–59)	Percentage	Black Challengers (1949–59)	Percentage
Gus Lesnevich	74.4	Ezzard Charles	91.3
Pat Valentino	75	Joe Walcott	76.7
Freddie Beshore	78.4	Joe Louis	98.4
Nick Barone	82.7	Joe Walcott	76.1
Lee Oma	68.5	Joe Walcott	75
Joey Maxim	78.9	Ezzard Charles	91.4
Rocky Marciano	100	Joe Walcott	74.6
Roland LaStarza	94.6	Ezzard Charles	88.5
Roy Harris	100	Ezzard Charles	87.6
		Archie Moore	83.7
		Floyd Patterson	96.8
		Archie Moore	84.3
		Tommy Jackson	86.5
Average	83.6 %	Average	85.5%

*Pete Rademacher, who fought for the world title in his first professional fight, represents a statistical anomaly. With some of the measures used, the validity of including Rademacher's non-existent record is questionable. It is easy enough to include figures of zero for his number of fights, wins-losses-draws, knockouts, Top Ten victims, entries into the Top Ten, time spent waiting in the ratings for his title shot, length of career in months, as well as his age, status as an unranked challenger, and his performance in defeat. It would be less meaningful to include averages that do not exist, like average individual winning percentage, KO percentage, his rate of previous fighting (none), average ranking when fighting for the title and the ratio of ranked contenders who challenged (he was not ranked), as well as ranked and unranked previous opponents and opponents' average record, for he had none.

White Challengers (1960–69)	Percentage	Black Challengers (1960–69)	Percentage
Tom McNeely	100	Sonny Liston	97.1
Jerry Quarry	83.9	Floyd Patterson	94.6
Dave Zyglewicz	96.6	Cassius Clay	100
Jerry Quarry	83.8	Sonny Liston	94.6
		Floyd Patterson	92.7
		Ernie Terrell	90
		Eddie Machen	87
		Doug Jones	80.6
		Floyd Patterson	86.8
		Cleveland Williams	91.5
		Ernie Terrell	90.7
		Zora Folley	87.1
		Jimmy Ellis	83.3
		Joe Frazier	100
		Buster Mathis	100
		Floyd Patterson	91.5
Average	91.1%	Average	92%

White Challengers (1970–83)	Percentage	Black Challengers (1970–83)	Percentage
Terry Daniels	84.8	Joe Frazier	100
Ron Stander	92	Jimmy Ellis	84.4
Chuck Wepner	73.2	Bob Foster	91.1
Scott LeDoux	68.4	Muhammad Ali	100
Gerry Cooney	100	George Foreman	100
Scott Frank	95.2	Ken Norton	93.8
		Muhammad Ali	95.7
		Ron Lyle	91.2
		Joe Frazier	94.1
		Jimmy Young	73.9
		Ken Norton	92.5
		Earnie Shavers	89.7
		Leon Spinks	85.7
		Muhammad Ali	94.8
		Larry Holmes	100
		Mike Weaver	70.4
		Earnie Shavers	87.7
		Leroy Jones	96
		Muhammad Ali	94.9
		Leon Spinks	71.4
		Renaldo Snipes	100
		Tim Witherspoon	100
		John Tate	100
		Mike Weaver	70
		James Tillis	100
		Michael Dokes	96.2
		Mike Weaver	70.6
Average	86.4%	Average	90.5%

The privilege of being a world title challenger consistently called for a better record from aspiring blacks than whites. Across the three periods, the average pugilist from the former had outperformed the latter, 86 percent to 84 percent (1949–59), 92 percent to 91 percent (1960–69), and 91 percent to 86 percent (1970–83). The margins may not seem not large enough to constitute a significant discrepancy in opportunity, as it seems unlikely there was a pool of black fighters stranded on the beach between the white and black figures, at least in the first two periods. That all three periods saw black heavyweights having better credentials, and by a growing margin in the third time frame, is compelling, especially when one remembers that the difference of one loss has often been sufficient to forever deny a contender a title fight opportunity.

Knockouts

In each of the sub-periods, white challengers enjoyed the privilege with fewer knockouts than black ones. In the first decade of the post–Louis era, the margin was huge, with the average black vying for the crown with forty-eight KO's on their calling cards, more than twice the performance of the average white. Even when one removes the seeming anomalies of the ancient Archie Moore, the black sample's average is still more than double (43 to 21) the white figure. The gap shrank considerably in subsequent decades, but the black challengers still held a noticeable margin, twenty-five to sixteen in the 1960s, twenty-two to eighteen in the 1970s and early 1980s. Winning impressively by stopping one's opponents as often as possible seemed a safer bet for African Americans dreaming of title glory. No amount of judge's racial bias can wake up an unconscious white hope before the count of ten.

Knockouts Scored by World Title Challengers

White Challengers (1949–59)	KO's	Black Challengers (1949–59)	KO's
Gus Lesnevich	21	Ezzard Charles	41
Pat Valentino	20	Joe Walcott	28
Freddie Beshore	8	Joe Louis	51
Nick Barone	21	Joe Walcott	32
Lee Oma	28	Joe Walcott	32
Joey Maxim	20	Ezzard Charles	48
Rocky Marciano	37	Joe Walcott	33
Roland LaStarza	24	Ezzard Charles	55
Roy Harris	9	Ezzard Charles	55
		Archie Moore	105
		Floyd Patterson	21
		Archie Moore	113
		Tommy Jackson	13
Average >	188/9 = 21	Average	627/13 = 48

White Challengers (1960–69)	KO's	Black Challengers (1960–69)	KO's
Tom McNeely	18	Floyd Patterson	26
Jerry Quarry	15	Sonny Liston	23
Dave Zyglewicz	14	Floyd Patterson	29
Jerry Quarry	18	Cassius Clay	15
		Sonny Liston	25
		Ernie Terrell	18
		Eddie Machen	29
		Doug Jones	19
		Floyd Patterson	32
		Cleveland Williams	51
		Ernie Terrell	18
		Zora Folley	40
		Jimmy Ellis	12
		Joe Frazier	17
		Buster Mathis	17
		Floyd Patterson	35
Average	65/4 = 16	Average	406/16 = 25

White Challengers (1970–83)	KO's	Black Challengers (1970–83)	KO's
Terry Daniels	25	Joe Frazier	21
Ron Stander	15	Jimmy Ellis	12
Chuck Wepner	12	Bob Foster	35
Scott LeDoux	17	Muhammad Ali	25
Gerry Cooney	22	George Foreman	34
Randy Cobb	19	Ken Norton	23
Scott Frank	14	Muhammad Ali	31
		Ron Lyle	21
		Joe Frazier	27
		Jimmy Young	5
		Ken Norton	30
		Earnie Shavers	50
		Leon Spinks	5
		Muhammad Ali	37
		Larry Holmes	19
		Mike Weaver	13
		Earnie Shavers	55
		Leroy Jones	12
		Muhammad Ali	37
		Leon Spinks	8
		Renaldo Snipes	11
		Tim Witherspoon	11
		John Tate	15
		Mike Weaver	14
		James Tillis	16
		Michael Dokes	14
		Mike Weaver	15
Average	124/7 = 18	Average	596/27 = 22

Individual Knockout Rate

Placing equal weight on each of the fighters makes no difference in comparing the two group's knockout credentials. White heavyweights also fought their way into championship showdowns with a lower ratio of knockouts. In the 1950s, black challengers confronted the reigning champion having KO percentages more than 17 percent higher than white ones. This discrepancy cannot be glossed over in what it reveals about the nature of the black and white challengers in the 1950s. The black ones were emphatically winning, stopping their opponents well more than half of the time, the white ones were not even finishing two of every five rivals inside the distance. The 1960s saw this margin shrink to 7 percent, and the gap still existed through the last period, although it had dropped to 2 percent. Blacks needed to win more impressively than whites to reach their sport's final destination.

Knockout Percentage of World Title Challengers

White Challengers (1949–59)	KO Percentage	Black Challengers (1949–59)	KO Percentage
Gus Lesnevich	21/76 = 27.6	Ezzard Charles	41/69 = 60.3

Pat Valentino	20/56 = 35.7	Joe Walcott	28/60 = 46.7
Freddie Beshore	8/37 = 22.2	Joe Louis	51/61 = 83.6
Nick Barone	21/52 = 40.4	Joe Walcott	32/67 = 47.8
Lee Oma	28/92 = 30.4	Joe Walcott	32/68 = 47.1
Joey Maxim	20/95 = 21.1	Ezzard Charles	48/82 = 58.5
Rocky Marciano	37/42 = 88.1	Joe Walcott	33/71 = 46.5
Roland LaStarza	24/56 = 42.9	Ezzard Charles	55/97 = 57.3
Roy Harris	9/23 = 39.1	Ezzard Charles	55/98 = 56.7
		Archie Moore	105/173 = 60.7
		Floyd Patterson	21/31 = 67.7
		Archie Moore	113/185 = 61.1
		Tommy Jackson	13/35 = 37.1
Average	38.6%	Average	56.2%

White Challengers (1960–69)	KO Percentage	Black Challengers (1960–69)	KO Percentage
Tom McNeely	18/23 = 78.3	Sonny Liston	23/34 = 67.6
Jerry Quarry	15/31 = 48.4	Floyd Patterson	26/37 = 70.3
Dave Zyglewicz	14/29 = 48.3	Cassius Clay	15/19 = 78.9
Jerry Quarry	18/37 = 48.6	Sonny Liston	25/37 = 67.6
		Floyd Patterson	29/41 = 70.7
		Ernie Terrell	18/40 = 45
		Eddie Machen	29/52 = 55.8
		Doug Jones	19/36 = 52.8
		Floyd Patterson	32/47 = 68.1
		Cleveland Williams	51/71 = 71.8
		Ernie Terrell	18/43 = 41.9
		Zora Folley	40/85 = 47.1
		Jimmy Ellis	12/30 = 40
		Joe Frazier	21/24 = 87.5
		Buster Mathis	17/23 = 73.9
		Floyd Patterson	35/52 = 67.3
Average	55.9%	Average	62.8%

White Challengers (1970–83)	KO Percentage	Black Challengers (1970–83)	KO Percentage
Terry Daniels	25/33 = 75.8	Joe Frazier	21/24 = 87.5
Ron Stander	15/25 = 60	Jimmy Ellis	12/32 = 37.5
Chuck Wepner	12/41 = 29.3	Bob Foster	35/45 = 77.8
Scott LeDoux	17/38 = 44.7	Muhammad Ali	25/31 = 80.6
Gerry Cooney	22/25 = 88	George Foreman	34/37 = 91.9
Randy Cobb	19/23 = 82.6	Ken Norton	23/32 = 71.9
Scott Frank	14/25 = 66.7	Muhammad Ali	31/46 = 68.9
		Ron Lyle	21/34 = 61.8
		Joe Frazier	27/34 = 79.4
		Jimmy Young	5/23 = 21.7
		Ken Norton	30/40 = 75
		Earnie Shavers	50/58 = 86.2
		Leon Spinks	5/7 = 71.4
		Muhammad Ali	37/58 = 63.8
		Larry Holmes	19/27 = 70.4
		Mike Weaver	13/27 = 48.2
		Earnie Shavers	55/65 = 84.6
		Leroy Jones	12/25 = 48

		Muhammad Ali	37/59 = 62.7
		Leon Spinks	8/14 = 57.1
		Renaldo Snipes	11/22 = 50
		Tim Witherspoon	11/15 = 73.3
		John Tate	15/19 = 78.9
		Mike Weaver	14/30 = 46.7
		James Tillis	16/20 = 80
		Michael Dokes	14/26 = 53.8
		Mike Weaver	15/34 = 44.1
Average	63.9 %	Average	65. 7%

Age

The black fighters who challenged for the title were also older than the corresponding white boxers in all three time frames. In the first post–Louis decade, the difference was five years (34 years to 29 years), followed by a margin of four years and two months (28 years, six months versus 24 years, four months) in the 1960s. These represent huge discrepancies within the parameters of a typical boxing career. In far less than four years, many boxers decline from world class reputation to *opponent* status, as the once highly-regarded fighter reduced to a stepping stone adversary for young prospects on the way up. That black heavyweight title challengers were four to five years older than white ones over a twenty-year span was a huge obstacle for the former's attempts to reach boxing's pot of gold.

Through the early 1980s, the discrepancy was still significant, with the six white challengers averaging twenty-eight years, seven months, versus twenty-nine years and one month for the twenty-seven black contestants. The ever-present temptation to retire from such a demanding sport makes even an six-month gap significant in the number of black boxers who left the sport from 1970 to 1983, perhaps oblivious to a big opportunity that might have been just around the corner.

Average Age of World Title Challengers

White Challengers (1949–59)	Born	Fought for Title	Age
Gus Lesnevich	2/22/15	8/10/49	34/5
Pat Valentino	1/25/20	10/14/49	29/9
Freddie Beshore	9/22/22	7/15/50	27/10
Nick Barone	6/12/26	12/5/50	24/6
Lee Oma	3/?/16	1/12/51	35
Joey Maxim	3/28/22	5/30/51	29/2
Rocky Marciano	9/1/23	9/23/52	29/1
Roland LaStarza	5/12/27	9/24/53	26/4
Pete Rademacher	8/20/28	8/22/57	29
Roy Harris	6/29/33	7/18/58	25/1

Average 29 years

Black Challengers (1949–59)	Born	Fought for Title	Age
Ezzard Charles	7/7/21	6/22/49	27/11
Joe Walcott	1/31/14	6/22/49	35/5
Joe Louis	5/13/14	9/27/50	36/4
Joe Walcott	1/31/14	3/7/51	37/1
Joe Walcott	1/31/14	7/18/51	37/6
Ezzard Charles	7/7/21	6/5/52	30/11
Joe Walcott	1/31/14	5/15/53	39/3
Ezzard Charles	7/7/21	6/17/54	32/11
Ezzard Charles	7/7/21	9/17/54	33/2
Archie Moore	12/13/13	9/21/55	41/9
Floyd Patterson	1/4/35	11/30/56	21/11
Archie Moore	12/13/13	11/30/56	43
Tommy Jackson	7.9/31	7/29/57	26/1

Average 34 years

White Challengers (1960–69)	Born	Fought for Title	Age
Tom McNeely	2/27/37	12/4/61	24/9
Jerry Quarry	5/15/45	4/27/68	22/11
Dave Zyglewicz	9/23/43	4/22/69	25/7
Jerry Quarry	5/15/45	6/23/69	24/1

Average 24 years, 4 months

Black Challengers (1960–69)	Born	Fought for Title	Age
Floyd Patterson	1/4/35	6/20/60	25/6
Sonny Liston	5/8/32	9/25/62	30/5
Cassius Clay	1/17/42	2/25/64	22/1
Sonny Liston	5/8/32	5/25/65	33/1
Floyd Patterson	1/4/35	7/22/63	28/7
Ernie Terrell	4/4/39	3/5/65	25/11
Eddie Machen	7/15/32	3/5/65	32/8
Floyd Patterson	1/4/35	11/22/65	30/11
Doug Jones	2/27/37	6/28/66	29/4
Cleveland Williams	6/30/33	11/14/66	33/4
Ernie Terrell	4/4/39	2/6/67	27/10
Zora Folley	5/27/32	3/22/67	24/10
Jimmy Ellis	2/24/40	4/27/68	28/2
Joe Frazier	1/12/44	3/4/68	24/2
Buster Mathis	6/5/44	3/4/68	23/9
Floyd Patterson	1/4/35	9/14/68	33/8

Average 28 years, 6 months

White Challengers (1970–83)	Born	Fought for Title	Age
Terry Daniels	5/1/46	1/15/72	25/8
Ron Stander	10/17/44	5/25/72	27/7
Chuck Wepner	2/26/39	3/24/75	36/1
Scott LeDoux	1/7/49	7/7/80	31/6
Gerry Cooney	7/24/56	6/11/82	25/11
Scott Frank	3/30/58	9/10/83	25/5

Average 28 years, 7 months

Black Challengers (1970–83)	Born	Fought for Title	Age
Joe Frazier	1/12/44	2/16/70	26/1
Jimmy Ellis	2/24/40	2/16/70	30
Bob Foster	12/15/38	11/18/70	31/11
Muhammad Ali	1/17/42	3/8/71	29/2
George Foreman	1/22/48	1/22/73	25
Ken Norton	7/9/45	3/25/74	28/9
Muhammad Ali	1/17/42	10/30/74	32/9
Ron Lyle	2/11/42	4/23/71	29/2
Joe Frazier	1/12/44	10/1/75	31/9
Jimmy Young	11/14/48	4/30/76	27/5
Ken Norton	8/9/45	9/28/76	31/3
Earnie Shavers	7/31/45	9/29/77	32/2
Leon Spinks	7/11/53	2/15/78	24/7
Muhammad Ali	1/17/42	9/15/78	36/8
Larry Holmes	11/3/49	6/9/78	28/7
Mike Weaver	6/14/52	6/22/79	27
Earnie Shavers	7/31/45	9/28/79	34/2
Leroy Jones	2/10/50	3/31/80	30/2
Muhammad Ali	1/17/42	10/2/80	38/8
Leon Spinks	7/11/53	6/12/81	27/11
Renaldo Snipes	7/15/56	11/6/81	25/4
Tim Witherspoon	12/27/57	5/20/83	25/5
John Tate	1/29/55	10/20/79	24/9
Mike Weaver	6/14/52	3/31/80	27/10
James Tillis	7/5/57	10/3/81	24/3
Michael Dokes	7/10/58	12/10/82	24/5
Mike Weaver	6/14/52	5/20/83	30/11

Average 29 years, 1 month

Career Length

Black contenders were no worse off for the years they put in to break into the elite. Once they were there, however, becoming a challenger for the heavyweight title was an entirely different struggle. There was a yawning chasm between the career lengths of white and black challengers across the thirty-five year period, and this gap was still significant in the last sub-period. The 1949–1959 time frame saw a glaring discrepancy between the two races, white boxers landing title shots after only seven years and four months as professionals, black challengers averaging fifteen years and three months, a difference of almost eight years! Obviously, this discovery is partially an extension of the above measure revealing black 1950s challengers to be six years older than their white contemporaries. But to fully appreciate the fundamental difference between the background of white and black challengers at this time, one should emphasize the names of the men who vied for the title. Six fighters stood on the black side of the ledger. Floyd Patterson (four years, three months) and Tommy Jackson (five years) are the only two with what could be called average or short career lengths before their championship fight. In boxing terms, however, these men were relative babies compared to the other four African Americans who tried to win the world title. Joe Louis, Archie Moore, Ezzard Charles, and Joe Walcott, represent an almost ancient old guard of title challengers, accounting for eleven of the thirteen 1950s title challenges by black fighters. Walcott and Moore could each be called the Satchel Paige of boxing, representing two of the most famous stories of perseverance and patience in boxing history, both beginning their careers in the 1930s, doggedly honing their skills through years of being frozen out of the title picture. Like Paige, they were ready for their moment in the spotlight when opportunity finally knocked. That both men were able to fight competitively, by the time the championship door opened for them, was a remarkable accomplishment. Walcott won the heavyweight title on his fifth attempt, Moore claimed the light heavyweight crown and held it for a decade, in addition to challenging twice for the heavyweight title. For years, these two men had to fight and win on the margins of the boxing world until they were overqualified (or overripe) in their credentials to challenge for world supremacy. They had paid so many dues for so long, the powers that controlled boxing must have been too embarrassed to permanently leave them out in the cold.

In addition to Walcott and Moore, Ezzard Charles challenged for the title four times between the ninth and fifteenth years of his career, and Joe Louis unwisely defied the clock in an attempt to win back the belt sixteen years after his first fight. Thirteen opportunities to fight for the championship were allotted to African American men in the first ten years after Joe Louis stepped down, *but only six different black men actually received the privilege,* men who had been proving themselves in the ring for an average of over fifteen years. Ten different white men challenged for the title during this span. That each white challenger fought for the championship once, while men like Charles and Walcott were allowed through this door four times each, speaks volumes about the meting out of boxing opportunity in the immediate afterglow of the Joe Louis years. Being given multiple title fight chances does not mean Charles and Walcott were done any favors. These opportunities were the least their sport could have offered, for they earned them through hard-won credentials, patience, and their performance in the ring the first time they fought for the title. Walcott beat Louis in the ring in their 1947 showdown, then lost the crown minutes later in an embarrassingly slanted judge's decision for the Brown Bomber. Charles dominated Walcott two years later when they contested Louis's abandoned crown.

These numbers reflect a strong tendency of the boxing establishment to look longer and harder for talented young white contenders than black ones. With black title challenges made almost exclusively by aging veteran fighters, one must sadly ask how many qualified up-and-coming black heavyweights were left waiting while their careers passed in the 1950s? Can we believe there were no worthy title challengers among men like Bob Dunlap, Coley Wallace, Bob Baker, and Al Hoosman? Could one viable opponent for the champion not be found among Clarence Henry, Bob Satterfield, Jimmy Slade, and Johnny Summerlin. Were Charlie Powell, Tony Anthony, Alonzo Johnson, and Billy Hunter, all inferior to every white challenger in this decade? Were none of these twelve men at least as able as Pete Rademacher, who challenged Floyd Patterson on August 22, 1957, with credentials of having won the Olympic gold medal the previous year. This white opponent fought for the world heavyweight championship in his first professional fight! Joe Frazier, Muhammad Ali, Floyd Patterson, George Foreman, and Leon Spinks all won gold medals, but still had to earn their professional stripes the hard way, starting out in the general ranks of the division, and proving themselves with multiple victories for slowly increasing purses.

From the early 1960s to the early 1980s, this gap in the career lengths of white and black challengers did not disappear. The margin continued to be in favor of the former, whose average career was five years and seven months shorter from 1960 to 1969, and still two years shorter in the period 1970 to 1983. For thirty-five years beginning with the retirement of Joe Louis, the average white championship contestant was introduced to the crowd at a significantly earlier stage in their career then black challengers. Black heavyweights were stuck in a slower waiting room than white ones.

Career Length of Title Challengers

White Challengers (1949–59)	Pro Debut	Title Fight	Interval
Gus Lesnevich	5/5/34	8/10/49	15/3
Pat Valentino	1/15/40	10/14/49	9/9
Freddie Beshore	12/?/42*	7/15/50	7/7
Nick Barone	6/7/46	12/5/50	4/6
Lee Oma	11/13/39	1/12/51	11/2
Joey Maxim	1/13/41	5/30/51	10/5
Rocky Marciano	3/17/47	9/23/52	5/6
Roland LaStarza	7/7/47	9/24/53	6/3
Pete Rademacher	8/22/57	8/22/57	0
Roy Harris	4/26/55	7/18/55	3/3

Average 7 years, 4 months

*Beshore's first fight is listed only as being in December, 1942, in Philadelphia.

Black Challengers (1949–59)	Pro Debut	Title Fight	Interval
Ezzard Charles	3/15/40	6/22/49	9/3
Joe Walcott	9/9/30	6/22/49	18/9
Joe Louis	7/4/34	9/27/50	16/3
Joe Walcott	9/9/30	3/7/51	20/6
Joe Walcott	9/9/30	7/18/51	20/11
Ezzard Charles	3/15/40	6/5/52	12/3
Joe Walcott	9/9/30	5/15/53	22/8

	Pro Debut	Title Fight	Interval
Ezzard Charles	3/15/40	6/17/54	14/3
Ezzard Charles	3/15/40	9/17/54	14/6
Archie Moore	7/14/36	9/21/55	19/2
Floyd Patterson	9/12/52	11/30/56	4/3
Archie Moore	7/14/36	11/30/56	20/5
Tommy Jackson	7/14/52	7/29/57	5/0

Average 15 years, 3 months

White Challengers (1960–69)	*Pro Debut*	*Title Fight*	*Interval*
Tom McNeely	7/17/58	12/4/61	3/5
Jerry Quarry	5/7/65	4/27/68	3/0
Dave Zyglewicz	4/26/65	4/22/69	4/0
Jerry Quarry	5/7/65	6/23/69	4/2

Average 3 years, 8 months

Black Challengers (1960–69)	*Pro Debut*	*Title Fight*	*Interval*
Floyd Patterson	9/12/52	6/20/60	7/9
Sonny Liston	9/2/53	9/25/62	9/1
Floyd Patterson	9/12/52	7/22/63	10/10
Cassius Clay	10/29/60	2/25/64	3/4
Sonny Liston	9/2/53	5/25/65	11/9
Floyd Patterson	9/12/52	11/22/65	13/2
Ernie Terrell	5/15/57	3/5/65	7/10
Eddie Machen	3/22/55	3/5/65	9/11
Doug Jones	7/28/58	6/28/66	7/11
Cleveland Williams	12/22/51	11/14/66	14/11
Ernie Terrell	5/15/57	2/6/67	9/9
Zora Folley	9/22/53	3/22/67	13/6
Jimmy Ellis	4/19/61	4/27/68	7/0
Joe Frazier	7/16/65	3/4/68	2/8
Buster Mathis	6/28/65	3/4/68	2/8
Floyd Patterson	9/12/52	9/14/68	16/0

Average 9 years, 3 months

White Challengers (1970–83)	*Pro Debut*	*Title Fight*	*Interval*
Terry Daniels	2/10/69	1/15/72	2/11
Ron Stander	7/31/69	5/25/72	2/10
Chuck Wepner	7/5/64	3/24/75	10/9
Scott LeDoux	2/4/74	7/7/80	6/3
Gerry Cooney	2/15/77	6/11/82	5/4
Randy Cobb	1/21/77	11/26/82	5/10
Scott Frank	5/2/78	9/10/83	5/4

Average 5 years, 7 months

Black Challengers (1970–83)	*Pro Debut*	*Title Fight*	*Interval*
Joe Frazier	7/16/65	2/16/70	4/7
Jimmy Ellis	4/19/61	2/16/70	8/10
Bob Foster	3/27/61	11/18/70	9/8
Muhammad Ali	10/29/60	3/8/71	10/4

George Foreman	6/23/69	1/22/73	3/7
Ken Norton	11/14/67	3/25/74	6/4
Muhammad Ali	10/29/60	10/30/74	14
Ron Lyle	4/23/71	5/16/75	5/1
Joe Frazier	7/16/65	10/1/75	10/2
Jimmy Young	6/22/69	4/30/76	6/0
Ken Norton	11/14/67	9/28/76	8/10
Earnie Shavers	11/6/69	9/29/77	7/11
Leon Spinks	1/15/77	2/15/78	1/1
Muhammad Ali	10/29/60	9/15/78	17/11
Larry Holmes	3/21/73	6/9/78	5/3
Mike Weaver	9/14/72	6/22/79	6/9
Earnie Shavers	11/6/79	9/28/79	9/11
John Tate	5/7/77	10/20/79	2/5
Leroy Jones	7/30/73	3/31/80	6/8
Muhammad Ali	10/29/60	10/2/80	19/11
Mike Weaver	9/14/72	3/31/80	7/7
Leon Spinks	1/15/77	6/12/81	4/5
James Tillis	11/18/78	10/3/81	2/10
Renaldo Snipes	11/18/78	11/6/81	3
Michael Dokes	10/15/76	12/10/82	6/2
Tim Witherspoon	10/30/79	5/20/83	4/7
Mike Weaver	9/14/72	5/20/83	10/8

Average 7 years, 7 months

Immediate Top Ten Waiting Period

Another valid time frame for consideration is how long ranked challengers spent cooling their heels in the Top Ten before they were selected as championship combatants. If a Great White Hope meant little or nothing to white fans during the years 1949–1983, one would anticipate that rated black and white heavyweights would wait comparable periods before their turn came up. The cream, so to speak, would rise to the top equally fast, no matter its shade. If skill, performance and other non-racial factors (even corrupt, political ones) were what determined how long a stint boxers endured in the rankings, the average number of months a contender held their Top Ten status would be equitable, regardless of a fighter's race. If black heavyweights have been kept in a slower lineup taking the final step from ranked stature to a title opportunity, however, one would believe they have experienced the *glass ceiling* so often decried by women and minorities in America, a ceiling which narrows upward advancement to less than what it should fairly be.

Months Spent in Top Ten by Challengers Before Title Fight

White Challengers (1949–59)	*Months between Previous Ranking and First Title Challenge*	*Black Challengers (1949–59)*	*Months between Previous Ranking and First Title Challenge*
Gus Lesnevich	2	Ezzard Charles	9

Pat Valentino	12	Archie Moore	4
Joey Maxim	11	Floyd Patterson	6
Rocky Marciano	23	Tommy Jackson	40
Roland LaStarza	31		
Roy Harris	15		
Average	15.7	Average	14.8

There are multiple fighters in this study who fought for the world title several times after entering the ratings, some after unsuccessful first challenges, others after winning and then losing the title. Other boxers were dropped from the ratings and then re-entered before fighting for the title. Still others fought for the title, were dropped from the rankings, and then fought their way back into Top Ten status and another championship bout. All of these situations represent confounding variables that distort the simple question of how long white and black contenders wait on average for a title fight. For a valid measure of the waiting period experienced by heavyweights in the ratings before a championship opportunity, the only boxers who can be considered are those who fought for the title for *the first time* measured against their *immediately previous entry* into the Top Ten.

White Challengers (1960–69)	*Months between Previous Ranking and First Title Challenge*	*Black Challengers (1960–69)*	*Months between Previous Ranking and First Title Challenge*
Tom McNeely	10	Sonny Liston	49
Jerry Quarry	9	Ernie Terrell	45
		Eddie Machen	18
		Doug Jones	8
		Cleveland Williams	6
		Zora Folley	123
		Jimmy Ellis	8
		Joe Frazier	12
		Buster Mathis	1
Average 9.5		Average 30	

White Challengers (1970–83)	*Months between Previous Ranking and First Title Challenge*	*Black Challengers (1970–83)*	*Months between Previous Ranking and First Title Challenge*
Chuck Wepner	20	George Foreman	32
Scott LeDoux	3	Ken Norton	18
Gerry Cooney	31	Ron Lyle	33
Randy Cobb	13	Jimmy Young	13
		Earnie Shavers	6
		Larry Holmes	29
		Mike Weaver	5
		Leroy Jones	8
		Renaldo Snipes	1

Tim Witherspoon	13
John Tate	8
James Tillis	6
Michael Dokes	34
Average 15. 8	

Average 16.8

Black heavyweights usually had to wait no longer in *The Ring*'s ratings than white heavyweights before landing a title shot. In both the 1950s and the 1970s, black contenders had slightly shorter stints in the Top Ten waiting for their big chance. This indicates no conscious or unconscious racial bias on the part of boxing authorities and promoters to handpick white title challengers more quickly from the rankings than black heavyweights. Only in the 1960s was there a large advantage in favor of whites, with the average black title contestant having been rated more than three times as long as white ones. This discrepancy can only partly be explained by the legal troubles that blocked Sonny Liston from title contention. There is no white challenger in the entire study who had to sit in the ratings for as long as the ten-plus years Zora Folley waited for a championship bout. For a decade, this black Arizonan was left stranded just below boxing's summit. He waited longer for a championship fight than the total wait of white challengers in any of the three sub-periods!

Taken together, there is a general trend of white and black contenders having the same gestation period, so to speak, before receiving the ultimate opportunity. The glaring anomaly of Folley, however, is consistent with the broader trend revealed by many of this study's other measures. It is difficult to imagine a white contender being overlooked for title bouts this long.

Total Waiting Periods and Number of Top Ten Visits

One can take the above measure a step further by asking how many *total months* each challenger had under their belt when they fought for the heavyweight championship. Every single month spent in the rankings can be thought of as an elite caliber accomplishment for a boxer. As such, the total amount of time spent in the ratings over these boxer's entire careers, is a rough approximation of how many dues they paid for a title opportunity. One would expect that a heavyweight who had been in the ratings for a total duration of two to three years was more deserving and qualified for a championship challenge than one who had been ranked for five months. Do we find comparable numbers for black and white pugilists in this regard?

The black challengers across this study were emphatically more qualified in terms of the total number of months they had logged in the Top Ten ratings before their title fight opportunities. In all three eras, they had accumulated much more time in the elite class then their white counterparts.

From 1949 to 1959, they had spent more than twelve months longer (32.5 to 20.3 months) as ranked contenders, more than three times longer in the 1960s (33.5 to 10.4 months), and almost twice as long (19.4 to 10.3) after 1970. With this measure, tickets to the heavyweight championship ball had to be validated several times over by black fighters. The white challengers seemed to have barely parked their cars in the Top Ten before being waved through the championship receiving line.

Total Months Spent in Top Ten by Challengers Before Title Fight

White Challengers (1949–59)	Total Months	Black Challengers (1949–59)	Total Months
Gus Lesnevich	2	Ezzard Charles	12
Pat Valentino	26	Joe Walcott	46
Freddie Beshore	1	Joe Walcott	67
Nick Barone	0	Joe Walcott	70
Lee Oma	47	Archie Moore	4
Joey Maxim	48	Floyd Patterson	6
Rocky Marciano	27	Archie Moore	16
Roland LaStarza	38	Tommy Jackson	40
Pete Rademacher	0		
Roy Harris	14		
Average 20.3		Average 32.5	

Many of the champions in this study received title fight opportunities after they themselves had lost the title. Such scenarios undermine the validity of this measure, meant to isolate the worthiness of title challenger credentials based on their longevity in the Top Ten rankings. When former champions vie to win back their titles, the opportunity they receive is at least partially a result of their former prestige as an ex-champion. It is impossible to measure how much of a title fight opportunity for an ex-champ is the result of the former versus the latter, so those challenges by former titleholders will be excluded for this portion of the study. Only those challengers who were fighting for the championship for the first time, and those who had previously challenged unsuccessfully for the crown are considered.

White Challengers (1960–69)	Total Months	Total Black Challengers (1960–69)	Total Months
Tom McNeely	10	Sonny Liston	49
Jerry Quarry	9	Cassius Clay	25
Dave Zyglewicz	0	Ernie Terrell	22
Jerry Quarry	23	Eddie Machen	101
		Doug Jones	36
		Cleveland Williams	53
		Zora Folley	123
		Jimmy Ellis	11
		Joe Frazier	13

White Challengers (1970–83)	Total Months	Black Challengers (1970–83)	Total Months
		Buster Mathis	1
Average 10.5		Average 33.4	
Terry Daniels	0	George Foreman	32
Ron Stander	0	Ken Norton	18
Chuck Wepner	20	Ron Lyle	33
Scott LeDoux	8	Jimmy Young	12
Gerry Cooney	31	Ken Norton	49
Randy Cobb	13	Earnie Shavers	28
Scott Frank	0	Leon Spinks	2
		Larry Holmes	29
		Mike Weaver	5
		Earnie Shavers	42
		Leroy Jones	8
		Renaldo Snipes	1
		Tim Witherspoon	13
		John Tate	8
		Mike Weaver	14
		James Tillis	6
		Michael Dokes	30
Average 10.3		Average 19.4	

The numbers do not strongly support a consistent racial preference by boxing powers in choosing white heavyweights from *The Ring*'s Top Ten list, based on the number of times the magazine included them in its ratings.

The corresponding contender's measure compared the number of times heavyweights entered the ratings, assuming more entries by white fighters could mean a greater receptiveness on the part of *The Ring*'s editors for a future white champion. Like all the other challenger criteria in this study, the number of Top Ten entries, to whatever extent it can accurately measure racial dynamics in boxing, hones in on the promotional and governing powers shaping the opportunity of championship fights. There is no way of proving, much less quantifying, cooperation between this magazine and the power brokers of the sport. It is indisputable that for much of the 1949–1983 time period the writers, editors, and publishers of *The Ring* and the most dominant promoters and commissioners in boxing numbered more whites than blacks. Prior to the 1970s one would be hard-pressed to identify an influential black power figure in boxing (journalist, promoter or governing official) other than Don King. Furthermore, this study found examples where long-time contenders were conveniently slotted into a high Top Ten ranking concurrently with their signing of a contract to fight for the title, indicating a sometimes cozy, mutually back-scratching relationship between Nat Fleischer's monthly periodical and the world governing bodies that approved championship bouts.

One still cannot assume either *The Ring* or boxing commissions were completely beholden to the opinion of the other in recognizing heavyweight talent, *even if both shared a bias* (conscious or unconscious) in favor or white heavies. They could not have been completely on the same page in meting out opportunity, for *The Ring* was not uniformly supportive of all challengers sanctioned by the governing bodies for title fights, white or black. The magazine did not automatically allow its rankings to be used as a shill to legitimize championship promotions. It ranked Sonny Liston as the number one contender in the world for over two years before he finally broke through the legal and political barriers blocking his quest for a title fight.

With this in mind, the above measure, the number of Top Ten stints by each challenger before their title fight, must be interpreted differently from the analysis of how many visits into the rankings were made by the contenders. With the title challengers, more entries into the ratings were assumed to be possible evidence of a *racial bias in favor of white heavyweights*, of *The Ring* promoting (unconsciously, perhaps) white boxers as viable champions to a white audience. With this statistic, a greater number of entries into the Top Ten before landing a title fight must be seen as the lot of a disadvantaged heavyweight forced to pay higher dues on the penultimate plateau below boxing's promised land, *possibly because of their skin color*. By the time a fighter finally lands a championship fight, their having multiple visits in and out of the ratings raises the possibility that the boxing world had subjected them to an unfairly long wait before a title fight. If the average black title challenger had to enter the Top Ten more often than their white brethren, one must conclude the sport's establishment was more confident about promoting white challengers than black ones.

From this vantage point, the numbers send a mixed message. In the 1950s, white challengers averaged more than two sojourns in the Top Ten before getting a title fight opportunity, almost double that of the black heavies. The light-heavyweight Joey Maxim was inserted into the ratings by a fawning *Ring* on ten separate occasions, practically screaming of a racial infatuation, of a desire to groom a Great White Hope for Joe Louis's eventual retirement. Yet this bias did not extend to the powers actually shaping who got to fight for Louis title's in his twilight years. Maxim did not fight for Charles's championship until he had been ranked ten separate times.

From the 1960s through the early 1980s, the tables turned and it was the black contenders who were ranked considerably more often before getting their big chance. In both eras, the average African American had been in the Top Ten more than once while the average Caucasian had been ranked on less than a single occasion. The statistical trend over time for this measure was moving in favor of whites fighting for the title with fewer entries into the ratings.

5. For All the Marbles

Number of Top Ten Entries by World Title Challengers

White Challengers (1949–59)	Top Ten Visits	Black Challengers (1949–59)	Top Ten Visits
Gus Lesnevich	1	Ezzard Charles	2
Pat Valentino	2	Joe Walcott	1
Freddie Beshore	1	Joe Walcott	1
Nick Barone	0	Joe Walcott	1
Lee Oma	2	Archie Moore	1
Joey Maxim	10	Floyd Patterson	1
Rocky Marciano	2	Archie Moore	1
Roland LaStarza	2	Tommy Jackson	1
Pete Rademacher	0		
Roy Harris	1		
Average	2.1	Average	1.1

White Challengers (1960–69)	Top Ten Visits	Black Challengers (1960–69)	Top Ten Visits
Tom McNeely	1	Sonny Liston	1
Jerry Quarry	1	Cassius Clay	1
Dave Zyglewicz	0	Ernie Terrell	1
Jerry Quarry	1	Eddie Machen	2
		Doug Jones	2
		Cleveland Williams	2
		Zora Folley	1
		Jimmy Ellis	2
		Joe Frazier	2
		Buster Mathis	1
Average	.8	Average	1.5

White Challengers (1970–83)	Top Ten Visits	Black Challengers (1970–83)	Top Ten Visits
Terry Daniels	0	George Foreman	1
Ron Stander	0	Ken Norton	1
Chuck Wepner	1	Ron Lyle	1
Scott Ledoux	2	Jimmy Young	1
Gerry Cooney	1	Ken Norton	1
Randy Cobb	1	Earnie Shavers	3
Scott Frank	0	Leon Spinks	2
		Larry Holmes	1
		Mike Weaver	1
		Earnie Shavers	4
		Leroy Jones	1
		Renaldo Snipes	1
		Tim Witherspoon	1
		John Tate	1
		Mike Weaver	1
		James Tillis	1
		Michael Dokes	1
Average	.7	Average	1.4

Rate of Fighting Activity

The challenger's samples reveal no advantage to being white in the rate of fighting one undertook on the way to the heavyweight championship. In all three time frames, the numbers suggest the white fighters to have been more motivated and active in competitive activity. They fought at markedly higher monthly rates in the 1950s (1 fight per 1.7 months versus 1 every 2.3 months for black fighters) and 1960s (1 per 1.5 months versus 1 for 2.3 months), and were still competing at a slightly more consistent rate (2.3 to 2.4) in the final period. As with the contender's data, white challengers, at the very least, did not get an easier ride in terms of their rate of boxing activity.

Rate of Fighting by World Title Challengers

White Challengers (1949–59)	Months between Fights	Black Challengers (1949–59)	Months between Fights
Gus Lesnevich	183/77 = 2.4	Ezzard Charles	111/69 = 1.6
Pat Valentino	117/57 = 2.1	Joe Walcott	225/60 = 3.8
Freddie Beshore	92/37 = 2.5	Joe Walcott	20/7 = 2.9
Nick Barone	54/53 = 1.0	Joe Walcott	4/1 = 4
Lee Oma	134/93 = 1.4	Archie Moore	244/185 = 1.3
Joey Maxim	125/96 = 1.3	Archie Moore	14/12 = 1.2
Rocky Marciano	66/43 = 1.5	Floyd Patterson	51/31 = 1.7
Roland LaStarza	75/57 = 1.3	Tommy Jackson	60/323 = 1.7
Roy Harris	40/24 = 1.7		
Average	1.7 months	Average	2.3 months

As this is another measure aimed at determining how hard contenders have worked to receive their title shot, title challenges by former champions will be excluded. Normally, world champion boxers fight considerably less often than other boxers. Having spent years climbing the ranks of their profession, champions only defend their title a few times per year. With every defense, a champion risks losing the title he has worked so long to achieve. Most champions are tempted to enjoy their newfound wealth, an indulgence that makes the physical commitment of training a greater challenge. The time spent by fighters as champions represents a statistical aberration for the purposes of this measure, not consistent with the normal activity of a hungry, upwardly mobile contender. These periods of relative inactivity would count far more against the black subject group since all but one of the world champions since 1949 were black, and the only white titleholder, Marciano, retired as champion for good in 1956, never attempting to win back his title. Thus only challenges by those fighters who had never previously won the title

5. For All the Marbles

will be considered, a sample that will include two boxers who fought at least twice before winning the championship (Weaver and Walcott), and three more (Norton, Shavers, Moore) who challenged twice without winning the crown in the ring. The rate of fighting (months/bouts) for these five boxer's second or third challenges was measured from their previous unsuccessful title contests. For example, Archie Moore's rate of fighting for his 1956 title fight with Floyd Patterson was calculated by dividing the time elapsed from his 1955 challenge of champion Rocky Marciano (14 months) by the number of contests (12) he fought from that fight forward to the night he challenged Patterson.

White Challengers (1960–69)	*Months Between Fights*	*Black Challengers (1960–69)*	*Months Between Fights*
Tom McNeely	41/24 = 1.7	Sonny Liston	109/35 = 3.1
Jerry Quarry	36/32 = 1.1	Cassius Clay	40/20 = 2.0
Dave Zyglewicz	48/30 = 1.6	Ernie Terrell	94/41 = 2.3
Jerry Quarry	62/38 = 1.6	Eddie Machen	119/53 = 2.2
		Doug Jones	95/37 = 2.6
		Cleveland Williams	179/72 = 2.5
		Zora Folley	162/86 = 1.9
		Jimmy Ellis	84/31 = 2.7
		Joe Frazier	31/20 = 1.6
		Buster Mathis	33/24 = 1.4
Average	1.5 months	Average	2.3 months

White Challengers (1970–83)	*Months between Fights*	*Black Challengers (1970–83)*	*Months between Fights*
Terry Daniels	35/34 = 1.0	Bob Foster	116/46 = 2.5
Ron Stander	34/26 = 1.3	George Foreman	43/38 = 1.1
Chuck Wepner	129/42 = 3.1	Ken Norton	76/33 = 2.3
Scott LeDoux	77/38 = 2.0	Ron Lyle	49/35 = 1.4
Gerry Cooney	64/26 = 2.5	Jimmy Young	82/24 = 2.4
Randy Cobb	70/24 = 2.9	Ken Norton	30/8 = 3.8
Scott Frank	65/22 = 3.0	Earnie Shavers	95/59 = 1.6
		Leon Spinks	13/8 = 1.6
		Larry Holmes	63/28 = 2.3
		Mike Weaver	81/28 = 2.9
		Earnie Shavers	24/7 = 3.4
		Leroy Jones	80/26 = 3.1
		Renaldo Snipes	36/23 = 1.6
		Tim Witherspoon	43/16 = 2.7
		John Tate	29/20 = 1.5
		Mike Weaver	16/4 = 4
		James Tillis	34/21 = 1.6
		Michael Dokes	74/27 = 2.7
Average	2.3 months	Average	2.4 months

Ranking of Challengers

Since a higher-ranked contender is ostensibly a more qualified and deserving challenger for the title, one must look at the rankings of those who vied for the championship to provide further insight into boxing opportunity. The boxing public wants to see exciting, competitive fights when the champion decides to defend their crown. This logically dictates a higher-ranked contender over a lower one. One does not expect the tenth-ranked contender to be as capable a challenger, as great a threat to the champion, as the number one ranked heavyweight. Have black and white heavyweights had to climb to similar rungs before they could reap the opportunity and financial benefit of a title challenge? In a sport whose audience no longer yearned for a white hero, one would expect the typical black and white challengers to come from comparable average positionings in the rankings. This would be a higher average spot if world champions were risking their title the way the public wanted, or a lower one when such titleholders were more intent on hoarding their titles by fighting weak opposition. Where, then, in the Top Ten, does one find the average white and black challenger for the heavyweight crown over the 1949–83 period?

It is equally revealing to consider how many of the black and white challengers were not even in the rankings when they received the improbable opportunity of a title chance. Such fighters are a rare breed to enjoy this unearned largesse. Have such white and black boxers been equally rare?

Average Ranking by *The Ring* of Challengers Fighting for Title

White Challengers (1949–59)	Ranking	Black Challengers (1949–59)	Ranking
Gus Lesnevich	7	Ezzard Charles	1
Pat Valentino	7	Joe Walcott	2
Freddie Beshore	Unranked	Joe Louis	Unranked
Nick Barone	Unranked	Joe Walcott	6
Lee Oma	4	Joe Walcott	2
Joey Maxim	3	Ezzard Charles	1
Rocky Marciano	1	Joe Walcott	1
Roland LaStarza	1	Ezzard Charles	1
Pete Rademacher	Unranked	Ezzard Charles	1
Roy Harris	5	Archie Moore	1
		Floyd Patterson	2
		Archie Moore	1
		Tommy Jackson	3
Average	28/7 = 4	Average	22/12 = 1.8
Unranked	Challengers 3/10	Unranked	Challengers 1/13

White Challengers (1960–69)	Ranking	Black Challengers (1960–69)	Ranking
Tom McNeely	9	Floyd Patterson	3

Jerry Quarry	2	Sonny Liston	1
Dave Zyglewicz	Unranked	Floyd Patterson	1
Jerry Quarry	3	Cassius Clay	1
		Sonny Liston	1
		Floyd Patterson	1
		Ernie Terrell	3
		Eddie Machen	9
		Doug Jones	2
		Cleveland Williams	4
		Ernie Terrell	1
		Zora Folley	2
		Jimmy Ellis	3
		Joe Frazier	1
		Buster Mathis	10
		Floyd Patterson	Unranked
Average	14/3 = 4.7	Average	43/15 = 2.9
Unranked Challengers	1/4	Unranked Challengers	1/16

White Challengers (1970–83)	*Ranking*	*Black Challengers (1970–83)*	*Ranking*
Terry Daniels	Unranked	Joe Frazier	1
Ron Stander	Unranked	Jimmy Ellis	3
Chuck Wepner	9	Bob Foster	Unranked
Scott LeDoux	10	Muhammad Ali	1
Gerry Cooney	3	George Foreman	2
Randy Cobb	9	Ken Norton	4
Scott Frank	Unranked	Muhammad Ali	1
		Ron Lyle	8
		Joe Frazier	2
		Jimmy Young	3
		Ken Norton	2
		Earnie Shavers	6
		Leon Spinks	Unranked
		Muhammad Ali	1
		Larry Holmes	3
		Mike Weaver	8
		Earnie Shavers	3
		Leroy Jones	6
		Muhammad Ali	5
		Leon Spinks	3
		Renaldo Snipes	10
		Tim Witherspoon	10
		John Tate	3
		Mike Weaver	3
		James Tillis	8
		Michael Dokes	1
		Mike Weaver	2
Average	31/4 = 7.8	Average	99/25 = 4
Unranked	Challengers 3/7	Unranked	Challengers 2/27

It can be emphatically stated that black contenders from 1949 to 1983 have had to climb much higher in the Top Ten ratings to receive a title fight opportunity than white ones. The average ranking of black challengers was markedly better than the latter in all three eras. White challengers in the

1950s averaged a ranking of 4.0 in the Top Ten, while there was a mean of 1.8 for the black title contestants. The gap narrowed only slightly in the 1960s, with a 4.7 rating for the black contingent and 2.9 for whites. In the 1970s and early 1980s, however, the margin grew larger than ever, with white challengers averaging 7.8 in the Top Ten, while the measure was 4.0 for the black ones. The promotional powers that chose title combatants, the media that encouraged the selections, and the mostly white public that accepted them, created a scenario whereby white challengers were plucked from clearly lower echelons of the ratings.

The incidence of dubious, unranked contenders vying for the title further reveals a trend in favor of white opportunity. Three of the ten white contenders from 1949 to 1959, Nick Barone, Fred Beshore, and Pete Rademacher, were not even on *The Ring*'s Top Ten list. Beshore had been out of the ratings for seventeen months when he challenged Ezzard Charles in the summer of 1950. Even more eye-opening is that Barone and Rademacher were not only unranked when they fought against Charles and Patterson, respectively, *they never entered the Top Ten in their entire careers after that!* In August 1950, Bob Baker and Clarence Henry were ranked sixth and tenth respectively. Neither had ever fought for the title, or would ever do so. They did, however, witness Ezzard Charles defend against the unranked Beshore. This scenario was painfully repeated again four months later, when Barone vaulted over the entire Top Ten into boxing's greatest payday. In 1957, while Patterson sought out amateur star Pete Rademacher as a challenger, a rated black American contender like Bob Satterfield would never fight for the championship. Nor would Larry Middleton, an African American heavyweight who was rated in 1972, at the time when both Daniels and Stander were given the red carpet treatment to fight for Frazier's title.

There were, at the time of both fights, ranked white heavyweights who were snubbed in favor of Beshore and Barone (Woodcock, Baksi, Layne, Savold), and Rademacher (McMurtry and Pastrano). These, however, were white contenders passed over by black champions in favor of less threatening white opponents. They were unfairly rebuffed, to be sure, but it was never black boxers who crashed the gate in front of them, something that would need to be the case at least a few times to support the idea that race meant nothing in pursuing championship opportunities.

Only one of the thirteen black challengers had the windfall of fighting for the title without being ranked. That was one Joe Louis, former heavyweight champion of the world through twelve years and twenty-five defenses, even then popularly recognized as the greatest heavyweight king ever. Louis changed his mind about retirement a year after giving up his crown, and signed to fight his successor, Ezzard Charles. If anyone deserved the benefit of the doubt, if any fighter was entitled to go to the front of the championship line without slogging through the rankings over many months, it was Louis. He had paid his dues like few heavyweights ever had. One cannot easily rationalize Barone, Beshore, and Rademacher's unusual opportunities without remembering they were white.

In the 1960s, having white skin again greatly increased one's chances of fighting for the title without being rated. The entire decade saw one black and one white challenger who were unranked. But there were only four white heavyweights who cracked the Top Ten in this decade, a ratio four times better than ratio of one unranked black challenger from a group of sixteen rated African American boxers. The difference becomes even more glaring when one considers the identities of the white and black challengers. The black heavyweight who leapfrogged over ten contemporaries into a 1968 Stockholm showdown with Jimmy Ellis was Floyd Patterson, who not only was a former champion, but the first and only heavyweight at that time who had regained the title. However mediocre a champion Patterson had been compared to Louis, Liston, Frazier, and Ali, he still had the acumen and experience of a fighter who had competed against some of the world's best, a heavyweight who had paid his dues over sixteen years of combat. Patterson's legitimacy was further confirmed by his performance that night when, at thirty-three, he pushed the much younger champion Ellis to the distance and broke the latter's nose. Ellis won a hotly-disputed decision to keep his title.

The white challenger, in marked contrast, was Dave Zyglewicz, who in 1969 signed to fight the other splinter champion, Smokin' Joe Frazier. Zyglewicz's record was impressive on paper. He carried twenty-eight wins and only one loss when he entered the Astrodome that night. But his list of opponents included perhaps two recognizable names, former contenders Billy Daniels and Willie Besmanoff, long past their prime fighters who had forty-seven losses between them when they faced Ziggy. Dave Zyglewicz showed a bravery that few of his critics possessed, choosing to slug it out with Frazier from the opening bell. He was no Floyd Patterson, however, and it showed. Frazier ended his opponent's evening at ninety-six seconds of the first round.[1] Like Barone and Rademacher before him, Zyglewicz never found a home in the Top Ten ratings, even though he continued to fight for many years after his fifteen minutes of fame (minus thirteen minutes and twenty-four seconds) against Smoking Joe. In his next two fights, he lost and drew with two opponents, Charlie Polite and Willis Earls, who had fewer wins than losses on their records.

The same scenario unfolded from 1970 to 1983. No matter how great their talent or potential, almost all African American heavyweights had to reach a title fight the hard way. Only two of the twenty-seven black challengers were unranked, a minuscule ratio compared to the three out of seven unranked white challengers. The performances of the two sub-groups again demonstrated the only credible unrated challenger to be on the black side of the ledger. Light heavyweight champion Bob Foster was clearly in over his head when he moved up in weight class against heavyweight champion Joe Frazier. He was knocked out in the second round, but Foster's performance was not greatly inferior to that of the two white boxers who challenged Frazier in 1972. Terry Daniels and Ron Stander lasted two and three rounds longer than Foster against the champion before referees stopped the carnage. However overmatched Foster had been, his credentials included a growing reputation (even in 1970, after only two years as champion) as one of the superior light-heavyweight champions in history. Daniels and Stander were both durable and brave challengers, but once again, one is considering two heavyweights who never made it into the Top Ten, before or after their big night fighting for the title. These were not young heavyweights on the career upswing who lost to Frazier because of inexperience. They were as good as they would ever get. Before their big chance, Stander and Daniels had regional reputations, fighting most of their early bouts in their respective home states of Nebraska and Texas. Stander followed his unsuccessful title challenge by losing five of his next seven fights, and nineteen more in all after losing to Frazier. Daniels lost his next five fights in a row, and dropped twenty-five of his last thirty-one bouts! Such losing streaks cannot be solely attributed to the physical beating Frazier laid on these two. These men had no business leapfrogging over ten qualified challengers to fight for the world title. But these were the boxers Joe Frazier chose to defend against. Frazier was no more guilty of protecting his crown against dubious opposition than Muhammad Ali was in defending against men like Jean Pierre Coopman and Richard Dunn, than George Foreman was in fighting Jose Roman, or Patterson was in risking his crown against Rademacher. One can also not blame Daniels or Stander for being fast-tracked into this privilege, for who would disqualify themselves from the money involved in a title fight out of fairness to other boxers? The decision was made between a promoter and the respective managers that these fights would go over well with the ticket-buying public, and the contracts were duly signed.

The one unranked challenger who exceeded expectations was Leon Spinks, an African American Olympic gold medallist who was handpicked as a challenger by Muhammad Ali in 1978. Ali, the 1960 Olympic light heavyweight champion, chose Spinks for the novelty of having a victory over his fourth Olympic gold medallist (after Patterson, Frazier, and Foreman). But the champion badly miscalculated, assuming that Spinks's bland record of seven wins and one draw indicated an easy victim. Spinks scored a huge upset over the poorly conditioned and over-confident Ali. Spinks was the rare exception, the unranked challenger who really was of elite caliber and deserving of a title shot. That Foster was already a world champion (albeit at a lighter weight) and Spinks was an Olympic champion when they fought for the title, while Stander and Daniels were regional heavyweight entities who would ultimately retire with fifty-one losses between them, indicates the same trend evident in the 1950s and 1960s. Once in a lifetime opportunities fell into unqualified white laps more easily than black ones between 1949 and 1983.

For the first two decades after the Brown Bomber bid adieu to an adoring audience, the crops of white contenders produced a greater ratio of challengers than the cadres of black residents in the Top Ten. Whites who made it into the Top Ten already had a large part of the journey behind them in terms of the odds of landing a title shot. In the 1950s, a ranked white heavyweight had a better than one in four chance of confronting the world titleholder, while rated black heavies had less than a one in four chance. From 1960–69, two of the four rated whites vied for the crown, while only seven of twenty blacks had the honor. It appears, at first glance, that the last period saw a breakthrough in the rate of black contenders challenging relative to whites, but closer examination throws this conclusion in doubt. Although roughly two-thirds of the African Americans (16 of 23) and whites (4 of 6) fought for the championship, three of the black boxers challenged for an inferior version of the world title. Big John Tate, Quick Tillis, and Dynamite Dokes, all fought for the WBA title, when it was universally accepted that the better heavyweight king was WBC champion Larry Holmes.[2] Given that Tate and Tillis could not beat Mike Weaver (who lost to Holmes), and that Dokes was held to a draw by Weaver in their rematch and lost to Gerry Coetzee (who lost to Snipes, a victim of Holmes), it is clear these three were allowed second-rate championship title fight opportunities by the boxing establishment. Discounting their big nights as something less than the Real McCoy would lower the black ratio of contenders to challengers to clearly below that of the white group. It is particularly compelling that all three of the ranked white contenders who were fighting across much of Holmes championship reign (1978–85), fought for the Easton Assassin's recognized legitimate crown. Scott LeDoux, Gerry Cooney, and Tex Cobb, were one punch away from the real title. The white and never-ranked Scott Frank joined them. Their big chance was the real big chance. Tate, Tillis, and Dokes were not fighting for table scraps in pursuit of the WBA title, but it was not the same privilege as the others enjoyed.

Ratio of Challengers Over Contenders

One would expect that an increasingly color-blind white American boxing audience would result in roughly equal ratios of black and white contenders landing the privilege of fighting for the championship. Across the time span of this study, the white and black contender cohorts would have offered up equal representation for world title contests, if the skin color of the world titleholder meant progressively less to white boxing fans. Every generation of black and white contenders should reveal similar ratios of how many heavyweights made it into the rankings, compared to the smaller number who took the final step upward to challenge for the world belt. The Top Ten is the farm system from which title challengers are drawn. How many contenders generated how many challengers with the black and white samples of heavyweights?

Contenders Ranked by *The Ring* Who Fought for Title

White Contenders (1949–59)	Fought for Title	Black Contenders (1949–59)	Fought for Title
Bernie Reynolds	(No)	Al Hoosman	(No)
Gus Lesnevich	(Yes)	Turkey Thompson	(No)
Grant Butcher	(No)	John Holman	(No)
Roland LaStarza	(Yes)	Bob Baker	(No)
Rocky Marciano	(Yes)	Clarence Henry	(No)
Harry Mathews	(No)	Coley Wallace	(No)
Dan Bucceroni	(No)	Bob Dunlap	(No)
Roy Harris	(Yes)	Bob Satterfield	(No)
Pat McMurtry	(No)	Jim Slade	(No)
Mike DeJohn	(No)	Archie Moore	(Yes)
Charlie Norkus	(No)	Tom Jackson	(Yes)
Rex Layne	(No)	John Summerlin	(No)
Willie Pastrano	(No)	Young Jack Johnson	(No)
		Harold Carter	(No)
		Eddie Machen	(Yes)
		Tommy Harrison	(No)
		Floyd Patterson	(Yes)
		Zora Folley	(Yes)
		Wayne Bethea	(No)
		Harold Johnson	(No)
		Sonny Liston	(Yes)
		Charlie Powell	(No)
		Tony Anthony	(No)
		Alonzo Johnson	(No)
		Billy Hunter	(No)
		Bill Gilliam	(No)
Total 4/13		Total 6/26	

White Contenders (1960–69)	Fought for Title	Black Contenders (1960–69)	Fought for Title
Tom McNeely	(Yes)	Cleveland Williams	Yes
George Logan	(No)	Cassius Clay	Yes
Jerry Quarry	(Yes)	Billy Daniels	No
Boone Kirkman	(No)	Doug Jones	Yes
		Ernie Terrell	Yes
		Thad Spencer	No
		Amos Johnson	No
		Hubert Hilton	No
		Elmer Rush	No
		Amos Lincoln	No
		Johnny Persol	No

		Joe Frazier	Yes
		Jimmy Ellis	Yes
		Leotis Martin	No
		Buster Mathis	Yes
		Henry Clark	No
		Al Lewis	No
		Mac Foster	No
		Al Jones	No
		Roger Rischer	No
Total 2/4		Total 7/20	

White Contenders *(1970–83)*		*Black Contenders* *(1970–83)*	
Chuck Wepner	Yes	George Foreman	Yes
Duane Bobick	No	Ron Lyle	Yes
Randy Neumann	No	Ken Norton	Yes
Scott LeDoux	Yes	Earnie Shavers	Yes
Gerry Cooney	Yes	Jeff Merritt	No
Tex Cobb	Yes	Larry Middleton	No
		Jimmy Young	Yes
		Larry Holmes	Yes
		Johnny Boudreaux	No
		Howard Smith	No
		Stan Ward	No
		Leon Spinks	Yes
		Mike Weaver	Yes
		John Tate (WBA)	Yes
		Leroy Jones	Yes
		Michael Dokes (WBA)	Yes
		Greg Page	Yes
		Marty Monroe	No
		James Tillis (WBA)	Yes
		Renaldo Snipes	Yes
		Tim Witherspoon	Yes
		Pinklon Thomas	Yes
		S.T. Gordon	No
Total 4/6		Total 16/23	

Opponent's Records

Although the white and black contender samples climbed over the same caliber of opposition into the ratings, measured by opponent's wins and losses, this equality did not extend to the world championship level. Here, black heavyweights traveled a longer and more arduous road to stand in the opposite corner from the heavyweight champion. To ascend to this plateau, the average African American heavyweight looked back on a resume of opponents averaging 35–9–2 in the 1950s, considerably better than the average opponents faced by the white challengers (23–9–2) for that decade. In the 1960s, this gap was almost as large as black challengers had faced an average opponent with nine more wins (22 to 13) and one fewer loss (8 to 7) than their Caucasian contemporaries. Even from 1970 onward, the black title contestants had climbed through opponents with better numbers, their opponents having five more victories (18 to 13) and one less defeat (7 to 6) than the white challengers. In all three periods, white men fought for the title having competed against an inferior average opponent based on simple record of wins and losses.

Since the heavyweight crown has been held almost exclusively by African Americans since 1949, one might argue this measure is inherently slanted in favor of the black fighters. Many of the black champions had opportunities to regain the title after losing it. When they did so, they brought to their challenge a record of opponents that included their stints as champions. Since world champion boxers are under pressure to defend against top notch competition, Louis, Walcott, Charles, Patterson, Liston, Ali, and Frazier could be said to bring competitive numbers to the tally not available to the white study group, which consisted of only one champion who never attempted to regain his title. When the above men were champions, their defenses (by virtue of being world title defenses) were against men who could be presented to the ticket-buying public (though not always persuasively) as legitimate threats to usurp the champion. Such challengers were more likely to have records with more wins and fewer losses than the average opponent of a contender who never wins the title.

This argument loses weight when one calculates the numbers again, leaving out the average opponent records for black champions after they won the title, only including those fighters they fought on their way to winning the title for the first time. Even this calculation speaks of white advantage and greater black effort to earn a title fight. In the 1950s the gap barely shrank at all as black challengers had virtually the same record (33–9–2) even without the ex-champion's title reign opponents included, still far better than the tally (24–10–2) for whites. The 1960s average for blacks (19–7–2) was still clearly better than that (13–7–1) of whites. Only in the final era did the removal of such former champion's title defense opponents bring the average record (14–7–1) almost equal to the figure (13–7–1) for white challengers.

Average Opponent Records of World Title Challengers

White Challengers (1949–59)	*Opponents' Average Record*	*Black Challengers (1949–59)*	*Opponents' Average Record*
Gus Lesnevich	27–10–2	Ezzard Charles	39–9–3
Pat Valentino	23–8–2	Joe Walcott	26–8–1
Freddie Beshore	19–8–2	Joe Louis	43–9–3
Nick Barone	25–12–1	Joe Walcott	34–8–1
Lee Oma	27–9–2	Joe Walcott	34–8–1
Joey Maxim	27–10–2	Ezzard Charles	42–10–3
Rocky Marciano	23–10–2	Joe Walcott	36–8–1
Roland LaStarza	15–9–1	Ezzard Charles	40–10–3
Roy Harris	20–6–1	Ezzard Charles	41–10–3
		Archie Moore	37–10–3
		Floyd Patterson	27–11–3
		Archie Moore	36–10–3

5. For All the Marbles

		Tommy Jackson	23–7–1
Average >	23–9–2	Average >	35–9–2

White Challengers (1960–69)	Opponents' Average Record	Black Challengers (1960–69)	Opponents' Average Record
Tom McNeely	11–6–1	Sonny Liston	22–9–2
Jerry Quarry	15–6–1	Floyd Patterson	30–10–2
Dave Zyglewicz	12–10–2	Cassius Clay	28–7–1
Jerry Quarry	15–6–1	Sonny Liston	3–8–2
		Floyd Patterson	29–9–2
		Ernie Terrell	16–6–1
		Eddie Machen	25–8–4
		Doug Jones	20–6–1
		Floyd Patterson	30–8–2
		Cleveland Williams	15–8–1
		Ernie Terrell	17–6–1
		Zora Folley	18–7–2
		Jimmy Ellis	26–10–2
		Joe Frazier	17–7–1
		Buster Mathis	6–5–1
		Floyd Patterson	31–9–2
Average 13–7–1		Average 22–8–2	

White Challengers (1970–83)	Opponents' Average Record	Black Challengers (1970–83)	Opponents' Average Record
Terry Daniels	12–10–1	Joe Frazier	20–6–1
Ron Stander	10–8	Jimmy Ellis	26–9–2
Chuck Wepner	13–5–1	Bob Foster	24–11–3
Scott LeDoux	17–6–1	Muhammad Ali	34–7–1
Gerry Cooney	13–6–1	George Foreman	12–8–1
Randy Cobb	16–6	Ken Norton	13–7–1
Scott Frank	11–9–1	Muhammad Ali	35–6–1
		Ron Lyle	24–11–2
		Joe Frazier	24–5–1
		Jimmy Young	16–7–1
		Ken Norton	15–7–1
		Earnie Shavers	13–9–1
		Leon Spinks	15–9
		Muhammad Ali	34–5–1
		Larry Holmes	12–5–1
		Mike Weaver	12–3
		Earnie Shavers	14–9–1
		Leroy Jones	11–6
		Muhammad Ali	33–5–1
		Leon Spinks	23–6–1
		Renaldo Snipes	9–5–1
		Tim Witherspoon	9–3
		John Tate	4–8–1
		Mike Weaver	13–3–1
		James Tillis	11–8–1
		Michael Dokes	12–4
		Mike Weaver	13–3–1
Average 13–7–1		Average 18–6–1	

Top Ten Victims

There was a large discrepancy, as well in the number of elite conquests on the records of black and white challengers. In terms of earning a Top Ten rating as measured by fighting elite opponents, black title contestants had to go through a relative marine boot camp compared to white ones. At the championship level, the measures reveal a strong tendency for white heavyweights to land title opportunities with fewer gems on their career sheets. The ten whites from 1949 to 1959 collected eighteen wins over ranked fighters on their way to boxing's peak, a modest average of almost two wins per fighter. But their thirteen black counterparts had 108 such notches on their belts at the same stage, an average (8.3) *almost five times greater*. This gap never approached equitability in the years to come. From 1960 to 1969, the black average dropped markedly (4.6), but was still more than three times that of the four white contenders, who had five such victims among them. The ratio soared like never before in the last time frame, as seven white heavyweights were ranked with a total of three such triumphs on their resumes, an average (0.4) *one-thirteenth* of the roughly four average elite victims claimed by African American pugilists. The white pathway along boxing's rainbow had few detours here. The black heavyweight road had considerably more dangerous pitfalls.

Victories Over Top Ten Opponents by World Title Challengers

White Challengers (1949–59)	Top Ten Victims	Black Challengers (1949–59)	Top Ten Victims
Gus Lesnevich	Mauriello (2)	Ezzard Charles	Bivins (3) Baksi, Maxim, Fitzpatrick, Ray
Pat Valentino	Knox, Thompson	Joe Walcott	Baksi, Oma, Gomez, Bivins, Maxim (25)*
Freddie Beshore	None	Joe Louis	
Nick Barone	None	Joe Walcott	Above five, plus Agramonte
Lee Oma	Nova, Mauriello Baksi, Flynn	Joe Walcott	Above six
Joey Maxim	Walker, Muscato Walcott, Bivins	Ezzard Charles	Above seven, plus Layne
Rocky Marciano	LaStarza, Layne Louis, Mathews	Joe Walcott	Above six
Roland LaStarza	Layne	Ezzard Charles	Above eight, Plus Layne Wallace, Satterfield, and Bivins

5. For All the Marbles

Pete Rademacher	None	Ezzard Charles	Above twelve
Roy Harris	Pastrano	Archie Moore	Riley, Valdes, Bivins (3), Dunlap
		Floyd Patterson	Slade (2), Jackson
		Archie Moore	Above six
		Tommy Jackson	Henry, Layne, Baker, Bucceroni, Charles (2)
Average 18/10 = 1.8		Average 108/13 = 8.3	

When he challenged Ezzard Charles to regain his title, Joe Louis counted the following Top Ten heavyweights as victims; Lee Ramage, Patsy Perroni, Natie Brown, Primo Carnera, Kingfish Levinsky, Max Baer, Charley Retzlaff, Jack Sharkey, Al Ettore, Bob Pastor, James Braddock, Tommy Farr, Nathan Mann, Max Schmeling, Tony Galento, Bob Pastor, Johnny Paychek, Arturo Godoy, Red Burman, Buddy Baer, Billy Conn, Lou Nova, Buddy Baer, Abe Simon, Billy Conn, Tami Mauriello, and Jersey Joe Walcott (twice).

White Challengers (1960–69)	Top Ten Victims	Black Challengers (1960–69)	Top Ten Victims
Tom McNeely	None	Floyd Patterson	Above three, plus Jackson Harris, London
Jerry Quarry	Patterson	Sonny Liston	Folley, Harris
	Spencer		DeJohn, Machen
Dave Zyglewicz	None	Cassius Clay	Lavorante, Jones, Cooper Moore
Jerry Quarry	Above two plus Mathis	Sonny Liston	Above four plus Patterson (2)
		Floyd Patterson	Above six, plus Johannson
		Ernie Terrell	Williams, Folley
		Floyd Patterson	Above seven, plus Machen, Chuvalo
		Eddie Machen	Valdes, Holman, Jackson, DeJohn, Hunter, Miteff,

		Doug Jones	Folley, Daniels
		Cleveland Williams	Miteff, Daniels (2)
		Ernie Terrell	Above two, plus Chuvalo Jones
		Zora Folley	Machen Daniels Cooper Cleroux (2)
		Jimmy Ellis	Persol Martin Bonavena
		Joe Frazier	Chuvalo Bonavena
		Buster Mathis	None
		Floyd Patterson	Above nine, plus Cooper
Average	> 5/4 = 1.3	Average	> 73/16 = 4.6

White Challengers 1970–83	Top Ten Victims	Black Challengers 1970–83	Top Ten Victims
Terry Daniels	None	Joe Frazier	Above two plus Mathis
Ron Stander	None		
Chuck Wepner	Terrell		Ramos
Scott LeDoux	None		Bonavena
Gerry Cooney	Norton		Quarry
Scott Frank	Snipes	Jimmy Ellis	Quarry
Randy Cobb	None		Martin
			Persol
			Bonavena
		Bob Foster	None
		Muhammad Ali	Above four plus Liston (2) Patterson Chuvalo Cooper Mildenber Williams Terrell Folley Quarry Bonavena
		George Foreman	Kirkman Chuvalo
		Ken Norton	Ali
		Muhammad Ali	Above fifteen plus Ellis, Quarry Foster Patterson Bugner Norton Frazier

5. For All the Marbles

	Ron Lyle	Bonavena
		Middleton
	Joe Frazier	Above six,
		plus Quarry
		Ali, Bugner
	Jimmy Young	Lyle
	Ken Norton	Above one
		plus Kirkman
		Quarry
	Earnie Shavers	Ellis
	Leon Spinks	Righetti
	Muhammad Ali	Above
		twenty-two
		plus
		Foreman Frazier
		Lyle
		Young
		Norton
		Wepner
		Shavers
		Bugner
	Larry Holmes	Shavers
	Mike Weaver	None
	Earnie Shavers	Above one
		Norton
	Leroy Jones	Weaver
	Muhammad Ali	Above
		Thirty
		plus Spinks
	Leon Spinks	Ali
		Mercado
		Evangelista
	Renaldo Snipes	Coetzee
	Tim Witherspoon	None
	John Tate	Knoetzee
	Mike Weaver	LeDoux
	James Tillis	None
	Michael Dokes	Ocasio
	Mike Weaver	Above one
		plus LeDoux
		Tate, Tillis
		Coetzee
Averag 3/7 = .4	Average 144/27 = 5.3	

Ranking of Previous Opponent

The final opponents beaten by the black heavyweights before their big chance were decidedly superior to the preparatory adversaries of the white ones. In the 1950s, the former group's rivals averaged a ranking almost three spots higher (4.8 to 1.9) in the Top Ten than the victims of the latter. The 1960–69 span saw the quality of the two samples' last opponents become equal, as the fighters from both groups typically defeated boxers situated at number four in the ratings. After 1970, however, the gap in favor or white heavyweights glaringly returned, with the average white being offered a championship bout immediately after beating men ranked ninth, while the black challenger had cleared a higher hurdle through defeating rivals rated more than four positions higher (4.9) on the scale. Such large quality gaps in the black and white resumes over two of the three eras can only have sifted out some black contenders more qualified than the average white challenger, but not up to the higher standard of their black brethren.

White challengers also enjoyed a clear advantage in the number of unranked conquests they had just fought before their title chance. In none of the three periods did the black boxers enjoy an edge with this measure. The first era saw five of the nine white challengers contest the world championship after beating an unranked foe, whereas only five of thirteen black men bidding for the crown had the same softer warm-up fight. The following decade saw equality rein again as the white and black boxers were equally likely (2 of 4, 8 of 16) to have bested unranked opposition prior to a title challenge. This was not a harbinger for sustained parity. From 1970 through 1983, all but one of the seven white challengers were introduced as title contestants having recently conquered pugilists out of the ratings. Gullick, Mac, Hinki, Shelburg, and Arlt did not spell out as stiff pre-championship tests for Daniels, Stander, Wepner, Cobb, and Frank. LeDoux's victory, before his attempt to take Larry Holmes's title, was at least respectable in that he beat a future ranked contender in Marty Monroe, while Cooney's victim, however faded, was Ken Norton, the former outstanding heavyweight and onetime title claimant. The twenty-seven African American challengers were nowhere near as likely to land a title shot after consuming such pastries as the above. Only twelve had beaten unranked foes prior to their challenge, the other fifteen typically had beaten top-notch opposition beforehand.

Ranking of Last Opponent Beaten by World Title Challengers

White Challengers (1949–59)	Previous Opponent and Ranking	Black Challengers (1949–59)	Previous Opponent and Ranking
Gus Lesnevich	Maxim (5)	Ezzard Charles	Maxim (4)
Pat Valentino	Thompson (7)	Joe Walcott	Louis (0)*
Freddie Beshore	Oma (3)	Joe Louis	Walcott (1)
Nick Barone	Beau (UNR)	Joe Walcott	Layne (UNR)
Lee Oma	Satterfield (UNR)	Joe Walcott	Charles (0)
Joey Maxim	Hood (UNR)	Ezzard Charles	Kahut (UNR)
Rocky Marciano	Mathews (6)	Joe Walcott	Marciano (1)
Roland LaStarza	Layne (3)	Ezzard Charles	Satterfield (7)
Pete Rademacher	NA	Ezzard Charles	Marciano (0)*
Roy Harris	Besmanoff (UNR)	Archie Moore	Olson (UNR)
		Floyd Patterson	Jackson (2)
		Archie Moore	Shire (UNR)
		Tommy Jackson	Mederos (UNR)
Average Ranking 24/5 = 4.8		Average Ranking 15/8 = 1.9	
Unranked Opponents 5/9		Unranked Opponents 5/13	

5. For All the Marbles

For the purposes of this measure, bouts against the world champion will use the numerical value of zero to designate the ranking/quality of such an opponent. This value is appropriate because it numerically represents a slightly lower value than the ranking of the number one rated challenger, and will have a similarly valid impact on the overall totals, given that the lower the ranking number, the more impressive the quality of performance concluded.

White Challengers (1960–69)	Previous Oppt and Ranking	Black Challengers (1960–69)	Previous Oppt and Ranking
Tom McNeely	Lave (UNR)	Floyd Patterson	Johannson (1)
Jerry Quarry	Spencer (2)	Sonny Liston	Westphal (UNR)
Dave Zyglewicz	Sanchez (UNR)	Floyd Patterson	Liston (1)
Jerry Quarry	Mathis (6)	Cassius Clay	Cooper (9)
		Sonny Liston	Ali (1)
		Ernie Terrell	Wallitsch (UNR)
		Floyd Patterson	Herring (UNR)
		Eddie Machen	Patterson (7)
		Doug Jones	Bailey (UNR)
		Cleveland Williams	Herring (UNR)
		Ernie Terrell	Jones (2)
		Zora Folley	Joyner (UNR)
		Jimmy Ellis	Bonavena (3)
		Joe Frazier	Conners (UNR)
		Buster Mathis	DeBruyn (UNR)
		Floyd Patterson	Quarry (8)
Average 8/2 = 4		Average 32/8 = 4	
Unranked Opponents 2/4		Unranked Opponents 8/16	

White Challengers (1970–83)	Previous Oppt. and Ranking	Black Challengers (1970–83)	Previous Oppt and Ranking
Terry Daniels	Gullick (UNR)	Joe Frazier	Quarry (3)
Ron Stander	Mac (UNR)	Jimmy Ellis	Patterson (6)
Chuck Wepner	Hinki (UNR)	Bob Foster	Tessman (UNR)
Scott LeDoux	Monroe (UNR)	Muhammad Ali	Bonavena (3)
Gerry Cooney	Norton (9)	George Foreman	Sorrels (UNR)
Randy Cobb	Shelburg (UNR)	Ken Norton	Ali (3)
Scott Frank	Arlt (UNR)	Muhammad Ali	Frazier (2)
		Ron Lyle	Young (UNR)
		Joe Frazier	Ellis (UNR)
		Jimmy Young	Roman (UNR)
		Ken Norton	Middleton (UNR)
		Earnie Shavers	Smith (7)
		Leon Spinks	Righetti (7)
		Muhammad Ali	Spinks (UNR)
		Larry Holmes	Shavers (7)
		Mike Weaver	Phillips (UNR)
		Earnie Shavers	Porette (UNR)
		Leroy Jones	Beattie (UNR)
		Muhammad Ali	Spinks (9)
		Leon Spinks	Mercado (7)
		Renaldo Snipes	Coetzee (6)
		Tim Witherspoon	Snipes (10)

	John Tate	Knoetzee (3)
	Mike Weaver	LeDoux (9)
	James Tillis	Fischer (UNR)
	Michael Dokes	Thomas (UNR)
	Mike Weaver	Dokes (1)
Average 9/1 = 9	Average 74/15 = 4.9	
Unranked Opponents 6/7	Unranked Opponents 12/27	

Challengers' Performance

How well challengers have done on their big night also offers potential insight as to how deserving white and black boxers were for the privilege of contesting the world championship. By looking at the results of title bouts, the average performance of the challengers should not be drastically different if fighters of the same quality and credentials were receiving this honor. How many of the white and black contestants lasted the full distance when the bell rang? For the ones who did not go the limit, how far into the fight did the average Caucasian and African American challenger go before being stopped?

Since all but one of the heavyweight champions in this study's time frame were black, there is no point in including those African American fighters who won the title. To do so would simply reinvent the wheel, so to speak, as to the relative quality of black and white boxers over this span. It would be worthwhile, though, to compare the performances of all losing challengers, black and white. Statistically isolating the unsuccessful pugilists would place a narrow focus on the qualifications of the average boxer from both races, as any higher standard found for black challengers could not be rationalized as the simple expression of black America generating the best elite boxers, and thus numerically swamping the white sample group by virtue of having mostly monopolized the title for decades.

Losing Performances of World Title Challengers

White Challengers (1949–59)	Result	Black Challengers (1949–59)	Result
Gus Lesnevich	KO'd in 10th	Joe Walcott	15 Round Decision
Pat Valentino	KO'd in 8th	Joe Louis	15 Round Decision
Freddie Beshore	KO'd in 14th	Joe Walcott	15 Round Decision
Nick Barone	KO'd in 11th	Ezzard Charles	15 Round Decision
Lee Oma	KO'd in 10th	Joe Walcott	KO'd in 1st
Joey Maxim	15 Round Decision	Ezzard Charles	15 Round Decision
Roland LaStarza	KO'd in 11th	Ezzard Charles	KO'd in 8th
Pete Rademacher	KO'd in 6th	Archie Moore	KO'd in 9th
Roy Harris	KO'd in 12th	Archie Moore	KO'd in 5th
		Tommy Jackson	KO'd in 10th
Went Distance 1/9		Went Distance 5/10	

5. For All the Marbles

White Challengers (1960–69)	Result	Black Challengers (1960–69)	Result
Tom McNeely	KO'd in 4th	Floyd Patterson	KO'd in 1st
Jerry Quarry	15 Round Decision	Sonny Liston	KO'd in 1st
Dave Zyglewicz	KO'd in 1st	Eddie Machen	15 Round Decision
Jerry Quarry	KO'd in 7th	Doug Jones	15 Round Decision
		Floyd Patterson	KO'd in 12th
		Cleveland Williams	KO'd in 3rd
		Ernie Terrell	15 Round Decision
		Zora Folley	KO'd in 7th
		Buster Mathis	KO'd in 11th
		Floyd Patterson	15 Round Decision
Went the Distance 1/4		Went the Distance 4/10	

White Challengers (1970–83)	Result	Black Challengers (1970–83)	Result
Terry Daniels	KO'd in 4th	Jimmy Ellis	KO'd in 5th
Ron Stander	KO'd in 5th	Bob Foster	KO'd in 2nd
Chuck Wepner	KO'd in 15th	Muhammad Ali	15 Round Decision
Scott LeDoux	KO'd in 7th	Ron Lyle	KO'd in 11th
Gerry Cooney	KO'd in 13th	Joe Frazier	KO'd in 15th
Randy Cobb	15 Round Decision	Jimmy Young	15 Round Decision
Scott Frank	KO'd in 5th	Ken Norton	15 Round Decision
		Earnie Shavers	15 Round Decision
		Mike Weaver	KO'd in 12th
		Earnie Shavers	KO'd in 11th
		Leroy Jones	KO'd in 8th
		Leon Spinks	KO'd in 3rd
		Renaldo Snipes	KO'd in 11th
		Tim Witherspoon	12 Round Decision
		James Tillis	15 Round Decision
		Mike Weaver	15 Round Draw
Went the Distance 1/7		Went the Distance 7/16	

Even when one reduces this measure to losing title challenges, the black championship contestants appear to have been better qualified to vie for the championship. In all three periods, a higher ratio of African Americans went the distance with the champion, with the margin being huge in two eras. The 1950s saw only one of nine white challengers make it to the final bell against the heavyweight king, while half (5 of 10) black boxers did so. From 1960 to 1969, the difference was much smaller, with four of ten blacks pushing the contest to the scoring cards, while one of four whites avoided a knockout. The discrepancy soared again after 1970, with Randy "Tex" Cobb the only one of seven white challengers to be standing at the final bell, while almost half (8 of 18) of the black fighters accomplished this. Their performance in the ring speaks loudly in favor of black challengers being better qualified for the privilege of world title fight. African American contenders were far more likely to finish title fights on their feet, and such a large discrepancy of outcomes would not be the case if the mechanics of boxing were colorblind.

6. Has the Great White Hope Left the Building?

> BOXING PROMOTER: I'm proud to announce that sixty days from today, on March 17, St. Patrick's Day, James "The Grim Reaper" Roper, will defend his heavyweight title against the number eight ranked contender ... Irish Terry Conklin!
> TERRY CONKLIN: But I'm not Irish.
> PUBLICIST: It's boxing. It just means you're white.
>
> —*The Great White Hype, 1996*

This study focused on two levels of achievement in boxing, entry into the Top Ten rankings, and challenging for the world heavyweight title. These standards of accomplishment represent the two highest plateaus of accomplishment in boxing. Nineteen statistical measures for the challengers, and sixteen for the contenders were calculated over three sub-periods within the years 1949–1983.

The numbers indicate equal opportunity was the norm for black and white heavyweights aspiring to break into *The Ring*'s ratings through this era, but sharp discrepancy in the statistical profiles of the two racial samples of fighters contesting the world crown. To become a rated Top Ten contender by *The Ring*, blacks were at no disadvantage compared to whites. Their skin color did not adversely affect their chances of reaching this prestigious level, and did not act as a drag on their prospects of being recognized as one of the world's ten best pugilists. There was remarkable consistency across all three sub-periods in the statistical record, proving that opportunity at this level was color-blind. If there was a desire for a Great White Hope in white America from the late 1940s to the early 1980s, it had no impact on boxing at this level of performance and recognition. The climb was similar for black and white pugilists.

In the 1950s, eight of sixteen measures reflected white heavyweights becoming rated with lesser difficulty, with eight suggesting black advantage. From 1960–69, eight variables indicated an advantage for blacks, seven for whites, with one even. From 1970 to 1983, nine variables suggested greater ease for blacks entering the ratings with seven portraying whites having an easier time. In all, twenty-five measures spoke of black advantage, twenty-two of greater white opportunity, with one even, a very equitable picture.

Summary of Statistical Measures for Contenders Ranked in *The Ring*'s Top Ten Ratings

W > White heavyweights entered the ratings with lesser credentials.
B > Black heavyweights entered the ratings with lesser credentials.
E > White and black heavyweights landing title fights with equal credentials.

Measure	1949–59	1960–69	1970–83
Fights	B	W	B
Average Record	B	W	W
Average Individual Winning Percentage	B	W	W
Average KO's	B	B	B
Average Individual KO Percentage	B	B	W
Age	W	W	B
Career Length	B	W	B
Top Ten Victims	W	W	W
Number of Top Ten Entries	W	B	B
Average Top Ten Entry Rank	B	B	B
Average Top Ten Exit Ranking	W	W	W
Ranking of Previous Opponent	W	B	W
Unranked Previous Opponents	W	B	W
Records During and Between Top Ten Rated Periods	W (2 of 3)	B (2 of 3)	B (2 of 3)
Rate of Fighting	B	B	B
Average Records of Opponents	W	E	B
Totals	8 White	7 White	7 White
	8 Black	8 Black	9 Black
		1 even	

The rough equality of such measures lends itself to the conclusion that the doorway to this stage of boxing success has been equally wide open along racial lines. Whatever political machinations unfairly intruded on heavyweights' career advancement to this peak, they were not about black and white. *The Ring* magazine meted out Top Ten ratings as readily to African American heavyweights as to white ones from 1949 to 1983.

One might expect that a white American yearning for a Caucasian ring hero might have emerged later in this period, as elite white boxers became a rarity. This thinking would assume that a reflexive white public receptivity to a white fighter would not have emerged in the immediate aftermath of Joe Louis's career, for it was not apparent then the sport would become a mostly black one. The white disappearance from the ring in general, and from the world title specifically, did not occur, much less enter the consciousness of white fans overnight. With this in mind, it is reasonable that statistical evidence may reflect equal opportunity early in the thirty-five year span, but the trend moved toward a black disadvantage later on, as white fans felt a more visceral need to latch on to whichever elite white heavyweights were left in a shrinking pool. But the measures speaking of equal opportunity are consistent across all three eras, with roughly half showing whites being rated more easily, and half with blacks hitting the Top Ten with lesser credentials.

The privilege of fighting for the world heavyweight championship, however, speaks to an opposite conclusion. The measures defining the championship challengers show a huge discrepancy in the pathway taken, in the dues paid by white and black title contestants. This chasm screamed out that black heavyweights had to be better, work harder, and do more to earn an opportunity to contest a world championship bout. Forty-nine of fifty-seven variables support this interpretation, a one-sided picture that defies any reservations about the validity of specific measures, or the smallness of some numerical gaps. The greater opportunity white heavyweights have enjoyed was equally evident across the three time spans. Coincidence cannot account for six of every seven measures pointing toward the advantage of white fighters over black ones. The chance of these numbers being sheer coincidence is little more persuasive than random luck explaining American boardrooms being 95 percent white, or that the average young black male has a greater chance of entering prison than college.

In the 1950s, sixteen of nineteen variables showed black heavyweights having better numbers or a more demanding path to a championship fight. The 1960s witnessed even starker white advantage, with only one statistic favoring black opportunity, two even, and sixteen again reflecting Caucasian privilege. After 1970, decades after white America had stopped using the term Great White Hope, seventeen of nineteen measures spoke of a steeper road for black heavyweights dreaming of a world title fight.

Summary of Statistical Measures for World Heavyweight Title Challengers

W > white heavyweights landing title fights with lesser credentials.
B > black heavyweights landing title fights with lesser credentials.
E > white and black heavyweights landing title fights with equal credentials.

Measure	1949–59	1960–69	1970–83
Fights	W	W	W
Average Record	W	W	W
Average Individual Winning Percentage	W	W	W
Average KO's	W	W	W

6. Has the Great White Hope Left the Building?

Average Individual KO Percentage	W	W	W
Age	W	W	W
Length of Career	W	W	W
Opponent's Average Record			
Top Ten Victims Average Ranking	W	W	W
Top Ten Victims Average Ranking	W	W	W
Unranked Challengers	W	W	W
Top Ten Wait	B	W	B
Total Top Ten Wait	W	W	W
Number of Top Ten Entries	B	W	W
Ranking of Previous Opponent	W	E	W
Unranked Previous Opponents	W	E	W
Ratio of Contenders Challenging	W	W	W
Rate of Fighting	B	B	B
Average Performance	W	W	W
Opponent's Average Record	W	W	W
Totals	16 White 3 Black	16 White 1 Black 2 even	17 White 2 Black

Even less than three decades ago, there was a desire on the part of whites for a white heavyweight champion. Perhaps this desire was unconscious but if there had been no such sentiment, there would have been a much more equitable number of measures portraying the white and black pursuit of the crown. If the vast majority of statistical measures show white heavyweights between 1949 and 1983 landing title shots with less achievement behind them, one must take such numbers at face value, concluding that the mechanisms divvying out championship opportunity, however complex, are partially influenced by the perception of white enthusiasm for a white ring hero. *These numbers do not lie.* Although some of the measures offer margins that border on minuscule within the context of boxing statistics, and other variables are undoubtedly less valid than others, the fact that forty-nine statistical arrows pointed toward white heavyweights having better opportunity while only six variables smiled on black contenders in the same manner leaves no doubt that white heavyweights enjoyed what Muhammad Ali once called "the complexion to get the connection"[1] in their pursuit of boxing fame and fortune.

One can rightly ask whether the conclusions do justice to opportunity within the larger context of American society in general. It could legitimately be argued this is a story of tremendous social advancement toward equality, one with a happy ending. The above numbers prove the glass of equal racial opportunity in boxing is far more full than empty, and that is where the focus should be. Boxing has come a long way since Jack Johnson and Jim Jeffries played out a symbolic racial drama under a searing Nevada sun in 1910. If racial inequality has been reduced to the point where black heavyweights need a handful more wins, one or two more quality opponents on their victim list, or have to wait an average of several months longer to contest the world championship, that is small historical potatoes compared to the injustice that scores of elite black heavyweights faced in the late nineteenth and early twentieth centuries, fighting beneath an invisible ceiling called a color line. One can only wish that other corners of American society experienced anywhere near the progress in boxing. Mammoth in comparison are the gaps between black and white Americans in regards to poverty, unemployment, imprisonment, and public health indicators, as well as representation in many professional occupations. Americans, white and black, can celebrate the almost equal opportunity of a sport like boxing. By the early 1980s, truly elite black fighters were almost certain to become rated, and very likely to receive a chance to fight for the championship. In the 1920s, a black boxer of sterling quality like Harry Wills was forever on the outside looking in at Jack Dempsey's title, for no other reason than his race. Less than sixty years later, African American pugilists below the level of greatness—John Tate, Michael Dokes, Renaldo Snipes, Marvis Frazier, James Tillis, and Mike Weaver—all fought for the championship. This, along with similar progress in other American sports, truly calls for Americans, white and black, to pat themselves on the backs.

An equally valid retort to the above is that the seeming progress made by the 105 black boxers who became rated or fought for the title between 1949 and 1983 may be as much about white biases being overwhelmed by sheer numbers as it was by a voluntary change in acceptance or tolerance. From the 1950s forward, the number of black elite heavyweights competing in America has far outstripped that of whites. A threshold may have been reached in which simple practicality dictated that a white audience's preference for a white champion be submerged, rather than disappear. At some point, those white American boxing fans who felt a psychological need for a Great White Hope may have had to choose between rooting for black fighters, or withdrawing their patronage of the sport entirely. Black numerical dominance in boxing may have simply swept aside the floodgates of white preference, as opposed to any genuine change in white attitudes. If, during these thirty-five years, more than 90 percent of the best heavyweights visible to the boxing public were black, and there was no apparent concern or complaint from white America, greater racial tolerance is surely only one contributing factor. As mentioned earlier, the hugely disproportionate ratio of black to white heavyweights has left little room for Great White Hope sentiment to grow. Much of the ability to steer opportunity toward whites may have been walled into a smaller and smaller corner, as the shrinking circle of white heavyweights left fewer plausible Great White Hopes from which to choose. It is worth pointing out that, while the gap between black and white opportunity clearly shrank from the time of Johnson versus Jeffries, the last white American heavyweight to challenge for the true world title, Scott Frank, was unranked when he fought for Larry Holmes's crown in 1983. Just as unranked as Beshore and Barone were when they tried to lift Ezzard Charles's belt in 1950, as Rademacher was in fighting Patterson in 1957, and as Zyglewicz, Stander, and Daniels were in confronting Frazier in 1969 and 1972. Larry Holmes and his managers clearly agreed to fight Frank because they were convinced there was enough public sentiment in the white challenger's home state of New Jersey to make it a viable promotion, just as Joe Frazier had agreed years earlier to fight Zyglewicz and Stander in their hometowns.

What these statistical findings depict about the attitudes of America toward black success or domination of sports was not the focus of this study. To ask what emotional need a Great White Hope would satisfy in the hearts and minds of white boxing fans is a study in itself, one that must draw on extensive social and psychological research into white-black relations in late twentieth century America. In 1997, twenty-six years after its first controversial foray into the topic, *Sports Illustrated* revisited race and sports performance with an extensive article questioning, "What Ever Happened to the White Athlete?"[2] The investigation delved deeply into a seeming national phenomenon in which white youth were showing up on fewer and fewer football fields and basketball courts. The rationale offered for this was a belief had entrenched itself in the minds of white America that it could not compete equally in such sports with black athletes, that blacks could jump higher, run faster, and hit harder than whites. This assumption was offered as an explanation why droves of white teenagers were playing in newer, nontraditional sports to which black athletes had less economic access, presumably activities like mountain biking, skateboarding, snowboarding, field hockey, and roller hockey. The implied image of white suburban teenagers cutting themselves from basketball and football teams even before tryouts began in favor of whitebread pursuits that ostensibly allowed them a chance at victory is one manifestation of white discomfort with black success in athletic competition. The statistical evidence revealed in this study, suggesting white heavyweight fighters had an easier time chasing success even into the early 1980s, is another. But what is the exact nature of this threat to the white psyche? It would be ludicrous to suggest that a significant number of white sports fans want to return to segregation in sports, or any other corner of society. Whatever Great White Hope urge still survives is a different creature, quantitatively, from what existed in 1910, when Americans were arrested, injured, or killed because a black man conquered a white one. There is no danger of sporadic racial violence flaring across America in response to black heavyweight champions trouncing white contenders. White America has had plenty of opportunities to get used to this scenario since 1949. Most of white America long ago learned to separate what happens in a boxing ring from their feelings and thoughts about everyday life. It has been decades since any mainstream Caucasian worried about a bloody race war on American soil. The mere suggestion might well elicit the same eye-rolling ridicule that greets the philosophies of backwoods constitutional militarists who occasionally creep into the daily news. This study's findings, then, cannot be attributed to any crude fear of the white race losing a race war.

Perhaps the yearning is a mostly innocent twinge of racial pride, a desire white America is no less entitled to than any other minority race in her population. Seeing a white face with the title "world heavyweight champion" underneath it on a television screen may be a reward in itself, with little or no implication beyond boxing. Role models are somewhat easier to identify with and follow when they come from one's own race, a reality extending far beyond American society.

At a more insecure end of a psychological continuum, the remaining advantage white heavyweights had into the early 1980s may testify to a white insecurity, no matter how vague, subconscious or illogical, that black domination in sports may soon extend to the boardrooms, classrooms, courtrooms, hospitals, and city halls of America. Some whites may be completely tolerant of someday living in an America of completely equal opportunity, but be unnerved at the black domination they see in the NBA, NFL, Olympics, or boxing rings. Such sports fans, however irrationally, might wonder whether black progress will stop at equality. If whites feel this way, rooting for a white fighter to win the title might represent a desire to "hold the line" on this growing encroachment on white success, privilege and prosperity. Such individuals may not have the slightest ill will toward blacks or any other racial minority, but are favorable to white athletic heroes like Great White Hopes as symbols that bolster their self-confidence, as images that remind them that their kind has not become soft in a modern world.

If whites make up three-quarters of this nation's 285 million people, and several tens of millions are hardcore or casual boxing fans, one has to acknowledge that some scream for white boxers to beat black ones because of a naked resistance to black advancement everywhere, a greater comfort to returning the heavyweight title back to where they think it belongs. Such individuals may see any and all opportunity in America as a zero sum game, where black advancement equates to white loss. Far more focussed research would be needed to unravel what was going through the minds of a white audience whose preferences resulted, even as late as 1983, in white and black heavyweights following unequal paths to the same goal.

By the early 1980s, it is certain that mainstream whites needing a Great White Hope did not feel this way; they did not want to disenfranchise blacks from the polls, bring back legally segregated neighborhoods, or outlaw interracial marriage. If nothing else, it can be said that America's racial majority has almost completely left behind those pillars of an institutionally racist society. Tens of millions of white American sports fans have enthusiastically cheered for African American athletes since 1947. Hundreds of millions, as well, have voted for Republican and Democratic candidates in support of, or at least not opposed to, civil rights legislation that mandates racially equal opportunity. Black doctors, lawyers, professors, business executives, engineers, mayors, senators, representatives, police, and military generals long ago stopped eliciting hostility from all but a racist white fringe. That white boxers were consistently reaching plateaus of opportunity with lesser credentials than black pugilists does not testify to anything so large as a campaign to bring back official white supremacy. A nation in which Condoleezza Rice is the National Security Advisor, Colin Powell is Secretary of State and a potential presidential candidate, and Tiger Woods and Michael Jordan are global corporate entities in and of themselves is in no danger of returning to signs that say "Colored Water Fountain" or "Whites Only."

Support for a Great White Hope was once a manifestation of a desire to push back the goals and assertions of black America. As early as 1949, through to 1983, it is much more plausible that the idea of a Caucasian ring hero became something whites favored to deal with their own insecurities, to sort out their own feelings about whiteness in an increasingly complex and racially integrated society.

Through this period, even the mere mention of the term Great White Hope gradually became an embarrassment in American sporting discourse. The expression more and more was used in an ironic, tongue-in-cheek manner, with fewer and fewer whites openly using it to convey their wishes for boxing. It became a phrase more often uttered in a distant, abstract manner, the white speaker or writer making sure the listener was aware that the the former did not himself or herself buy into the thinking as it was historically understood. Perhaps that must stand as the most positive development in this story, that virtually any use of the expression by whites in recent decades has had a furtive quality to it, in which most whites would look over their shoulders in mixed company before broaching the topic. The paucity of white

Americans who still use the term in a deadpan, unapologetic manner, indicates a general consciousness that it is socially unacceptable to crassly cheer for white boxers out of open hostility toward blacks rights or opportunity. But here again, we are talking about the public behavior and discourse of America's white majority. What was going on inside their hearts and minds from 1949 to 1983, and even today, two decades later, could be a different story. Whereas a hundred million plus Caucasian Americans may have been as uninterested in a Great White Hope privately as they were publicly, the statistical discrepancies uncovered in this study suggest much of the white boxing audience, and undoubtedly some of the general sporting audience, retained some such sentiment, however politely they have kept it hidden.

To confirm that the concept of the Great White Hope burns brightly under the surface of sporting interest, one need only log on to numerous boxing fan forums on the web. One can find in such chat rooms passionate debates as to whether Tye Fields and Baby Joe Mesi are Great White Hopes with inflated records and strong promotional teams, or fighters worthy of respect. Fields is a six-foot-nine, 285-pound mountain of muscle. In his first twenty-five fights, he is 24–1 with twenty-three knockouts, with twenty-two in the first round! Yet in his one loss, Fields was himself knocked out in the first round, raising doubts about the quality of his victims. Fields is presently nowhere near a Top Ten ranking, and will not be until he moves up a qualitative notch in competition. This has not stopped Fields from already having a modest cult following, thanks to cable boxing shows. Fields has a larger following among boxing fans in his home state of Iowa. Casual white boxing fans who could not name more than a handful of black heavyweights (dozens of whom are more established than Fields) recognize Fields's name. Few black heavyweights ranked outside the Top Ten have their own fan website, as Fields does.

The other white heavyweight of note is Baby Joe Mesi of Buffalo. Mesi appears to be considerably closer to Top Ten quality than Fields, sporting an undefeated record of 25–0, only having to win two fights by decision. His New York hometown has embraced his career, giving him a local celebrity status unknown to any black Buffalo heavyweight in extended memory. Mesi is ranked seventeenth by the World Boxing Council,[3] so it is possible that his career path may land him in the top tier of his profession.

Where white America is in terms of its feelings toward a Great White Hope cannot be assessed until a white fighter like Mesi or Fields is good enough to move within striking distance of the heavyweight title. Such a heavyweight will need to be packaged and promoted enough so that white boxing fans can be persuaded they actually have a chance to succeed where Quarry, Cooney, Morrison, Wepner, Harris, McNeely, Daniels, Stander, LeDoux, Cobb, and Frank all fell short. If such a contender can be presented to the white audience, only then will enthusiasm for a white heavyweight hero be flushed out. It will be become clearer as to how far, if at all, mainstream white America has moved beyond a need to have a white champion simply by virtue of his race.

Conclusion: Limitations, Assumptions, and Methodological Problems

The 105 boxers in this study were defined as heavyweights because they either challenged for the heavyweight championship or were ranked in the Top Ten listings of *The Ring* for at least one month between 1949 and 1983. Yet a sizable minority were light heavyweights for part or most of their careers. Since the modernization of boxing in 1892, it has been commonplace for fighters to move from one weight division to another, usually from a lower weight to a heavier one. Sometimes, boxers make this leap for better financial opportunity, as some weight classes are more marketable to the public, thus offering larger purses. This has been particularly true of the heavyweight division, by far the category with the most money to be made. Other boxers move up the ladder when they realize they have previously not been fighting at their natural fighting weight. Young boxers are often still filling out physically, and may find it increasingly difficult to make the official weight limit of their class. For these fighters, the decision to move up is made for them by their genes. Finally, some boxers shift to a heavier competitive class simply due to a lack of discipline in training. These boxers eat their way across arbitrary weight distinctions. In addition to all the above, it also happens that boxers compete across weight divisions, fighting heavier opponents if the money is attractive, and taking on lighter ones for competitive advantage.

Even a casual glance at this sample of boxers reveals a light heavyweight flavor to the competitive measures. Archie Moore and Bob Foster fought in the 160–175 pound range virtually their entire careers, with heavyweight title challenges counting for most of their activity in the higher division. Jimmy Ellis was a mediocre light heavyweight for his first twenty bouts, before the removal of his tonsils made him grow into a far more accomplished heavyweight. Henry Mathews spent more than a decade competing under 175 pounds before trying his hand in the upper division. There are nineteen boxers in this study who fought more than half of their pre-ranked or pre-challenge bouts against light heavyweight opposition, which is why they were listed in *The Ring Record Book and Boxing Encyclopedia's* as light heavyweights themselves:

Doug Jones	Billy Hunter
Jimmy Ellis	Harry Mathews
Johnny Persol	Willie Pastrano
Jimmy Slade	Gus Lesnevich
Tommy Harrison	Grant Butcher
Joey Maxim	Bob Satterfield
Nick Barone	Tony Anthony
Bob Foster	Archie Moore
Harold Johnson	Floyd Patterson
Dan Bucceroni	

Almost one-fifth of the fighters under scrutiny fought as light heavyweights. What impact would this variable have on the interpretation of statistics meant to evaluate heavyweight credentials? The numerical measures used were supposed to be of heavyweights, for heavyweights, and about heavyweights. Statistics meant to define heavyweight credentials could well be distorted if light heavyweight success had little or no relevance to heavyweight excellence. It could be argued that a 165-pound boxer defeating a same-sized opponent is a comparable accomplishment, worthy of the same reverence, as a 220-pounder defeating his physical equal. The effort and skill required is relatively the same. The smaller victor had to sweat as hard and receive as much pain to emerge triumphant. In this light, it seems logical that a light heavyweight's record should be accepted at face value when he moves upward.

On the other hand, one can question whether a light heavyweight entering the heavyweight class with a spotless record of thirty wins and no losses, deserves the same accolades as a career 200-pounder with the same numbers. It has been proven time and again that a heavyweight is more than just a light heavyweight who added thirty pounds of muscle. Only once since 1908 has the light heavyweight titleholder successfully challenged for the ultimate crown, and Michael Spinks's victory was a highly controversial decision over a fading thirty-four-year-old Larry Holmes. Other light heavyweights have dreamed big and crashed hard in chasing this dream. Georges Carpentier was destroyed by Jack Dempsey, John Henry Lewis and Billy Conn by Joe Louis, Archie Moore by Rocky Marciano, and Bob Foster by Joe Frazier. That it has been almost unheard of for the second-heaviest champion to win the crown jewel of boxing proves that some boxers are natural heavyweights, with bodies genetically meant to carry over 200 pounds, without any loss of speed or coordination. There is more than a weight classification that separates heavyweights and light heavyweights. Something is lost when the latter try to become the former, so their credentials are worth somewhat less fighting at the heavier weight. Given this, one is tempted to go through the 3,500 bouts of the 105 boxers with a statistical formula that would bestow more credibility for victories over heavyweights, less value for wins over smaller opposition. A system was considered in which heavyweight victims would count for a value of 1.0, light heavyweights and middleweights for .85 and .7, respectively. Such a system proved impractical. Not all boxers in *The Ring Record Books* even have a weight designation listed under their name. An even greater methodological problem is that for the majority of boxers whose division is listed, the classification is no guarantee their entire fighting activity for the year was at that weight. There is nothing in boxing to prevent a fighter from moving up and down repeatedly in weight from one fight to the next. This is a familiar story for boxers with rollercoaster weight fluctuations. There is no realistic way of knowing the exact weight of all 3,500 boxers fought against the 105 heavyweights under analysis when the fights occurred. It would take years to determine this by moving one step further away from the sample fighters, finding the weight of the perhaps 50–60,000 opponents for the 3,500 primary opponents, and even then one would not be able to confirm the relative weight of the heavyweight competitive activity. With each degree of separation, one would merely be acquiring a bigger data base, not a more reliable set of information.

The artificial nature of this study's sub-period divisions is a further potential distortion of its data analysis. There is no historical justification for this periodization. It was arbitrarily chosen to provide a view of statistical change over time, if such numbers would present themselves. The years 1949 to 1983 saw a seismic change in American race relations in sports as well as the nation in general. Within these three-plus decades, the white American public could have changed its mind several times over about Great White Hopes, evolving from more interest to less or visa versa. Three sub-periods can only identify a maximum of two reversals in what their study's measures might indicate about its primary question. Choosing another set of dates might have revealed a somewhat different statistical picture from which to draw conclusions.

This study assumes *The Ring* magazine provides a looking glass for white sensitivities and racial preferences as expressed by which boxers they preferred to root for between 1949 and 1983. If white fans wanted a Great White Hope at the contender level, it is assumed a major boxing magazine like *The Ring* would be hard-pressed to ignore this wish. A mainstream boxing magazine in 1949–1983 America translates into an essentially white magazine, written mostly (if not exclusively) by white editors and journalists, for a mainstream white audience, and about a white view of boxing. No matter how fairly *The Ring* publicized black boxers, no matter how passionately it spoke against Great White Hopes, praised Joe Louis, or spoke out against racism in boxing on its pages, no matter how many black boxing fans picked this magazine off the shelf during these thirty-five years, the magazine's publishers had to know their market was mostly white. Knowing which side their financial bread was buttered on could scarcely have helped but have some impact (if not an overwhelming one) on *The Ring*'s system of picking which fighters to rate each month, if millions of its white readers were susceptible to the promotion of Great White Hopes. If its Caucasian readership was itching to read about a white ring hero, it could only have resulted in a quantifiable discrepancy in how hard white and black heavyweights worked to reach the big time of boxing.

This study made no attempt to define the exact nature of how opportunity is meted out in boxing, primarily because the unregulated, politically charged nature of boxing has inherently lent itself to a competitive infrastructure that defies any simple formula. The forces that control which heavyweights become rated, or have a chance to fight for the title, have never existed in a vacuum. They are unlikely to have ever been completely disconnected from the values, sentiments, and preferences of a mostly white society. Boxing, by its very definition, has always been as commercial an endeavor as any other professional sport. Whatever the exact web of factors shaping boxing opportunity, one cannot help but find within the web a supreme motivation to promote boxers and sanction title fights that make the most money for the sport's many agents. Like any other profit motive enterprise, this can be done much more easily by pandering to what the public already wants.

Sportswriters, promoters, and boxing governing officials all steer championship opportunity toward some boxers at the expense of others, and if the white mainstream has continued to want a white champion, such agents would have no choice but to be influenced by this, at least partially. In 1982, a white newspaper sports journalists unimpressed with Gerry Cooney's credentials to fight for Larry Holmes's title would have been hard-pressed to snub this bout on principle, given the immense pressure that would have been brought to bear by his or her editors to sell papers by giving in to the clamoring of the white audience. A promoter in 1969 may have been fully aware there were myriad black heavyweights more deserving to challenge champion Joe Frazier than Dave Zyglewicz, but taking the moral high road would have left him or her out in the cold when Frazier and Zyglewicz generated hundreds of thousands of dollars in gate receipts. In 1961, the ruling officials of the world boxing body that sanctioned the Patterson-McNeely fight may have held their noses at Patterson's choice of a challenger (snubbing the lethal Sonny Liston), but unfairness to Liston did not stop the cash registers from ringing loudly on the night of December 4, 1961.

For the purpose of this study, all that needs to be acknowledged is that fairness has taken many holidays from the ring, commonly referred to as the red-light district sport of American sport. This unfairness has resulted in many deserving boxers being passed over for title contention. However many forms of unfairness have characterized less deserving boxers moving to the front of the competiive line, race was once one of the most prominent manifestations. Thus the rationalization for this study, to see if, or how much of a remnant of this factor continued into the early 1980s, a time when it was easy for Americans to assume the age of the Great White Hope was long dead. Whatever the exact web of factors and agents that have been at work in doling out opportunity in boxing, a potential white preference for a Great White Hope would hitch a ride on these mechanisms, subsequently working to the advantage of white boxers. If one can visualize opportunity in boxing as a pinball bouncing chaotically off the walls and corners of an arcade game, whatever circuitous route the ball takes to its final destination (the granting of Top Ten status or the offering of a title fight to a contender), a yearning by white America for a Great White Hope (if it still existed) would accompany the ball to the end. This hope would register on the pinball machine's scoreboard (through comparative statistics), no matter how complex the journey, or how many other factors had their own influence.

Appendix 1: Records of Opponents

The following is a summary of the records for the opponents of this study's boxers, when they fought against the 105 subject heavyweights.

Muhammad Ali

1960	Tunney Hunsaker	6-6
	Herb Siler	1-0
1961	Tony Esperti	9-4-2
	Jim Robinson	0-1
	Donnie Fleeman	34-11-1
	Lamar Clark	47-2-1
	Duke Sabedong	15-11-1
	Alonzo Johnson	19-7
	Alex Miteff	24-10
	Willie Besmanoff	43-26-7

Entered Top Ten 198-78-12 / 10 = 20-8-1

1962	Sonny Banks	12-2
	Don Warner	12-6-2
	George Logan	22-6-1
	Billy Daniels	16-0
	Alejandro Lavorante	19-3
	Archie Moore	182-23-10
1963	Charlie Powell	22-6-1
	Doug Jones	21-3-1
	Henry Cooper	27-8-1

Challenged for Title 531-135-28 / 19 = 28-7-1

1964	Sonny Liston	35-1
1965	Sonny Liston	35-2
	Floyd Patterson	44-4
1966	George Chuvalo	34-11-2
	Henry Cooper	33-11-1
	Brian London	35-13
	Karl Mildenberger	49-2-3
	Cleveland Williams	65-5-1
1967	Ernest Terrell	39-4
	Zora Folley	74-7-4

1970	Jerry Quarry	37-4-4
	Oscar Bonavena	46-6-1

Challenged for Title 1,057-205-35 / 31 = 34-7-1

1971	Joe Frazier	26-0
	Jimmy Ellis	30-6
	Buster Mathis	29-2
	Jurgen Blin	28-8-6
1972	Mac Foster	28-1
	George Chuvalo	66-17-2
	Jerry Quarry	43-5-4
	Al Lewis	28-4
	Floyd Patterson	55-7-1
	Bob Foster	49-5
1973	Joe Bugner	43-5-1
	Ken Norton	29-1
	Ken Norton	30-1
	Rudi Lubbers	20-1
1974	Joe Frazier	30-1

Challenged for Title 1,591-269-45 / 46 = 35-6-1

	George Foreman	40-0
1975	Chuck Wepner	30-9-4
	Ron Lyle	31-2-1
	Joe Bugner	51-7-1
	Joe Frazier	32-2
1976	Jean Pierre Coopman	24-3
	Jimmy Young	17-4-2
	Richard Dunn	33-9
	Ken Norton	37-3
1977	Alfredo Evangelista	14-1-1
	Earnie Shavers	52-5-1
1978	Leon Spinks	6-0-1

Challenged for Title 1,958-314-59 / 58 = 34-5-1

	Leon Spinks	7-0-1
Challenged for Title	1,965-314-60 / 59 = 33-5-1	

Tony Anthony

1952	George Boddie	15-8
Incomplete (December 8, 1949)		
	Lou Ford	*Unavailable*
1953	Gordon Perry	5-0
	Joe Shaw	2-3-2
	Abe Hillard	3-1
	Ronnie Moore	4-10
	Al Niang	6-6-2
Incomplete (April 18, 1952)		
	Jose Contreras	18-27-3
	Miguel Mendevil	24-11-4
	Johnny Brown	6-6-3
	Jimmy Champagne	11-13-3
	Henry Lee	14-11-1
Incomplete (December 30, 1952)		
	Al Heath	3-5-1
	Eddie Dixon	10-1-2
	Al Warner	9-9-2
	Eddie Dixon	10-2-2
	Tommy Smith	16-10
	Roy Alston	14-8
1954	Richie Anderson	7-6-1
	Jacques Royer-Crecy	33-19-4
	Andy Mayfield	11-7-1
	Wilfredo Miro	46-14-5
	Lou King	29-19-3
	Terry Moore	39-13-3
	Willie Troy	26-2
1955	Said Khelfu	2-8
	Claude Chapman	12-1
	Bobby Boyd	33-6-2
	Lloyd Triplett	23-8-5
1956	Clarence Floyd	5-2
	Frank McGary	7-3-2
	Tony Johnson	23-7-8
	Clarence Hinnant	21-8
	Gordon Wallace	31-11-1
1957	Chuck Spieser	19-4-1
	Yvon Durelle	65-18-2
	Archie Moore	171-24-2
1958	Yvon Durelle	72-18-3
	Artie Miller	6-4-1
	Orville Pitts	5-1
	Calvin Brad	16-9-1
	Archie McBride	21-13
	Archie McBride	21-14
	Sonny Ray	17-5-5
1959	Reuben Vargas	17-6

	Sonny Ray	18-6-5
	Jesse Bowdry	26-3
	Bob Young	18-7-1
	Alonzo Johnson	17-2
Entered Top Ten	1,027-400-81 / 48 = 21-8-2	

Bob Baker

1949	Ray Bassett	*Unavailable*
	Jim Fulton	1-3
Incomplete (September 25, 1947)		
	Bob Golden	4-0
	Ben Skelton	5-5
Incomplete (October 14, 1947)		
	Willie Champion	0-4
	Joe Modzele	14-3
	Pedro Bradley	10-4
	Pedro Bradley	10-5
	Grady Welch	7-8-1
	Walter Hafer	15-16-1
	Marty Marshall	4-1-1
1950	Henry Jones	5-18-1
	Johnny Flynn	41-27-2
	Rusty Payne	37-14-1
Entered Top Ten	153-108-7 / 13 = 12-8-1	

Nick Barone

1946	Eddie McGill	*Unavailable*
	Harley Thume	0-0
	Billy Oden	*Unavailable*
	Leroy Kenney	0-0
	Leroy Kenney	0-1
	Bobby Hynds	*Unavailable*
	Bobby Vowles	*Unavailable*
	Jackson Bradley	3-4
	Tony DeMicco	18-2
	Jackie Turner	*Unavailable*
1947	Al Mitchell	7-12
Incomplete (October 16, 1945)		
	Al Johnson	16-13-1
	Jack McCurry	*Unavailable*
	Willie Davis	7-11
	Jim Roussee	1-0
	Johnny DeNero	8-1-1
	Willie Davis	8-13-1
	Cleve Bailey	14-17-1
	Cleve Bailey	14-19-1
	Jim Roussee	2-3
	Shed Bell	6-3
Incomplete (November 2, 1945)		
	Pat Richards	16-0-3

1948	Victor Buttin	Unavailable
	Charley Babcock	11-2
	Danny Martin	33-22-3
	Ossie Harris	39-46-5
	Russ Baxter	41-27-2
	J.C. Wilkins	26-14-4
	Shelton Bell	9-11-1
	Prentiss Hall	27-6
	Billy Grant	51-57-8
	George Kochan	44-21-11
	Chuck Hunter	36-10-1
1949	Freddie Flores	18-33-10
	Joe Taylor	13-4-2
	Tommy Yarosz	70-5
	Joe Taylor	15-4-2
	St. Paul	41-25-2
	Phil Muscato	55-17
	Tommy Yarosz	75-6
	Dick Wagner	25-7-4
	Chubby Wright	17-16-2
	Dave Whitlock	24-2-1
	Dick Wagner	25-9-4
1950	Bob Satterfield	22-9-2
	Reuben Jones	32-10-1
	Phil Muscato	55-21
	Gino Buonvino	15-2-1
	Tommy Yarosz	78-8-1
	Lee Oma	60-26-4
	Joe Taylor	23-8-2
	Jimmy Beau	25-3

Challenged for Title   1,125-530-81 / 45 =25-12-1

Fred Beshore

1942	Dan Biggers	Unavailable
1944	Joe Levy	Unavailable
	Dan Biggers	4-15
1946	Jimmy Wilson	2-7-2

Incomplete (November 12, 1945)

	Easy Flowers	Unavailable
	Bill McClure	3-4
	Nick Moreno	2-0
	Jack Glover	0-1
	Babe Edwards	14-2-3
	Jack Glover	2-6
	Jesse McGowen	0-4

Incomplete (April 15, 1946)

	Horace Thompson	Unavailable
	Carlton Perry	2-12-2
	Carlton Perry	3-13-2
	Babe Edwards	17-2-4
1947	Bobby Bonger	20-4

Incomplete (December 16, 1946)

	Charley Riggs	14-5

	Ernie Rios	9-7-3
	Bill McClure	13-9-2
	Al Jordan	15-12-1
	Dick Underwood	Unavailable
	Ernie Rios	10-9-3
	Francisco De La Cruz	9-8
	Tommy Garland	27-6-2
1948	George Millich	16-3-1
	Dutch Culbertson	17-1-2
	Tiger Jack Fox	115-16-9
	Bobby Zander	14-8-1
	Roland Spencer	9-4-6
	Pat Valentino	39-10-4
1949	Joe Weiden	20-4-1
	Tony Bosnich	30-8-1
	Bob Dunlap	12-1
	Dutch Culbertson	18-6-3
	Lee Oma	59-25-2
1950	Lee Oma	60-25-2

Challenged for Title   575-237-56 / 31 = 19-8-2

Wayne Bethea

1954	Rue Williams	0-2
	Elle Rogelle	4-4
	Henry Hawkins	0-0-1
	Howie Turner	11-0-2
	Robert Graves	3-0
	Rico Hackney	1-0
	Bob Biehler	8-2
	Harold Carter	11-0
1955	Joey Rowan	23-6
	Harold Carter	13-1
	Harold Carter	15-1
	Harold Carter	16-1-1
	Julio Mederos	18-10-2
	Mickey Carter	10-6-1
1956	Ernie Cab	5-4-1
	Ezzard Charles	93-17-1
	Jimmy Slade	24-15-4
	Joe Bygraves	32-7
	Howie Turner	20-2-5
	Zora Folley	26-2-1
1957	Zora Folley	27-2-1
	Jeff Dyer	15-8
	Bert Whitehurst	23-10-2
	Paul Andrews	32-7
	Harold Johnson	54-7

Entered Top Ten   484-114-22 / 25 = 19-5-1

Duane Bobick

1973	Tommy Burns	8-8-1
	Willie Anderson	0-0
	Jim Williams	Unavailable

	Clyde Brown	7-8
	Doug Kirk	13-4-1
	Sylvester Murphy	1-1
	Ned Edwards	1-14
	Chuck Borden	3-3
	G. G. Maldonado	8-3-2
	Manuel Ramos	24-23-3
	Ron Draper	0-0
	Orvin Veazey	16-7
	Roger Russell	11-13-2
	John Hudgins	12-18-2
	Reco Brooks	5-5-1
1974	Orville Qualls	11-7-1
	Jimmy Summerville	10-4-4
	Jimmy Cross	18-6-1
	Ted Gullick	16-6-1
	Billy Daniels	23-19-1
	Lou Bailey	17-41-5
	Art Robinson	2-3
	Donnie Nelson	4-2
	Mike Weaver	6-5
	Harold Carter	16-29-2
1975	Cookie Wallace	19-19-2
	Raul Gorosito	12-8-1
	Ernie Lassiter	3-2-1
	Oliver Wright	12-10
	Pat Duncan	33-8-2
	Rochelle Norris	11-3
	George Johnson	19-19-4
	Randy Neumann	31-5

Entered Top Ten 372-303-39 / 32 = 12-9-1

Johnny Boudreaux

1973	Elgie Waters	3-16
	Elgie Waters	3-17
	Charlie Lee	1-6-1

Incomplete (January 17, 1966)

	Jack Johnson	2-7-1
	Art Bradford	1-3
	Memo Vargas	*Unavailable*
1974	Charles Atlas	1-3
	Oliver Wright	10-4
	Terry Daniels	32-12-1
	Bob Avery	13-9-2

Incomplete (March 27, 1972)

	George Johnson	20-17-3
	Tommy Howard	2-13-1
	Koli Vailea	5-3
	Leon Shaw	4-4-1
1975	Stan Ward	2-0
	Cookie Wallace	18-18-2
	Tony Doyle	40-14-1
	Charles Atlas	6-6
1976	Brian O'Melia	14-26-2

	Joe Gholston	13-10-2

Entered Top Ten 190-188-17 / 19 = 10-10-1

Dan Bucceroni

1947	Bob Payne	1-3-1
	Paris Lennon	*Unavailable*
	Charley Smith	*Unavailable*
	Jimmy Long	8-25
1948	Jimmy Long	8-26
	Fred Ramsey	7-9-1
	Herman Badger	18-7-1
	John Calcinore	6-0
	Dick Lee	1-3
	Booker Robinson	*Unavailable*
	Tony Jess	1-1-1
	John Calcinore	6-1
	Dick Wagner	17-6-4
1949	Billy Norris	*Unavailable*
	Guy Manayunk	*Unavailable*
	Billy Guy	1-7
	Vernon Williams	9-3-2
	Billy Guy	1-8
	Ted Calaman	7-0
	Harry Daniels	0-3-1
	Jerome Richardson	2-1
1950	Rocky Jones	2-0
	Wylie Burns	22-4-3
	James Walls	11-17-2
	Mike Jacobs	12-11-2
	Doc Bee	*Unavailable*
	Shamus O'Brien	23-20-2

Incomplete (November 10, 1948)

	Sony Parisi	15-2
	James J. Parker	8-1-2
1951	Jimmy Bell	25-25-3

Incomplete (November 17, 1948)

	Jimmy Roussee	3-2-2
	Bob Murphy	54-4
	Dick Wagner	26-13-4
	Earl Sabotin	15-0
	Augustino Guedes	18-12-3
	Rocky Jones	7-3
	Kevin Allen	2-3-1
	Roland LaStarza	47-11
1952	Aaron Wilson	19-6
	Roland LaStarza	47-11
	Dave Davey	22-1
	Danny Nardico	42-7-4
1953	Rocky Jones	10-8-11

Entered Top Ten 526-255-50 / 37 = 14-7-1

Grant Butcher

1948	Sam Jordan	4-0-4

Records of Opponents

	Frank Buford	4-2-1
	Andy Walker	1-3-3
	Frank Buford	6-2-2
1949	Dave Whitlock	19-0-1
	Johnny O'Neill	12-6-3
	Charley Riggs	16-7

Incomplete (December 10, 1947)

	Remo Polidori	10-1-1
	Dave Whitlock	22-1-1
	Johnny O'Neill	12-7-3
	Lloyd Marshall	56-15-5
	Joe Kahut	39-9-8
	Dave Whitlock	24-2-1

Entered Top Ten 225-55-33 / 13 = 17-4-2

Harold Carter

1953	Joey Rowan	12-2
	Clyde Thompson	Unavailable
	Al Roberts	Unavailable
	Ike Thomas	2-4
	Ike Thomas	2-5
1954	Dick Reddick	Unavailable
	Joe Lindsay	24-6-2
	Bob Slaughter	6-1-1
	Bob Slaughter	6-2-1
	Bob Golden	9-5
	Earl Haines	3-3

Incomplete (July 12, 1950)

	Wayne Bethea	5-1-1
1955	Ike Thomas	2-7-2
	Bob Slaughter	7-5-2
	Wayne Bethea	6-2-1
	Julio Mederos	44-9-7
	Wayne Bethea	6-3-1
	Julio Mederos	44-10-7
	Wayne Bethea	6-3-2
1956	Bob Satterfield	40-20-3

Entered Top Ten 224-88-30 / 17 = 13-5-2

Ezzard Charles

1940	Medley Johnson	Unavailable
	Jimmy Brown	Unavailable
	John Reeves	Unavailable
	Charley Banks	Unavailable
	Kid Ash	Unavailable
	Charley Banks	Unavailable
	Remo Ferdandez	Unavailable
	Eddie Fowler	Unavailable
	Pat Wright	Unavailable
	Frankie Williams	Unavailable
	John Reeves	Unavailable
	Bradley Lewis	Unavailable

	Marty Simmons	43-17-6
	Bill Hood	Unavailable
	Charley Jerome	Unavailable
1941	Billy Bengal	Unavailable
	Slaka Cavrich	Unavailable
	Floyd Howard	Unavailable
	Joe Sutka	Unavailable
	Rudy Kozole	Unavailable
	Ken Overlin	112-13-5
	Al Gilbert	7-5-3
	Pat Mangini	11-11
	Teddy Yarosz	107-13-3
1942	Anton Christoforidis	44-10-7
	Ken Overlin	120-13-6
	Billy Pryor	Unavailable
	Evelio Tunero	70-22-14
	Charley Burley	51-5-1
	Charley Burley	52-6-1
	Steve Mamakos	21-12-1
	Booker Beckwith	19-2
	Jose Basora	34-6-2
	Mose Brown	20-8-1
	Joey Maxim	20-5
	Joey Maxim	20-6
1943	Jimmy Bivins	31-5
	Lloyd Marshall	32-6-2
1946	Al Sheridan	7-10-1
	Tee Hubert	14-5
	Billy Duncan	45-11-3
	George Parks	13-18-2
	Tee Hubert	14-6
	Archie Moore	76-12-6
	Shelton Bell	7-4
	Lloyd Marshall	52-13-3
	Billy Smith	21-5-1
	Jimmy Bivins	52-7-1
1947	Billy Smith	23-6-2
	Jimmy Bivins	56-8-1
	Erv Sarlin	8-2
	Archie Moore	80-13-8
	Fitzie Fitzpatrick	38-8-3
	Elmer Ray	60-7-2
	Joe Matisi	12-3-2
	Lloyd Marshall	54-14-3
	Al Smith	2-1
	Clarence Jones	13-18-1
	Teddy Randolph	17-21-5
	Fitzie Fitzpatrick	39-10-3
1948	Archie Moore	85-14-8
	Sam Baroudi	37-9-3
	Elmer Ray	64-7-2
	Erv Sarlin	10-6-1
	Jimmy Bivins	66-12-1
	Walter Hafer	14-12-1
	Joe Baksi	51-7-4
1949	Johnny Haynes	22-11
	Joey Maxim	62-15-4

Challenged for Title 1,928-460-123/49 = 39-9-3

	Jersey Joe Walcott	46-13-1
	Gus Lesnevich	58-13-5
	Pat Valentino	42-10-4
1950	Freddie Beshore	28-6-2
	Joe Louis	60-1
	Nick Barone	43-8-1
1951	Lee Oma	63-27-3
	Jersey Joe Walcott	51-15-1
	Joey Maxim	75-16-14
	Jersey Joe Walcott	51-16-1
	Rex Layne	34-2-2
	Joey Maxim	76-17-14
	Joe Kahut	54-18-7

Challenged for Title 2, 609-622-178/62 = 42-10-3

1952	Jersey Joe Walcott	51-16-1
	Rex Layne	38-5-2
	Bernie Reynolds	52-9-1
	Cesar Brion	39-7
	Jimmy Bivins	82-23-1
	Frank Buford	21-17-5
1953	Wes Bascom	15-4
	Tommy Harrison	18-6-1
	Rex Layne	40-6-2
	Bill Gilliam	23-18-2
	Larry Watson	12-8
	Nino Valdes	23-8-2
	Harold Johnson	42-5
	Coley Wallace	19-2
1954	Bob Satterfield	32-14-2

Challenged for Title 3, 116-770-197/77 = 40-10-3

	Rocky Marciano	45-0

Challenged for Title 3161-770-197/78 = 41-10-3

Henry Clark

1964	Joey Orbillo	0-0
	Johnny Gordon	13-3-2
	Jimmy Harryman	1-0
	John Balla	11-2-2

Incomplete (June 18, 1962)

	Manuel Ramos	4-1
	John Balla	10-3-2
	James Taylor	8-3-2
	Tom Pawlaski	3-0
1965	Matt Jackson	11-12-3

Incomplete (September 25, 1959)

	Dave Furch	10-16-3
	George Johnson	5-4-1
1966	Amos Lincoln	32-4-3
	Bobby Stintinato	24-12-1
	Zora Folley	70-7-4
1967	Bill McMurray	20-15-2

	Steve Grant	9-0
	Fred Lewis	17-4-1
	Eddie Machen	60-9-3
	Steve Grant	9-1
	Roger Rischer	26-10-2
1968	Leotis Martin	25-3

Entered Top Ten 369-109-31 / 21 = 18-5-1

Tex Cobb

1977	Pedro Vega	*Unavailable*
	Tyrone Harbee	1-0
	Trinidad Escamilla	*Unavailable*
	Earnest Smith	3-13

Incomplete (March 23, 1977)

	David Wynne	6-0-1
	Dave Martinez	0-3

Incomplete (September 13, 1977)

	Don Hinton	*Unavailable*
1978	Dave Martinez	0-3
	Paul Solomon	6-3-1

Incomplete (February 15, 1977)

	Rodell Dupree	9-11
1979	Zack Ferguson	0-2
	Jesse Crown	4-2
	Don Halpin	5-4
	Terry Mims	7-5
1980	Eusebio Hernandez	19-2
	Cookie Wallace	24-29-2
	Robert Echols	14-4-1
	Earnie Shavers	58-9-1
	Ken Norton	41-6-1
1981	Michael Dokes	19-0-1
	Harry Terrell	15-8

Entered Top Ten 231-98-8 / 16 = 14-6-1

	Bernardo Mercado	28-3
1982	Jeff Shelburg	22-4

Entered Top Ten 281-105-15 / 18 = 16-6

Gerry Cooney

1977	Bill Jackson	0-1
	Jimmy Robertson	*Unavailable*
	Jose Rosario	*Unavailable*
	Matt Robinson	4-9-4

Incomplete

	Joe Maye	2-15
	Quinnie Locklear	3-5

Incomplete (August 7, 1978)

	Jimmy Sykes	1-2
1978	Terry Kidd	0-1
	Austin Johnson	*Unavailable*

Records of Opponents

	Gary Bates	16-17-2
Incomplete (January 25, 1977)		
	S.T. Gordon	1-2
	G.G. Maldonado	12-6-2
	Charley Polite	15-32-3
	Sam McGill	2-1
	Grady Daniels	6-1
1979	Eddie Lopez	12-1
	Charlie Johnson	14-3
	Tom Prater	19-10-1
	Broderick Mason	10-3
	Malik Dozier	4-2-1
	Dino Dennis	35-2-1

Entered Top Ten 156-118-14 / 18 = 9-7-1

	Leroy Boone	12-3
1980	Jimmy Young	25-9-2
	Ron Lyle	40-6-1
1981	Ken Norton	42-6-1

Challenged for Title 275-142-18 / 22 = 13-6-1

Billy Daniels

1960	Don Lee	*Unavailable*
	Richie Lee	*Unavailable*
	Ralph Giss	*Unavailable*
	Ken Kelly	6-1
	Nat Hammer	*Unavailable*
	Charlie Jones	6-7
1961	John Byrd	6-5
	Tommy Sims	24-16-3
	Willie Bell	10-4-1
	Wilfredo Avellez	10-2
	Johnny Jenkins	15-4-5
	Claude Chapman	24-5-1
	John Massey	9-1-2
	Jeff Davis	4-1
	Don Warner	11-5-2
1962	Claude Chapman	25-7-1
	Cassius Clay	13-0
	Mike DeJohn	44-9-1

Entered Top Ten 207-67-16/ 14 = 15-5-1

Terry Daniels

1969	Charles Burnett	*Unavailable*
	Bob Johnson	*Unavailable*
	Kenny Kinney	*Unavailable*
	Lamar Thompson	*Unavailable*
	Joe Sharlow	0-2
	Floyd Casey	3-13-2
	Gilbert Riggs	*Unavailable*
	Joe Sharlow	0-4
	Leroy Caldwell	5-2
	Dickie Willis	7-7-1

	Joe Sharlow	0-5
1970	Dickie Willis	7-7-1
	Kenny Hayden	*Unavailable*
	Leo Bennett	*Unavailable*
	Sonny Moore	20-33-2
	Sonny Moore	20-33-3
	Glenn Kurtiza	*Unavailable*
	Woody Parks	1-2
	Joe Harris	1-2-1
	Terry Sorrels	0-3
	Paul Nielsen	10-7
	Amos Lincoln	39-12-3
	Joe Byrd	11-13-1
1971	Willis Earls	12-11-3
	Tony Doyle	35-8-1
	Bob Scott	3-0
	Freddie Williams	5-12-1
	Floyd Patterson	49-7
	Clyde Brown	4-0
	Manuel Ramos	24-16-3
	Jack O'Halloran	19-12-2
	Sonny Moore	21-36-3
	Ted Gullick	16-3

Challenged for Title 312-244-26 / 25 = 12-10-1

Mike Dejohn

1950	Mike Barron	*Unavailable*
	Hank Thompson	*Unavailable*
	Harry Mazier	*Unavailable*
	Sonny Parker	*Unavailable*
	Jackie Batson	*Unavailable*
1951	Ted Alexander	0-2
	Bill Bailey	0-1

Incomplete

	Pete Graham	0-0
	Rufe Williams	*Unavailable*
	Russell Session	4-1
	Joey Evans	*Unavailable*
	Norvel Gaddes	*Unavailable*
	Syl Kuchinski	6-3-1

Incomplete (November 14, 1950)

1954	Art McCann	*Unavailable*
	Hal McNeely	*Unavailable*
	Johnny Kasmier	*Unavailable*
	Ernie Cab	1-2-1
	Jimmy Cousins	4-1
	Ponce DeLeon	2-15-4
	Chuck Syers	8-4-2
	Max Cox	*Unavailable*
1955	Jimmy Williams	7-4-4
	Jack Jacobs	5-4-1
	Moses Graham	2-0
	Jimmy Wells	21-32-2
	Emil Brtko	16-2

	Gene Jackson	0-1
	Jack Taylor	3-2-3

Incomplete (August 11, 1954)

	Jimmy Bivins	84-25-1
	Bobby Robbins	*Unavailable*
1956	Emil Brtko	17-3
	Roy Bullock	5-4-1
	Moses Graham	2-3
1957	Jack Jacobs	11-8-2
	Leo Petras	3-4
	Julius Griffin	6-1
	Neal Welch	2-9-1
	Alex Miteff	12-0

Entered Top Ten   221-131-23 / 25 = 9-5-1

Michael Dokes

1976	Al Byrd	1-2
1977	Sergio Rodrigues	0-1
	Dave Wilson	3-0

Incomplete (December 10, 1976)

	Charlie Jordan	12-32-2
	Ed Turner	16-7-1
1978	George Holden	0-5

Incomplete (January 17, 1978)

	Abdul Khan	0-2-1

Incomplete (October 20, 1977)

	Dan Johnson	2-9
	Terry Mims	7-1
	Eugene Green	4-2-1
	Ira Martin	4-3
1979	Wendell Bailey	9-0
	Greg Sorrentino	15-4-1
	Willie McIntyre	0-1
	Jimmy Young	23-8-2
1980	Earl Tripp	13-3
	Lucien Rodriguez	25-5

Entered Top Ten   134-85-8 / 17 = 8-5

	Osvaldo Ocasio	15-1
	Osvaldo Ocasio	15-1-1
	Tom Fischer	26-5
1981	Tex Cobb	17-1
	John Gardner	34-2
	Harry Terrell	15-9
	George Chaplin	17-4-1
1982	Lynn Ball	18-5
	Franco Thomas	24-3

Challenged for Title   315-116-10 / 26 = 12-4-1

Bob Dunlap

1948	Bobby Green	*Unavailable*

	Smiley Burnette	7-2-5

Incomplete (September, 1946)

	Lee Sponsell	*Unavailable*
	Lloyd Delucchi	5-8-6
	Andy Walker	0-2-1
	Dave Whitlock	17-0-1
	Jess Slocum	4-3-2
	Champ Millich	17-10-1

Incomplete (February 11th, 1949)

	Obie Wooten	9-19-4
	Hank Thurman	6-3-3
	Lee Upshaw	2-1
1949	Frank Buford	6-3-2
	Eddie Sims	
	Freddie Beshore	24-2-1
	Harry Wills	19-14-6
	Dave Whitlock	22-1-1
	Lloyd Marshall	56-17-3
	Andy Walker	9-4-4
1950	John McFalls	9-0-2
	Jack Warren	3-5-4

Incomplete (July 26, 1948)

	Jay Lambert	8-2-1
	Frank Buford	11-7-4
	Dutch Culbertson	18-11-3
	Rex Layne	19-1
	Clarence Henry	19-2-1
1951	Ponce DeLeon	1-6-2
	Al Smith	
1952	Rafael Iglesias	*Unavailable*
	Ron Whittle	21-11-6
	Cesar Brion	39-6

Entered Top Ten   351-140-63 / 25 = 14-6-3

Jimmy Ellis

1961	Arley Seifer	15-11-1
	Gene Leslie	12-4-1
	Johnny Morris	21-4
	Wilf Greaves	34-19-1
	Clarence Riley	17-21-5
	Holly Mims	48-21-6
1962	Rory Calhoun	45-14-2
	Johnny Alford	14-3-3
	Holly Mims	49-21-6
	Rudolph Bent	30-25-4
	Charlie Glover	14-10-1
	Sammy Poe	1-2
	Henry Hank	52-16-3
	Leroy Green	18-15-2
1963	Johnny Halahifi	50-11-5
	Lou Gutierrez	54-4-4
1964	Rubin Carter	18-4
	Joe Spencer	4-0

Records of Opponents

	Don Fullmer	31-11-2
	George Benton	51-9-2
1955	Joe Blackwood	Unavailable
	Chuck Leslie	9-7
1966	Hubert Hilton	13-3-2
	Lewina Wacqua	18-2-1
	Billy Daniels	20-14-1
	Eddie Dembry	9-2
	Tommy Sims	32-26-4
1967	Johnny Persol	17-3-1

Entered Top Ten 696-282-56 / 27 = 26-10-2

	Leotis Martin	24-1
	Oscar Bonavena	29-3

Challenged for Title 749-286-55 / 29 = 26-10-2

1968	Jerry Quarry	26-1-4
	Floyd Patterson	46-6-1

Challenged for Title 821-293-34 / 31 = 26-9-1

Zora Folley

1953	Jimmy Ingram	7-8
	Cal Chambers	3-2-1
	K.O. Brown	Unavailable
	Lonnnie Malone	21-10-2
1954	Howard King	13-2-3
	Battling Blackjack	14-2

Incomplete (July 12, 1950)

	Jackie Condon	14-26-5
	Johnny Rebel	Unavailable
	Frank Buford	22-24-3
	Kirby Seals	5-2
	Kid Percy	0-1
	Sandy McPherson	17-27-3
	Georgie Woods	4-0-1
	Jimmy Ingram	13-11-1
	Kid Zanzibar	32-7
1955	J.B. Reed	4-2-1
	Kirby Seals	5-6-1
	Calvin Brad	6-4-1
	Howard King	21-4-4
	Johnny Summerlin	24-4-2
	Jake Williams	5-3-2
	Ted Calaman	17-2

Incomplete (1950)

	Reuben Wilson	6-3-1
	Young Jack Wilson	10-5-1
1956	Watson Jones	33-23-5

Incomplete (September 19, 1953)

	Ponce DeLeon	2-19-4
	Don Robinson	12-3

Incomplete

	Roger Rischer	13-4-2

	Nino Valdes	35-13-2
	Wayne Bethea	13-4-2

Entered Top Ten 371-221-49 / 28 = 13-8-2

1957	Wayne Bethea	13-5-2
	Howie Turner	20-3-5
	Johnny Hollins	7-10-1
	Sports Harvey	10-11
	Jim Woods	Unavailable
	Julius Griffin	6-3
	Jeff Dyer	15-9
	Edgardo Romero	24-5-2

Incomplete

	Monroe Ratliff	6-7-4
	Duke Sabedong	13-5-1
	Edgardo Romero	24-7-2

Incomplete

1958	Garvin Sawyer	13-4
	Eddie Machen	24-0
	Art Swiden	28-11-1
	Pete Rademacher	0-1
	Henry Cooper	15-7-1
	Joe Bygraves	36-11-1
1959	Alex Miteff	16-2-1
	Hank Thurman	24-16-4
	Willie Besmanoff	38-14-8
	Alvin Williams	53-25-6
	Howard King	34-16-7
	Monroe Ratliff	13-12-4
	Alonzo Johnson	17-3
1960	Eddie Machen	31-1-1
	Clarence Williams	2-2
	Sonny Liston	29-1
	Willie Besmanoff	41-21-8
1961	Norm Letcher	1-1
	Alejandro Lavorante	12-1
	Ben Marshall	3-6

Incomplete

	Sonny Moore	11-15-2
	Henry Cooper	22-7-1
1962	Mike DeJohn	41-9-1
	Robert Cleroux	31-2-1
	Paul Andrews	37-9
	Doug Jones	19-2
	Al Gonzalez	13-1
	Dave Furch	8-9-2
	Doug Jones	20-3-1
1963	Dean Bogany	23-7-2
	Robert Cleroux	39-4-1
	Ernie Terrell	31-4
	John Collins	5-4
	Billy Daniels	18-3
1964	George Chuvalo	25-7-2
	Tod Herring	24-2
	Karl Mildenberger	39-2-1
	Gerhard Zech	25-2-1

1965	Oscar Bonavena	8-0
	Bob Foster	21-3
1966	Jefferson Davis	28-8-1
	Henry Clark	8-2-3
	Jefferson Davis	28-10-1
1967	Floyd Joyner	19-11-4

Incomplete (August 18, 1965)
Challenged for Title 1,482-567-143 / 82 = 18-7-2

George Foreman

1969	Don Waldheim	5-4-1
	Fred Askew	1-6-1
	Sylvester Dullaire	6-1
	Chuck Wepner	18-4-2
	John Carroll	0-2
	Cookie Wallace	5-10-1
	Vernon Clay	6-3
	Roberto Davila	10-12
	Leo Petersen	10-12
	Max Martinez	5-7
	Bob Hazelton	3-2
	Levi Forte	19-19-1
	Gary Wiler	3-4
1970	Charlie Polite	10-14-3
	Jack O'Halloran	18-5-2
	Gregorio Peralta	73-5-7
	Rufus Brassell	13-2
	James J. Woody	14-5-1
	Aaron Eastling	19-7-2
	George Johnson	14-12-3

Entered Top Ten 252-136-24 / 20 = 13-7-1

	Roger Russell	11-7-2
	George Chuvalo	59-15-2
	Lou Bailey	14-28-5
	Boone Kirkman	22-1
	Mel Turnbow	8-9
1971	Charlie Boston	3-0
	Stamford Harris	5-6
	Gregorio Peralta	73-5-8
	Vic Scott	1-2

Incomplete

	Leroy Caldwell	11-8-1
	Ollie Wilson	16-30-1
	Luis Pires	18-7-1
1972	Murphy Goodwin	0-9
	Clarence Boone	2-16
	Ted Gullick	16-5-1
	Miguel Angel Paez	41-17-9
	Terry Sorrels	0-5

Challenged for Title 452-306-54 / 37 = 12-8-1

Bob Foster

1961	Duke Williams	*Unavailable*

	Clarence Ryan	1-5-1
	Billy Johnson	3-1-1

Incomplete (June 1, 1960)

	Ray Bryan	7-9-2
	Floyd McCoy	10-11
	Ernie Knox	8-6-1

Incomplete (May 5, 1961)

	Clarence Floyd	10-11
1962	Billy Tisdale	0-3-1
	Bert Whitehurst	31-25-6
	Doug Jones	19-3-1
1963	Richard Benjamin	*Unavailable*
	Curtis Bruce	16-12-1
	Mauro Mina	40-2-2
	Willie Besmanoff	44-27-8
1964	Dave Bailey	14-10-3
	Allen Thomas	19-3-2
	Ernie Terrell	34-4
	Norm Letcher	6-4
	Don Quinn	22-8
	Henry Hank	55-19-4
1965	Robert Rascon	29-5-1
	Dave Russell	7-13-3
	Chuck Leslie	8-5
	Henry Hank	56-20-4
	Zora Folley	69-7-4
1966	Leroy Green	19-20-3
1967	Jim Robinson	10-21

Incomplete (October 14, 1963)

	Andres Selpa	118-41-26
	Eddie Cotton	57-22-5
	Henry Mathews	6-2-1
	Levan Roundtree	12-3
	Eddie Vick	11-9-3
	Sonny Moore	19-26-2
1968	Dick Tiger	58-15-3
	Charley Polite	8-8-3
	Eddie Vick	11-12-3
	Roger Rouse	30-6-4
1969	Frank De Paula	18-6-3
	Andy Kendall	27-4-5
	Levan Roundtree	1307
	Chuck Leslie	17-18-4
1970	Bill Hardney	10-11-1
	Cookie Wallace	6-11-2
	Roger Rouse	32-10-4
	Mark Tessman	30-1

Challenged for Title 1,020-466-117 / 43 = 24-11-3

Mac Foster

1966	Jim Gilmore	0-1
1967	Bert Birmingham	4-2-1
	Sam Wyatt	1-2
	L.J. Wheeler	2-2-1

Records of Opponents 195

	Lou Phillips	2-1
	Lino Armenteros	26-23-7

Incomplete (June 8, 1964)

	Floyd Joiner	19-14-4

Incomplete (May 25, 1967)

	Ray Ellis	3-5
	Roy Wallace	3-2-1
1968	Hubert Hilton	17-7-2
	Steve Grant	9-3
	Sonny Moore	19-27-2
	Curtis Bruce	27-20-1
	Tommy Burns	7-2
	Tommy Fields	16-13-3
	Joe Hemphill	0-1-1

Entered Top Ten 155-125-22 / 16 = 10-8-1

Scott Frank

1978	Joe Maye	9-18-1
	Robert Colay	0-1
	Johnny Blaine	1-12-1
	John McGrath	*Unavailable*
	Chuck Wepner	35-13-2
	Charles Harris	10-24-1
1979	Guy Casale	10-1-3
	James Reid	2-1
	Don Martin	4-4
	Bill Connell	11-3-1
1980	Ron Stander	36-15-2
	C.J, Bar Brown	4-15-2
	Randy Willis	*Unavailable*
1981	Al Brooks	5-4
	Eddie Mallard	2-5-2
	Johnny Blaine	3-23-2
1982	Renaldo Snipes	22-1
	Mark Lee	15-5
	Mike Jameson	9-4
1983	Steve Zouski	23-4
	Ken Arlt	18-10

Challenged for Title 219-163-18 / 19 = 11-9-1

Joe Frazier

1965	Woody Goss	2-2
	Mike Bruce	3-1
	Ray Staples	11-4
	Abe Davis	5-17

Incomplete (May 25, 1965)

1966	Mel Turnbow	6-2
	Dick Wipperman	30-5-1
	Charley Polite	3-4-1
	Don Smith	8-3-1
	Chuck Leslie	10-9-1
	Memphis Al Jones	3-5

	Billy Daniels	20-13-1
	Oscar Bonavena	21-2
	Eddie Machen	51-8-2

Entered Top Ten 173-75-7 / 13 = 13-6-1

1967	Doug Jones	29-8-1
	Jeff Davis	29-11-1
	George Johnson	8-8-3
	George Chuvalo	47-13-2
	Tony Doyle	18-4-1
	Marion Conners	24-8-1

Challenged for Title 328-127-16 / 19 = 17-7-1

1968	Buster Mathis	23-0
	Manuel Ramos	20-6-2
	Oscar Bonavena	38-4
1969	Dave Zyglewicz	28-1
	Jerry Quarry	31-2-4

Challenged for Title 468-140-22 / 24 = 20-6-1

1970	Jimmy Ellis	27-5
	Bob Foster	41-4
1971	Muhammad Ali	31-0
1972	Terry Daniels	28-4-1
	Ron Stander	23-1-1
1973	George Foreman	37-0
	Joe Bugner	43-6-1
1974	Muhammad Ali	43-2
	Jerry Quarry	49-6-4
1975	Jimmy Ellis	39-11-1

Challenged for Title 829-179-30 / 34 = 24-5-1

Bill Gilliam

1943	Roy Taylor	5-1
	Roy Taylor	5-2
1946	Gilley Ferrion	*Unavailable*
	Jimmy Robinson	2-0
	Moose Kennedy	6-3
1947	Howard Chard	4-5
	Ken Shaw	14-6-2
	Roy Thomas	7-1
	Mickey Carter	3-0
	Adam Spencer	11-7-1
	Mickey Carter	5-1-1
	Eddie Franklin	11-3-1
1948	Gene Jones	25-5-1
	Red Applegate	9-6
	Lee Jackson	7-0-2
	Red Applegate	9-7
	Roy Thomas	10-4-2
	Jim Walker	7-2
1949	Maynard Jones	7-3-1
	Colion Chaney	46-25-7
	Earl Hines	*Unavailable*
	Willie Bean	18-9-2
	Willie Bean	18-10-2
1950	Joe Lindsay	18-2-2

	Abel Cestac	37-7-1
	Omelio Agramonte	28-6
1951	Bob Baker	23-0
	Jack Flood	10-7-1
	Art Henri	13-20-1
	Rocky Jones	7-5
1952	Omelio Agramonte	37-14
	Eddie Polly Smith	6-4-2
	Charles Lester	4-2-2
	Gene Jones	43-8-3
	Kid Riviera	27-8-2
	Bob Baker	25-1-1
	Bob Baker	26-1-1
	Bob Baker	27-1-1
1953	Bob Baker	27-2-1
	Harold Johnson	40-5
	Nino Valdes	22-6-2
	Ezzard Charles	82-8-1
	Coley Wallace	18-2
1954	Chubby Wright	23-29-3
	Leonard Morrow	27-7-1

Entered Top Ten   789-242-47 / 41 = 19-6-1

S.T. Gordon

1977	Alvaro Lopez	3-2
	Howard Gilmore	Unavailable
	Al Merazini	Unavailable
	Richard Dean	Unavailable
	Richard Jensen	Unavailable
	Dick Hernandez	Unavailable
	Howard Snyder	Unavailable
	Hector SoDono	Unavailable
	John Crece	Unavailable
	Big Boy Brown	Unavailable
	Junior Alvarado	Unavailable
	Dave Ochoa	Unavailable
1978	Gerry Cooney	10-0
	Via Sufoa	0-1

Incomplete (December 19, 1979)

	Eddie Lopez	9-1
	Earl Tripp	7-1
	Young Sanford Houpe	12-2
1979	Earl Tripp	10-2
	Bobby Gatewood	Unavailable
1980	Eric Sedillo	13-1
	Niua Tofaeno	9-0
	Ivy Brown	24-9
	Earl Tripp	16-4
1981	Harry Terrell	15-7
	King David Smith	13-19-5
	Alvaro Lopez	54-11
1982	Carlos DeLeon	31-1-1
1983	Jesse Burnett	25-14-2
	Trevor Berbick	22-2-1

Entered Top Ten   273-77-9 / 17 = 16-5-1

Roy Harris

1955	Tommie Smith	16-10
	I.H. Harvey	9-8
	Ted Donald	4-1
	Bobby Watson	Unavailable
	Chuck Connor	Unavailable
	Lajuin Burke	0-1
	Dick Smith	Unavailable
	Fred Taylor	0-2-1
	Buddy Turman	11-1
	Ponce DeLeon	2-18-4
1956	Don Tucker	9-3
	Johnny Bullard	Unavailable
	Alvin Williams	49-13-6
	Calvin Butler	7-4
	Oscar Pharo	25-4
	Charlie Norkus	26-13
	J.D. Marshall	5-1
1957	Claude Chapman	22-4-1
	Joey Rowan	28-12-1
	Bob Baker	71-23-2

Entered Top Ten   284-118-15 / 16 = 18-7-1

	Willie Pastrano	41-5-4
	Willie Besmanoff	36-8-7

Challenged for Title   361-113-26 / 18 = 20-6-1

Tommy Harrison

1951	Earl Keel	12-8
	Lou Newman	2-3
	Frankie Crane	16-3
	Frankie Crane	16-4
	Frankie Crane	17-4
	Bill McNeece	3-0
	Paul Pargo	1-0
	Al Timmons	Unavailable
	Al Timmons	Unavailable
	Frankie Crane	17-5
	Frankie Crane	19-5
	Sonny Boy Harris	Unavailable
	Paul Pargo	3-6
	Abel Fernandez	4-3-1
	Abel Fernandez	4-4-1
1952	Al Callaghan	2-0
	Al Callaghan	Unavailable
	Bobo Olson	42-4
	Abel Fernandez	6-5-1
	Frankie Crane	20-6
	Paul Andrews	15-1
	Rocky Jones	8-7-1
	Charley Norkus	17-9
	Jimmy Bivins	81-23-1

	Wes Bascom	15-3
1953	Ezzard Charles	80-7-1
	Jimmy Bivins	81-25-1

Entered Top Ten   481-135-7 / 23 = 21-6

Clarence Henry

1948	Al Timmons	14-14-3
	Don Wagner	Unavailable
	Tommy Jessen	3-1-1
	Billy Kinard	Unavailable
	John Curtis	13-2-2
	John Curtis	13-4-2
	Harry Wills	14-9-4
1949	Don Angen	Unavailable
	Billy McClure	17-14-5
	Dutch Culbertson	18-7-3
	Jay Lambert	6-0-1
	Jimmy Bivins	71-17-1
	Battling Blackjack	12-4
	Billy Smith	37-13-1
1950	Frankie Daniels	15-3-1
	Battling Brown	37-4-3
	Bob Murphy	41-2
	Al Spaulding	16-17-1
	John Holman	13-3

Entered Top Ten   340-114-28 / 16 = 21-7-2

Hubert Hilton

1963	Arthur Minor	Unavailable
	Orin Johnson	4-0
	Wendell Newton	7-5-1
	Orin Johnson	4-1
	Luther Murphy	6-2-1
	Luther Murphy	7-2-1
	Wendell Newton	8-6-1
1964	Ray Batey	7-6-1
	Wildredo Avellez	11-4

Incomplete (January 19 1962)

	Joe Sheldon	7-5-1
	Willie Jackson	7-4-1
	Billy Daniels	18-5
1965	Roberto Davila	2-1
	Johnny Prescott	26-5-3
	Jack Bodell	20-5

Entered Top Ten   134-51-10 / 14 = 10-4-1

John Holman

1947	Joe Dawson	2-0
	Bill Zaier	8-1-2
	John Lester	
1948	Sterling Ingram	8-3

Incomplete (December 15, 1947)

	Fred Ford	6-7-1
	Jackie Thompson	6-10-3
	Acie Talbert	5-1
	Tiny Robinson	Unavailable
	Gene Jones	28-6-1
1949	Elmer Ray	66-9-1
	Johnny Haynes	22-13
	Sid Peaks	31-9
	Dale Hall	13-5-3
	Willie Bean	21-11-2
1950	Turkey Thompson	46-9-2

Entered Top Ten   262-84-15 / 13 = 20-6-1

Larry Holmes

1973	Rodell Dupree	2-2
	Art Savage	0-0
	Curtis Whitner	Unavailable
	Don Branch	1-4
	Bob Bozic	10-1
	Jerry Judge	14-3-1
	Kevin Isaacs	2-0
1974	Howard Darlington	1-17-1
	Bob Mashburn	7-6-2
	Joe Hathaway	Unavailable
1975	Charley Green	14-14
	Oliver Wright	12-8
	Robert Yarborough	
	Ernie Smith	2-3
	Obie English	15-5
	Charlie James	3-3
	Rodney Bobick	34-5
	Leon Shaw	7-7-1
	Billy Joiner	10-10-3
1976	Joe Gholston	13-9-2

Entered Top Ten   147-97-10 / 17 = 9-6-1

	Fred Askew	14-12-1
	Roy Williams	21-4
1977	Tom Prater	17-3-1
	Horacio Robinson	4-2
	Young Sanford Houpe	12-1
	Ibar Arrington	21-3-1
1978	Earnie Shavers	52-6-1

Challenged for Title   288-128-13 / 24 = 12-5-1

Al Hoosman

1943	Herb Narvo	13-2-1
	Bill Biddle	10-11-4
	Bill Biddle	11-12-4
	Alabama Kid	103-15-2
	Alabama Kid	103-16-2
	Joe Gladden	0-0
1944	Herb Narvo	17-4-1

1945	Johnny Davis	4-13
	Cleo Everett	7-13-2
	J. D. Turner	37-28-51
	Lee Savold	58-23
1946	Lee Savold	60-23
	Colion Chaney	28-17-4
	Vern Escoe	13-6
1947	Bill Poland	36-5-3
	Buddy Walker	70-24-5
	Dusty Wilkerson	2-1
	Buddy Walker	73-27-5
1948	John Hibbard	17-8-3
1949	Billy McClure	17-14-6
	Jerry McSwain	21-6-1
	Ray Stevens	26-4
	Al Spaulding	13-13-1

Entered Top Ten 737-284-49 / 22 = 34-13-2

Billy Hunter

1954	Tony Lomonaco	15-6
	Tony Lomonaco	17-6-1
	Foneda Cox	2-1
1955	John Riggins	4-0
	Jackie King	11-2
	John Riggins	6-0
	Elmo Smith	4-10-1
	Sonny Wilcox	1-6-1

Incomplete (September 16, 1953)

	Calvin Butler	4-3
1957	Moses Graham	2-4
	Fritz Zack	*Unavailable*
	Johnny Jenkins	11-2-4
	Johnny Gray	13-7-1
1958	Sonny Liston	14-1
	Otis Fuller	4-6-1
	Norm Bolden	1-5-1

Incomplete (June 26, 1957)

1959	Nat Dixon	3-3
	Bob Baker	51-14-1
	Alonzo Johnson	14-1
	Don Warner	7-1
	Alex Miteff	19-3-1
	Tony Anthony	41-7-1

Entered Top Ten 244-88-13 / 21 = 12-4-1

Tommy Jackson

1952	Terry Halpine	*Unavailable*
	Jimmy Middleton	*Unavailable*
	Gene Brien	*Unavailable*
	Jack Jacobs	2-0
	Phil Alston	22-9-2
	Jimmy Dilenge	16-2-1

	Shirley Pembleton	6-1
1953	Roy Thomas	15-13-5

Incomplete (March 27, 1952)

	Elmo Lincoln	2-0-1
	Bob Golden	8-4
	Joe Lindsay	24-4-2
	Bert Whitehurst	12-2
	Joe Lindsay	24-5-2
	Archie McBride	19-5
1954	Rex Layne	41-9-2
	Clarence Henry	34-5-1

Entered Top Ten 225-58-16 / 13 = 17-4-1

	Dan Bucceroni	46-3
	Jimmy Slade	18-9-4
	Charley Norkus	23-9
	Nino Valdes	30-8-2
	Keene Simmons	9-19-1
1955	Leo Johnson	8-7-1
	Roy Thomas	15-14-5

Incomplete

	Kid Saucer	11-4
	Archie McBride	19-8
	Jimmy Slade	20-13-4
	Ezzard Charles	90-13-1
	Ezzard Charles	90-14-1
	Rex Layne	41-9-2
	Jimmy Slade	22-14-2
	Bob Baker	44-5-2
	Johnny Williams	57-8-3

Challenged for Title 768-215-44 / 33 = 23-7-1

Alonzo Johnson

1957	Tony Sinabaldi	*Unavailable*
	Solomon McTier	3-0
	Kenny Davis	*Unavailable*
	Ollie Wilson	6-8
	Cortez Stewart	8-2
	Julius Griffin	6-2
	Neal Welch	2-10-2
	Matt Jackson	10-7-3
1958	Cal Butler	12-9
	Al Lane	1-1
	Emil Brtko	23-9
	Shirley Pembleton	12-7-2
	Rudy Williams	10-4-1
1959	Charlie Forest	5-1-2
	Jimmy Slade	26-16-4
	Billy Hunter	12-5-1
	Nino Valdes	48-16-2

Entered Top Ten 184-97-17 / 15 = 12-6-1

Amos Johnson

1960	Cordell Jones	0-0-1

Records of Opponents

	Opponent	Record
	Jim Anderson	5-1
	Dave Furch	3-1-1
1961	Ocie Chatman	7-6
	Willie Gill	7-6
1963	Waban Thomas	10-7
	Billy Joiner	2-0
	Willie Besmanoff	44-28-8
1964	Jefferson Davis	19-4-1
	Lou Bailey	11-20-5
	Willie Williams	6-7-1
	Mert Brownfield	4-1
	Cody Jones	11-4-2
	Willie Williams	6-8-1
	Chip Johnson	7-5
	Billy Joiner	6-1
	Mack Harrison	7-2
	Karl Mildenberger	40-2-2
1965	Tiger Gorman	3-0

Entered Top Ten 202-104-22 / 19 = 11-5-1

Harold Johnson

	Opponent	Record
1955	Joe Riley	*Unavailable*
1956	Charley Lester	*Unavailable*
	Jack Simon	*Unavailable*
	Randy Ingram	0-2
1947	Frank Lowry	11-10-3
	Chappie Manning	4-6-3
	Jimmy Holden	10-7-2
	Joe Van Loan	*Unavailable*
	Tony Gillo	15-36-7
	Leon Szymurski	16-7
	Fred Lester	2-2
	Tommy Ruth	13-1
	Al Pinel	31-53-4
	Eddie Beazley	5-0
	Randy Ingram	0-3
	Jimmy Moore	9-9
	Herbie Katz	59-23-2
	Kid Wolfe	5-8-3
1948	Kenny Harris	13-1
	Kenny Harris	13-2
	Vernon Williams	3-0-1
	Augustino Guedes	15-6-2
	Jim Holden	18-15-5
	Willie Brown	4-11
1949	Arturo Godoy	85-17-9
	Archie Moore	99-18-8
	Henry Hall	40-10-4
	Henry Hall	40-12-4
	Jimmy Bivins	72-16-1
	Bert Lytell	66-18-7
1950	Joe Walcott	47-14-1
	Harry Daniels	0-0
1951	Dusty Wilkerson	8-9
	Chuck Hunter	42-15-1
	Elkins Brothers	26-7-1

	Opponent	Record
	Chubby Wright	22-24-2
	Archie Moore	122-19-2
	Archie Moore	124-19-4
1952	Archie Moore	124-20-9
	Clarence Henry	31-2-2
	Bob Satterfield	27-13-2
	Leonard Morrow	21-6-1
	Bob Satterfield	28-13-2
	Nino Valdes	22-4-2
1953	Jimmy Slade	15-4-2
	Bill Gilliam	22-13-2
	Toxie Hall	8-6-2
	Ezzard Charles	84-9-1
	Henry Hall	47-16-5
	Chubby Wright	25-28-3
1954	Jimmy Slade	18-8-4
	Charlie Williams	36-14
	Paul Andrews	23-2
	Archie Moore	142-20-9
	Billy Smith	56-20-7
	Julio Mederos	15-5-2
	Marty Marshall	15-2-1
1955	Paul Andrews	29-4
	Julio Mederos	17-8-2
1956	Bert Whitehurst	22-9-2
	Bob Satterfield	46-22-4

Entered Top Ten 1,912-648-140 / 57 = 33-11-2

Young Jack Johnson

	Opponent	Record
1953	Kirby Seals	0-1
	Fred Taylor	0-1-1
	Harland Kelly	0-0
	Sonny Andrews	12-8
	Sonny Andrews	12-8-1
	Gene Brown	9-5
	Frankie Daniels	22-7-1
1954	Frankie Buford	21-23-5
	Willie Bean	39-18-4
	Willie Bean	39-19-4
	Frankie Buford	22-26-4
1955	Willie Bean	41-21-4
	Gene Thompson	10-6-3
	Johnny Summerlin	23-4-2
	Willie Bean	41-23-4
	Marty Marshall	20-7-2
	Zora Folley	21-1-1
	Ezzard Charles	92-16-1

Entered Top Ten 424-211-37 = 24-12-2

Al Jones

	Opponent	Record
1964	Duke Johnson	8-11-1
	Willie Johnson	2-0-1
1965	Lee Andrews	1-0
1966	Willie Thomas	17-26-6

	Wayne Bunyan	3-3		Erich Schoppner	34-0-3
	Duke Johnson	10-13-4		Bob Foster	8-0
	Aaron Beasley	3-3		Zora Folley	65-5-2
	Gene Idolette	0-1-1	*Entered Top Ten* 489-104-23 / 24 = 20-4-1		
	Joe Louis White	2-3-1	1963	Cassius Clay	17-0
	Chip Johnson	10-11-1		Billy Daniels	18-2
	Chip Johnson	10-12-1	1964	Tom McNeely	30-6
	Willie Johnson	7-4-1		Leroy Green	17-16-4
	Levi Forte	15-11-1		Billy Daniels	18-5-1
	Jeff Davis	28-9-1		George Chuvalo	27-9-2
	Sonny Moore	18-22-2	1965	Prentice Snipes	18-6
1967	Levi Forte	16-13-1		Cody Jones	11-7-2
	Archie Ray	19-9-2		Chip Johnson	10-9-1
	Ollie Wilson	16-28		Archie McBride	24-17-2
Incomplete (December 12, 1964)			1966	Lou Bailey	13-23-5
	Everette Copeland	4-10-3	*Challenged for Title* 692-206-40 / 35 = 20-6-1		
	James Beattie	26-3			
	Al Jones	17-0	## *Leroy Jones*		
	Bob Stallings	9-9			
1968	Matt Blow	6-2	1973	Otis Scroggins	0-1
	Lee Batts	10-1	1974	Larry Frazier	6-0
	Roosevelt Eddie	4-3-2		Joe Anderson	*Unavailable*
	Zora Folley	76-9-5		Paul Solomon	6-1-1
	Matt Blow	6-3	*Incomplete* (July 13, 1971)		
	Jim Howard	9-1		Lou Rogan	3-2
1969	Cleveland Williams	71-7-1		Bob Crutison	0-8
	Henry Clark	17-4-3		Jimmy Gilmore	5-9
	Jack O'Halloran	17-4-1		Henry Culpepper	3-2
Entered Top Ten 457-235-39 / 31 = 15-7-1			*Incomplete* (April 1, 1972)		
				Koli Vailea	4-2
## *Doug Jones*				Chu Hernandez	*Unavailable*
			1975	Reco Brooks	5-9-1
1958	Jimmy McNair	2-2		Jimmy Gilmore	5-11
	Vince Ferguson	5-0		George Johnson	20-19-3
	Andre Tessier	2-0		Larry Frazier	6-0
1959	Edmund George	7-8-3		Arthur Robinson	3-7
Incomplete (March 8th, 1957)			1976	Jody Ballard	21-4
	Frank Lapola	*Unavailable*		Mongol Ortiz	20-11
	Gunner Doerner	5-0	*Incomplete* (October 3, 1975)		
	Rudy Corney	6-5-2		Pedro Lovell	17-2-1
	Sonny Boykins	6-6-1	1977	Cookie Wallace	20-24-2
	Richie Hill	7-4		John Dennis	27-1-1
	Chuck Whittley	4-5		Greg Johnson	7-6
	Juan Pomare	11-6	1978	Mike Weaver	13-7
1960	Clarence Floyd	9-7	1979	Fili Moala	5-2-1
	Leroy Green	16-9-2		Harry Terrell	12-4
	Von Clay	11-1-2		Jim Beattie	37-9
	Von Clay	11-2-2	*Entered Top Ten*		
	Bobo Olson	74-10	*Challenged for Title* 245-141-10 / 23 = 11-6		
1961	Floyd McCoy	10-10			
	Pete Rademacher	13-3-1	## *Boone Kirkman*		
	Von Clay	15-4-2			
	Eddie Machen	39-4-1			
1962	Harold Johnson	67-8			
	Zora Folley	62-5-2	1966	Lou Phillips	0-0

| | Gale Wright | 4-0-2 |
| | John Collins | 5-6 |

Incomplete (February 6, 1964)

	Al Carter	3-8-1
	Archie Ray	19-5-1
	Archie Ray	19-6-2
1967	Bowie Adams	17-2-1
	Bert Leroy	*Unavailable*
	Wayne Heath	9-5
	Lars Norling	13-11-4
	Eddie Machen	60-10-3
	Doug Jones	29-9-1
	Doug Jones	30-9-1
	Bill Neilsen	22-11-2
	Wayne Heath	9-7
	Archie Ray	19-13-2
1968	Mike Lanum	10-6

Incomplete

	Everette Copeland	4-13-3
	Bill MacMurray	21-19-2
1970	Mike Bruce	8-24-1
	Ollie Wilson	15-22

Incomplete

	Bill McMurray	23-22-2
	Amos Lincoln	38-11-3
	George Foreman	23-0
1971	Fred Lewis	37-11-1
	Richard Gosha	10-15
	Bill Drover	32-15-3
	Steve Carter	15-5
	Jack O'Halloran	32-16-3
	Roby Harris	5-9-1
	Lou Bailey	17-39-4
1974	Larry Renaud	12-6
	Al Jones	6-20
	Ken Norton	30-3
	Ron Lyle	29-1-1
	Randy Neumann	29-5

Entered Top Ten 654-364-45 / 35 = 19-10-1

Roland LaStarza

| 1947 | Dave Glanton | 1-6 |
| | Jack Johnson | 2-2-1 |

Incomplete

	Al Zapalla	0-2
	Jim Dodd	6-5-2
	Jim Johnson	3-15-1
	Zeke Brown	*Unavailable*
	Matt Mincey	0-2
	Jimmy Evans	12-3
	Loren McCarthy	1-3
	Matt Mincey	0-4
	Fred Ramsay	7-6-1

| | Luther McMilliam | 12-16-1 |
| 1948 | Mike Belluscio | 10-6-1 |

Incomplete (June 30, 1947)

	Frankie Reid	0-4
	Jimmy White	8-14
	Steve King	3-1-1
	Claude McClintock	*Unavailable*
	John Holloway	2-8
	Freddie McManus	5-8-1
	Ben Rusk	9-0
	Tony Gangemi	12-14-2
	Oscar Goode	39-21-2
	Teddy George	*Unavailable*
	Mel McKinney	6-9-1
	Don Mogard	14-0
	Mike Jacobs	11-6-2
	Don Mogard	15-1
	Gene Gosney	13-1
1949	Bill Weinberg	40-16-14
	Gino Buonvino	13-1-1
	Eldridge Eatman	14-16-3
	Jimmy Carollo	38-14-2
	Harry Haft	11-5
	Jackie Lyons	23-16-1
	Joe Domonic	17-8
	Walter Hafer	15-15-1
	Cesar Brion	28-2

Entered Top Ten 390-250-38 / 34 = 11-7-1

1950	Rocky Marciano	25-0
	James Walls	11-18-2
	George Fuller	7-10-1
	Keene Simmons	7-5-1
	Dulio Spagnolo	12-5-3
1951	Ted Lowry	51-56-9
	Curt Kennedy	25-4-1
	Keene Simmons	8-8-1
	Vern Mitchell	56-11-1
	Gene Felton	10-13-1
	Ted Lowry	51-60-9
	Dan Bucceroni	35-2
1952	Bill Wilson	16-12-1
	Ralph Schneider	16-4-2
	Joe McFadden	4-2-1
	Dan Bucceroni	37-2
	Rocky Jones	9-7-1
	Rocky Jones	10-7-1
1953	Rex Layne	40-5-2

Challenged for Title 819-481-75 / 53 = 15-9-1

Rex Layne

1949	Jim Watkins	0-0
	Jim Watkins	0-1
	Hank Thurman	9-7-3
	George Abinet	4-4-1

	Joe Williams	0-2	1977	Johnny Boudreaux	19-1-1
	Lee Bearcat Carter	8-11-3		Pedro Soto	14-2-3
Incomplete (November 29, 1948)				Tom Prater	18-5-1
				Duane Bobick	38-1
	Buddy Thomas	4-17-4		Leon Spinks	5-0
Incomplete (June 12,1947)			1978	Bill Sharkey	18-2
	Lee Bearcat Carter	8-12-3		Sylvester Wilder	4-30
Incomplete (November 29, 1948)				James Brown	*Unavailable*
				Joe Donatto	3-4
	Gene Pierce	*Unavailable*	1979	Jim Beattie	37-7
	Harry Wills	19-15-6		Ron Lyle	37-5-1
	Willie McCoy	*Unavailable*		Ken Norton	41-6
	Ponce DeLeon	1-1	*Entered Top Ten* 563-204-21 / 34 = 17-6-1		
	Floyd Gibson	21-4-1			
	Sonny Orrocks	1-3-1		Mike Weaver	20-10
	Joe Sandell	0-2		Marty Monroe	20-0-1
1950	Bob Golden	4-2	*Challenged for Title* 603-214-22 / 36 = 17-6-1		
	Dave Whitlock	27-2-1			
	Dave Whitlock	27-3-1			
	Grant Butcher	11-3-2			
	Dave Whitlock	28-4 1	1934	Justin Hoffman	*Unavailable*
	Willie Parker	*Unavailable*		Sid Cohen	*Unavailable*
	Bob Dunlap	18-4-1		Jimmy Calabrese	*Unavailable*
	Jack Huber	2-5-1		Willie Klein	*Unavailable*
	Bob Blevins	0-1		Roy Frisco	*Unavailable*
	Joe Kahut	44-12-5		Tony Kalb	*Unavailable*
	Turkey Thompson	46-11-2		Nicky Williams	*Unavailable*
Entered Top Ten 282-134-36 / 36 = 12-6-2				Charley Weisse	*Unavailable*
				Mark Hough	*Unavailable*
				Tom Chester	*Unavailable*
				Jackie Aldare	7-6-7
				Stan Willardson	*Unavailable*
1974	Arthur Pullens	0-0		Jackie Aldare	8-6-7
	Floyd Cox	1-2	1935	Bucky Lawless	34-26-4
Incomplete (November 11, 1968)				Jackie Aldare	8-7-7
	Steve Patterson	*Unavailable*		John Anderson	23-7-11
	Reggie Flemmings	2-3		John Anderson	23-8-11
	Larry Penniger	2-0		Mark Hough	*Unavailable*
	Joe Batton	4-5-1		Charley Weisse	*Unavailable*
	Tom Berry	10-4		Tony Celli	2-4-1
	Ron Draper	0-1		Butch Lynch	*Unavailable*
	Lou Rogan	7-4	1936	Eddie Kid Whalen	*Unavailable*
	John L. Johnson	7-2		Frankie Caris	*Unavailable*
1975	C.J. Brown	1-0-1		Frankie Caris	*Unavailable*
	Larry Renault	13-11		Sammy Christian	*Unavailable*
	CookieWallace	18-19-2		Lou Rogers	*Unavailable*
	Rodney Bobick	33-4		Ray Actis	36-4-5
	Terry Daniels	34-19-1		Carmen Barth	6-1
	George Johnson	20-20-3		Marty Simmons	26-6-2
	Brian O'Melia	14-25-2		Young Stuhley	62-14-26
	Ron Stander	27-7-2		Freddie Steele	73-2-6
1976	Bill Carson	10-5-1	1937	Tony Celli	4-9-1
	Larry Middleton	22-7-2		Young Corbett	110-10-17
	Duane Bobick	34-0		Young Stuhley	62-16-26
	John Dennis	27-0-1		Atilio Sabatino	26-4-4
	George Foreman	42-1		Alabama Kid	57-9-3
	Junior Bentley	1-1		Allan Mathews	62-5-3

Scott LeDoux

Gus Lesnevich

Records of Opponents

	Herbie Katz	27-3-1
1938	Joey Parks	26-3-2
	Ben Brown	*Unavailable*
	Jack Kirkland	*Unavailable*
	Lou Brouillard	46-16-1
	Buddy Ryan	7-7-2
	Stanley Hasrato	16-7-4
	Ron Richards	81-18-6
	Ambrose Palmer	57-6-2
1939	Alabama Kid	63-12-3
	Bob Olin	52-26-5
	Larry Lane	26-2-2
	Dave Clark	20-2-2
	Billy Conn	49-8
1940	Dave Clark	23-4-2
	Billy Conn	51-8
	Wally Sears	9-9

Incomplete

	Henry Cooper	19-22-2
	Al Delaney	41-16-6
	Jack Marshall	8-4-2
1941	Nathan Mann	62-7-6
	Antoine Christoforidis	42-9-6
	Tami Mauriello	32-1
	Tami Mauriello	32-2
1942	Bob Pastor	49-6-4
	Jimmy Bivins	25-4
1946	Joe Kahut	24-2-3
	Lee Oma	42-17-1
	Freddie Mills	63-11-6
	Bruce Woodcock	27-1
1947	Billy Fox	43-0
	Melio Bettina	79-11-4
	Tami Mauriello	73-9-1
	Tami Mauriello	75-10-1
1948	Billy Fox	50-1
	Freddie Mills	71-15-6
1949	Eldridge Eatman	14-15-3
	Joey Maxim	63-16-4

Entered Top Ten
Challenged for Title 2,113-454-228 / 54 = 39-8-4

Al Lewis

1966	Art Miller	0-0
	Gene Hunt	0-4
	John Hall	*Unavailable*
	Vic Brown	3-5
	Larry McGee	0-0
	Mack Harrison	*Unavailable*
	Mert Brownfield	4-3

Incomplete

	Mert Brownfield	4-4

Incomplete

1967	Buddy Moore	0-0
	Earl Averette	4-3
	Aaron Eastling	11-1-1
	Willie McMillian	2-0
	Don Toro Smith	10-5-1
	Dick Wipperman	32-10-1
	Dick Wipperman	32-11-1
	Bob Stallings	9-10
1968	Dave Russell	1-1
	Bob Stallings	11-15
	Johnny Featherman	26-10
	Eduardo Corletti	25-2-5

Entered Top Ten 174-84-9 / 17 = 10-5-1

Amos Lincoln

1954	Duke Sabedong	0-0
	Bobby Jackson	0-3-1

Incomplete (June 9, 1953)

	Junior Washington	13-22
	George Tavares	3-0
	Gene Brixon	15-5-2
1955	Duke Sabedong	3-1
	Bill Lanza	54-18-3
	Ernie Smith	*Unavailable*
	Bill Parker	*Unavailable*
	Bill Little	4-2

Incomplete (August 26, 1954)

	Bill Brixon	*Unavailable*
	Wally Cox	*Unavailable*
	Gus Bruno	3-7
	Duke Sabedong	11-2-1
	Frank Buford	23-28-5

Incomplete (August 26, 1955)

1956	George Tavares	8-3-2
	Roger Rischer	11-4-1
	Howard King	28-9-5
	Frank Williams	3-3
	George Woods	*Unavailable*
	Babe Hunt	0-7
	Charley Que	7-4-2
	Barrie Jackson	7-1

Incomplete (May 4, 1954)

1957	Bill Mathias	1-9

Incomplete (May 16, 1955)

	Hank Thurman	24-15-3

Incomplete (October 9, 1952)

	Marty Marshall	21-10-2
1961	Eddie Jackson	2-4-1
	Otis Fuller	7-11-4
	Young Jack Johnson	21-13-1
1962	Ernie Terrell	24-4
1964	Jim Fletcher	4-2-3

	Chuck Leslie	6-3
	Thad Spencer	22-2
1965	Jim Fletcher	5-3-3
	Sante Amonte	51-5-3
	Roberto Davila	1-2
	George Johnson	5-3-1
	Roberto Davila	3-3
	Thad Spencer	25-3

Entered Top Ten 415-211-42 / 34 = 12-6-1

Sonny Liston

1953	Don Smith	2-0
	Ponce DeLeon	2-13-4
1954	Martin Lee	*Unavailable*
	Stan Howlett	2-0
	John Summerlin	18-2-2
	John Summerlin	18-3-2
	Marty Marshall	16-4-2
1955	Neil Welch	2-2
	Marty Marshall	19-6-2
	Emil Brtko	15-1
	Calvin Butler	4-2
	Johnny Gray	9-3-1
	Larry Watson	13-13
1956	Marty Marshall	21-8-1
1958	Billy Hunter	8-4-1
	Ben Wise	8-7-1
	Bert Whitehurst	24-13-2
	Julio Mederos	21-18-3
	Wayne Bethea	17-8-3
	Frankie Daniels	33-15-2

Entered Top Ten 252-122-26 / 19 = 13-6-1

	Bert Whitehurst	24-14-2
	Ernie Cab	10-8-1
1959	Mike DeJohn	36-5-1
	Cleveland Williams	43-2
	Nino Valdes	48-17-2
	Willie Besmanoff	41-16-8
1960	Howard King	34-19-8
	Cleveland Williams	45-3
	Roy Harris	30-1
	Zora Folley	51-3-2
	Eddie Machen	34-2-1
1961	Howard King	36-21-8
	Albert Westphal	19-44-3

Challenged for Title 703-277-62 / 32 = 22-9-2

	Floyd Patterson	39-2
1963	Floyd Patterson	39-3
1964	Muhammad Ali	19-0

Challenged for Title 800-282-62 / 35 = 23-8-2

George Logan

1957	Buster Keyser	*Unavailable*

	Billy Reese	0-2
	Larry Williams	*Unavailable*
1958	Dick Tanner	0-1
	Bill Lanza	14-9-1
	Andy Walker	17-17-7
1959	Al Noriega	2-11-1
	Joe Sullivan	5-4-1
	Jackie Torme	11-3-1
	Walter Robinson	4-12

Unavailable

	Joe Habana	*Unavailable*
	Ezzard Charles	96-23-1
	Tommy Jackson	31-7-1
	Herman Henry	8-5
1960	Tom McNeely	15-0
	Billy Fields	3-8-2
	Willie Besmanoff	41-20-8
	Donnie Fleeman	33-8-1
	Tom McNeely	20-0
	Tom McNeely	21-0
1961	Dave Roy	5-7
	Frankie Daniels	34-20-4
	Calvin Butler	12-13
	Calvin Butler	12-14
	Young Jack Johnson	21-14-1
	Pete Rademacher	13-3-1
	Johnny Riggins	23-9
	Tony Alongi	27-0
	Alejandro Lavorante	18-1

Entered Top Ten 486-211-30 / 25 = 19-8-1

Joe Louis

1934	Jack Kracken	*Unavailable*
	Willie Davis	*Unavailable*
	Larry Udell	*Unavailable*
	Jack Kranz	*Unavailable*
	Buck Everett	39-12-3
	Alex Borchuk	9-0
	Adolph Wiater	17-0-2
	Art Sykes	*Unavailable*
	Jack O'Dowd	*Unavailable*
	Stanley Poreda	35-9-2
	Charley Massera	27-6-3
	Lee Ramage	41-8-4
1935	Patsy Perroni	56-3-6
	Hans Birkie	14-22-5
	Lee Ramage	41-9-4
	Donald "Red" Barry	47-19-13
	Natie Brown	49-6-2
	Roy Lazer	44-2
	Biff Bennett	*Unavailable*
	Roscoe Toles	2-1-1
	Willie Davis	*Unavailable*
	Gene Stanton	24-17
	Primo Carnera	81-7

Records of Opponents

	Kingfish Levinsky	63-20-6
	Max Baer	41-8-1
	Paulino Uzcudun	51-14-3
1936	Charley Retzlaff	61-8-7
	Max Schmeling	48-7-4
	Jack Sharkey	39-11-4
	Al Ettore	34-7-1
	Jorge Brescia	8-0
	Eddie Sims	36-17-2
1937	Steve Ketchell	Unavailable
	Bob Pastor	21-1-2
	Natie Brown	49-6-8
	James Braddock	53-22-10
	Tommy Farr	56-12-11
1938	Nathan Mann	40-4-3
	Harry Thomas	54-5-2
	Max Schmeling	48-7-4
1939	John Henry Lewis	79-7-5
	Jack Roper	26-22-6
	Tony Galento	76-24-5
	Bob Pastor	38-4-4
1940	Arturo Godoy	48-9-6
	Johnny Paychek	47-3-2
	Arturo Godoy	48-10-6
	Al McCoy	66-17-5
1941	Red Burman	49-6-1
	Gus Dorazio	36-9-2
	Abe Simon	34-7
	Tony Musto	23-9-1
	Buddy Baer	48-5
	Billy Conn	59-8
	Lou Nova	25-2-5
1942	Buddy Baer	46-5
	Abe Simon	36-7
1946	Billy Conn	62-9
	Tami Mauriello	69-7-1
1947	Jersey Joe Walcott	46-11-1
1948	Jersey Joe Walcott	46-12-1

Challenged for Title 2, 235-472-174/52 = 43-9-3

Ron Lyle

1971	A.J. Staples	10-4
	Art Miller	14-23-2
	Gary Bates	16-13-2
	Edmundo Stewart	1-5
	Leroy Caldwell	11-6-1
	Frank Niblett	14-38-11
	Eddie Land	6-10
	Manuel Ramos	24-18-3
	Joe. E. Lewis	2-1-1
	Jack O'Halloran	21-12-2
	Bill Drover	32-10-3
1972	Chuck Leslie	19-22-4
	George Johnson	15-14-3
	Mel Turnbow	8-10
	Mike Boswell	13-8

	Vincente Rondon	37-6-1

Entered Top Ten 243-200-33 / 16 = 15-13-2

	Buster Mathis	30-3
	Luis Pires	18-8-1
	Larry Middleton	20-2-1
1973	Jerry Quarry	44-6-4
	Bob Stallings	13-20
	Gregorio Peralta	86-7-8
	Wendell Newton	14-8-2
	Lou Bailey	17-35-5
	Jose Luis Garcia	22-4-2
	Jurgen Blin	30-10-6
	Larry Middleton	20-3-1
	Gregorio Peralta	88-8-8
1974	Oscar Bonavena	51-8-1
	Jimmy Ellis	39-9
	Boone Kirkman	32-4
	Memphis Al Jones	8-20
1975	Jimmy Young	13-4-2

Challenged for Title 788-359-74 / 33 = 24-11-2

Eddie Machen

1955	Raul Flores	1-0
	Ed Robert	Unavailable
	George Kennedy	0-2-1
	Clarence Williams	1-1
	Artie Lucido	2-1
	Shamus Jones	3-2-1
	Frank Buford	22-27-5
	Bill Davis	Unavailable
	Howard King	24-6-4
	Max Chris	21-2
	Benny Wise	2-2
1956	Julio Mederos	19-11-2
	Nino Valdes	34-11-2

Entered Top Ten 129-65-15 / = 12-6-1

	Matt Jackson	9-5-2
	Nino Valdes	35-12-2
	Julio Mederos	19-13-2
	John Holman	30-12-1
	Johnny Summerlin	31-6-2
1957	Joey Maxim	82-23-14
	Joey Maxim	82-24-14
	Bob Baker	47-10-1
	Walter Hafer	19-23-1

Incomplete

	Edgardo Romero	24-6-2

Incomplete

	Tommy Jackson	29-6-1
1958	Zora Folley	39-2-1
	Ingemar Johannson	20-0
1959	Young Jack Johnson	16-11-1
	Clarence Williams	2-5

Incomplete (December 10, 1955)

	Reuben Vargas	18-6
	Reuben Vargas	18-7
	Garvin Sawyer	14-8
	Willie Besmanoff	41-15-8
	Pat McMurtry	33-3-1
1960	Zora Folley	49-3-2
	Billy Hunter	15-6-2
	Alex Miteff	22-5-1
	Alonzo Johnson	18-5
	Sonny Liston	30-1
	Wayne Bethea	21-12-2
1961	Garvin Sawyer	14-11
	Mike DeJohn	41-7-1
	Harold Johnson	64-8
	Mike DeJohn	41-8-1
	Brian London	24-7
	Doug Jones	19-0
1962	Bert Whitehurst	31-23-6
	Roger Rischer	20-6-2
	Cleveland Williams	53-4
1963	Ollie Wilson	15-19

Incomplete

	Alonzo Johnson	22-10
	Bill McMurray	16-8
	Dave Bailey	14-9-3
1964	Duke Sabedong	16-14-2
	Floyd Patterson	40-4

Challenged for Title 1,322-432-90 / 52 = 25-8-4

Rocky Marciano

1947	Lee Epperson	5-1
1948	Harry Bilzarian	3-6
	John Edwards	*Unavailable*
	Bobby Quinn	8-0
	Eddie Ross	15-0-1
	Jimmy Weeks	*Unavailable*
	Jerry Jackson	*Unavailable*
	Bill Hardemann	1-3
	Gil Cardione	*Unavailable*
	Bob Jefferson	2-2
	Pat Connolly	8-5
	Gilley Ferron	*Unavailable*
1949	Johnny Pretzie	7-5
	Artie Donato	7-5
	James Wall	9-13-1
	Jimmy Evans	17-5-1
	Don Mogard	15-8
	Harry Haft	11-6
	Pete Louthis	23-11-3
	Tommy Giorgio	9-9
	Ted Lowry	48-47-9
	Joe Domonic	18-10
	Pat Richards	19-5-5

	Phil Muscato	55-20
	Carmine Vingo	16-1
1950	Roland LaStaza	37-0

Entered Top Ten 333-162-20 / 21 = 16-8-1

	Eldridge Eatman	14-17-3
	Gino Buonvino	15-3-1
	Johnny Shkor	28-18-2
	Ted Lowry	51-55-9
	Bill Wilson	15-7-1
1951	Keene Simmons	8-7-1
	Harold Mitchell	0-10-2
	Art Henri	12-16-1
	Red Applegate	10-14-2
	Rex Layne	34-1-2
	Freddie Beshore	31-11-2
	Joe Louis	68-2
1952	Lee Savold	72-30-3
	Gino Buonvino	17-6-2
	Bernie Reynolds	51-9-1
	Harry Mathews	78-3-6

Challenged for Title 837-371-58 / 37 = 23-10-2

Leotis Martin

1962	Bobby Warthen	2-0
	Bob Rutherford	*Unavailable*
	German Hernandez	*Unavailable*
	Joe Washington	*Unavailable*
1963	Buddy Moore	2-3
	Mannie McCoy	3-1
	Frank Davis	*Unavailable*
	Johnny Alford	15-8-3
	Bill Johnson	3-3-1
	Floyd McCoy	14-14-1
1964	Allen Harmon	21-8-4
	Dave Russell	7-12-3
1965	Dave Bailey	14-11-3
	Earl Battles	4-3
	Don Warner	13-12-3
	Sonny Banks	20-—-6
	Curtis Bruce	19-17-1
	Von Clay	19-13-2
1966	Amos Johnson	14-5-1
	Roberta Davila	7-5
1967	Mariano Etchevarria	23-37-5
	Colrado King	*Unavailable*
	Ulric Regis	7-3
	Lee Carr	8-4
	Billy Daniels	21-16-3

Entered Top Ten 236-181-30 / 20 = 12-9-2

Harry Mathews

1937	Bud Hutchinson	*Unavailable*
	Ira Bruner	*Unavailable*

	Spec Andrews	Unavailable		Watson Jones	26-17-4
1938	Joey Parks	Unavailable		Reuben Jones	33-10-1
	Harry Bean	Unavailable		Phil Muscato	55-22
	Truman Kennedy	Unavailable		Aanton Raadik	37-17-3
	Truman Kennedy	Unavailable		Jose Ochea	3-1
	Truman Kennedy	Unavailable		John Thomas	25-16-1
	Leo Jordan	Unavailable		Sonny Andrews	8-3-1
	Powder Proctor	Unavailable		Anton Raadik	37-18-3
	Johnny Canadeo	Unavailable		Frank Ronkovich	14-7-4
	Celly Royabaugh	Unavailable		Windmill Pearce	5-6
	Mike Cleary	Unavailable	1951	Bob Murphy	54-3
	Wally Miles	Unavailable		Ron Whittle	18-9-6
	Eddie Norris	Unavailable		Frank Buford	19-13-4
1939	Pete Blanchard	Unavailable		Freddie Beshore	30-10-2
	Chief Ballard	Unavailable		Bill Petersen	51-38-8
	Jackie Burke	15-10-2		Dutch Culbertson	19-16-4
1940	Tait Cain	Unavailable		Lloyd Marshall	64-23-4
	Caesar Romero	Unavailable		Jose Basora	74-18-7
	R.J. Lewis	Unavailable		Dave Whitlock	27-9-2
	Teddy White	Unavailable		Grant Butcher	16-6-2
	Jack Hibbard	Unavailable		Grant Butcher	16-7-2
1941	Al Penna	Unavailable		Dave Whitlock	27-10-2
	Bud Peterson	Unavailable		Maynard Jones	12-7-2
	Booker T. Washington	Unavailable		Danny Nardico	33-5-4
	Al Globe	Unavailable		Art Henri	14-21-1
	Bud Smith	Unavailable	1952	Charley Eagle	14-12-3
	Red Shannon	Unavailable		George Kaplan	22-7
	Jimmy Casino	8-9-4		Rex Layne	38-4-2
	Dan Gill	Unavailable			
	Bob Reid	Unavailable	*Entered Top Ten* 1,355-537-174 / 56 = 24-10-3		
1942	Al Hostak	58-6-3			
	Al Hostak	58-7-3	**Buster Mathis**		
1943	Jack Chase	21-3-3			
	Eddie Booker	64-4-7	1965	Bob Maynard	Unavailable
1946	Manuel Jones	Unavailable		Johnny Shore	2-0
	George Evans	26-6-8		Gerald Couturier	Unavailable
	Benny Droll	13-11-8		Bob Stallings	4-3
1947	Bernie Reynolds	19-1		Charley Lee	0-2
	Paul Banks	15-11-6	1966	Chuck Wepner	4-1-2
	Milo Savage	14-5-5		Mike Bruce	4-2-1
	Bobby Volk	18-3		Charley Polite	3-3-1
1948	Remo Polideri	7-0-1		Tom Swift	Unavailable
	Tom Fair	Unavailable		Everett Copeland	4-7-3
	Jackie Burke	3-1-1		Charlie Chase	1-1
	Bobby Ward	7-13-6		Mert Brownfield	0-1
	Bobby Seamon	1-1-1		Bob Stallings	9-4
	Pedro Jimenez	26-22-22		Earl Averette	0-0
	Milo Savage	21-9-8		Johnny Barazza	6-8
1949	Bobby Castro	18-28-5		Sonny Andrews	3-5
	Jackie Burke	5-2-1	1967	Waban Thomas	12-11
	Henry Lee	4-1-1		Ed Hurley	7-6
	George Sherman	22-5		Sonny Moore	18-24-2
	Bobby Joe Walcott	6-5-3		Wayne Heath	9-5
	Billy Davis	16-8-1		Ron Marsh	22-1
1950	Tony Elizondo	45-10-1		Roberto Davila	7-7
	Freddie Fiducia	46-14-1		Gerrie DeBruyn	7-1-2
	Jack Flood	8-4-1			
	Gene Pierce	0-3	*Entered Top Ten*		

Appendix 1

Challenged for Title 122-90-11 / 20 = 6-5-1

Joey Maxim

Year	Opponent	Record
1941	Bob Berry	*Unavailable*
	Frank McBride	*Unavailable*
	Orlando Trotter	*Unavailable*
	Bob Berry	*Unavailable*
	Tony Paoli	*Unavailable*
	Johnny Trotter	*Unavailable*
	Lee Oma	8-7-1
	Nate Bolden	28-9-3
	Bill Peterson	14-3-1
	Oliver Shanks	13-6-1
	Red Burman	52-9-1
1942	Booker Beckwith	17-1
	Herbie Katz	47-14-1
	Lou Brooks	16-2
	Frank Green	*Unavailable*
	Charles Roth	*Unavailable*
	Charles Roth	*Unavailable*
	Jimmy Bivins	26-5
	Lou Brooks	19-—-3
	Curtis Shepherd	14-12-1
	Altus Allen	14-7-1
	Jack Marshall	14-11-2
	Shelton Bell	2-0
	Hubert Hood	0-0
	Larry Lane	39-7-5
	Ezzard Charles	31-2-1
	Ezzard Charles	32-2-1
1943	Clarence Brown	0-1
	Clarence Brown	0-2
	Curtis Shepherd	16-13-2
	Curtis Shepherd	17-13-1
	Al Jordan	4-1-1
	Nate Bolden	45-16-4
	Buddy Scott	35-11-5
	Claude Villar	9-11-1
1944	Georgie Parks	4-7-2
	Buddy Walker	56-14-5
	Bob Garner	25-6-2
	Frank Androff	2-0-1
	Lloyd Marshall	44-10-3
	Johnny Flynn	19-17-2
1945	Johnny Flanagan	5-0
	Clarence Brown	8-7
	Cleo Everett	9-14-2
1946	Howard Williams	*Unavailable*
	John Thomas	20-8-1
	Ralph De John	37-13-3
	Buddy Walker	66-22-5
	Phil Muscato	33-10
	Charley Eagle	11-11-2
	Phil Muscato	35-10
	Phil Muscato	35-12
	Henry Cooper	21-42-7
	Jersey Joe Walcott	43-9-1
	Clarence Jones	13-13-1
	Bearcat Jones	2-13
	Jim Ritchie	2-0
	Jimmy Webb	50-15-4
	Al Velez	18-4-1
Incomplete (December 3, 1945)		
	Jack Marshall	20-28-2
Incomplete (December 5, 1944)		
1947	Jersey Joe Walcott	43-11-1
	Marty Clark	26-5-1
	Charley Roth	13-14-1
	Jersey Joe Walcott	45-11-1
	Clarence Jones	13-17-1
	John Thomas	23-13-1
	Bob Foxworth	15-1
	Billy Thompson	24-3-2
1948	Olle Tandberg	18-4-1
	Bob Sikes	21-4
	Tony Bosnich	28-4-1
	Pat Valentino	39-9-2
	Louis Berlier	3-1
	Francisco De La Cruz	10-9
	Roy Hawkins	16-2-1
	Pat Valentino	39-10-3
	Joe Kahut	41-6-4
	Bill Peterson	44-24-7
	Bill Peterson	46-25-7
	Joe Kahut	42-7-4
	Bob Satterfield	20-6-3
	Jimmy Bivins	68-14-1
1949	Ezzard Charles	62-5-1
	Gus Lesnevich	58-11-5
	Joe Kahut	46-10-5
	Pat McCafferty	65-7
Incomplete (January 14, 1949)		
	Bill Peterson	49-30-8
1950	Freddie Mills	73-16-6
	Joe Dawson	2-2
Incomplete		
	Bill Peterson	50-33-8
	Johnny Swanson	14-10-1
Incomplete (September 25, 1950)		
	Bill Peterson	50-34-8
	Big Boy Brown	14-19-2
	Dave Whitlock	27-7-2
1951	Hubert Hood	15-19-4
Incomplete		

Challenged for Title 2, 252-856-167/84 = 27-10-2

Pat McMurtry

Year	Opponent	Record
1954	Tommy Demers	1-2

Incomplete (June 16, 1950)

	Al Kelly	0-0
	Billy Carter	15-18-2
	Bill Mathias	0-2
	Max Chris	10-0
	Nat Washington	Unavailable
	Jimmy Murphy	6-1
	Bill Boatsman	10-4
	Jack Nelson	23-9-1
	Chuck Ross	17-8-4
	Gene Brixon	15-3-2
	Kirby Seals	5-4-1
1955	Chuck Woodsworth	13-4-1
	Hans Friedrich	9-6-6
	Murray Bennett	3-21-2
	J.B. Reed	4-4-1
	Bob Albright	19-2
	Jimmy Walls	21-35-2
	Bob Dunlap	30-11-1
1956	Cordell Jones	3-5-1
	Matt Jackson	9-4-2
	Ezzard Charles	94-18-1
	Willie Pastrano	35-4-4
	Joey Rowan	28-10-1
1957	Reuben Vargas	11-2
	Edgardo Romero	24-4-2

Incomplete (October 1, 1954)
Entered Top Ten 405-181-34 / 25 = 16-7-1

Tom McNeely

1958	Richie Norton	0-8

Incomplete (October 22, 1956)

	Bob Harris	1-2
	Temple Jones	Unavailable
	Eddie Walker	5-6

Incomplete (November 29, 1959)

	Eddie Allen	Unavailable
	Moses Walker	6-2
	Bob Halpern	Unavailable
1959	Art Maryorga	10-5
	Cornelius Brown	2-12
	Leo Pinto	Unavailable
	Charlie Lopes	Unavailable
	Jeff Holmes	Unavailable
	Cardell Farmos	10-3-1
	Lou Jones	3-8
	Lou Jones	3-10
1960	George Logan	12-1-1
	Willie Besmanoff	41-18-8
	Tunney Hunsaker	5-5
	Uli Ritter	20-2-5
	Jimmy Wiley	1-2
	George Logan	15-2-1
	George Logan	15-3-1

Entered Top Ten 149-89-17 / 16 = 9-6-1

	Kitone Lave	40-16-3

Challenged for Title 189-105-20 / 17 = 11-6-1

Jeff Merritt

1968	Ronnie Williams	0-0
	Joe Belton	Unavailable
	Bobby LeHines	Unavailable
	Milton Torres	3-3-2

Incomplete (January 19, 1965)

	Al Singletary	2-8-1
	John Gause	1-0
	Jimmy Patterson	Unavailable
1969	Roy Williams	7-0
	Charlie Harris	7-3-1
	Mike Bruce	7-20-1
	Roger Russsell	11-4-2
	Henry Clark	19-5-3
1970	Johnny Hudgins	6-4
	Eddie Vick	11-14-3
	Charley Polite	11-15-3
	George Dulaire	13-15-4
	Willie McMillian	16-9-1
	Al Banks	8-11

Entered Top Ten 122-111-21 / 15 = 8-7-1

Larry Middleton

1965	Jimmy Hayes	1-0
	Matt Robinson	Unavailable
	Jerry O'Neal	Unavailable
	Wiley Farmer	
1966	Melvin Pierce	0-0
	Melvin Pierce	0-1
1968	Phil Smith	4-1-1
	Billy Moore	Unavailable
1969	Roy Williams	7-1
	Cleo Daniels	7-16-1
	Bill Hardney	9-6-1
	Orvin Veazey	3-9-2

Incomplete (August 17, 1965)

1970	Phil Smith	10-3-1
	Mike Lanum	10-7

Incomplete

	Harold Darlington	1-7-1
	Gene Owens	2-0
1971	Cleo Daniels	7-20-1
	Mack Harrison	8-9

Incomplete (April 21, 1971)

	Joe Bugner	34-3-1
1972	Tony Doyle	38-10-1

Entered Top Ten 141-93-10 / 16 = 9-6-1

Marty Monroe

1974	King David Smith	2-3-2	
	Lee Thomas	*Unavailable*	
1975	Ron Draper	0-2	
	Tony Pulu	14-2	
	Tony Pulu	15-2-1	
	Fernando Jones	2-3	
	Dwayne Bonds	1-0	
	Tony Pulu	15-3-1	
	Mel Rush	*Unavailable*	
1976	Greg Johnson	5-0	
	Willie Moore	3-5	

Incomplete

	Randy Mack	1-2
1977	C.J. Bar Brown	6-3-2
	Joe Gholston	13-13-3
1978	Fraser Memela	*Unavailable*
	Larry Cruz	1-0
1979	Gary Gahan	0-6-1

Incomplete

	Leroy Boone	11-1
	Jimmy Ingram	8-6-2
	Henry Lumpkin	1-2
1980	Grady Daniels	7-5
	Scott LeDoux	25-8-4
	Lynn Ball	13-3
	Eddie Lopez	15-2-2

Entered Top Ten 158-71-18 / 22 = 7-3-1

Archie Moore

1936	Murray Allen	*Unavailable*
	Speedy Schaefer	*Unavailable*
	Murray Allen	*Unavailable*
	Sammy Jackson	*Unavailable*
	Sammy Jackson	*Unavailable*
1937	Dynamite Payne	*Unavailable*
	Johnny Davis	*Unavailable*
	Joey Huff	*Unavailable*
	Ham Pounder	*Unavailable*
	Charlie Dawson	*Unavailable*
	Karl Martin	*Unavailable*
	Frank Hatfield	*Unavailable*
	Al Dublinsky	*Unavailable*
	Nathan Logan	*Unavailable*
	Billy Adams	*Unavailable*
	Sammy Slaughter	18-15-2

Incomplete

	Sammy Christian	*Unavailable*
	Sammy Jackson	*Unavailable*
1938	Carl Lautenschgler	*Unavailable*
	Frank Rowsey	46-16

Incomplete

	Jimmy Brent	*Unavailable*
	Ray Vargas	*Unavailable*
	Johnny Romero	*Unavailable*
	Johnny Sikes	*Unavailable*
	Lorenzo Pedro	*Unavailable*
	Johnny Romero	*Unavailable*
	Tom Henry	*Unavailable*
	Bobby Yannes	*Unavailable*
	Ray Lyle	*Unavailable*
	Irish Bob Turner	32-29-5
1939	Jack Moran	*Unavailable*
	Domenic Ceccarelli	4-11-1
	Marty Simmons	41-9-6
	Teddy Yarosz	97-10-3
	Jack Coggins	*Unavailable*
	Bobby Seamen	*Unavailable*
	Honeyboy Jones	44-13-1
	Shorty Hogue	13-1
1940	Jack McNamee	1-2-1
	Ron Richards	92-20-6
	Atilio Sabatino	30-11-7
	Joe Delaney	40-24-12
	Frank Lindsay	4-4
	Fred Henneberry	52-14-5
	Ron Richards	93-21-6
	Pancho Ramirez	*Unavailable*
	Shorty Hogue	30-1-2
1941	Clay Rowan	*Unavailable*
	Shorty Hogue	33-1-2
	Clay Rowan	*Unavailable*
	Eddie Booker	46-2-4
1942	Bobby Britton	22-29-5
	Guero Martinez	*Unavailable*
	Jimmy Casino	8-11-4
	Shorty Hogue	46-10-3
	Tabby Romero	*Unavailable*
	Jack Chase	15-0-1
	Eddie Booker	63-3-7
1943	Jack Chase	18-2-3
	Big Boy Hogue	23-14-3
	Eddie Cerda	67-12-9
	Jack Chase	22-3-3
	Aaron Wade	21-4
	Kid Hermosillo	*Unavailable*
	Jack Chase	26-3-4
1944	Amelio Rodrigues	6-6-2
	Eddie Booker	67-5-7
	Roman Starr	11-4-3
	Charley Burley	52-9-3
	Kenny Lasalle	32-19-3

Incomplete

	Louis Mays	*Unavailable*
	Jimmy Hayden	1-2

Records of Opponents

Incomplete

	Battling Monroe	1-6-1
	Nate Bolden	50-22-4
1945	Joey Jones	*Unavailable*
	Bob Jacobs	21-8-1
	Nap Mitchell	6-8-2
	Nate Bolden	54-23-4
	Teddy Randolph	12-12-5
	Lloyd Marshall	49-10-4
	George Kochan	36-6-10
	Lloyd Marshall	49-11-4
	Jimmy Bivins	46-5-1
	Cocoa Kid	150-42-10
	Holman Williams	133-20-10
	O'Dell Riley	3-0-2
	Holman Williams	134-20-11
	Colion Chaney	27-16-5
1946	Curtis Shephard	35-23-2
	Georgie Parks	13-17-2
	Vern Escoe	14-6
	Ezzard Charles	38-4-1
	Shamus O'Brien	21-9-1
	Billy Smith	21-6-1
	Jack Chase	44-14-6
1947	Jack Chase	44-15-7
	Rusty Payne	21-6
	Ezzard Charles	46-3-1
	Curtis Shephard	47-27-2
	Bert Lytell	45-11-4
	Bobby Zander	14-6
	Jimmy Bivins	60-10-1
	George Fitch	25-13-1
1948	Ezzard Charles	54-4-1
	Dusty Wilkerson	12-3
	Doc Williams	14-2
	Billy Smith	29-8-2
	Leonard Morrow	10-2-1
	Jimmy Bivins	66-11-1
	Tiger Ted Lowry	45-34-7
	Billy Smith	31-11-2
	Henry Hall	35-8-3
	Lloyd Gibson	20-2-1
	Henry Hall	36-8-3
	Bob Amos	32-2-5
	Doc Williams	21-3
1949	Alabama Kid	121-28-9
	Bob Satterfield	21-7-2
	Alabama Kid	121-30-9
	Dusty Wilkerson	15-4
	Jimmy Bivins	68-12-1
	Harold Johnson	25-0
	Clinton Bacon	14-3-2
	Bob Sikes	23-10-1
	Esco Greenwood	5-16
	Phil Muscato	55-19
	Bob Amos	34-6-4
	Doc Williams	29-5

	Leonard Morrow	19-4-1
1950	Bert Lytell	68-19-7
	Vernon Williams	12-4-3
1951	Billy Smith	38-13-4
	John Thomas	25-17
	Jimmy Bivins	75-16-1
	Abel Cestac	39-10-1
	Herman Harris	10-6-1
	Art Henri	12-18-1
	Abel Cestac	39-11-3
	Karel Sys	64-13-7
	Alberto Lovell	36-7-3
	Vincente Quiroz	*Unavailable*
	Victor Carabajal	*Unavailable*
	Americ Capitanelli	*Unavailable*
	Rafael Miranda	*Unavailable*
	Alfredo Lagay	20-8-10

Incomplete (July 20, 1950)

	Embrell Davidson	20-2
	Harold Johnson	34-2
	Chubby Wright	22-25-2
	Harold Johnson	34-3
1952	Harold Johnson	35-3
	Jimmy Slade	14-3-2
	Bob Dunlap	23-6-1
	Clarence Henry	32-3-2
	Clint Bacon	21-5-2
	Joey Maxim	78-18-4
1953	Toxie Hall	8-3-2
	Leonard Dugan	5-0
	Sonny Andrews	12-7-1
	Nino Valdes	22-5-2
	Al Spaulding	20-23-1
	Frank Buford	21-19-5
	Joey Maxim	79-19-4
	Reinaldo Ansaloni	2-0
	Dogomar Martinez	24-0-1
1954	Joey Maxim	79-20-4
	Bob Baker	31-4-1
	Bert Whitehurst	18-3
	Harold Johnson	47-5
	Nino Valdes	33-8-2

Entered Top Ten 4, 651-1, 312-362/125 = 37-10-3

| 1955 | Carl Olson | 63-6 |

Challenged for Title 4, 714-1,318-362/126 = 37-10-3

	Rocky Marciano	48-0
1956	Howard King	27-7-5
	Bob Dunlap	30-12-1
	Frankie Daniels	27-11-1
	Howard King	28-8-5
	Willie Bean	41-24-4
	George Parmentier	15-11-4
	Sonny Andrews	14-11-2
	Gene Thompson	10-10-4
	Yolande Pompey	31-2-2

	James Parker	28-5-4
	Roy Shire	

Challenged for Title 4,998-1, 418-394/137 = 36-10-3

Randy Neumann

1969	Jeff Marxs	0-0
	Junior Wilkerson	0-0
	George Simpson	0-2
	Junior Wilkerson	1-1
	Junior Wilkerson	1-2
1970	Angel Rivera	*Unavailable*
	Tony Gagliardo	13-9-3
	Lenore Couture	0-4
	Sonny Brown	3-3-2

Incomplete (March 19, 1970)

	Edmundo Stewart	1-1
	Edmundo Stewart	1-2
1971	Jimmy Harris	1-2
	Jimmy Harris	2-2
	Tony Norris	14-3
	Raul Gorosito	1-0
	Brian O'Melia	9-5
	Bob Castle	2-4
	Raul Gorosito	5-1
	Chuck Wepner	22-8-2
1972	Jimmy Young	7-2
	Chuck Wepner	22-9-2
	Alex Carr	1-1-1
	G.G. Maldonado	5-2-2
1973	Jerry Quarry	43-5-4
	Doug Kirk	13-2
	Pedro Agosto	23-4
	Raul Gorosito	11-4-2
1974	Chuck Wepner	27-9-2
	Carl Baker	8-12-1
1975	Larry Beilfuss	11-6
	Bob Scott	1-1
	Larry Renault	12-14
	Bill Aird	17-8-4
	Wendell Joseph	2-8

Incomplete

	Boone Kirkman	32-5
	Bobby Walker	7-3
	Duane Bobick	32-0

Entered Top Ten 350-144-25 / 36 = 10-4-1

Charlie Norkus

1948	James Walls	3-8-1
	James Walls	4-8-1
1949	Eddie Brown	1-2
	Jimmy Hill	5-1
	Howard Bergen	7-11

Incomplete (December 2, 1947)

	Eddie Blair	*Unavailable*
	George Washington	4-13
	Johnny Pretzie	7-6
	James Walls	10-14-1
	Jack LaBroad	1-1
	Tommy Giorgio	9-6
	Clifton Murphy	0-3
	Buddy Moore	14-7-2
	George Washington	8-14
	Ricky Ronci	18-5-1
	Eddie Davis	1-5
	Sonny Parisi	8-0
1950	Curt Kennedy	21-3-1
	Curt Kennedy	23-3-1
	Cesar Brion	28-3
	Dulio Spagnolo	12-6-3
1951	Caesar Brion	35-6
	Keene Simmons	8-12-1
	Lalu Sabotin	18-2
	James J. Parker	13-2-2
1952	Dave Davey	21-1
	Tommy Harrison	15-6-1
1953	Ernie Shephard	6-3
	Ike Thomas	1-4
	Matt Daniels	0-3
	Ray Wilding	41-3-4
	Hal Buolston	14-1-1
1954	Danny Nardico	48-10-4
	Danny Nardico	48-11-4
	Tommy Jackson	15-2-1
	Caesar Brion	46-10
	Charley Powell	11-0-1
	Roland LaStarza	53-5

Entered Top Ten 577-200-30 / 37 = 16-5-1

Ken Norton

1967	Grady Brazell	*Unavailable*
1968	Sam Wyatt	4-6-2
	Harold Dutra	6-0
	Jimmy Gilmore	2-2
	Wayne Kindred	5-2
	Cornell Nolan	*Unavailable*
1969	Joe Hemphill	0-2-1
	Wayne Kindred	5-2
	Pedro Sanchez	5-9
	Bill McMurray	22-21-2
	Gary Bates	16-9-2
	Julius Garcia	*Unavailable*
1970	Aaron Eastling	18-6-2
	Stamford Harris	4-2
	Bob Mashburn	4-2-2
	Ray Ellis	6-8
	Jose Luis Garcia	11-2-1
	Cookie Wallace	8-12-2

	Chuck Leslie	18-20-4		Big Boy Brown	10-5-1
	Roby Harris	3-5-1		Buddy Walker	46-11-5
1971	Steve Carter	14-3		Dusty Wilkerson	7-1
	Vic Brown	22-16		George Parks	4-5
	James J. Woody	16-8-1		Buddy Walker	50-11-5
1972	Charlie Harris	7-14-1		Willie Thomas	5-7-1
	Jack O'Halloran	22-13-2		Larry Lane	46-12-7
	Herschel Jacobs	27-18-2		George Parks	4-6-2
	James J. Woody	16-10-1		Herb Marshall	29-15-5
			1944	George Fuller	2-6

Entered Top Ten   261-192-26 / 24 = 11-8-1

	Henry Clark	23-7-5		Wallace Cross	23-16-3
	Charley Reno	7-6-1		Johnny Denson	18-13-2
1973	Muhammad Ali	41-1		Larry Lane	48-12-7
	Muhammad Ali	41-2		Earl Lowman	12-12
				Danny Cox	13-13-6

Challenged for Title   373-207-32 / 28 = 13-7-1

				Herb Marshall	29-16-5
				Buddy Knox	87-22-5
1974	George Foreman	39-0		Lou Nova	41-6-6
	Boone Kirkman	32-3		Billy Nitchy	13-10-1
1975	Reed Brooks	9-19-1		Billy Nitchy	14-10-1
	Jerry Quarry	50-7-4		Teddy Randolph	7-7-5
	Jose Luis Garcia	28-7-1		Tami Mauriello	56-6-1
1976	Pedro Lovell	16-1-1		Al Blake	15-5-1
	Ron Stander	29-8-2		Tami Mauriello	57-6-1
	Larry Middleton	23-8-2	1945	Joe Baksi	40-3-4
				Tami Mauriello	57-7-1

Challenged for Title   599-260-43 / 39 = 15-7-1

				Earl Lowman	17-25
				Larry Lane	51-18-8
				Jackie Saunders	7-6

Lee Oma

				Prentiss Hall	14-2
1939	Al Globe	Unavailable	1946	Jimmy Bell	21-9-3
	Altus Allen	2-1		Phil Muscato	32-9
	Bob Ray	Unavailable		Gus Lesnevich	52-9-5
	Altus Allen	2-2		Jersey Joe Walcott	41-9-1
1940	Billy Mundune	Unavailable		Phil Muscato	38-13
	Altus Allen	2-2-1		Joe Muscato	23-15-1
	Tiger Warrington	59-7-5		Fitzie Fitzpatrick	34-7-2
	Bert Hardy	Unavailable	1947	Phi Muscato	39-13
	Hobo Williams	Unavailable		Pat Comiskey	53-8-1
	Ira Hughes	Unavailable		Colion Chaney	41-24-6
1941	Orlando Trotter	Unavailable	1948	Henry Flake	21-2-1
	Erv Sarlin	11-3		Henry Flake	22-2-1
	Orlando Trotter	Unavailable		Walter Hafer	13-11-1
	Booker Beckwith	13-0		Ted Lowry	45-32-6
	Bob Sikes	Unavailable		Red Applegate	10-10-2
	Lou Campbell	Unavailable		Howard Chard	6-14
	Joey Maxim	5-1		BruceWoodcock	31-2
	Johnny Denson	1-0		Tommy Gomez	64-7-1
	Jack Marshall	14-11-2	1949	Angel Sotillo	34-19-10
	Panther Williams	Unavailable		Ted Lowry	47-39-8
1943	Louis Jones	Unavailable		Johnny Flynn	37-24-2
	Dan Biggers	2-3		Phil Muscato	55-15
	Dan Aldrich	4-1		Omelio Agramonte	20-4
	Leon Ford	Unavailable		Augustino Guedes	15-8-3
	Larry Scalone	Unavailable		Fitzie Fitzpatrick	43-15-1
	Jimmy Gordon	Unavailable		Jo Weiden	22-5-1
	Dusty Wilkerson	4-0		Enrico Bertola	33-7-1
	George Parks	4-3		Freddie Beshore	28-4-2

214   Appendix 1

1950	Freddie Beshore	28-5-2
	Vern Mitchell	50-6-1
	Bill Weinberg	41-20-4
	Bob Satterfield	24-9-4
	Nick Barone	41-7
	Bob Satterfield	25-9

Challenged for Title 2,074-720-161 / 76 = 27-9-2

Greg Page

1979	Dan Martin	4-3

Incomplete (December 19, 1978)

	Jerry McIntyre	*Unavailable*
	James Knox	0-0
	Oliver Phillips	2-3
	Frankie Brown	3-1

Incomplete

	James Reid	4-1
	Ira Martin	4-4
1980	Victor Rodrigues	9-3
	Clayman Parker	27-5-1
	George Chaplin	16-1-1
	Larry Alexander	16-7-2

Entered Top Ten 85-28-4 / 10 = 9-3

Willie Pastrano

1951	Domingo Rivera	4-6-1
	Frank Speed	1-3
	Jimmy Connino	*Unavailable*
	Domingo Rivera	4-7-1
1952	Alvin Boudreaux	0-2-1
	Alvin Pelligrini	5-0
	Buzz Brown	16-10-2

Incomplete (June 29, 1948)

	John Chaney	7-2-1
	Al McCoy	17-10
	Jim Carter	1-2-1
	Sonny Luciano	52-16-4
	Sonny Luciano	52-17-4
	Johnny Capitano	10-3-2
	Alvin Pelligrini	7-1-1
	Lonnie Rylant	3-0
	Alvin Pelligrini	9-1-1
	Alvin Boudreaux	1-4-1
	Alvin Pelligrini	9-2-1
1953	Alfredo Griffin	8-10-2
	Emerson Butcher	15-7-7
	Chic Boucher	29-12-3
	Roger Trevine	6-2-3
	Chato Hernandez	2-2
	Johnny Cesario	81-12-4
	Del Flanagan	60-8-2

	Elmer Beltz	26-7-2
	Elmer Beltz	26-7-3
	Halo Scortichini	22-11-3
1954	Jimmy Martinez	48-7-3
	Jacques Royer-Crecy	34-19-4
	Tommy Hatcher	4-13-1
	Tommy Bazzano	52-32-7
	Jimmy Martinez	52-10-3
	Jackie LaBua	23-4
	Bobby Dykes	95-15-6
1955	Tony Johnson	22-5-7
	Al Andrews	32-10-2
	Willie Troy	30-—-3
	Joey Maxim	81-22-4
	Chuck Spieser	15-2
	Paddy Young	49-10-3
	Joey Rowan	25-6-1
	Rex Layne	45-16-4

Entered Top Ten 1,080-338-95 / 42 = 26-8-2

Floyd Patterson

1952	Eddie Goodbold	5-13-1
	Sammy Walker	32-27-4
	Lester Jackson	5-10-2
	Lalo Sabotin	21-6
1953	Chester Mieszala	16-6
	Dick Wagner	29-15-4
	Gordon Wallace	22-3-1
	Wesbury Bascom	16-7-1
	Dick Wagner	29-16-4
1954	Yvon Durelle	20-4-1
	Sam Brown	3-1

Incomplete (June 1, 1950)

	Jesse Turner	36-15-5
	Joey Maxim	79-21-4
	Jacques Royer-Crecy	35-15-1
	Tommy Harrison	22-9-2
	Alvin Williams	43-10-6
	Esau Ferdinand	39-10-7
	Joe Gannon	31-2
	Jimmy Slade	20-10-4
1955	Willie Troy	30-2
	Don Grant	16-1
	Esau Ferdinand	40-11-7
	Yvon Durelle	28-9-2
	Archie McBride	20-9
	Alvin Williams	48-11-6
	Dave Whitlock	33-14-3
	Calvin Brad	8-5-1
	Jimmy Slade	23-14-4
1956	Jimmy Walls	21-36-2
	Alvin Williams	49-12-6

Entered Top Ten 819-324-78 / 30 = 27-11-3

	Tommy Jackson	27-4-1

Challenged for Title 846-328-79 / 31 = 27-11-3

	Archie Moore	156-21-8
1957	Tommy Jackson	29-5-1
	Pete Rademacher	0-0
1958	Roy Harris	21-0
1959	Brian London	22-4
	Ingemar Johannson	21-0

Challenged for Title 1,095-358-88 / 37 = 30-10-2

1960	Ingemar Johannson	22-0
1961	Ingemar Johannson	22-1
	Tom McNeely	23-0
1962	Sonny Liston	33-1

Challenged for Title 1,195-360-88 / 41 = 29-9-2

1963	Sonny Liston	34-1
1964	Sante Amonti	47-4-2
	Eddie Machen	47-4-2
	Charley Powell	25-9-3
1965	George Chuvalo	29-8-2
	Todd Herring	26-3

Challenged for Title 1,403-389-97 / 47 = 30-8-2

1965	Muhammad Ali	21-0
1966	Henry Cooper	33-12-1
1967	Willie Johnson	13-11-1
	Bill McMurray	20-16-2
	Jerry Quarry	23-1-3
	Jerry Quarry	24-1-4

Challenged for Title 1,537-430-108 /49 = 31-9-2

Johnny Persol

1963	Don Turner	6-5
	Bobo Reckly	14-0-4
	Mike Campbell	8-5-1

Incomplete (December 2, 1957)

	Herschel Jacobs	15-4
	Charley Jordan	9-5-2
	Mel Fulgham	12-7-2
	Herchel Jacobs	15-6
	Willie Giles	8-1-2
	Johnny Alford	15-9-3
	Allen Thomas	19-2-1
1964	Eddie Cotton	50-14-1
	Eddie Cotton	50-15-1
	Bobo Olson	87-13-2
	Henry Hank	56-19-3
	Roger Rouse	18-3-2
1965	Chic Calderwood	40-6-1
	Jimmy Dupree	16-2-1
1966	Harold Johnson	72-9
	Herschel Jacobs	19-11-2
	James J. Woody	10-0
	Amos Lincoln	35-4-3

Entered Top Ten 574-140-31 / 21 = 27-7-1

Charley Powell

1953	Fred Taylor	0-1
1954	Bob Sherman	1-2-2
	Bill Mathias	0-1
	Al Winn	0-3-1
	Joe Hayward	Unavailable
	Ozzie Hubbard	Unavailable
	Harland Kelly	1-1-1
	Frank Buford	22-23-5
	Al Spaulding	20-25-5
	Rocky Jones	10-11-1
	Sandy McPherson	17-27-4
	Keene Simmons	9-18-1
	Charley Norkus	24-12
1955	Hans Friedrich	8-4-6
	Johnny Summerlin	22-4-2
1956	Charley Que	6-3
	Charley Que	6-3-2
	Neal Welch	2-6-1
	Roger Rischer	11-4-2
1958	Sam Edwards	1-2
	Johnny Haywood	0-2
	Bob Biehler	18-10-1
	Charlie Jones	5-4
	Charlie Norkus	32-18
1959	Nino Valdes	47-15-2

Entered Top Ten 262-199-36 / 23 = 11-9-2

Jerry Quarry

1965	Gene Hamilton	6-27

Incomplete (December 12, 1961)

	John Henry Jackson	8-8-2
	Lance Holmberg	0-2
	Dave Centi	7-0
	Willie Davis	Unavailable
	Ray Ellis	1-0
	John Henry Jackson	8-9-2
	J.P. Spencer	0-0
	Ray Ellis	2-1
	Melvin Manley	0-1
	Al Carter	3-7-1
	Ray Crear	3-4
	Tony Doyle	11-2
	Ray Crear	3-5
1966	Eddie Land	0-3
	Prentice Snipes	18-7
	Tony Alongi	38-2-1
	Eddie Machen	48-8-3
	Bill Neilsen	22-10-2
	Leslie Borden	12-7-2
	Joey Orbillo	10-1-1
1967	Memphis Al Jones	3-8
	Brian London	35-14
	Alex Miteff	25-12-1

	Floyd Patterson	46-5
Entered Top Ten	354-158-20 / 27 = 13-6-1	
	Floyd Patterson	46-5-1
1968	Thad Spencer	32-5
Challenged for Title	432-168-21 / 29 = 15-6-1	
	Jimmy Ellis	25-5
	Bob Mumford	0-12-2
	Willis Earls	4-8-1
1969	Charley Reno	3-2
	Aaron Eastling	17-3-2
	Buster Mathis	29-1
Challenged for Title	510-199-26 / 35 = 15-6-1	

Bernie Reynolds

1946	David Glunton	*Unavailable*
	Jimmy Maxwell	4-1
	Jimmy Letty	0-0
	Billy Beauford	2-11
	Tommy Giorgio	1-0
	Hugh Walker	0-3
	Billy Beauford	2-11
	Jim Letty	0-4
	Johnny Davis	5-20
	Joe Peters *Unavailable*	
	Jimmy Hooper	3-0
	George Haywood	0-1
	Tom Reddington	43-11-1
	Willie Hayes	4-6
	George Haywood	0-4
1947	Willie Hayes	4-7
	George Haywood	0-5
	Jim White	8-6
	Willie Brown	0-0
	Jackie Cranford	24-5-1
	Kid Roscoe	4-1
	Walter Hafer	11-5-1
	Bob Miller	3-8
	Babe O'Blenis	*Unavailable*
	Earl Lowman	22-37
	Leo Matricinni	15-0
	Eldridge Eatman	13-10-3
	Eldridge Eatman	13-11-3
	Jackie Cranford	29-7-1
1948	Jackie Cranford	30-7-1
	Kid Roscoe	8-6
	Eddie Blunt	35-19-6
Incomplete (July 11, 1946)		
	Ted Waters	*Unavailable*
	Jim Neville	3-2
	Nathan Mann	72-9-6
	Bill Weinberg	40-14-3
	Renato Totino	12-4-3
	Angel Sotillo	2-5
	Roscoe Howard	*Unavailable*

	Leo Matricinni	20-4-1
	Leo Matricinni	21-4-1
	Harry Bernstsen	21-12-1
1949	Mike Jacobs	12-9-2
	Gene Gasney	13-2
	Gene Felton	10-12-1
	Walter Hafer	14-14-1
Entered Top Ten	523-297-36 / 41 = 13-7-1	

Roger Rischer

1953	Bill Boatman	9-2
	Tommy White	*Unavailable*
1954	Walter Robinson	2-1
	Sylvester Stewart	*Unavailable*
	Jim Marzano	*Unavailable*
	George Kennedy	0-0
	Bob Battista	*Unavailable*
	Carlos Martinez	0-1
	Harland Kelly	1-2-1
	Howard King	18-3-3
1955	Bob Wise	3-9-2
	Reuben Vargas	5-0
	Raul Flores	2-1
	Howard King	23-6-4
	Howard King	25-7-4
1956	Howard King	26-7-4
	Amos Lincoln	13-1-2
	Charlie Powell	15-2-2
	Young Jack Johnson	12-7-1
	Zora Folley	24-2-1
1957	Reuben Vargas	12-3
	Archie Moore	164-21-6
1959	Joe Louis III	12-13-2
Incomplete (June 24, 1958)		
1960	Frank Haynes	14-20-3
1961	Young Jack Johnson	22-14-1
	Kirk Barrow	22-6-1
	Monroe Ratliff	14-18-4
1962	Howard King	37-23-7
	Eddie Machen	41-4-1
1963	Kirk Barrow	27-9-1
	Cleveland Williams	58-5-1
1964	Bill McMurray	16-11-1
	Charley Powell	25-8-3
	Bill McMurray	17-11-1
	Willie Richardson	14-2-1
	Henry Cooper	28-9-1
Entered Top Ten	701-228-58 / 32 = 22-7-2	

Elmer Rush

1962	John Riggins	3-7-7
1963	Keno Carlos	*Unavailable*
	Tom Cummins	*Unavailable*

	Dave Furch	9-12-2		Harold Johnson	37-5
1964	Archie Ray	14-2-2	1953	Murray Bennett	3-13-2
	Bill McMurray	16-10		Gene Brown	9-4
	Bill McMurray	16-10-1		Bob Baker	30-2-1
	Al Carter	3-6-1			
	Bill McMurray	16-13-1			

Entered Top Ten   1,317-346-88 / 46 = 29-8-2

1965	Todd Herring	25-3
	Charlie Howard	Unavailable
	Tony Anchonado	0-0
	Roy Rogers	6-1
	Eddie Machen	48-6-1
	Todd Herring	26-4

Entered Top Ten   182-74-8 / 12 = 15-6-1

Earnie Shavers

1969	Red Howell	1-1
	George Holden	7-4-2
	Stan Johnson	6-0
	Lee Roy	Unavailable
	J.D. McCauley	1-0
	Chico Francano	Unavailable
	Gene Idolette	4-7-1

Incomplete

Bob Satterfield

1945	Young Mitchell	0-0
	Arthur McWhorter	2-0-1
	Mike Parshay	1-4
	Charlie Roth	1-1
	Johnny Vorce	7-7-1
	Herman Hayes	Unavailable
	Vecre Van	11-3-1
	Curley Denton	4-4-1
	Oscar Boyd	10-5-1
	Charley Polk	8-6
	Bob Garner	31-9-3
	Collins Brown	16-2-1
	Denny McCombs	12-4
1946	Johnny Clark	26-7-1
	Holman Williams	138-22-11
	Vince Pimpinella	38-55-9
	Jake LaMotta	60-11-2
1947	Willie Moore	9-2-1
	Bob Foxworth	9-1
	Willie Moore	10-3-2
	Al Johnson	12-6-2
	Chuck Hunter	10-3-2
	Al Johnson	14-8-3
1948	Sam Baroudi	36-9-3
	Art Swiden	18-3
	Billy Smith	30-9-2
	Richard Hagan	13-1-2
	Bob Amos	32-2-1
1949	Archie Moore	98-17-5
	Henry Hall	39-9-4
	Sylvester Perkins	29-7-1
1950	Nick Barone	38-5-1
	Tommy Gomez	75-8-2
	Lee Oma	60-25-4
	Lee Oma	61-26-4
	Vern Mitchell	56-8-1
1951	Elkins Brothers	25-5-1
	Rex Layne	29-1-2
	Wes Bascom	11-0
1952	Clarence Henry	30-2-2
	Harold Johnson	36-4

1970	Tiger Brown	2-8
	Joe Byrd	10-7
	Tiger Brown	2-9
	Art Miller	13-15-1
	Ron Asher	0-6

Incomplete (February 4, 1970)

	Frank Smith	Unavailable
	Ron Stander	9-0
	Jim Daniels	Unavailable
	Don Branch	1-2
	Johnny Hudgins	10-7
	Johnny Mac	5-3
	Bunky Adkins	5-0
1971	Lee Estes	6-16-3
	Nat Shaver	Unavailable
	Johnny Mac	5-4
	Richard Gosha	10-9
	Steve Carter	14-2
	Young Agabab	Unavailable
	Mack Harrison	8-8

Incomplete

	Willie Johnson	18-16-2
	Jimmy Brown	3-8-2

Jimmy Brown (October 26,1970)

	Chuck Leslie	19-21-4
	Bill Hardney	12-17-1
	Bill McMurray	23-23-3
	Pat Duncan	17-3-1
	Charlie Boston	4-3

Incomplete

	Elmo Henderson	18-11
	Cleo Daniels	7-23-2
	Del Morris	Unavailable
1972	Ted Gullick	16-4-1
	Elgie Waters	2-9
	Charlie Polite	12-19-3
	Bob Felstein	14-10-1

	Lou Bailey	17-35-5
	Vincente Rondon	37-7-1
	A.J. Staples	11-5
	Leroy Caldwell	13-12-2
1973	Jimmy Young	5-3
	Harold Carter	14-25-2
	Jimmy Ellis	38-7

Entered Top Ten 419-369-37 / 40 = 10-9-1

	Jerry Quarry	47-6-4
1974	Cookie Wallace	13-17-2
	Bob Stallings	17-21
	Jimmy Young	7-3
1975	Leon Shaw	4-5-1
	Rochelle Norris	11-1
	Oliver Wright	12-9
	Ron Lyle	31-3-1
	Tommy Howard	2-15-2
1976	Henry Clark	32-8-5
	Henry Clark	32-9-5
	Roy Williams	21-5
1977	Howard Smith	17-1-1

Challenged for Title 665-472-58 / 53 = 13-9-1

	Muhammad Ali	54-2
1978	Larry Holmes	26-0
	Harry Terrell	8-3
	John Gerowski	19-15-1
	Harold Carter	23-46-3
	Ken Norton	41-5
	Eddie Porette	2-2

Entered Top Ten 838-545-62 / 60 = 14-9-1

Jimmy Slade

1949	Joe Lindsay	13-1-2
	Grant Hodges	8-1-2
	Grant Hodges	8-2-2
	Harry Daniels	0-2-1
	Freddie Fiducia	45-13-1
	Jack Porter	11-7-2

Incomplete

	Joe Lindsay	16-2-2
1950	Mickey Carter	1-1
	Lee Baldwin	4-3
	Doc Williams	29-6
	Chubby Wright	19-18-2
	Doc Williams	29-7
	Bert Lytell	79-20-7
	Ted Lowry	51-53-9
	Chubby Wright	20-19-2
1951	Earl Walls	12-6
	Henry Hall	40-14-6
	Julian Keene	32-5
	Doc Cockell	50-8-1
1952	Archie Moore	128-19-6
	Charley Lester	6-4-2

	Yolande Pompee	14-0-2
1953	Harold Johnson	39-5
	Yolande Pompee	15-0-3
	Herbie Hayes	9-4
	Tommy Harrison	20-8-1
	James J. Parker	23-4-2
	Dan Bucceroni	43-3
	Herman Harris	11-12-1
	Rocky Jones	10-10-1
1954	Harold Johnson	45-5

Entered Top Ten 830-262-57 / 31 = 27-8-2

Howard Smith

1971	George Gray	5-2
	Cannibal Nuapia	Unavailable
	Don Koontz	12-4

Incomplete (February 17, 1967)

1972	Henry Culpepper	2-1
	Mike Weaver	0-0
	Mike Weaver	0-1
	Dan Johnson	1-1
1973	Al Evans	8-4

Incomplete (July 19, 1971)

	Jack O'Halloran	32-16-2
	Steve Carter	15-6
1974	Tony Doyle	40-13-1
	Jack O'Halloran	35-20-2
	Raul Gorosito	12-7-2
1975	Larry Middleton	21-5-2
1976	John Jordan	0-0
	Dan Johnson	2-4
	Dan Johnson	2-5
	Johnny Boudreaux	19-0-1

Entered Top Ten 206-89-10 / 17 = 12-5-1

Renaldo Snipes

1978	Carl Haliburton	0-2
	Hal Emerson	Unavailable
1979	Sam Miller	0-5

Incomplete

	Ron Hope	Unavailable
	Dave Smith	0-3-1

Incomplete (June 13, 1978)

	Barry Funches	1-0
	Charles Cox	4-0

Incomplete (October 27, 1978)

	Eugene Green	4-3-1
	Mike Tarasewich	5-5-1
	Tyrone Harlee	10-11-1
1980	Dave Johnson	13-4

	James Reid	4-2
	Johnny Warr	4-10
	Robert Coley	4-5-1

Incomplete (June 6, 1980)

| | Larry Alexander | 16-8-2 |
| | Rodell Dupree | 11-13 |

Incomplete

	Malik Dozier	4-3-1
	Dwaine Bonds	10-6-1
1981	Leroy Boone	13-6
	Jumbo Cummings	14-0
	Eddie Muhammad	38-4-1
	Gerrie Coetzee	24-2

Entered Top Ten
Challenged for Title 179-92-10 / 20 = 9-5-1

Thad Spencer

1960	Frankie Rowe	*Unavailable*
	Theo Lolanzo	*Unavailable*
1961	Harvey Taylor	26-11-3

Incomplete (January 10, 1957)

	Frank Haynes	14-24-3
	Roy Smith	18-10-5
	John Riggins	22-6
	Shirley Pembleton	12-8-2

Incomplete (September 30, 1958)

	Jerry Gaines	*Unavailable*
	Lou Bailey	8-15-5
	Dave Furch	7-6-2
1962	Art Wright	3-10

Incomplete (August 23, 1958)

	John Riggins	23-10
	Otis Lee	6-0
	Willie McDonald	9-3-1
	Leonard Dugan	6-1

Incomplete (April 1, 1953)

1963	Al Carter	1-1
	Monroe Ratliff	13-16-4
	Jeff Davis	17-3
	Jimmy Fletcher	3-1-3
	Charley Leslie	4-2
1964	Ray Shiel	18-14-2
	George Johnson	3-1-1
	Ollie Wilson	16-25
	Tom McNeely	33-8
	Amos Lincoln	25-3-3
1965	Chuck Leslie	7-4
	Billy Daniels	19-7-1

Entered Top Ten 313-189-35 / 24 = 13-8-1

Leon Spinks

| 1977 | Bobby Smith | 6-5-2 |

Incomplete

	Peter Freeman	13-7
	Jerry McIntyre	4-2
	Pedro Agosto	25-8-1
	Bruce Scott	9-36-1
	Scott LeDoux	21-6-1
	Alfio Righetti	27-0

Entered Top Ten
Challenged for Title 105-64-3 / 7 = 15-9

1978	Muhammad Ali	55-3
	Muhammad Ali	55-4
1979	Gerry Coetzee	21-0
1980	Alfredo Evangelista	33-4-2
	Eddie Lopez	15-2-1
	Kevin Isaac	14-6-2
	Bernardo Mercado	27-2

Challenged for Title 325-83-8 / 14 = 23-6-1

Ron Stander

1969	Bobby Street	1-1
	Red Ferris	*Unavailable*
	Lee Estes	4-7
	Willie Elbert	1-3

Incomplete (October 23, 1967)

	Joe Byrd	10-6
1970	Roy Rodrigues	*Unavailable*
	Lee Powell	0-9
	Joe Harris	0-1-0
	Woody Parks	1-0
	Earnie Shavers	12-1
	Eddie Dembry	11-6

Incomplete (December 4, 1968)

	Ray Ellis	7-9
	Bill Hardney	13-17-1
	Manuel Ramos	26-13-2
	Murphy Goodwin	0-3
1971	Thad Spencer	32-11-1
	Frank Bullard	8-9
	Lee Carr	9-7
	Jack O'Halloran	19-11-2
	Manuel Ramos	27-18-3
	Jesse Crown	22-12-1
	Clyde Brown	5-4
1972	Reco Brooks	7-10
	Mike Boswell	13-6
	Johnny Mac	7-11

Entered Top Ten 235-1745-10 / 23 = 10-8

Johnny Summerlin

| 1950 | Harvey Pack | 0-0 |

	Lloyd Michigan	6-7
	George McDonald	7-4
	Norman Smith	*Unavailable*
	John Cidone	*Unavailable*
	George McDonald	7-6
	Mike Rock	*Unavailable*
1951	Bob Hershey	*Unavailable*
	Ronnie Wulf	3-2
	Bill Roberts	11-3
	Bill Roberts	11-4
	Bob Masterson	*Unavailable*
	Richard Hagen	21-6-4
	Charley Lester	2-3
	Wes Bascom	8-0
	Ponce DeLeon	1-7-2
	Ralph Schneider	15-5-2
1952	Vern Escoe	19-11
	Bob Johnson	4-1
1954	Oscar Pharo	15-1
	Oscar Pharo	15-2
	Sonny Liston	5-0
	Sonny Liston	6-0
	George Powell	11-3
	Toxie Hall	10-11-3
1955	Arthur Wright	14-7
	Al Hunter	4-4
	Willie Coleman	3-1
	Charley Powell	12-1-1
	Young Jack Johnson	8-4-1
	Zora Folley	18-0-1
	Bert Whitehurst	21-8-2
	Neal Welch	3-6-1
	Ernie Cab	5-2-1

Entered Top Ten   265-109-19 / 29 = 9-4-1

John Tate

1977	Jerry Thompkins	7-3
	Norm Kues	0-0
	Baker Tinsley	2-0
	Walter Santemore	5-0
	Eddie Lopez	8-0
	Lou Esa	16-2-1
	Frank Schram	13-8
	Charlie Jordan	12-39-2
1978	James Dixon	4-5-1
	Leon Shaw	17-11-1
	Harold Carter	24-43-3
	Raul Gorosito	16-12-7
	Bernardo Mercado	20-0
	Walter Santemore	5-1
	Johnny Boudreaux	21-4-1
	Cookie Wallace	23-30-2
	Ron Draper	2-9
	Duane Bobick	48-2

Entered Top Ten   242-169-18 / 18 = 13-9-1

	Kallie Knoetzee	17-2
	Gerry Coetzee	22-0

Challenged for Title   279-161-17 / 20 = 14-8-1

Ernie Terrell

1957	Norman Bolden	0-2-1
	Andy Bonds	4-4
	Ray Griggs	0-2-1
	Neal Welch	3-12-2
	Ted Poole	5-6
1958	Cal Butler	12-9
	Emil Brtko	20-8
	Johnny Harper	5-7
	Johnny Gray	14-8-1
	Bill Pickett	3-3
	Joe Hemphill	9-0
	John Hobart	5-5-1
	Sid Peaks	42-18
1959	Willie Coleman	5-3
	Johnny Gray	15-8-1
	Tunney Hunsaker	6-1
	Chuck Garrett	3-4

Incomplete (June 10, 1959)

1960	Clay Thomas	10-1-1
	Lee Williams	10-0-1
	Frankie Daniels	34-17-7
	Joe Hemphill	17-1
	Wayne Bethea	20-12-2
1961	Ernie Cab	10-12-1
	Willie Coleman	7-5
	Chuck Garrett	6-5

Incomplete (March 27, 1961)

	Ernie Cab	12-14-1
1962	Herb Siler	11-3
	Cleveland Williams	51-4
	Amos Lincoln	25-1-4
	Eddie Jackson	4-6-1
	Ray Lopez	9-3
	Young Jack Johnson	24-18-1
1963	Young Jack Johnson	24-19-1
	Herb Siler	14-6
	Cleveland Williams	56-4-1

Entered Top Ten   495-231-38 / 35 = 14-7-1

	Zora Folley	63-3-6
	Gerhard Zech	24-1-1
	Jeff Davis	20-5-1
	Bob Foster	14-2
	Henry Wallitsch	14-10

Challenged for Title   633-255-43 / 40 = 16-6-1

1965	Eddie Machen	46-6-2
	George Chuvalo	33-9-2
	Doug Jones	29-6-1

Challenged for Title   741-276-48 / 43 = 17-6-1

Pinklon Thomas

1978	Ken Arlt	7-1
	Mustafa El Amin	5-5-1
1979	Roger Braxton	0-1
	Lew Lockwood	3-5
	Elmo Henderson	17-11

Incomplete (October 21, 1975)

	Fonia Leota	6-2-1
	Lee Holloman	0-10-1
	George Jerome	11-12-5
	Willie Stoglin	1-5
	Leroy Caldwell	21-18-4

Incomplete (July 11, 1979)

	Bobby Jordan	5-2
1980	Jerry Williams	2-0
	Frank Brown	3-4

Incomplete

	Jerry Williams	2-2
1981	Lee Mitchell	1-8-1

Incomplete

	Curtis Whitner	3-6
1982	Johnny Warr	6-17-1
	Luis Acosta	15-3
	Jerry Williams	5-6
	James Tillis	22-1

Entered Top Ten 108-96-13 / 20 = 5-5-1

Turkey Thompson

1939	Bobby Seamon	*Unavailable*
	Bobby Yannes	*Unavailable*
	Bobby Pacho	102-49-17
	Bobby Yannes	*Unavailable*
	Bobby Seamon	*Unavailable*
1940	Johnny B. Romero	5-10
	Lorenzo Pedro	*Unavailable*
	Angelo Puglisi	55-7-4
	Teddy Yarosz	101-14-3
	Johnny Romero	6-12
	Johnny Romero	6-13
	Glenn Lee	35-13
	Pancho Ramirez	*Unavailable*
	Chief White	*Unavailable*
	Junior Munsell	58-8-1
1941	Tommy Martin	49-8-2
	Bob Pastor	41-6-4
	Tony Musto	23-10-1
	Bob Pastor	43-6-4
	Buddy Knox	80-14-5
	Neville Breech	15-6-1
	Abe Simon	36-8
	Irvin Proctor	*Unavailable*
1942	Henry Cooper	20-32-2
	Pat Valentino	16-4-1
	Pat Valentino	16-5-1
	Ernie Nordman	2-7
	Gus Dorazio	45-14-2
	Gus Dorazio	45-15-2
	Ernie Nordman	3-10
1943	Jack Marshall	15-13-2
	Eddie Blunt	34-14-6
	Clayton Worlds	1-0
	Robert Jones	*Unavailable*
	Ben Moroz	15-8
	Elmer Ray	3-0
	Elmer Ray	3-1
	Chuck Crowell	38-17-5
	Clayton Worlds	2-1-1
1944	Perk Daniels	2-1
	Perk Daniels	3-1
	Lee G. Murray	32-6-2
	Al Hart	22-10-2
1947	Ralph Hooker	6-3
	Johnny Haynes	17-6
	Kid Riviera	15-5-1
	Arturo Godoy	79-16-4
1948	Jimmy Bivins	64-12-1
	Tony Bosnich	29-5-1
	Whitey Berlier	5-3-1
	Willie Bean	10-4-1
	Pat Valentino	41-10-4
1949	Roy Taylor	31-9-3
	Bill Petersen	48-27-8
	Lee Q. Murray	59-15-4
	Al Hart	*Unavailable*
	Al Spaulding	15-15-1

Entered Top Ten 1, 391-473-97 / 48 = 29-10-2

James Tillis

1978	Ron Stephany	*Unavailable*
	Al Bell	4-11-2
1979	Dave Watkins	0-0
	Sylvester Wilder	4-33
	Rocky Lane	0-0
	George Gofarth	1-0
	Henry Porter	6-0
	Charles Atlas	7-18
	Jimmy Cross	23-14-1
	Bob Whaley	0-0
	Harry Terrell	12-6
	Memphis Al Jones	0-1
1980	Cookie Wallace	24-27-2
	Ron Stander	36-16-2
	Frank Schram	1-3
	Walter Santemore	7-8
	Eric Sedillo	13-2
	Mike Koranicki	22-6-2
	Domingo D'Elia	23-1-3
1981	Tom Fischer	26-6

Entered Top Ten
Challenged for Title 209-152-12 / 19 = 11-8-1

Pat Valentino

1940	Buddy Holzhauer	0-3

Incomplete

	Big Tiger Wade	*Unavailable*
	Mario Duchini	*Unavailable*
	Buddy Holzhauer	0-4

Incomplete

	Angelo Puglisi	3-8-1

Incomplete

	John Petry	*Unavailable*
	Charley Thomas	*Unavailable*
	Harold Blackshear	3-2
	Newsboy Millich	13-8-1
	Jack Dallas	*Unavailable*
	Ralph DeLeon	27-7-3
	Harold Blackshear	5-4
	Buddy Knox	78-8-31
1941	Tommy Martin	48-8-2

Incomplete

	Solly Krieger	79-20-7
	Bob Nestell	24-11
	Oscar Rankin	37-15-4
	O'Dell Pollee	*Unavailable*
	Melio Bettina	55-10-3
	Oscar Rankin	39-15-4
1942	Eddie O'Dooley	10-0
	Turkey Thompson	20-3-2
	Turkey Thompson	21-3-2
1943	Freddie Fiducia	41-10-1
	Jimmy Bivins	35-5
	Bob Smith	6-8-1
1944	Bob Smith	6-10-1
1946	Harry Wills	13-6-4
	John Donnelly	16-9-2
	Doug Ellison	10-9-3
	Jack Hannon Porter	10-2-2
	Willie Williams	1-11
	Jack Hannon Porter	11-3-2
	Tommy Galland	*Unavailable*
	Francis Ogg	15-12-4
	Jack Hannon Porter	11-4-2
	Willie Brown	6-3-2
	Eddie Powell	4-1
	Willie Brown	6-4-2
	Francisco de la Cruz	3-3
	Big Boy Brown	14-13-2
1947	Fitzie Fitzpatrick	34-7-3
	Rusty Payne	21-4
	Ernie Rios	9-6-3
	Jack Hannon Porter	11-6-2

	Billy McClure	14-9-2
	Billy McClure	14-10-2
	Jesse McSwain	16-1-2
	Tony Bosnich	27-4
1948	Tony Bosnich	27-4-1
	Joey Maxim	54-14-2
	Jimmy Bivins	65-11-1
	Joey Maxiim	57-14-3
	Freddie Beshore	25-22
	Tony Bosnich	30-6-1
	Turkey Thompson	41-8-3

Challenged for Title 1,117-368-85 / 48 = 23-8-2

Jersey Joe Walcott

1930	Cowboy Wallace	*Unavailable*
	Jimmy O'Toole	*Unavailable*
	Frankie Mathews	*Unavailable*
1931	Carl Mays	*Unavailable*
1933	Bob Norris	*Unavailable*
	Henry Taylor	*Unavailable*
	Henry Taylor	*Unavailable*
1935	Al Lang	*Unavailable*
	Lew Alva	*Unavailable*
	Pat Roland	*Unavailable*
	Joe King	1-5

Incomplete

	Roxie Allen	2-3

Incomplete

1936	Al Ettore	30-7-1
	Willie Reddish	2-2-1

Incomplete

	Joe Colucci	*Unavailable*
	Lou LaPage	*Unavailable*
	Phil Johnson	3-2-1
	Bill Ketchell	2-7

Incomplete

	Carmen Passarella	*Unavailable*
	Bill Ketchell	2-8-1

Incomplete

	Bill Ketchell	2-11-1

Incomplete

1937	Tiger Jack Fox	65-9-3
	Joe Lipps	2-10-1

Incomplete

	Elmer Ray	16-6

Incomplete

	George Brothers	*Unavailable*
1938	Freddie Fiducia	21-2-1
	Jim Whitest	*Unavailable*
	Art Sykes	1-13

Incomplete

	Lorenzo Pack	18-6-2
	Tiger Jack Fox	78-10-6
	Roy Lazer	47-6-1
	Bob Tow	5-10-1

Incomplete

1939	Al Boros	15-12
	Curtis Shephard	5-2
1940	Tiger Lewis	*Unavailable*
	Abe Simon	24-5
1941	Columbus Grant	*Unavailable*
1944	Felix Del Paoli	2-3-1
	Ellis Singleton	*Unavailable*
1945	Jackie Saunders	6-2
	Johnny Allen	7-10
	Austin Johnson	2-0-2
	Johnny Allen	9-10
	Joe Baksi	44-4-4
	Johnny Denson	23-26-3
	Steve Dudas	51-23-2
	Lee Q. Murray	39-8-2
	Curtis Shephard	35-22-2
1946	Johnny Allen	14-12
	Jimmy Bivins	52-5-1
	Al Blake	18-9-1
	Lee Oma	44-18-1
	Tommy Gomez	52-4-1
	Joey Maxim	40-12-1
	Elmer Ray	55-6-2
1947	Joey Maxim	46-12-2
	Elmer Ray	57-6-2
	Joey Maxim	48-13-2
	Joe Louis	58-1
1948	Joe Louis	59-1

Challenged for Title 1, 102-343-49 / 42 = 26-8-1

1949	Ezzard Charles	63-5-1
	Olle Tandberg	23-5-1
1950	Harold Johnson	29-1
	Omelio Agramonte	28-5
	Johnny Shkor	28-17-2
	Hein Ten Hoff	18-0-3
	Rex Layne	25-1-2

Challenged for Title 1, 277-304-52 / 38 = 34-8-1

| 1951 | Ezzard Charles | 69-5-1 |

Challenged for Title 1, 346-309-53 / 39 = 34-8-1

	Ezzard Charles	74-6-1
	Rocky Marciano	42-0

Challenged for Title 1, 462-315-54 / 41 = 36-8-1

Coley Wallace

1950	Willie Brown	4-14
	George Washington	9-9

	Eddie Brown	4-8
	Sylvester Salters	12-6-1
	Ben Harrison	4-6-1
	Jon Peters	*Unavailable*
	Scotty Twyman	*Unavailable*
	Joe Green	*Unavailable*
	Dulio Spagnolo	13-16-3
1951	Vern Mitchell	56-9-1
	Maynard Jones	12-6-2
	Elkins Brothers	25-7-1
	Billy Sawyer	1-0
	Aaron Wilson	19-3
1952	Aaron Wilson	19-4

Entered Top Ten 178-88-9 / 12 = 15-7-1

Stan Ward

1974	George Gray	20-9-2
	John Robinson	*Unavailable*
1975	Johnny Boudreaux	14-1
	Les Miller	5-1-1
	Pat Duncan	33-8-1
	Dwain Bonds	3-1
1976	Mac Foster	30-5
	Jeff Merritt	23-2

Entered Top Ten 128-27-4 / 7 = 18-4-1

Mike Weaver

1972	Howard Smith	3-1
	Howard Smith	4-1
1973	Carlos Lopez	*Unavailable*
	Billy Ryan	4-0
	Lynch Martin	3-0
	Toni Pulu	9-2
	Bob Swoopes	*Unavailable*
	Larry Frazier	5-0
1974	Ellis McKinley	*Unavailable*
	Rod Bobick	25-3
	Orville Qualls	11-8-1
	Duane Bobick	23-0
	Mani Vaca 13-2	*Incomplete*
1975	Tony Doyle	40-15-1
1976	Jodie Ballard	23-7
	Fonomonu Sekona	15-1
1977	Dwain Bonds	4-3
	Bill Sharkey	15-0
	Dave Martinez	*Unavailable*
	Pedro Lovell	18-2-2
1978	Stan Ward	8-1-2
	Leroy Jones	20-0-1
	Mike Creel	1-3
	Bernardo Mercado	20-1
	Abdul Khan	0-3

Incomplete (December 13, 1974)

224   Appendix 1

1979	Stan Ward	10-2-2
Entered Top Ten	274-55-9 / 22 = 12-3	
	Oliver Phillips	2-3
Challenged for Title	276-58-10/ 23 = 12-3	
	Larry Holmes	30-0
	Harry Terrell	12-5
	Scott LeDoux	25-7-4
Entered Top Ten	343-70-14 / 26 = 13-3-1	

Chuck Wepner

1964	George Cooper	*Unavailable*
	Rudy Pavesi	*Unavailable*
	Everette Copeland	1-6-1
	Jerry Tomasetti	0-0
1965	Ray Patterson	10-1
	Everette Copeland	2-7-2
	Bob Stallings	4-4
1966	Buster Mathis	5-0
	Jerry Tomasetti	0-1
	Cleo Daniels	7-13-1
	Johnny Deutsch	7-2
	Dave Centi	11-9
1967	Dan McAteer	19-7-2
Incomplete (August 7, 1963)		
	Jerry Tomasetti	3-2
	Charles Harris	0-2-1
1968	Clay Thomas	14-8-3
Incomplete (August 21, 1967)		
	Eddie Vick	11-11-3
	Mike Bruce	7-11-1
	Forest Ward	4-0-2
	Mert Brownfield	1-7
	Jerry Tomasetti	11-5
Incomplete (October 16, 1968)		
1969	Roberto Davila	10-9
	Mike Bruce	7-18-1
	Jose Roman	20-5-1
	George Foreman	3-0
	Pedro Agosto	17-1
1970	Manuel Ramos	22-9-2
	Sonny Liston	49-4
	Joe Bugner	26-2
1971	Jerry Judge	9-3-1
	Jesse Crown	21-8-1
	Mike Boswell	13-4
	Randy Neumann	16-1
1972	Randy Neumann	18-1
	John Clohessy	13-3
1973	Billy Narquart	7-3-2
Incomplete (March 24, 1969)		
	Ernie Terrell	46-7

Entered Top Ten	414-174-24 / 35 = 12-5-1	
1974	Billy Williams	6-6-1
Incomplete (May 25, 1972)		
	Randy Neumann	24-3
	Charley Polite	13-28-3
	Terry Hinki	38-3-3
Challenged for Title	495-202-30 / 39 = 13-5-1	

Cleveland Williams

1951	Lee Hunt	2-2-1
Incomplete (July 22, 1948)		
1952	Paul Banks	0-0
	Rudolph Wood	*Unavailable*
	Roosevelt Holmes	*Unavailable*
	Ray Banks	0-1
	Johnny Fowler	*Unavailable*
	Ray Brown	4-2
	Paul Favourite	*Unavailable*
	Harry Turner	*Unavailable*
	Eddie Joe Williams	*Unavailable*
	Jimmy Felton	*Unavailable*
	Lee Raymond	*Unavailable*
	Sam Harold	3-1
	Candy McDaniels	14-13
	Baby Booze	*Unavailable*
	Roosevelt Holmes	*Unavailable*
	Art Henri	16-23-1
	Joe McFadden	4-3-1
	Johnny Hollins	4-0-1
	Claude Rolfe	5-11-1
	Graveyard Walters	*Unavailable*
1953	Abie Gibson	*Unavailable*
	Ponce DeLeon	1-11-4
	Terry O'Conner	6-15-1
	Ponce DeLeon	1-12-4
	Omelio Agramonte	40-19
	Keene Simmons	8-17-1
	Sonny Jones	7-3
	Claude Rolfe	11-13-2
	Lloyd Willis	0-0
1954	Jimmy Walls	20-24-2
	Sylvester Jones	8-4
	Bob Satterfield	32-14-2
1956	John Hollis	6-5-1
1957	Johnny Mason	4-5
	J.D. Marshall	7-2
	Cliff Gray	2-6-1
	John Holman	31-16-1
	Bob Albright	21-6-3
	Frankie Daniels	30-13-2
1958	Gene White	17-12
	Dick Richardson	22-5-2
	Frankie Daniels	33-14-2
	Howie Turner	20-5-6

Incomplete (December 10, 1957)

1959	Ollie Wilson	8-13
	Sonny Liston	23-1
	Ernie Cab	10-9-1
	Curley Lee	16-1
1960	Sonny Liston	27-1
	Ben Marshall	3-5

Incomplete (August 5, 1957)

	George Moore	10-0

Incomplete

	Johnny Hayden	7-3
1961	Wayne Bethea	22-13-2
	Alex Miteff	23-8-1

Entered Top Ten 524-329-43 / 41 = 13-8-1

	Jim Wiley	2-4
1962	Ernie Terrell	23-3
	Alonzo Johnson	21-10
	Eddie Machen	41-5-1
	Dave Bailey	14-7-2
1963	Billy Daniels	18-1
	Young Jack Johnson	24-19-1
	Ernie Terrell	30-4
	Kirk Barrow	27-10-2
	Roger Rischer	21-7-2
1964	Tommy Fields	9-6-1
	Sonny Banks	20-5
	Billy Daniels	19-5-1
1966	Ben Black	2-1-1
	Mel Turnbow	6-3
	Sonny Moore	18-20-3
	Todd Herring	26-5

Challenged for Title 845-444-57 / 58 = 15-8-1

Tim Witherspoon

1979	Joey Adams	*Unavailable*
	Robert Ritchie	*Unavailable*
	Robert Evans	3-1-1
	Charles Cox	4-1
	Oliver Wright	15-12-1
	James Reid	4-3
1981	Ed Bednarik	4-0
	Marvin Stinson	12-0-3
	Dave Johnson	13-7
	Bobby Jordan	5-3

Incomplete (December 14, 1979)

	Jerry Williams	5-3
	Curtis Gaskins	2-2
	Alfonso Ratliff	13-0
1982	Louis Acosta	15-2

Entered Top Ten 95-34-5 / 12 = 8-3

	Renaldo Snipes	22-4-1

Challenged for Title 117-37-6 / 13 = 9-3

Jimmy Young

1969	Jimmy Gilmore	4-7
	Jim Jones	6-8-2
	Johnny Gause	2-1
1970	Clay Hodges	1-0
	Howard Darlington	1-9-1
1971	Roy Williams	10-2
	Andy Geiger	*Unavailable*
	Lou Hicks	10-19
1972	Jasper Evans	2-3-1
	Randy Neumann	18-1
1973	Earnie Shavers	42-2
	Obie English	7-1
	Mike Boswell	13-12
	Billy Aird	14-7-2
1974	Richard Dunn	26-6
	John Jordan	15-7-2
	Les Stevens	17-3
	Jose Luis Garcia	27-5-1
	Earnie Shavers	46-4
1975	Ron Lyle	31-1-1

Entered Top Ten 293-98-10 / 19 = 15-5-1

	Robert Lloyd	5-10-2
	Al Jones	8-22
1976	Jose Roman	45-13-3

Challenged for Title 351-144-15 / 22 = 16-7-1

Dave Zyglewicz

1965	James Oliver	5-4
	Jerry Keys	*Unavailable*
	Clarence Boone	2-7
	Ray Martin	10-5-1
1966	Ray Martin	10-6-1
	Bob Simmons	11-7-4
	Max Martinez	3-1
	Duke Johnson	10-15-4
	Bob Slaughter	0-4
	Sonny Moore	20-21-2
	Ray Vega	2-5-1
	Archie Ray	19-8-2
1967	Charley Hall	6-27-2
	Roy Rogers	7-3
	Dave Centi	11-10
	Billy Daniels	20-15-3
	Max Martinez	3-3
	Everette Copeland	4-9-3
	Eddie Parotte	0-0-1
	Willie Besmanoff	49-32-8
	Sonny Moore	20-25-2
	Mike Bruce	6-7-1
	Bill McMurray	21-17-2

1968	Johnny Featherman	26-9	Bob Felstein	13-4-1
	Sam Wyatt	5-7-2	Pedro Sanchez	5-7
	Levi Forte	18-17-1	*Challenged for Title*	322-294-43 / 28 = 12-10-2
	Willie Johnson	16-13-2		

APPENDIX 2: MISSING RECORDS

The following is a list of more than five hundred boxers, mostly American, between the 1930s and 1980s for whom complete records could not be found for the statistical purposes of this study. The Ring Record Book and www.boxrec.com *have already been consulted for the partial records they offer. If any of the following boxers themselves, friends, or surviving family spot their name, it would be greatly appreciated if confirmed and accurate records could be sent to the author in care of the publisher. Sports journalists, amateur boxing researchers, are also encouraged to send confirmed and accurate records. The hometowns of some of the boxers are included below.*

Boxer	Hometown	Need Record After
Joey Adams	Memphis	1979
Young Agabab		1971
Eddie Allen		1958
Junior Alvarado		1977
Joe Anderson		1974
Don Angen		1949
Marcelino Armenteros	Cuba	1967
Ron (Ray?) Asher	Wheeling, WV	1970
Wilfredo Avellez	Puerto Rico	1964
Bob Avery	Tucson	1974
Bill Bailey		1953
John Balla	San Francisco	1964
Mike Barron		1951
Ray Basset		1949
Gary Bates	Las Vegas	1978
Jackie Batson	Charlotte	1951
Bob Battista		1954
Earl Battles	Philadelphia	1965
Eddie Beazley	Paterson	1947
Doc Bee	Philadelphia	1950
Jimmy Bell	Fayetteville	1951
Shed (Shelton) Bell	Youngstown	1947
Mike Bellusco	Rye, New York	1948
Richard Benjamin		1963
Leo Bennett	Los Angeles	1970
Howard Bergen	Jersey	1949
Dan Biggers	Baltimore	1942
Joe Blackwood		1965
Eddie Blair	Jersey	1949
Eddie Blunt	Corona/Roper, NC	1948
George Boddie	Dayton	1952
Norm Bolden	Detroit	1958
Bobby Bonger	Chicago	1947
Grady Brazell	Mobile	1967
Bill Brixon		1955
Battling Brown		1950
Big Boy Brown		1977
Buzz Brown	St. Paul	1951
Frank Brown	Saginaw	1980
Jimmy Brown	West Oak, PA	1971
Clarence Boone	Fort Worth	1972
Baby Booze		1952
Gene Brien		1952
Dick Brown		1955
Frank Brown		1979
K.O. Brown		1953
James Brown		1978
Ray Brown	Chicago	1952

Name	Location	Year
Sam Brown	Newark	1954
Zeke Brown		1947
Mert Brownfield	Pittsburgh	1964
Frank Buford	Oakland	1955
Johnny Bullard		1956
Charles Burnett		1969
Smiley Burnette (George Sponsell)	Richmond	1948
Victor Buttin		1948
Ted Calaman	Philadelphia	1955
Leroy Caldwell	New Orleans	1971
Al Callaghan (Callihan)	San Bernardino	1952
Mike Campbell	Brooklyn	1963
Keno Carlos		1963
Al Carter	Los Angeles	1963
Lee Bearcat Carter	Indianapolis	1949
Steve Carter	Chicago	1973
John Cidone		1950
Henry Culpepper	Los Angeles	1974
Tom Cummins		1963
Robert Colay (Coley?)	Atlantic City	1978
John Collins	Boise	1966
Jimmy Connino		1951
Chuck Connor		1955
George Cooper		1964
Gerald Couturier		1965
Charles Cox	Boston	1979
Floyd Cox		1974
Mack Cox		1954
Wally Cox		1955
Jim Daniels		1970
Abe Davis	Hartford	1965
Frank Davis		1963
Kenny Davis		1957
Sergeant Willie (Bill) Davis	Philadelphia	1965
Joe Dawson	Chicago	1950
Richard Dean		1977
Eddie Dembry	Chicago	1970
Tommy Demers	Sands Point, ID	1954
Leonard Dugan	Los Angeles	1962
Rodell Dupree	Jersey City	1980
John Edwards	New Haven	1948
Willie Elbert		1969
Hal Emerson		1978
Trinidad Escamilla		1977
Al Evans	Detroit	1971
Joey Evans	New York	1953
Paul Favrot (Favourite?)	New Orleans	1952
Gene Felton	Los Angeles	1951
Jimmy Felton		1952
Red Ferris		1969
Tommy Fields	Los Angeles	1968
Easy Flowers		1946
Lou Ford		1952
Johnny Fowler		1952
Chico Francona (Froncano?)		1969
Jim Fulton		1949
Norvel Gaddes (Geddes?)		1953
Jerry Gaines		1961
Tommy Galland		1946
Julius Garcia		1969
Chuck Garrett	Chicago	1961
Bobby Gatewood		1979
Andy Geiger		1971
Edmund George	New York	1959
Teddy George		1948
Abie Gibson		1953
Howard Gilmore		1977
Tommy Giorgio	Schenectady, NY	1949
Ralph Giss		1960
David Glunton		1946
Joe Murphy Gordwin	Houston	1970
Bobby Green		1948
Joe Green	Washington	1950
Ted Gullick	Cleveland	1974
Walter Hafer	Washington	1957
Earl Haines	Philadelphia	1954
Carl Haliburton	Millington, WI	1978
John Hall	Pittsburgh	1966
Bob Halpern	Bronx	1958
Terry Halpine		1952
Gene Hamilton (Haskell E. Hamilton)	Brooklyn	1965
Nat Hammer	New York	1960
Sonny Boy Harris		1951
Mack Harrison	Akron	1966
Al Hart	Washington	1949
Joe Hathaway		1974
Kenny Hayden	Oklahoma City	1970
Herman Hayes	Oklahoma City	1945
Joe Hayward		1954
Elmo Henderson	San Antonio	1979
Chu Chu Hernandez		1974
Dick Hernandez		1977
Eusebio Hernandez		1980
German Hernandez		1962
Bob Hershey		1950
Don Hinton		1978
George Holden	Orlando	1978
Jeff Holmes		1959
Roosevelt Holmes		1952
Hubert Hood	Chicago	1951
Ron Hope		1979
Roscoe Howard		1948
Charlie Howard		1965
Ozzie Hubbard		1954
Lee Hunt	New Haven	1951

Missing Records

Bobby Hynds		1946
Eugene Idolette	Vero Beach, FL	1969
Rafael Iglesias		1952
Randy Ingram	Philadelphia	1946
Sterling Ingram	Denver	1948
Barrie Jackson		1956
Bobby Jackson	Denver	1954
Matt Jackson	Seattle	1965
Richard Jensen		1977
Austin Johnson		1978
Bill Johnson	New York	1963
Bob Johnson		1969
Jack Johnson	Trinidad, Guyana	1947
Temple Jones		1958
Watson Jones	Los Angeles	1956
Bobby Jordan	Norfolk	1981
Johnny Kasmier		1954
Harland Kelly	Los Angeles	1953
Jerry (Perry) Keys	Erie, Pa.	1965
Abdul Khan (Gary Gahan)	San Diego	1978
Billy Kinard	Orlando	1948
Colrado King (Caribbean)		1967
Kenny Kinney		1969
Ernie Knox	Baltimore	1961
Don Koontz	Bakersfield	1971
Syl Kuchinski	Buffalo	1953
Glenn Kurtiza (Kuritzka?)		1970
Frank LaPola		1959
Charlie Lee	Paterson, NJ	1973
Don Lee	Bronx	1960
Henry Lee	Seattle	1953
Richie Lee	Harlem	1960
Paris Lennon		1947
Bert LeRoy		1967
Charley Lester	Cleveland	1946
John Lester		1947
Joe Levy		1944
Bill Little	Morton, WA	1955
Quinnie Locklear	Baltimore	1977
Theo Lolanzo		1960
Carlos Lopez		1973
Charlie Lopes	Boston	1959
Joe Louis III	San Francisco	1959
Guy Manayunk		1949
Billy Marquart (Narquart?)	Paterson, NJ	1973
Ben Marshall	Oklahoma City	1960
Jack Marshall	Dallas	1946
Don Martin	Memphis	1979
Dave Martinez		1978
Jim Marzano		1954
Bob Masterson		1950
Bill Mathias	Eureka	1957
Bob Maynard (Menard?)	Montreal	1965
Harry Mazier		1951
Don McAteer	Newark	1967
Pat McCafferty	St. Louis	1949
Art McCann	New York	1954
Claude McClintock		1948
Willie McCoy (Billie Edwin)	Freeport, TX	1949
Jack McCurry		1947
Eddie McGee	Macon	1946
Jesse McGowen		1946
John McGrath		1978
Ellis McKinley		1974
Jerry McIntyre		1979
Willie McIntyre	Miami	1979
Hal McNeely		1954
Al Merazini		1977
Jimmy Middleton		1952
Sam Miller		1979
Champ Millich	Sacramento	1948
Arthur Minor		1963
Al Mitchell	Bronx	1947
Lee Mitchell	Los Angeles	1981
George Moore	Detroit	1960
Willie Moore	North Carolina	1976
Del Morris		1971
Bob Mumford	Los Angeles	1969
Al Niang	New York	1953
Cornell Nolan		1968
Billy Norris		1949
Richie Norton (Norden?)	Stamford	1956
Cannibal Nuapia		1971
Babe O'Blenis		1947
Shamus O'Brien	Harlem	1950
Dave Ochoa		1977
Terry O'Conner	Great Britain/ Lansing, MI	1953
Billy Oden		1946
Mongol Ortiz	Mexico	1976
Sonny Parker		1951
Willis Parker	California	1950
Eddie (Edmund) Parotte (Parotta)	Virgin Islands	1967
Steve Patterson		1974
Rudy Pavesi		1964
Shirley Pembleton	Philadelphia	1961
Joe Peters		1946
Jon Peters		1950
Bill Petersen	Portland	1951
Gene Pierce (Pearce?)		1949
Leo Pinto		1959
Jack Hannon Porter	Oakland	1947
Angelo Puglisi	Duluth	1940
Lee Raymond		1952
Johnny Rebel		1953
Dick Reddick		1954
James Reid	Richmond	1980
Charley Riggs	Akron	1949

Gilbert Riggs		1969
Joe Riley		1946
Robert Ritchie		1980
Bobby Robbins (Robert Dixon)	Boston	1955
Al Roberts		1953
Jimmy Robertson	Muncie, Indiana	1977
Booker Robinson	Philadelphia	1948
Don Robinson	Denver/California	1956
Jim Robinson	Philadelphia	1967
John Robinson	Kansas City	1974
Matt Robinson	Washington	1977
Tiny Robinson		1948
Mike Rock		1950
Roy Rodrigues		1970
Roy Rogers	Houston	1965
Jose Rosario		1977
Frankie Rowe		1960
Lee Roy		1969
Bob Rutherford		1962
Art Savage		1973
Vic Scott	Los Angeles	1971
Nat Shaver	Miami	1970
Jack Simon	Tampa Bay	1946
Eddie Sims	Cleveland	1949
Tony Sinabaldi		1957
Ben Skelton	Pittsburgh	1949
Al Smith	New York	1951
Bobby Smith	Miami Beach	1977
Charley Smith		1947
Dave Smith		1979
Dick Smith		1955
Ernie Smith	Dallas	1975
Ernie Smith		1955
Frank Smith		1970
Norman Smith	Monroe	1950
Tommie Smith	Providence	1955
Howard Snyder		1977
Hector SoDono		1977
Paul Solomon	San Francisco	1978
Lee Sponsell	Pacific Coast	1948
Gene Stanton	Cleveland	1935
Ron Stephany		1978
Cortez Stewart	New York	1957
Sylvester Stewart		1954
Via Sufoa		1978
Johnny Swanson	Cleveland	1950
Tom Swift		1966
Bob Swoopes		1973
Leon Szymurski		1947
Harvey Taylor	Los Angeles	1961
Jack Taylor	Newark	1955
James Taylor		1964
Buddy Thomas	Washington	1949
Clay Thomas	Brooklyn	1968
Roy Thomas	Jamaica, Great Britain	1953
Clyde Thompson		1953
Hank Thompson		1951
Horace Thompson		1946
Lamar Thompson		1969
Hank Thurman	Modesto, CA	1957
Al Timmons	Cleveland	1951
Roscoe Toles	Naftel, AL	1935
Jerry Tomasetti	Wilkes-Barre, PA	1968
Harry Turner		1952
Howard Turner	Brooklyn/Warren	1958
Jackie Turner		1946
Scotty Twyman		1950
Dick Underwood		1947
Mani Vaka		1974
Joe Van Loan		1947
Memo Vargas	Mexico	1973
Orvin Veazey	Stamford	1973
Pedro Vega		1977
Al Velez	Wichita	1946
Bobby Vowles		1946
Don Wagner	Portsmouth	1948
Eddie Walker	Detroit	1958
Ted Walters	New York	1948
Lewina Waqa	Fiji Islands	1966
Graveyard Walters		1952
Jack Warren	Los Angeles	1950
Joe Washington		1962
Nat Washington		1954
Bobby Watson		1955
Joe Weiden	Vienna	1949
Tommy White		1953
Curtis Whitner		1973
Sonny Wilcox	Cleveland	1955
Ray Wilding	Great Britain	1953
Dusty Wilkerson	Philadelphia	1951
Billy Williams	Vineland, NJ	1974
Duke Williams		1961
Eddie Joe Williams		1952
Howard Williams		1946
Jim Williams		1973
Rufe Williams		1953
Randy Willis		1980
Dave Wilson	Waterbury, CT	1976
Jimmy Wilson	West Indies	1946
Ollie Wilson	Hartford	1971
George Woods	Los Angeles	1956
Rudolph Wood(s)		1952
Art Wright	Detroit	1962
Robert Yarborough		1975
Fritz Zack (Jack?)		1955
Kid Zanzibar		1953

Missing Records 231

The following boxers, for whom confirmed records were not found, were opponents of Joe Louis, Jersey Joe Walcott, Ezzard Charles, Harry Mathews, Gus Lesnevich, Archie Moore, Joey Maxim, Turkey Thompson, Al Hoosman, and Pat Valentino between 1930 and 1944.

Billy Adams, Buffalo
Murray Allen
Roxie Allen
Lew Alva
Spec Andrews
Kid Ash
Chief Ballard
Harry Bean
Billy Bengal
Biff Benton, Fort Sheridan, IL
Dan Biggers
Hans Birkie, Hamburg, Germany
Pete Blanchard
Eddie Booker, San Jose
Alex Borchuk (Al Delany), Cleveland
Jimmy Brent
Bobby Britton, New York
George Brothers
Ben Brown
Ira Bruner
Jimmy Brown, Philadelphia
Jackie Burke, Pittsburgh
Clarence "Red" Burman, Baltimore
Trent Cain
Jimmy Calabrese
Lou Campbell
Johnny Canadeo
Frankie Caris, Philadelphia
Jimmy Casino, Los Angeles
Slaka Cavrich
Tony Celli, Leominster, MA
Tom Chester, Brooklyn
Sammy Christian (Speedy Schaefer)
Mike Cleary
Sid Cohen, Florida, NY
Joe Colucci
Danny Cox, New York
Willie Davis, Chicago
Charlie Dawson
Joe Delany
Al Dublinski
Remo Fernandez
Leon Ford
Eddie Fowler
Roy Frisco, East Beach
Dan Gill
Joe Gladden

Al Globe
Jimmy Gordon
Columbus Grant
Bert Hardy, Nova Scotia
Frank Hatfield
Jimmy Hayden, New York
Herman Hayes
Tom Henry
Kid Hermosillo, Obegon, Mexico
Jack Hibbard
Justin Hoffman, Flatbush, NY
Shorty Hogue, Jacumba, CA
Bill Hood, Orlando
Joey Huff
Floyd Howard
Bud Hutchinson
Sammy Jackson, Los Angeles
Charley Jerome
Charley Johnson, Los Angeles
Jack Johnson, Guyana
Medley Johnson
Phil Johnson, Bayonne
Louis Jones, Augusta
Leo Jorday
Robert Jones
Tony Kalb
Truman Kennedy
Billy Ketchel, Millville, NJ
Steve Ketchell, Hartford
Joe King, New Orleans
Jack Kirkland
Willie Klein
Rudy Kozole
Jack Kracken, Champaign
Jack Kranz
Al Lang
Kenny LaSalle, Houston
Carl Lautenschlger
Roy Lazer, Paterson, NJ
Lou Lepage
Joe Levy
Bradley Lewis
R.J. Lewis, Denver
Tiger "Red" Lewis, Richmond
Frank Lindsay
Nathan Logan, St. Louis
Joe Lipps, Charlotte
Ray Lyle
Butch Lynch, Plainfield, NJ
Jack Marshall, Dallas

Karl Martin
Guero Martinez
Charley Massera, Philadelphia
Frankie Mathews
Carl Mays
Louis Mays
Tommy Martin, Virgin Islands
Al McCoy, Winslow, ME
Wally Miles
Jack Moran, Chicago
Billy Muldune (Muldoon?)
Bob Norris
Jack O'Dowd, Detroit
Jimmy O' Toole, Bridgeton, N.J.
Bobby Pacho, Cleveland/ El Centro, CA
Joey Parks, St. Louis
Young Carmen Passarella
Dynamite Payne
Lorenzo Pedro
Al Penna
Bud Peterson
Ham Pounder
Irvin Proctor
Powder Proctor
Billy Pryor
Angelo Puglisi
Pancho Ramirez
Bob Ray
John Reeves
Bob Reid
Charley Retzlaff, Duluth, Minnesota
Lou Rogers
Pat Roland
Caesar Romero
Tabby Romero (Henry R. Ramirez) Phoenix
Johnny Romero, San Diego
Willie Reddish, Philadelphia
Clay Rowan
Frank Rowsey, Powder River, MT
Celly Royabaugh
Larry Scalone
Bobby Seamon
Wally Sears, Minersville, PA
Red Shannon
Bob Sikes, Little Rock
Johnny Sikes, Bismarck

Ellis Singleton
Sammy Slaughter, Terre Haute
Gene Stanton, Cleveland
Joe Sutka, Detroit
Art Sykes, Elmira, New York
Henry Taylor, Philadelphia
Harry Thomas
Lee Thomas
Roscoe Toles, Naftel, AL
Bob Tow
Orlando Trotter
Larry Udell
Cowboy Wallace
Booker T. Washington,
　Sacramento
Charley Weisse
Eddie Kid Whalen, Brooklyn
Teddy White
Chief White
Jim Whitest
Stan Willardson
Charles Hobo Williams,
　Alexandria
Frankie Williams
Nicky Williams
Panther Williams
Pat Wright
Bobby Yannes
Ray Vargas, California

NOTES

1. American Boxing in Black and White

1. Phillip, M. Hoose, Necessities: Racial Barriers in American Sports (New York: Random House, 1989), xxiv; Joyce Carol Oates, On Boxing (Garden City, New York: Dolphin/Doubleday, 1987), 65; and David Wiggins, "The Notion of Double-Consciousness and the Involvement of Black Athletes in America Sport," in Ethnicity and Sport in North American History and Culture, ed. George Eisen and David Wiggins (Westport, Connecticut: Greenwood, 1994), 134.

2. The 1890s stand as the decade when notions of white purity and black inferiority gained a legitimacy across America they had never had before, a legitimacy that sanctioned both formalized segregation across much of the nation, and brutal mistreatment of non-whites both within and beyond America's borders. While many hundreds of African Americans had been murdered since the Civil War, the lynching toll of the century's last decade clearly testified to an obsessive desire to keep blacks in their place. The annual rate of blacks being lynched soared from an average annual rate of 67 for most of the 1880s (1882–89) to over 111 in the century's final decade. The figure dropped to 79 and 57 per year for the first two decades of the twentieth century. Whatever combination of anger, fear, and hatred in white minds conspired to create a typical race lynching, they were in peak supply as the century wound down. See Harry A. Plosky and James Williams, ed. The Negro Almanac: A Reference Work on the African American (Detroit: Gale Research, 1989), 368. It was in this decade that whites first encountered a generation of blacks with no memory of slavery or the deference that came with it, and thus some states felt the need to put into law what had previously been assumed social custom. The first Southern states disenfranchised their black populations with combinations of voting requirements like the poll tax, the grandfather clause, and the understanding test. The process of southern states disenfranchising black voters with various election rules is discussed in detail in Joel Williamson, The Crucible of Race: Black-White Relations in the American South Since Emacipation (New York: Oxford, 1984), 224–58. The Supreme Court handed down the ultimate expression of racial inequality, the Plessy versus Ferguson ruling, in 1896. This sentenced blacks to a separate public existence than whites. White Americans in the 1890s, along with other caucasian races, were talking about the "white man's burden," alluded to by Rudyard Kipling: the belief that it was whites' shared destiny to civilize the world's darker and backward peoples. America specifically alluded to this sacred duty in sanctioning their first great expansionist impulse into far away lands like Samoa, Hawaii, Cuba, Puerto Rico, and the Phillipines. Belief in the "white man's burden" is recounted in Nell Irvin Painter, Standing at Armageddon: The United States,

1877–1919 (New York: W.W. Norton, 1987), 141–69. White journalists, ministers, doctors, and politicians alike expounded on the "scientifically proven" preeminence of the white specimen, and on the limitations of blacks, natives, and Asians; thus the rationale for denying such groups equal rights and a political voice. For a brief account of the Plessy versus Ferguson decision, as well as the worsening plight of black Americans in the 1890s, see Sean Dennis Cashman, America in the Gilded Age: From the Death of Lincoln to the Rise of Theodore Roosevelt (New York: New York University, 1984), 207–13.

3. John Lucas and Ronald A. Smith, Saga of American Sport (Philadelphia: Lea and Febiger, 1978), 270–79.

4. Randy Roberts, Papa Jack: Jack Johnson and the Era of White Hopes (New York: Macmillan, 1983), 60–1 and Ashe, 15. An illustration of just how confident white fighters were that skin color almost guaranteed victory over black opponents can be seen in accounts of the Marvin Hart-Jack Johnson fight and the Johnson-Burns world title fight. See Roberts, 36 and 61–62.

5. David Wiggins, Glory Bound: Black Athletes in a White America (Syracuse: Syracuse University Press, 1997), 35; Jeffrey Sammons, Beyond the Ring: The Role of Boxing in American Society (Urbana: University of Illinois Press, 1988), 32–33; and Michael Isenberg, John L. Sullivan and his America (Urbana: University of Illinois Press, 1988), 290–93.

6. Roberts, 1983, 19, 35, 39, and 44.

7. Johnson's anger at the white dominated society around him began at a young age, and is best illustrated by the battle royal contests that poor southern black youths were forced to fight for the entertainment of white men. In these melees, multiple boys would earn pennies by fighting in demeaning circumstances, chaotic free-for-alls with masks or bags over their heads in front of jeering spectators. Not being allowed to fight for the true heavyweight title as a black adult could hardly have been viewed by Johnson as anything but an extension of this same indignity. See Roberts, 1983, 6–8 and 28.

8. Benjamin Rader, American Sports: From the Age of Folk Games to the Age of Televised Sports (Upper Saddle River, New Jersey: Prentice Hall, 1999), 5–9.

9. It is difficult to think of a sport more tailor-made to offend nineteenth century middle class sensitivities than boxing. Two men pounding each other's bloody faces with their fists represented the complete opposite of discipline and self-control, worshipped by most reformers. A screaming, swearing, and fighting audience full of spectators, many with knives and guns on their persons and drawn from the same blue-collar sporting fraternity despised by middle class moralists, threatened the latter's vision of an orderly society. Gambling, as common in boxing as in any other sport, was a means for immediate gratification, something that made a mockery of Puritan beliefs about the value of self-denial, hard work, and moderation. See Steven Riess, Sport in Industrial America: 1850–1920 (Wheeling, Illinois: Harlan Davidson, 1995), 7, 9, 44, and 57; and Rader, 40–41.

10. John Richard Betts, America's Sporting Heritage: 1850–1920 (Reading, Massachussets: Addison-Wesley, 1974), 167.

11. Isenberg, 70–74.

12. Sammons, 6 and Melvin Adelman, A Sporting Time: New York City and the Rise of Modern Athletics, 1820–1870 (Urbana: University of Illinois, 1986), 236–37.

13. Rader, 26 and 27.

14. At various times in American history, the strongest attacks on sports have come from a moralizing middle class, while the upper and lower classes have more often been enthusiastic participants. Puritan opposition in seventeenth century England and early New England is discussed in Nancy Struna, People of Prowess: Sport, Leisure and Labor in Early Anglo-America (Urbana: University of Illinois, 1996), 26–33. This general class breakdown of attitudes toward sports was also evident in the Progressive Era at the be-

ginning of the twentieth century, with particular middle class attention devoted to eradicating professional boxing along with numerous other immoral activities in America. See Rader, 19 and 21, and Riess, 108.

15. Dale Somers, The Rise of Sports in New Orleans: 1859–1900 (Baton Rouge: Louisiana State Press, 1972), 160.

16. Sammons, 19–20 and 24.

17. Sammons, 16–29.

18. The relative minority of Americans in 1908 who felt their Caucasian race was the undisputed pinnacle of ruggedness clearly had never seen a hockey game on a Saskatchewan pond, or endured a Manitoba winter. A decade later, this view would seem even more amusing at Vimy Ridge.

19. Sammons, 35.

20. Denzil Batchelor, Jack Johnson and His Times (London: Phoenix Sports Books, 1956), 72; Robert H. deCoy, The Big Black Fire (Los Angeles: Holloway, 1969), 68–71; and Sal Fradella, Jack Johnson (Boston: Branden, 1990), 35.

21. Roberts, 1983, 28, 32, 46–47 and Randy Roberts, Jack Dempsey: The Manassa Mauler (Baton Rouge: Louisiana State University, 1979), 26. Finis Farr, Black Champion: The Life and Times of Jack Johnson (New York: Charles Scribner's Sons, 1964), 26.

22. Farr, 30; Roberts, 1983, 22 and 75; Richard Bak, Joe Louis, The Great Black Hope (Dallas: Taylor, 1996), 72; Al-Tony Gilmore, Bad Nigger: The National Impact of Jack Johnson (Port Washington, New York: Kennikat, 1975), 12–18; deCoy, 60, and Fradella, 24.

23. Chris Mead, Champion: Joe Louis, Black Hero in White America (New York: Charles Scribner's Sons, 1985), 24.

24. Gilmore, 14; Roberts, 74 and Ploskey and Williams, 368.

25. Exactly how much America was focused on the racial symbolism of this bout was evident in white and black ministers calling for the Lord's intervention to ensure the victory of Johnson or Jeffries. Roberts, 1979, 23, Gilmore, 38–39, and Bak, 72.

26. Gilmore, 42–44 and Los Angeles Times. Editorial, 6 July 1910.

27. Roberts, 1983, 145, 151–52.

28. Roberts, 1979, 51.

29. Ocania Chalk, Pioneers of Black Sport (New York: Dodd, Mead and Company, 1975), 163. A detailed discussion of the backroom New York State politics involved in the controversy over holding a Dempsey-Wills title fight in New York can be found in Roberts, 1979, 213–219.

30. Mark D. Coburn, "America's Great Black Hope," American Heritage 29, no. 6 (1978): 84.

31. Coburn, 84 and 88.

32. Mead, 62–63 and 98.

33. Mead, 259.

34. Mead, 52–53.

35. Mead, xii.

36. Mead, 296.

37. Chalk, 180.

2. Segregation in American Sports Is Dead, but...

1. Richard Lapchick, *Five Minutes to Midnight: Race and Sport in the 1990s* (New York: Madison, 1991), 270.

2. Richard Lapchick, *Broken Promises: Racism in American Sports* (New York, St. Martin's, 1984), 207; Edna and Art Rust, Jr. *Art Rust's Illustrated History of the Black Ath-*

lete (Garden City, New York: Doubleday, 1985), 243; Jules Tygiel, *Baseball's Great Experiment: Jackie Robinson and His Legacy* (New York: Oxford, 1997), 91 and 285–332.

3. Richard O. Davies, *America's Obsession: Sports and Society Since 1945* (New York: Harcourt Brace, 1994), 58.

4. Tygiel, 340 and 352, and Jack Olsen, *The Black Athlete: A Shameful Story: The Myth of Integration in American Sport*. (New York: Time-Life, 1968), 182–84.

5. See Hoose, xxii.; James C. Harris, "It's Time for the NFL to Give Black Coaches Opportunity," *New York Amsterdam News*, 1 March 1997, 46 and 48 and Gary Sailes, "Betting Against the Odds: An Overview of Black Sports Participation," in Gary Sailes, *African Americans in Sport: Contemporary Themes* (New Brunswick, N.J.: Transaction, 1998), 30–31.

6. Harry Blauvel and Jack Carey, "Black Coaches Still Find Doors Closed," *USA Today*, 2 August 1995, Sec. 3, p. 3.

7. Gary Sailes, "The African American Athlete: Social Myths and Stereotypes," in *Racism in College Athletics: The African American Athlete's Experience*, ed. Dana Brooks and Ronald Althouse (Morgantown: Fitness Informational Technology, 2000), 55 and 157; Richard Lapchick, "Race and College Sports: A Long Way to Go," in *Sport in Society: Equal Opportunity or Business as Usual?* ed. Richard Lapchick (Thousand Oaks: Sage, 1996), 2; In Big Ten schools, this trend was particularly apparent, with white athletes graduating in four years (1990–94) at more than twice the rate of their black teammates, 61 percent to 27 percent at Ohio State, 77 percent to 34 percent at Michigan. See Matt Markey, "Black College Athletes Losing in Battle for a Degree," *The Toledo Blade*, 25 March 2001, Sec. A, p. 9.

8. Harry Edwards, *The Revolt of the Black Athlete* (New York: Collier-MacMillan, 1969), 11–16; Olsen, 56–57 and 118–38.

9. Olsen, 155–56 and 162–64.

10. Lapchick, 1984, 176, and Wiggins, 110. Perhaps the most poignant example of the second-class status of black college athletes is seen in the fate of the nation's third-leading rusher in 1964, Junior Coffey of the University of Washington Huskies football team. Coffey was warned to stop dating a white co-ed, refused, and shortly thereafter became a second-string player, never to be a starter again. See Davies, 52.

11. Edwards, xv and Davies, 185–94.

12. D. Stanley Eitzen, *Sport in Contemporary Society: An Anthology* (New York: St. Martin's, 1996), 249–250.

13. Lapchick, 239.

14. Lapchick, "The 1994 Racial Report Card," in Lapchick, 1996, 47–48 and Kenneth Shropshire, *In Black and White: Race and Sports in America* (New York: New York University Press, 1996), 21–22.

15. For extensive discussion of the racist practices of professional golf, see Charlie Sifford and James Gullo, *Just Let Me Play: The Story of Charlie Sifford, the First Black PGA Golfer* (New York: British American Publishing, 1992). The 1962 Montreal episode cited is recounted on 175, the infamous Greensboro tournament in which Sifford was publicly harassed is remembered on pages 117–24. Further references can be found in Lapchick, 271 and Davies, 42–43.

16. Jon Entine, *Taboo: Why Black Athletes Dominate Sports and Why We Are Afraid to Talk About It* (New York: Public Affairs, 2000), 275 and Brooks and Althouse, 45.

17. For a detailed examination of the obstacles faced by aspiring black NFL quarterbacks, see Hoose, 51–69; Farai Chideya, *Don't Believe the Hype: Fighting Cultural Misinformation About African-Americans* (New York: Penguin, 1995), 157.

18. For an in-depth account of the racial hostility Aaron encountered during his 1973–74 pursuit of Ruth's home run crown, see Hank Aaron and Lonnie Wheeler, *I Had a Hammer: The Hank Aaron Story* (New York: Harper, 1991), 310–73

19. Chalk, 118. For a compelling example of how black athletes were left on the bench because one more black on the field would have been one too many, see Aaron and Wheeler, 217–8. One of Aaron's Braves teammates in the early 1960s reminisces about being the best player for a given position on the team's roster but his presence on the field would have tilted the racial count to five blacks and four whites, stranding him on the bench more often than the Braves could afford.

20. See Arthur A. Ashe, Jr., *A Hard Road to Glory: The African American Athlete in Basketball.* (New York: Amistad, 1988), 46, Harry Edwards, *The Sociology of Sport* (Homewood, Illinois: Dorsey, 1973), 214; Shropshire, 44 and Lapchick, 1991, 287; Lawrence Kahn and Peter D. Sherer, "Racial Discrimination in the National Basketball Association," in *The Business of Professional Sports*, ed. Paul D. Staudohor and James A. Mangan, (Urbana: University of Illinois, 1991), 72 and 88–9; Randy Roberts and James S. Olson, *Winning Is the Only Thing: Sports in America Since 1945* (Baltimore: Johns Hopkins Univerity, 1989), 42 and 44.

21. Henderson, 4–5. A summary of studies indicating selective recruitment of black athletes in football, baseball, and basketball is found in Jay Coakley, *Sport in Society: Issues and Controversies* (St. Louis: Times Mirror/Mosby, 1986), 161–3 and in the early 1990s, it was found that 52 percent of the NBA's black players were averaging more than ten points per game, while only 20 percent of the league's white players were doing so. In baseball, 25 percent of the major league's black players were hitting better than .281, almost double the portion (13 percent) of white players hitting this well. See Lapchick, 1991, 283–85.

22. Olsen, 186.

23. Walter LaFeber, *Michael Jordan and the New Global Capitalism* (New York: W.W. Norton and Company, 1999), 45.

24. Lapchick, 1991, 45, 276, and 287, and Mikaela Dufur, "Race Logic and 'Being Like Mike': Representations of Athletes in Advertising, 1985–94," in *African Americans in Sport: Contemporary Themes* ed. Gary A. Sailes (New Brunswick, U.S.A.: Translation, 1998), 74–76.

25. Lapchick, 1991, 243.

26. Edwards, 22–23 and Donald Chipman, Randolph Campbell and Robert Calvert, *The Dallas Cowboys and the NFL* (Norman: University of Oklahoma, 1970), 139–40.

27. Ron Thomas, "Black Faces Still Rare in the Press Box," in Lapchick, 1996, 224 and Lapchick, 1991, 248.

28. Billy Hawkins, "The Dominant Images of Black Men in America: The Representation of O.J. Simpson," in Sailes, 1998, 39–51.

29. Lapchick, 180.

30. Hoose, 4 and Wiggins, 197.

31. Hoose, 10–12.

32. Buck O'Neil, Steve Wulf and David Conrads, *I Was Right on Time* (New York: Simon & Schuster, 1996), 216.

33. Between 1992 and 2001, African Americans accounted for yearly national averages between 6.9 and 8.0 percent of the enrolment of US medical schools, sitting at 7.2 percent in 2001. Look for the *Association of American Medical Colleges* website at *www.aamc.org-data/facts/famg82001.htm* . During the same period, American law schools included black enrolments between 6.4 percent and 7.0 percent. See the Legal Education Statistics section on the American Bar Association website at *www.abanet.org/legaled/statistics/stats.html*

34. Brooks and Althouse, 2000, 44. A high-profile news story that illustrated this frustration felt by black athletes unfolded in the wake of the Detroit Pistons 1987 playoff loss to the Boston Celtics. Pistons guard Isaiah Thomas (in agreement with fellow black teammate Dennis Rodman) railed at how the exploits of white stars like Celtic Larry Bird were

attributed to hard work, while theirs were consistently explained in genetic or God-given terms. Thomas stated that the media created the impression that he came out of his mother's womb dribbling a basketball. See Wiggins, 218–19.

3. The Great White Hope ... Extinct or Dormant?

1. Harry Mullan, *The Book of Boxing Quotations* (London: Stanley Paul, 1991), 190.
2. Chalk, 163.
3. Roberts, 1983, 18, and Wiggins, 54.
4. Larry Holmes and Phil Berger, *Larry Holmes: Against the Odds* (New York: St. Martin's 1998), 205–6.
5. Oates, 68. It is obvious in trying to determine serious challengers for the world title from among recent white American contenders. Tom McNeely vied for Floyd Patterson's title in 1961. This dubious fight drew howls of contempt from the media. Whatever the odds, McNeely put in a performance that would have made any barroom brawler proud. He was knocked down, but got up *eight times in less than four rounds* of mayhem before the referee mercifully intervened. In 1969, Joe Frazier signed to defend his splinter version of the heavyweight crown against Dave "Ziggy" Zyglewicz. For whatever motivational value it offered, the fight took place in the Astrodome, in Zyglewicz's hometown of Houston. The home crowd advantage, Frazier's historic reputation as a slow starter, and Zyglewicz's courageous attempt to take the fight to the champ, combined to push the fight to a length of ninety-six seconds, in which Zygelwicz was knocked down twice. One Frazier punch hit the challenger with such numbing force, he actually lifted him upward before depositing him on the canvas. One can actually see the sickening impact as Zyglewicz's feet lift off the ground when Frazier's hook lands. This observation is emphasized in the Joe Frazier biography shown on ESPN Sports Classic network.

Twice in the late 1960s, Jerry Quarry fought for splintered versions of the championship, losing a decision to Jimmy Ellis for the WBA belt in 1968, then being stopped by Joe Frazier for the New York State sanctioned world title in 1969. In both fights, Quarry was competitive. The decision against Ellis was close, with one judge calling the fight even, another scoring Ellis only one round ahead. The Quarry-Frazier bout was a brutal slugfest in which the white challenger courageously (though unwisely) stood toe to toe in an effort to knock out Frazier. In spite of dishing out considerable punishment, Quarry played into Frazier's hands almost perfectly, fighting exactly the type of brawling, unscientific war the Philadelphian preferred. He was eventually worn down by the more durable champion. The ring doctor ultimately ended the bout after the seventh round when Quarry's face was almost unrecognizably swollen. Quarry later lamented using the wrong strategy to slug it out with a slugger, attributing his impetuous game plan to his "Irish temper" and a proud determination to prove his courage to doubting media journalists who had questioned his grit after his loss to Ellis a year earlier.

After Quarry fell short of the championship, overmatched white fighters Ron Stander and Terry Daniels vainly challenged Frazier in 1972, fights whose outcomes were doubted by no knowledgeable boxing observers. Neither Daniels nor Stander had ever been ranked in the Top Ten before fighting Frazier, nor would either ever become rated contenders afterward. Both were bludgeoned. Daniels was knocked down numerous times; Stander was pummeled into a bloody mess. In a memorable quote from the world of boxing, *Stander's own wife admitted her husband had as much chance of beating Frazier as a Volkswagen Bug had of winning the Indianapolis 500.*

In 1975, neither boxing insiders nor white America sang the praises of Chuck Wepner very loudly as he trained to fight Muhammad Ali. The New Jersey heavyweight had a less-than-stellar record of thirty wins and nine losses. Ironically, Wepner exceeded all expectations, taking Ali into the fifteenth round before being knocked out. Before the fight,

Wepner had promised his wife that she would be sleeping with the world heavyweight champion that very evening. At bedtime, she asked her husband if she should visit Ali's room, or if the champ would come to her.

Ali never again defended his title against a white American opponent. Before fighting Cooney, Larry Holmes had fought a game, but outclassed Scott LeDoux in 1980. Like Wepner, LeDoux's record (26–8–4) testified to a journeyman fighter, albeit a tough one, who was in over his head against a champion of Holmes's caliber. After taking considerable punishment, the fight was stopped in the seventh round. Randy "Tex" Cobb was the next white pugilist to try to upend Holmes, but his sole accomplishment was in grittily lasting the full fifteen rounds against a quicker champion who boxed circles around him all night. Cobb's challenge was less notable for any suspense about the outcome than how the fight's one-sided nature prompted a disgusted Howard Cosell to swear off ever again commentating for boxing fights. Ever the comedian, Cobb quipped he would happily go another fifteen rounds with Holmes to remove Cosell from Monday Night Football as well. Finally, Scott Frank, unranked just like Daniels and Stander years earlier, challenged Larry Holmes in 1983, coming away a decisive loser.

6. Holmes and Berger, 194.
7. Holmes and Berger, 211.
8. Muhammad Ali was one of the greatest boxing champions America has ever had, and (after he moved away from the militant Black Muslim sect) one of this nation's most admirable humanitarians, sportsmen (in the ring), and public-friendly celebrities. Yet in the 1970s, his worldwide adulation as a counterculture icon in a liberal age, combined with his marketable appeal as boxing's greatest cash cow, clearly weighed on the minds of judges scoring several of his big fights. Against Frazier in 1974, Ali clutched and grabbed Frazier like an octopus over 130 times in twelve rounds, in spite of the fact that constant holding is an infraction that is supposed to count against a fighter on the cards, or even result in disqualification if it is too blatant. Yet neither the referee nor the two other judges batted an eye at this unfair tactic, and Ali took the decision. That Frazier had landed far more meaningful blows can be confirmed by any objective viewing of the bout. Every time Frazier landed a body blow, Ali would hug for his life, whereas Ali only stunned Frazier once, in the second round, making it crystal clear who was dishing out the most hurt. Without Frazier's workmanlike performance, there would have been virtually no fight for the Madison Square Garden crowd to watch that night, as Ali's grabbing limited the fighting to isolated flurries.

Beginning in 1976, Ali lost his title to Jimmy Young, Ken Norton, and Earnie Shavers, but on all three occasions his crown was rescued courtesy of generous gift decisions from judges intoxicated by the Ali mystique. Ali was repeatedly awarded rounds in which he did little but hang on the ropes or back away from more aggressive adversaries. Perhaps Ken Norton was the most poignant victim of the Ali legend. The scorecards revealed that all three judges had this fight in a dead heat entering the final round, a ridiculous tally that could not have been more unfairly slanted in Ali's favor if the judges had been sitting beside Angelo Dundee in Ali's corner throughout the bout. The popular boxing axiom, that by this point in the champion's career a challenger had to knock him out to win by a decision, seems appropriate.

Pro-Ali judging was also in evidence in bouts he lost. On March 31, 1973, a largely unheralded Ken Norton confronted Ali in the former's hometown of San Diego. In what was expected to be a warm-up match for the former champion's quest to win back the title, a hungry and better-conditioned Norton beat his legendary adversary to the punch over all twelve rounds. The fight was so one-sided, even Ali's own ring doctor, Ferdie Pacheco, openly admitted as a ring commentator that his client was losing round after round throughout, simply trying to survive. Barely standing at the end of twelve rounds, Ali was actually awarded the fight by one morally challenged judge. Five years later, when Ali finally lost his crown to Leon Spinks, a judge again replaced what they saw with their own eyes with the Ali mystique, awarding the fight to the champion. Even Ali openly accepted the decision, for Spinks had carried the fight to the aging and rusty champion, beating him on the ropes constantly, while Ali never took charge. Poorly trained for a fight he overconfidently expected to win easily, Ali gave away almost every round in the vain hope the more aggressive Spinks would tire. Even his most ardent admirers could not argue with a straight face that Ali won the contest. No one can blame the Louisville Lip for receiving this scoring largesse from wide-eyed judges. Yet a more even-handed assessment of Ali's greatness must wait for a day when the debate includes more than infatuated admirers who bitterly rail at any questioning of this fighter's stature.

9. Mullan, 66.

10. Floyd Patterson and Milton Gross, *Victory Over Myself* (New York: Scholastic, 1962), 101.

11. Holmes and Berger, 191.

12. The reputation of *The Ring* took a hit in credibility in the late 1970s from which some think it has never completely recovered. The magazine lent its name to the promotion of an American boxing tournament organized by Don King, with the former's rankings used to seed the participants. The tournament was a public relations disaster as the media uncovered multiple improprieties in the boxers' résumés, as well as the choices of who was included and excluded from the competition. This blow to *The Ring's* reputation created a void in the sport's rankings structure, resulting in the ascendancy of various world boxing commissions influence over the sport.

13. Mullan, 186–87.

14. John Major, *Prize Possession: The United States and the Panama Canal, 1903–79*. (New York: Cambridge, 1993), 31; Tindall, George B. and David E. Shi, *America: A Narrative History* (New York: W.W. Norton, 1993), 31.

15. In 1910, the year when Johnson beat Jeffries, the racial composition of the United States almost entirely consisted of a white majority and a black minority of about 10 percent. Asians and Hispanics do not even register on graphs showing racial breakdowns until years later. Donald B. Dodd, *Historical Statistics of the States of the United States: Two Centuries of the Census, 1790–1970*. 104; Jeffrey S. Passel and Barry Edmonston, "Immigration and Race: Recent Trends in Immigration to the United States," in *Immigration and Ethnicity: The Integration of America's Newest Arrivals*, ed. Barry Edmonston and Jeffrey S. Passel (Washington, Urban Institute Press, 1994), 79.

16. Frequent references are made to the handful of black heavyweights competing in America during the first two decades of the century. Wills, McVey, Langford, Jeanette, Jeff Clark and Jim Barry fought each other multiple times due to the color line that often prevented them from fighting notable white contenders. See Roberts (1983), 45.

17. Mullan, 190–91.

18. Stephen Brunt, *Mean Business: The Creation of Shawn O'Sullivan* (Markham: Viking, 1987), 76.

19. Holmes and Berger, 197.

20. Brunt, 76.

21. Quarry had decision victories over Top Ten contenders like Buster Mathis, Thad Spencer, Ron Lyle, Brian London, Larry Middleton, Randy Neumann, and former heavyweight champion, Floyd Patterson. His signature victories included a knockout over undefeated Mac Foster, and an electrifying first-round stoppage of an up-and-coming Earnie Shavers, a brutal puncher with over forty knockouts (including seventeen in the first round). Yet except for his loyal fans, and knowledgeable boxing aficionados, Quarry is typically remembered as a frustrated white boxer who choked in big fights.

22. These one-liners from the Johnny Carson show in the aftermath of the Norton-Bobick fight were cited in Ken Norton, Marshall Terrill, and Mike Fitzgerald, *Going the Distance* (Champaign: Sports Publishing, 2000), 135.

23. James P. Dawson, "Charles Rated 1–4 to Defeat Beshore," *New York Times*, 15 August, 1950, 35.
24. James P. Dawson, "Charles Stops Beshore in Fourteenth Round and Retains NBA Heavyweight Title," *New York Times*, 16 August 1950, 35.
25. James P. Dawson, "Charles Knocks Out Barone in Eleventh to Retain Title," *New York Times*, 6 December 1950, 47.
26. *New York Times*, August 1958.
27. Arthur Daley, "Patterson Knocks Out Harris in Twelfth at Los Angeles to Retain Crown," *New York Times*, 19 August 1958, 32.
28. Arthur Daley, "Patterson Halts McNeely in Fourth Round and Retains Heavyweight Title," *New York Times*, 5 December 1961, 54.
29. Joseph C. Nichols, "Marciano, Floored in Second Round, Stops Moore in Ninth," *New York Times*, 22 September 1955, 37.
30. Dave Anderson, "The Super Weekend," *New York Times*, 15 January 1972, 21.
31. Joe Frazier and Phil Berger, *Smokin' Joe: The Autobiography of a Heavyweight Champion of the World: Smokin' Joe Frazier* (New York: MacMillan, 1969), 124–25.
32. Red Smith, "Frazier Stops Daniels in Fourth and Retains Title," *New York Times*, 16 January 1972, Section 5, p.1.
33. Council Bluffs, Iowa is directly across the state line from Omaha, Nebraska. Stander was hailed as a hometown hero in the nearby larger city.
34. Dave Anderson, "Frazier's Foe Has 2 Goals: Win Title and Fight Ali." *New York Times*, 24 May 1972, 40; Dave Anderson, "Frazier Heavy Choice Tonight," *New York Times*, 25 May 1972, 63.
35. Frazier and Berger, 127.
36. Dave Anderson, "Daniels' Credits Fall Short at College and in the Ring," *New York Times*, 14 January 1972, 23.
37. Dave Anderson, "Frazier's Foe Has Two Goals: Win Title and Fight Ali," *New York Times*, 24 May 1972, 40.
38. Dave Anderson, "Ali Scales 223 1/2, High for Title Bout," *New York Times*, 24 March 1975, 43 and 45.
39. "Holmes Eyes Louis Record in Title Bout with Le Doux," *New York Times*, 6 July 1980, 4S. It is likely the author of this article was *Times* correspondent Michael Katz. No attribution for the story was given, but Katz was the credited writer for articles about the fight for the next two days, including the day after the fight. Newspapers typically send one correspondent to important championship boxing fights.
40. Michael Katz, "Holmes Stops LeDoux in 7th to Retain W.B.C. Heavyweight Title," *New York Times*, 8 July 1980, B11.
41. Peter Alfano, "Scott Frank's Dial-A-Fight Challenge," *New York Times*, 7 September 1983, B11 and B15.
42. Peter Alfano, "Holmes Has a Goal Beyond Perfection," *New York Times*, 10 September 1983, 17.
43. Peter Alfano, "Holmes Halts Outclassed Frank in 5th to Keep Title," *New York Times*, 11 September 1983, S3.

4. Approaching the Summit

1. Bill Gilliam of Newark, New Jersey, was born in May of 1924, but his exact birth date is missing from *The Ring Record Book*. Anyone familiar with this man is invited to mail his birth date to the address listed at the beginning of the appendix.
2. Jeff Merritt was born in Macon County, Georgia, ostensibly on January 1, 1946, according to the BoxRec website. He fought out of New York City in the late 1960s and

early 1970s. Anyone who can confirm Merritt's birth date is invited to send such information to the address listed at the beginning of the appendix.

3. In one comical scenario, both Eddie Machen and Zora Folley were recognized as legitimate challengers for Patterson's crown. D'Amato seemingly caved to public pressure when he finally agreed to let Patterson fight the winner of a 1958 contest between the two. When the two fought to a draw, D'Amato reneged on his offer, claiming that the two had eliminated each other from title contention! See www.boxrec.com under Floyd Patterson's record.

4. Phil Pepe, Come Out Smokin': Joe Frazier — The Champ Nobody Knew (New York: Coward, McCann and Geoghegan, 1972), 63.

5. Frazier and Berger, 75.

5. For All the Marbles

1. Frazier and Berger, 69.

2. In 1978, political squabbling between the World Boxing Council (WBC) and World Boxing Association (WBA) resulted in the bifurcation of the heavyweight title. Leon Spinks, after toppling Muhammad Ali's undisputed crown, rankled the WBC by refusing to fight the contender (Ken Norton) that organization deemed as most worthy. The WBC responded by stripping Spinks of the title and awarding it to Norton. The WBA continued to recognize Spinks. Within seven months, Spinks had lost his WBA crown in a rematch with Ali, Norton had his WBC belt taken by Larry Holmes. Ali retired immediately, prompting the WBA to recognize a series of champions while Larry Holmes would monopolize the WBC title for six years (1978–84). When Holmes was stripped by the WBC in 1984 for not defending against a challenger deemed worthy, he formed his own boxing governing body, the International Boxing Federation (IBF) which conveniently recognized him as the heavyweight champion, a status that was probably still accurate until 1985–86. This splintering effect would only get worse, to the dismay of loyal boxing fans. Over the last quarter century, boxing organizational chaos has ensued with champions recognized in every division by a dozen or so self-anointed, alphabet soup (WBO, WBU) governing bodies whose only authority is in their own minds and bestowed by a gullible press.

6. Has the Great White Hope Left the Building?

1. Holmes and Berger, 194.

2. S.L. Price and G. Cornelius, "Whatever Happened to the White Athlete?" *Sports Illustrated*, 8 December 1997, 30–55.

3. www.wbcboxing.com.

REFERENCES

Books

Aaron, Hank and Lonnie Wheeler. *I Had a Hammer: The Hank Aaron Story*. New York: Harper, 1991.

Adelman, Melvin. *A Sporting Time: New York City and the Rise of Modern Athletics, 1820–70*. Urbana: University of Illinois, 1986.

Ashe, Arthur, Jr. *A Hard Road to Glory: The African American Athlete in Basketball*. New York: Amistad, 1988.

Bak, Richard. *Joe Louis, the Great Black Hope*. Los Angeles: Holloway, 1969.

Batchelor, Denzil. *Jack Johnson and His Times*. London: Phoenix Sports Books, 1956.

Betts, John Richard. *America's Sporting Heritage*. Reading, Massachussets: Addison-Wesley, 1974.

Brooks, Dana and Ronald Althouse. *Racism in College Athletics: The African American Athlete's Experience*. Morgantown: Fitness Informational Technology, 2000.

Campbell, Randolph and Robert Calvert. *The Dallas Cowboys and the NFL*. Norman: University of Oklahoma, 1970.

Chalk, Ocania. *Pioneers of Black Sport*. New York: Dodd, Mead and Company, 1975.

Chideya, Farai. *Don't Believe the Hype: Fighting Cultural Misinformation About African-Americans*. New York: Penguin, 1995.

Coakley, Jay. *Sport in Society: Issues and Controversies*. St. Louis: Times Mirror/Mosby, 1986.

Davies, Richard O. *America's Obsession: Sports and Society Since 1945*. New York: Harcourt Brace, 1994.

Dodd, Donald B. *Historical Statistics of the States of the United States: Two Centuries of the Census, 1790–1970*. Westport, Connecticut: Greenwood, 1993.

Edwards, Harry. *The Revolt of the Black Athlete*. New York: Collier and MacMillan, 1969.

Edwards, Harry. *The Sociology of Sport*. Homewood, Illinois: Dorsey, 1973.

Eisen, George and David Wiggins, eds., *Ethnicity and Sport in North American History and Culture*. Westport, Connecticut: Greenwood, 1994.

Eitzen, D. Stanley. *Sport in Contemporary Society: An Anthology*. New York: St. Martin's, 1996.

Entine, Jon. *Taboo: Why Black Athletes Dominate Sports and Why We Are Afraid to Talk About It*. New York: Public Affairs, 2000.

Farr, Finis. *Black Champion: The Life and Times of Jack Johnson.* New York: Charles Scribner's Sons, 1964.
Fradella, Sal. *Jack Johnson.* Boston: Branden, 1990.
Frazier, Joe and Phil Berger. *Smokin' Joe: The Autobiography of a Heavyweight Champion of the World, Smokin' Joe Frazier.* New York: MacMillan, 1996
Gilmore, Al-Tony. *Bad Nigger: The National Impact of Jack Johnson.* Port Washington, New York: Kennikat, 1975.
Hauser, Thomas. *Black Lights: Inside the World of Professional Boxing.* Toronto: Simon & Schuster, 1991.
Hoose, Phillip. *Necessities: Racial Barriers in American Sports.* New York: Random House, 1989.
Holmes, Larry and Phil Berger. *Larry Holmes: Against the Odds.* New York: St. Martin's, 1998.
Isenberg, Michael. *John L. Sullivan and His America.* Urbana: University of Illinois, 1988.
LaFeber, Walter. *Michael Jordan and the New Global Capitalism.* New York: W.W. Norton, 1999.
Lapchick, Richard. *Broken Promises: Racism in American Sports.* New York: St. Martin's, 1984.
_____, ed., *Sport in Society: Equal Opportunity or Business as Usual.* Thousand Oaks: Sage, 1996.
_____. *Five Minutes to Midnight: Race and Sport in the 1990's.* New York: Madison, 1991.
Lucas, John and Ronald A. Smith. *Saga of American Sport.* Philadelphia: Lea and Febiger, 1988.
Major, John. *Prize Possession: The United States and the Panama Canal, 1903–79.* New York: Cambridge, 1993.
Mullan, Harry. *The Book of Boxing Quotations.* London: Stanley Paul, 1991.
Mead, Chris. *Champion: Joe Louis, Black Hero in White America.* New York: Charles Scribner's Sons, 1985.
Norton, Ken. *Going the Distance.* Champaign: Sports Publishing Inc., 2000.
Oates, Joyce Carol. *On Boxing.* Garden City, New York: Dolphin/Doubleday, 1987.
O'Neil, Buck, Steve Wulf and David Conrads, *I Was Right on Time* New York: Simon & Schuster, 1996.
Passel, Jeffrey and Barry Edmonston, "Immigration and Race: Recent Trends in Immigration to the United States," in *Immigration and Ethnicity: The Integration of America's Newest Arrivals,* ed. Barry Edmonston and Jeffrey S. Passel, page reference. Washington: Urban Institute Press, 1994.
Patterson, Floyd and Milton Gross. *Victory Over Myself.* New York: Scholastic, 1962.
Rader, Benjamin. *American Sports: From the Age of Folk Games to the Age of Televised Sports.* Upper Saddle River, New Jersey: Prentice Hall, 1999.
Riess, Steven. *Sport in Industrial America: 1850–1920.* Wheeling, Illinois: Harlan Davidson, 1995.
Roberts, Randy. *Jack Dempsey: The Manassa Mauler.* Baton Rouge: Lousiana State University, 1979.
_____. *Papa Jack: Jack Johnson and the Era of White Hopes.* New York: MacMillan, 1983.
Roberts, Randy and James S. Olson. *Winning Is the Only Thing: Sports in America Since 1945.* Baltimore: Johns Hopkins, 1989.
Rust, Edna and Art Rust, Jr. *Art Rust's Illustrated History of the Black History of the Black Athlete.* Garden City, New York: Doubleday, 1985.

Sailes, Gary. *African Americans in Sport: Contemporary Themes*. New Brunswick, New Jersey: Transaction, 1998.
Sammons, Jeffrey. *Beyond the Ring: The Role of Boxing in American Society*. Urbana: University of Illinois, 1988.
Shropshire, Kenneth. *In Black and White: Race and Sports in America*. New York: New York University, 1996.
Sifford, Charlie and James Gullo. *Just Let Me Play: The Story of Charlie Sifford, the First Black PGA Golfer*. New York: British American Publishing, 1992.
Somers, Dale. *The Rise of Sports in New Orleans: 1859–1900*. Baton Rouge: Louisiana State University, 1972.
Staudohor, Paul D. and James A. Mangan. *The Business of Professional Sports*. Urbana: University of Illinois, 1991.
Struna, Nancy. *People of Prowess: Sport, Leisure and Labor in Early Anglo-America*. Urbana: University of Illinois, 1996.
Tindall, George B. and David E. Shi, *America: A Narrative History*. New York: W.W. Norton, 1993.
Tygiel, Jules. *Baseball's Great Experiment: Jackie Robinson and His Legacy*. New York: Oxford, 1997.
Wiggins, David K. *Glory Bound: Black Athletes in a White America*. Syracuse: Syracuse University, 1997.

Magazines and Newspapers

Los Angeles Times, Editorial, July 6, 1910.
New York Amsterdam News, March 1, 1997
New York Times, August 15 & 16, December 6, 1950; September 22, 1955; August 19, 1958; December 5 1961; January 14 & 15, May 24 & 25, 1972; March 24, 1975; July 6 & 8, 1980; September 7, 10 & 11, 1983.
Price, S. L. and G. Cornelius, "Whatever Happened to the White Athlete?" *Sports Illustrated*, 8 December 1997, 30–55
The Ring, Volumes 9ñ62, New York
The Toledo Blade, March 25, 2001, "Black College Athletes Losing in Battle for a Degree" Section A, page 9.
U.S.A. Today, August 2, 1995.

Websites

www.aamc.org/data/facts/famg82001.htm. Association of American Medical Colleges.
www.abanet.org/legaled/statistics/stats.html. American Bar Association.
www.boxrec.com. Boxrec.
www.wbcboxing.com. World Boxing Council

INDEX

Aaron, Hank 33
Ali, Muhammad 42, 45, 49, 53, 72–73, 76, 113, 173
Anderson, Dave 73
Anthony, Tony 141
Arum, Bob 62–63
Ashe, Arthur 45

Baer, Max 17
Baker, Bob 141
Balboa, Rocky 42
Barone, Nick 69–70, 154
Baseball: black alienation 26; integration 23–25
Beshore, Fred 69, 154
Besmanoff, Willie 155
Bethea, Wayne 125
Bird, Larry 46
Bobick, Duane 67, 126
Bonavena, Oscar 119
Borzov, Valeri 57
Boxer's occupations 8
Boxing: colorline 10–11, 16; opponents 8; popularity, among upper class 9–10; supporters 8–10; white collar fans 9
Braddock, Jim 17, 55
Brown, Simon 63
Brunt, Stephen 64
Burns, Tommy 7

Carnera, Primo 17
Carter, Harold 125
Chamberlain, Wilt 37
Charles, Ezzard 84, 90, 99, 140, 154
Chuvalo, George 119

Clemens, Roger 46
Coaching: racial diversity, professional sports 26; college sports 27
Cobb, Rand (Tex) 157, 169
College athletes: academic underachievement 27; accusations of discrimination 29; Cincinnati Bearcats basketball 30; Connie Hawkins scandal 30; isolation of black athletes 28
Connors, Jimmy 45, 89
Cooney, Gerry 48–49, 68, 157
Coopman, Jean-Pierre 156
Corbett, James 6, 56

Daley, Arthur 70–71
D'Amato, Cus 100
Daniels, Billy 118, 155
Daniels, Terry 71–72, 156
Dawson, James P. 70
Dempsey, Jack 16–17, 84
DeJohn, Mike 110
De La Hoya, Oscar 65
Dokes, Mike 110
Dunlap, Bob 141
Dunn, Richard 156
Duran, Roberto 103

Ellis, Jimmy 121, 155
Evert, Chris 89

Fields, Tye 178
Firpo, Luis 59
Fleischer, Nat 147
Folley, Zora 90, 99, 100–101, 125, 145
Foreman, George 90

Foster, Bob 156
Foster, Mac 121
Frank, Scott 74, 157
Frazier, Joe 42, 49, 50, 71–72, 118–119

Golf 31
Grange, Red 84
Great White Hope Search 14
Great White Hype 75
Gwynn, Tony 84

Harris, Roy 70
Hart, Frank 5
Hart, Marvin 7
Henry, Clarence 141
Holmes, Larry 48–50, 63, 73–74, 103, 157
Hoosman, Al 141
Hunter, Billy 141

Individualism 9

Jackson, Peter 6
Jeanette, Joe 16, 58
Jeffries, Jim 7
Jeter, Derek 46
Jim Crow 5
Johannson, Ingemar 57
Johnson, Alonzo 141
Johnson, Jack 7, 11–13
Jones, Doug 118
Jordan, Michael 177

King, Billie Jean 89
King, Don 62–63

Langford, Sam 58
Law school enrollments (African American) 39
Laver, Rod 89
LeDoux, Scott 73–74, 126
Leonard, Sugar Ray 103
Lesnevich, Gus 125
Lewis, Butch 63
Liston, Sonny 99, 145
Louis, Joe 17–21, 84

Machen, Eddie 100–101, 119
Mann Act 15
Marciano, Rocky 61, 71, 85, 121
Marshall, George Preston 24

Mathews, Harry 121
Maxim, Joey 121, 125, 148
Mays, Willie 37
McGwire, Mark 84
McKey, Sam 16, 58
McNeely, Tom 70
Media: diversity 37; portrayals of black athletes 24, 37–38
Mesi, Joe 178
Middleton, Larry 154
Molyneaux, Tom 4
Monroe, Marty 166
Montana, Joe 46
Moore, Archie 71, 99, 140
Moorer, Michael 90
Morrison, Tommy 55–56
Murphy, Isaac 5, 46

National Basketball Association 33–34
National Football League 24, 26
Negro Heavyweight Championship 7
Neumann, Randy 126
New York Yankees 24
Norton, Ken 49, 53, 126

O'Neill, Buck 39
O'Sullivan, Shawn 63

Parrish, Robert 121
Patterson, Floyd 50, 57, 70, 100, 103, 155
Perkins, Don 37
Persol, Johnny 121
Powell, Charlie 177
Professional sports: Al Campanis controversy 30; front office diversity 30–31
Promotional opportunities 35–36

Quarry, Jerry 66–67, 113, 119, 121, 126
Quarterbacks, black under-representation 32

Racial violence 14
Radmacher, Pete 154
Ramos, Manuel 72
Rice, Condoleezza 177
Rice, Jerry 46
Richmond, Bill 4
Rickard, Tex 16
Robeson, Paul 46

Robinson, Jackie 25
Roosevelt, Theodore 58
Root, Jack 7

Satterfield, Bob 125, 141
Savarese, Lou 45
Schmeling, Max 17
Sharkey, Jack 17
Shavers, Earnie 49
Slade, Jimmy 141
Sosa, Sammy 84
Spinks, Leon 156
Sports Illustrated 37, 38, 175
Stacking (racial) 32
Stander, Ron 72, 156
Sullivan, John L. 56
Summerlin, Johnny 141

Tate, Big John 157
Tate, Sam 16
Taylor, Marshall 5
Terrell, Ernie 63, 121
Tillis, Quick 157

Tunney, Gene 84
Tyson, Mike 45, 85

Urban political machines 8

Walcott, Jersey Joe 90, 99
Walker, Moses 5, 46
Wallace, Coley 141
Weaver, Mike 157
Wepner, Chuck 42–43, 45, 72, 121
White stereotypes (of black traits) 5
White supremacy theory 5–6
White teenager athletes (abandonment of sports) 175
Willard, Jess 15–16
Williams, Cleveland 90
Wills, Harry 16–17, 58
Woods, Tiger 45, 65, 177

Young, Jimmy 49

Zyglewicz, Dave 155

www.ingramcontent.com/pod-product-compliance
Ingram Content Group UK Ltd.
Pitfield, Milton Keynes, MK11 3LW, UK
UKHW040610160426
5217IPUK00034B/496